Costs and Benefits of Economic Integration in Asia

Costs and Benefits of Economic Integration in Asia

Edited by
Robert J. Barro and Jong-Wha Lee

OXFORD
UNIVERSITY PRESS
2011

OXFORD
UNIVERSITY PRESS

Oxford University Press, Inc., publishes works that further
Oxford University's objective of excellence
in research, scholarship, and education.

A co-publication of the Oxford University Press and the Asian Development Bank:

Oxford University Press   Asian Development Bank
www.oup.com   www.adb.org

The first edition published in 2011 by:

Oxford University Press   Asian Development Bank
198 Madison Avenue,   6 ADB Avenue, Mandaluyong City,
New York, NY 10016,   1550 Metro Manila,
USA   Philippines

Library of Congress Cataloging-in-Publication Data

Costs and benefits of economic integration in Asia / edited by Robert J. Barro
and Jong-Wha Lee.
    p. cm.
    Includes bibliographical references and index.
    ISBN 978-0-19-975398-7 (cloth : alk. paper) 1. Asia—Economic integration.
2. Asia—Economic policy—21st century. I. Barro, Robert J. II. Lee, Jong-Wha.
    HC412.C6487 2010
    337.1′5—dc22   2010009167

1   3   5   7   9   8   6   4   2

Printed in the United States of America
on acid-free paper

Contents

Foreword

The Asian Development Bank (ADB) has long recognized that regional cooperation and integration is key to regional economic development. In fact, this is elucidated in the *Agreement Establishing the Asian Development Bank* (the Charter), where it is stated that the Bank's purpose is " ... to foster economic growth and cooperation in the region ... and contribute to the acceleration of the process of economic development of the developing member countries in the region, collectively and individually." In 1994, ADB adopted for the first time a policy to articulate its approach in promoting regional cooperation. This was replaced in 2006 by the *Regional Cooperation and Integration Strategy.*

The changed global and regional economic landscapes, especially after the 1997–1998 Asian financial crisis, led to the feeling that a more comprehensive and effective way of channeling the ADB's support for ongoing and future initiatives of regional cooperation and integration would be essential. The Office of Regional Economic Integration (OREI), which has its roots in the Regional Economic Monitoring Unit created after the Asian crisis, is now the focal point for regional cooperation and integration initiatives undertaken by the ADB.

One of the key roles of OREI is to conduct research and serve as a knowledge hub for regional cooperation issues. In recent years, several monographs on Asian regional economic integration were published by OREI: in 2004, the two-volume *Monetary and Financial Integration in East Asia;* in 2005, *Asian Economic Cooperation and Integration: Progress, Prospects and Challenges;* in 2008, *Emerging Asian Regionalism: A Partnership of Shared Prosperity;* and more recently in 2009, *Pan-Asian Integration: Linking East and South Asia*; and *National Strategies for Regional Integration: South and East Asian Case Studies*. In general, the focus of these publications was to assess the evolution and existing levels of integration and cooperation, and to recommend ways to promote closer ties. Apart from some short-term issues of concern, greater regional cooperation was viewed as inevitable and, through it, the region as a whole would benefit and global welfare would also be improved.

This book, however, pauses to ask whether quantifiable results from cooperation and integration can be substantiated in the areas of trade, investment, and finance in Asia. Selected prominent economists were offered the challenge of quantifying the costs and/or benefits of economic and financial integration in the region. This book will add insights to both the current consensus and differences regarding Asian economic integration. Readers will gain from having an objective and thorough analysis of a range of initiatives that promote regional economic integration and that are beneficial to countries individually. I greatly appreciate the efforts of the excellent team of authors, led by Robert J. Barro and Jong-Wha Lee.

Currently, the global economy appears to be recovering from the deep recession, pulled by the strong performance of developing Asian economies. In the aftermath of the global crisis, the global economic landscape will change dramatically, and Asia must play a constructive role in shaping its future. Asian countries must continue "open regionalism" and enhance regional and global cooperation. A regionally well-integrated and globally connected Asian economy will help in building a more vibrant and prosperous world.

Haruhiko Kuroda
President
Asian Development Bank

Acknowledgments

This volume is a knowledge product of the Office of Regional Economic Integration (OREI) of the Asian Development Bank (ADB). It was funded by the ADB Regional Technical Assistance 6500 ("Quantifying the Costs and Benefits of Regional Economic Integration in Asia"). From inception to completion, Hsiao Chink Tang led the project, with Josephine Duque-Comia providing excellent administrative assistance. Various people who assisted at different periods of the project deserve a special mention: Jayant Menon and Wilhelmina Paz and Iloila Tan for assisting in the preparation of the technical assistance paper; Vivian Francisco for organizing the joint workshop with Hong Kong Institute for Monetary Research (HKIMR); Liza Cruz for arranging the seminars at ADB Headquarters; Richard Niebuhr for editorial assistance; Lyndree Malang for overall coordination at the later stage of the project; and Carolyn Dedolph Cabrera and Priscila Del Rosario for facilitating the publication of this volume.

The book has benefited from valuable comments and feedback from participants at the ADB-HKIMR workshop and seminars at ADB Headquarters. Special thanks go to Hans Genberg and his team at the HKIMR, particularly Patrick Yu, for organizing the joint workshop.

The views expressed in this volume are those of the authors; they do not represent those of ADB or other institutions with which the authors are affiliated.

Robert J. Barro
Jong-Wha Lee

Contributors

Pol Antràs
Harvard University
United States

Robert J. Barro
Harvard University
United States

Eduardo Borensztein
Inter-American Development Bank
United States

Hector Calvo-Pardo
University of Southampton
United Kingdom

Caroline Freund
World Bank
United States

C. Fritz Foley
Harvard Business School
United States

Robert Koopman
United States International Trade
    Commission
Unites States

Jong-Wha Lee
Korea University
Republic of Korea

Prakash Loungani
International Monetary Fund
United States

Kris James Mitchener
Santa Clara University
United States

Emanuel Ornelas
London School of Economics
United Kingdom

Andrew K. Rose
University of California, Berkeley
United States

Anthony J. Venables
University of Oxford
United Kingdom

Hans-Joachim Voth
Universitat Pompeu Fabra
Spain

Zhi Wang
United States International Trade
    Commission
United States

Shang-Jin Wei
Columbia University
United States

Acronyms and Abbreviations

ACU	Asian Currency Unit
ADB	Asian Development Bank
ADBI	Asian Development Bank Institute
AFTA	ASEAN Free Trade Agreement and/or Area
AIO	Asian International Input-Output Tables
AMS	Asian monetary system
AMU	Asian monetary union
ASEAN	Association of Southeast Asian Nations
ASEAN+3	ASEAN plus People's Republic of China, Japan, and Republic of Korea
BCS	business cycle synchronization
BEA	Bureau of Economic Analysis
BEC	Broad Economic Categories
BK	Baxter-King filter
CAREC	Central Asia Regional Economic Cooperation
CEPR	Centre for Economic and Policy Research
CIA	Central Intelligence Agency
CIDER	Center for International and Development Economics Research
CIF	cost, insurance, and freight
CIS	Commonwealth of Independent States
CFA	African French Franc zone (*Coopération Financière en Afrique Centrale*)

CMIM	Chiang Mai Initiative Multilateralization
COW	Correlates of War
CPIS	Coordinated Portfolio Investment Survey
CRRA	constant relative risk aversion
CU	customs union
CUSTA	Canada–United States Free Trade Agreement
DOTS	Direction of Trade Statistics
DVA	domestic value-added
EAEC	Eurasian Economic Community
EBRD	European Bank for Reconstruction and Development
ECCA	Eastern Caribbean Currency Area
ECU	European Currency Unit
EMS	European Monetary System
EMU	European Monetary Union and/or Economic and Monetary Union
ER	exchange rate
ERM	exchange rate mechanism
EU	European Union
FDI	foreign direct investment
FOB	free on board
FTA	free trade agreement
FVA	foreign value-added
G3	Germany, Japan, and the Unites States
G7	G3 plus Canada, France, Italy, and the United Kingdom
GDP	gross domestic product
GE	General Exceptions
GMM	generalized method of moments
HKIMR	Hong Kong Institute for Monetary Research
HP	Hodrick-Prescott filter
IDE	Institute of Development Economies
IL-FT	Inclusion List-Fast Track
IL-N	Inclusion List-Normal
IMF	International Monetary Fund
IO	input-output
IRIO	interregional input-output
ISER	Institute of Social and Economic Research
IT	inflation targeting
IV	instrumental variables
IZA	Institute for the Study of Labor
Lao PDR	Lao People's Democratic Republic
LDC	less developed countries
MERCOSUR	Southern Common Market (*Mercado Común del Sur*)
MFN	most favored nation
MNE	multinational enterprises

MID	militarized interstate disputes
MU	monetary union
NAFTA	North American Free Trade Agreement
NATO	North Atlantic Treaty Organization
NBER	National Bureau of Economic Research
NBS	National Bureau of Statistics
NCCR	National Centre of Competence in Research
NTB	non-tariff barrier
OCA	optimum currency area
OECD	Organisation for Economic Co-operation and Development
OLS	ordinary least squares
OxCarre	Oxford Centre for the Analysis of Resource Rich Economies
PPE	property, plant, and equipment
PPI	producer price index
PPP	purchasing power parity
PRC	People's Republic of China
PWT	Penn World Tables
Q1	first quarter
Q4	fourth quarter
RMS	root-mean-squared
RTA	regional trade agreement
SL	Sensitive List
TEL	Temporary Exclusion List
UN	United Nations
UK	United Kingdom
US	United States
UN BEC	United Nations Broad Economic Categories
VAR	vector autoregression
VS	vertical specialization
WDI	World Development Indicators
WITS	World Integrated Trade System
WTO	World Trade Organization

Costs and Benefits of Economic Integration in Asia

1

Introduction

Robert J. Barro and Jong-Wha Lee

The global financial crisis of 2008–2009 raised concerns that the world would move toward protectionism and isolationism. One fear was that tariffs and other barriers to international trade would increase, thereby reducing exports and imports of goods and services. In addition, restrictions on international financial flows might grow, thereby lowering cross-border asset holdings and amounts of foreign direct investment (FDI). Increases in trade and financial protectionism clearly pose threats to Asian economies, which rely heavily on external demand as an impetus to growth and are closely linked to global financial markets.

A crisis can also have an impact on trade and financial integration among the economies within the region. Asian economies are becoming closely intertwined, through trade, investment, and financial transactions. The regional integration that we are witnessing today in Asia emerged largely in response to the contagious impacts of the 1997–1998 Asian financial crisis. Another important influence has been the strong growth of the People's Republic of China (PRC) as a market for other Asian economies. For Asia, it is reasonable to worry about a potential reversal in the upward trend toward regional and global integration—in trade, financial flows, and production structures.

To study these and related issues, in 2008 the Asian Development Bank (ADB) initiated a project titled "Quantifying the Costs and Benefits of Regional Economic Integration in Asia." In January 2009, ADB and the Hong Kong Institute for Monetary Research (HKIMR) jointly organized a conference in Hong Kong, China, on the costs and benefits of economic integration.

The papers presented at the conference assess the economic consequences of deepening trade and financial and monetary integration in the region. A common theme of the research relates to the costs and benefits of economic integration at the regional and global levels. The idea is to quantify these costs and benefits for various dimensions of trade, investment, and finance.

The present volume includes updated versions of eight of the papers presented at the conference. These studies deal with time patterns in trade barriers, volumes of trade, cross-border asset holdings and flows, foreign direct investment, currency regimes, and production structures between countries. They emphasize developments in Asia since the early 1990s, but parts of the analysis relate to longer-term Asian history. The focus on the 1990s is particularly advantageous for assessing the effects of the 2008–2009 global financial meltdown, because the sample includes the Asian financial crisis of 1997–1998. Although this earlier event was more localized than the 2008–2009 crisis, the reactions observed within Asia in the late 1990s provide useful information about likely responses in Asia and elsewhere to the 2008–2009 event.

Eduardo Borensztein and Prakash Loungani, in "Asian Financial Integration: Trends and Interruptions" (chapter 3 of this volume), examine financial integration in Asian countries from the mid-1980s through early 2009. The overall trend has been toward more integration, judging by patterns in equity returns and interest rates and also by quantities of cross-border asset holdings. The speed of convergence in Asian financial patterns toward those in the world's richest countries is comparable to Eastern Europe but faster than Latin America. Although Asian regional financial integration is clearly increasing, its financial markets are more closely linked to global markets than they are to one another. However, gains from global diversification are likely to be higher than those achievable only by regional diversification.

An important point is that the movement toward Asian financial integration was interrupted by the crisis of 1997–1998, but this interruption proved to be only temporary. In fact, one beneficial effect of the crisis was to spur the development of Asian bond markets, featuring securities denominated in local currencies. Borensztein and Loungani document another interruption in Asian financial integration in 2008–2009 because of the global financial crisis. However, given the behavior observed in the 1990s, one can reasonably project that this latest turnabout in Asian financial integration will likely again be temporary (assuming that the global financial crisis itself does not last forever!).

The study by Hector Calvo-Pardo, Caroline Freund, and Emanuel Ornelas, "The ASEAN Free Trade Agreement: Impact on Trade Flows and External Trade Barriers" (chapter 6 of this volume), examines the interplay in Asia among regional free trade agreements, external tariff barriers, and the volume of international trade. The emphasis is on the impact of the ASEAN Free Trade Agreement (AFTA) of 1992 on developments from 1993 to 2007. This regional pact initially comprised six Asian countries but later in the 1990s it was extended to cover four more.

A major finding is that AFTA led not only to an expansion of trade between member countries but also between AFTA and nonmembers. One key observation is that reductions in preferential tariffs among member countries seemed to cause reductions in external (most favored nation) tariffs. This result sheds light on the long-standing debate about whether regional free-trade agreements enhance trade and welfare overall. The usual concern is that trade diversion from nonmember countries might more than offset the expansion of trade between members. However, in the Calvo-Freund-Ornelas study, the expansion of trade (and reduced trade barriers) involving nonmembers reinforces the overall favorable impact of the regional agreement. This finding supports the view that regionalism can be a "building block" toward global free trade. Another result is that the Asian Financial Crisis of the 1990s led to only a temporary interruption of trade involving the ASEAN countries. In most cases, the countries did not react to the crisis by raising tariffs for nonmembers, with the exception of Thailand in 1998–1999. However, even in this case, the rise in external tariffs was only temporary. By 1999, there was a resumption in the downward path of most favored nation tariffs, which apply to the nonmembers.

Anthony Venables, in "Economic Integration in Remote Resource-Rich Regions" (chapter 7 of this volume), provides a framework to think about the political economy of regional versus multilateral free-trade agreements. Given the assumed absence of monopoly power in internationally traded goods, a region such as central Asia does best overall under multilateral free trade. However, distributional effects arise that may generate political support for trade restrictions or liberalizations limited to a region. Countries close to places abundant in an exported natural resource such as oil benefit if the resource-rich nation restricts its trade with the rest of the world. In effect, resource-poor neighbors gain by exporting produced goods (or labor) to the resource-abundant country—and more of this gain arises when the abundant country chooses to restrict imports from the rest of the world. This effect underscores the idea that regional integration can help to spread benefits of unevenly distributed resource wealth among the region's economies. However, there are other channels for spreading these benefits. An even better outcome, for example, is for the resource-rich country to (efficiently) implement free trade with the rest of the world but provide foreign aid to its neighbors. Other effects involve the distribution of factor incomes within resource-rich countries. Non-owners of the exported natural resource can benefit from the imposition of tariffs on trade with neighboring countries or the world overall. However, these benefits could also be garnered by (efficiently) allowing free trade and then taxing natural-resource production.

Pol Antràs and Fritz Foley, in "Regional Trade Integration and Multinational Firm Strategies" (chapter 8 of this volume), observe that free-trade agreements and the volume of international trade interact with the determination of FDI. They use a theoretical model of this interaction to assess empirically the effects of the 1992 AFTA on the numbers of US firms involved in FDI in Asian countries. They also assess changes in the numbers and sizes of the Asian affiliates of the US companies. (The analysis focuses on US-origin FDI because of the availability of detailed data on this activity from the benchmark surveys of 1989, 1994, and 1999).

The key findings from the comparison of 1989 (pre-AFTA) to 1994 (post-AFTA) are that the AFTA countries showed sharp increases in the number of US parent firms, the number of Asian affiliate companies, and the average size of these affiliates, compared to non-AFTA Asian countries. This expansion in various dimensions of FDI activity is a counterpart of the increase in international trade documented by Calvo, Freund, and Ornelas. Interestingly, Antràs and Foley find from the 1999 survey that the Asian Financial Crisis interrupted the FDI expansion in the AFTA countries. To know whether this interruption was only temporary—as found by Borensztein and Loungani for financial-market integration in Asia—we will have to consult the 2004 FDI survey, which has yet to be studied. This extension will also provide guidance on whether the 2008–2009 global financial crisis, which likely caused another interruption of FDI expansion in the AFTA countries, will have only temporary retarding effects.

Jong-Wha Lee and Robert Barro, in "East Asian Currency Union" (chapter 2 of this volume), apply previous models of optimal currency areas to assess whether an East Asian currency union is likely to be desirable and, if so, what form it should take. Some of the issues involve Robert Mundell's classic trade-off between benefits from a common currency—such as promotion of trade in goods, services, and financial claims—against costs from the loss of an independent monetary policy and possibly from forgoing seigniorage revenue. Another consideration is that linking to a stable nominal anchor currency can provide the discipline needed to achieve low and stable inflation. This study adds the idea that a satisfactory monetary union requires political negotiation, for example to determine a common monetary policy and share seigniorage revenue. Hence, the more the partner countries are politically aligned, the more attractive a common currency will be. Finally, the important role of rare macroeconomic disasters, such as the global financial crisis of 2008–2009, suggests that monetary union will be more worthwhile if linking diminishes the probability and potential size of disaster events, including financial crises and wars.

Judging by standard criteria, it is unclear that East Asia would benefit overall from forming a currency union. The large amount of intra-region trade is a favorable factor, but the low degree of output co-movement is unfavorable (because it raises the likely costs from relinquishing independent monetary policies). Another troublesome feature is the weak political proximity (gauged by voting patterns at the United Nations) between Japan and other East Asian countries. A quantitative calibration exercise suggests that most countries in East Asia would gain in welfare by forming a currency union involving a broad group of East Asian economies. However, the benefit would be much more substantial if a currency union were to reduce the probability and size of disaster events, including wars.

Andrew Rose, in "Understanding Business Cycle Synchronization: Is Inflation Targeting Paving the Way to Asian Monetary Union?" (chapter 4 of this volume), focuses on the extent of business-cycle synchronization, that is, output co-movement between countries. As already noted, this co-movement is a major determinant of optimal currency areas in the framework pioneered by Mundell and used by Lee and Barro. Joining a currency union implies the loss of an independent monetary policy. The cost of losing independent monetary policy is, however, significantly lessened if business cycles are synchronized among member countries, for in this case the common monetary policy can be as good as individual monetary policy for each country's stabilization.

Rose explores the two-way causation between trade and business-cycle synchronization. Although the effect of trade on synchronization is ambiguous in theory (because trade can increase specialization and lead, thereby, to less output co-movement), the empirical relationships from an array of prior studies are overwhelmingly in the positive direction. There is also clear evidence from previous research that monetary union leads to higher synchronization but little evidence that inflation targeting (IT) works in a similar way. That is, the increased rates of adoption of IT since New Zealand began to target inflation in 1990 have not led to decoupling of business cycles across countries. This pattern also holds in the sample of dyads that includes at least one Asian country. In the wake of the Asian financial crisis, the majority of the crisis-affected East Asian economies, including Indonesia, the Republic of Korea, the Philippines, and Thailand, switched to an IT regime. Rose concludes that IT may be an attractive way station on the road toward monetary union in Asia. In other words, aside from other desirable characteristics as a monetary regime, IT has the attraction of enhancing business-cycle synchronization. Through this channel, monetary union itself becomes more desirable and thereby, more likely to materialize. However, Rose observes that European monetary union took many years to construct and that the case for Asian monetary union, although plausible, is less compelling than Europe's. Thus, a monetary union for Asia is unlikely in the near future.

Kris Mitchener and Hans-Joachim Voth, in "Trading Silver for Gold: Nineteenth-Century Asian Exports and the Political Economy of Currency Unions" (chapter 5 of this volume), study pre–World War I Asian monetary systems. This historical analysis provides an excellent counterpoint to the Lee-Barro and Rose studies, which consider the workings of modern monetary regimes in Asia and elsewhere. The Mitchener-Voth findings add further evidence on how currency unions—in this case, based on silver or gold—affect the volume of international trade. The major result is that currency union promotes trade but that some unions are better than others. Most of the Asian countries were on the silver standard around 1870, but many shifted to gold between 1870 and 1913. Moreover, many of these shifts were driven by decisions of colonial powers or by the politics of silver and were, therefore, largely exogenous to economic events in the Asian countries. Mitchener and Voth find that, although silver was better for trade than paper, gold was better still—presumably because much of the rest of the world was on gold in this period. The Asian countries that abandoned their ties to the silver standard early during the late nineteenth century saw large increases in their trade volume.

The study by Robert Koopman, Zhi Wang, and Shang-Jin Wei, "A World Factory in Global Production Chains: Estimating Imported Value-Added in Exports by the People's Republic of China" (chapter 9 in this volume), investigates the impact of integration through production on the economies in Asia. Their focus is on the PRC, which is a hub of global production networks.

The Koopman-Wang-Wei study constitutes an important methodological breakthrough in the computation of the extent of foreign and domestic content in a country's exports. The analysis requires detailed input-output tables at a disaggregated level. Using this information, the authors isolate the special role of imported inputs in the country's export-processing sectors and also consider that imported inputs may indirectly have some content by the PRC involving earlier stages of production and trade. The final result from a detailed and careful analysis is a set of estimates of foreign content in merchandise exports by the PRC, broken down by sector and source country. One conclusion is that the share of foreign content in the PRC's overall merchandise exports was already high by 1997 (48%), then changed little up to 2006, when it reached 49%. However, this stability reflected two opposing trends—a diminishing share of processing exports in total merchandise exports (falling from 60% to 54%) and a change in the overall composition of exports toward more sophisticated goods that, however, extensively used imported components as inputs. Within Asia, the most important source countries for the PRC were Japan and Hong Kong, China. Outside Asia, the most important were the United States and the European Union. Overall, the basic picture for the PRC is one of considerable integration of production structures for exported goods with the world economy. However, the extent of this integration has not been rising significantly in recent years.

This volume is organized around two broad topics and four subtopics. The main areas are: Monetary and Financial Cooperation and Integration; and Trade and Investment Cooperation and Integration. The first of these includes two subtopics: Asian Currency Union and Monetary/Exchange Rate Policy Cooperation and Financial Integration. The second broad area also includes two subtopics: Free Trade Agreements and Integrating Production.

Most of the contributions in this book were prepared as background and analytical papers for the Asian Development Bank's Regional Technical Assistance Project Number 6500, "Quantifying the Costs and Benefits of Regional Economic Integration in Asia." The authors are prominent scholars of Asian economic development and policy, well-recognized in Asian academic and policy circles, and are drawn from leading universities and think tanks throughout the region and beyond.

We believe that this volume will become an essential reference on current consensus and controversy in the debate on economic integration, particularly as applied to Asia. Its appeal should be wider than to a purely academic audience, since government officials and other policy makers would gain from having an authoritative diagnosis of various initiatives that seek to promote regional economic integration.

2

East Asian Currency Union

Jong-Wha Lee and Robert J. Barro

We are grateful to Jeffrey Frankel, Ross Garnaut, Francis Lui, Changyong Rhee, Yunjong Wang, and seminar participants at the American Economic Association annual meeting, the Australian National University, and the Bank of Korea for helpful comments on an earlier draft. Jong Suk Han and Joo Hyun Pyun provided able research assistance. The views expressed in this chapter are the authors' and do not necessarily reflect the views or policies of the Asian Development Bank.

1 Introduction

The choice of an appropriate exchange rate regime has been one of the most fundamental policy issues in East Asian economies since the 1997 financial crisis. Prior to the crisis, the majority of East Asian economies adopted de facto United States (US) dollar peg systems for exchange rate arrangements.[1] In the wake of the crisis, however, the majority of the crisis-affected East Asian economies, including Indonesia, Republic of Korea (Korea), the Philippines, and Thailand, switched to floating exchange rate regimes. It is not yet clear whether the new exchange rate system provides enough confidence to these economies, and thus in the long run can serve as a permanent choice. Much concern has been raised about the undesirable aspects of increased instability in the foreign exchange market. East Asian countries have kept their exchange rates, even if formally floating, pegged to the US so as to moderate excessive volatility of rates due to a "fear of floating" against the US dollar (Calvo and Reinhart, 2002). Critics also assert that East Asian central banks tend to intervene heavily in the foreign exchange market in order to keep exchange rates undervalued in pursuit of an "export-led growth strategy," which results in accumulating an unlimited amount of low-yielding dollar-denominated assets (Dooley et al., 2003 and Roubini, 2007).

This post-crisis experience has provoked calls for alternative exchange rate arrangements in East Asia. Dornbusch and Park (1999), Williamson (1999), and Ogawa and Ito (2002) advocate a common-basket exchange rate peg for the East Asian region. They argue that East Asian countries outside Japan can expect to stabilize their overall export competitiveness by pegging their currencies to a basket consisting of the yen, dollar, and euro. This system would not only provide exchange rate stability vis-à-vis major trading partners, but also intra-region stability. Others propose the creation of an Asian monetary system (AMS), in which each currency is pegged to a common currency unit similar to the European Currency Unit (ECU); the value of the Asian unit would be based on a basket of specified amounts of Asian currencies and its bilateral exchange rate would be allowed to fluctuate within a limited band around a central exchange rate.[2] However, critics argue that even if participating countries could agree on a common basket peg, in reality it would be difficult to decide on a set of specific rules by which exchange rate policy could be managed with adherence to the basket as a numeraire.

On the other hand, there is increasing discussion about the need to create a monetary union in the region. Many researchers and policy makers there suggest that a monetary union is the ultimate goal to achieve intra-region exchange rate stability and economic integration of East Asia. McKinnon (1999) has proposed a currency union with the US dollar as the common currency. Others suggest that East Asia can emulate the European experience of monetary integration by taking the necessary steps to build requisite institutions and policies, which would eventually lead to the formation of an East Asia–wide monetary union with a new currency (Kawai and Motonishi, 2005).

As pointed out by Alesina et al. (2002) and Barro (2004), there has been a trend toward evolution of currency unions in the world. A recent example is the West African monetary zone involving six West African states. They note that several global developments are stimulating interest in currency unions around the world. One development is globalization involving integration in trade and financial transactions, trends that raise the benefits from currency unions. Another factor is the growing awareness of the importance of monetary stability. As monetary authorities increasingly value price stability over active macroeconomic stabilization, countercyclical monetary policy becomes less important. Hence, the cost of giving up independent monetary policy decreases. These developments provide a favorable environment for a currency union in East Asia.

The purpose of this chapter is to assess the feasibility of a common currency arrangement in East Asia, particularly compared to the euro area, and then gauge the economic impact of a currency union on individual East Asian economies. First, we ask whether East Asia has favorable conditions to share a common currency. We empirically investigate whether East Asia meets the criteria for an optimum currency area (OCA). Included here are the symmetry of output and price shocks across countries, commitment to price stability, and trade and financial integration. We also discuss the political proximity among the East Asian countries, particularly as compared to that of European countries.

Several studies have assessed the feasibility of a currency union in East Asia. An early study by Eichengreen and Bayoumi (1999) shows that, on pure OCA grounds, East Asia is a plausible candidate for a common currency area, analogous to the euro area. However, they point out that the lack of political proximity in East Asia may hinder efforts to form a currency union in the region. Other studies, such as Kwan (1998), Baek and Song (2002), Lee et al. (2004), and Kawai and Motonishi (2005), also used empirical and theoretical analyses to evaluate whether East Asia—either as a whole or as subregions—has favorable conditions to form a currency union according to traditional OCA criteria. This study adopts the approach suggested by Alesina et al. (2002) and uses updated data to assess the feasibility of an East Asian currency union. New data are also used to measure political proximity in the region. No empirical paper to date has systematically assessed the degree of political proximity among East Asian economies in the context of forming a currency union.

Second, this chapter assesses welfare effects of various types of currency unions, including a dollar bloc and a new regional currency bloc for East Asian economies. The potential benefits and costs of joining a currency union are evaluated. A currency union increases trade among countries adopting the same currency, contributes to growth of output and consumption, and thereby generates positive welfare effects. However, increasing price and output fluctuations due to the loss of monetary policy independence incur welfare costs. Based on calibrations of a representative consumer model, we assess the welfare gains from increasing consumption growth rates and the costs of increasing aggregate consumption volatility that currency unions are expected to bring about in East Asia. The model allows rare but large declines in consumption as in Barro (2006a). In an economy where major disasters such as wars or financial crises can occur, the high volatility from these disasters can generate large welfare costs, compared to those from normal disturbances. We demonstrate that the welfare implications of a currency union involve the probability and size of such disasters.

The remainder of this chapter is organized as follows. Section 2 discusses the benefits and costs of currency unions, and reviews the conditions for an optimum currency area. Section 3 measures the extent to which the East Asian economies satisfy the optimum currency area criteria, particularly as compared to European countries. We then evaluate whether East Asia is an optimum currency area. Section 4 assesses the welfare effects from various types of currency unions in East Asia. Concluding remarks are presented in Section 5.

2 The Benefits and Costs of an East Asian Currency Union

2.1 Benefits and Costs of Currency Unions

Each country can decide whether to join a currency union by comparing the associated costs and benefits. Adoption of another country's money as a nominal anchor is an extreme form of a fixed exchange rate system. Frankel (2004) summarizes the four advantages of fixed exchange rate regimes over floating regimes: the fixed exchange rate system (i) provides a nominal anchor for monetary policy and thus represents a more credible commitment to fight inflation; (ii) promotes trade and investment by reducing uncertainty and transaction costs; (iii) prevents competitive devaluation; and (iv) avoids speculative bubbles in exchange rates. In addition to these conventional benefits from fixed exchange rate regimes, a currency union would help a developing country increase its access to long-term financing. The typical developing country cannot borrow internationally on a long-term basis in its own currency because foreign investors require a very high risk premium to compensate for the potential loss in real value due to devaluation and domestic inflation. Dollarization would assist in avoiding this "original sin."

However, a fixed exchange rate regime such as a currency union involves costs: it (i) results in loss of independent monetary policy; (ii) hinders automatic adjustment to external shocks since exchange rates cannot respond to adverse developments while sticky prices and wages may prolong the needed adjustment; and (iii) may provide neither seigniorage revenue nor a lender-of-last-resort capability.

2.2 Optimum Currency Area (OCA) Criteria

An OCA can be defined as a region that would be better off using a common currency. The theory of an optimum currency area, pioneered by Mundell (1961) and McKinnon (1963), establishes criteria for the creation of a common currency area in a region. The important factors include trade openness, the symmetry of shocks across countries, labor mobility and wage flexibility, financial integration, the tendency for inflation, and political proximity.

2.2.1 Trade Openness

A high degree of trade integration is likely to increase the efficiency gain from using a common currency to lower transaction costs for trade. In addition, the cost of losing monetary policy independence can be attenuated when the country is more open. As countries achieve higher levels of trade integration, an independent monetary policy plays a more limited role in macroeconomic stabilization.

2.2.2 Symmetry of Shocks

As pointed out by Mundell (1961), the major cost of joining a currency union is the loss of an independent monetary policy. This cost, however, is significantly lessened if business cycles are synchronized among member countries, for in this case the common monetary policy can play a stabilizing role just as well as individual monetary policy. In this context, the currency union is more attractive if countries have similar production structures, and thereby are subject to common shocks and react similarly to global events.

As Alesina et al. (2002) pointed out, what turns out to matter is not the correlation of output per se, but rather the variance of the ratio of the client country's output to the anchor country's output. This variance depends on the individual variances of output in addition to the correlation of outputs. If a client country's variance of output is much greater than that of the anchor country, then the anchor country's monetary policy may not be appropriate for the client country.[3]

Another important feature for an OCA is the speed of adjustments to shocks. Even if disturbances are asymmetric across economies, a faster adjustment to shocks helps an economy mitigate the costs of relinquishing independent monetary policy.

2.2.3 Labor Mobility

A traditional OCA criterion is the ease of labor movement between the country in question and its potential currency area partners. If labor is highly mobile between the countries, workers are able to respond to adverse local shocks by moving across borders to obtain jobs. In that case, there is less need by a country for its own expansionary monetary or currency devaluation policies. Moreover, fiscal transfers from currency partners can compensate for loss of such discretionary policies.

2.2.4 Financial Integration

Countries with close financial linkages benefit from a common currency. As in trade, a common currency brings benefits such as lower transactions costs and elimination of the risk of exchange rate changes associated with trading in financial instruments between countries with different currencies. Financial integration among a group of countries could facilitate the formation of a common currency area for the group, as it reduces the cost of adjustment to shocks to demand and supply by facilitating cross-border movements of capital.

However, capital market integration may have offsetting effects on forming a currency union. As suggested by Kalemli-Ozcam et al. (2001), better income insurance attained through greater capital-market integration may induce greater specialization of production and hence larger asymmetric shocks across countries. If stronger capital-market integration leads to reduced synchronization of business cycles, candidate countries would be less willing to join a currency union. As argued by Imbs (2004), however, if capital flows are correlated internationally, financial integration may help to synchronize output co-movement.

In any case, given the extent of asymmetric shocks, greater capital-market integration is more beneficial for the formation of a currency union by facilitating risk sharing among heterogeneous economies.

2.2.5 Inflation and the Variability of Relative Prices against Anchor Country

An OCA criterion that began to be emphasized in the 1990s is the need to import monetary stability. Alesina and Barro (2002) discuss the idea that a currency union commits clients to a stable monetary policy. Specifically, by adopting the currency of a credible anchor, an inflation-prone country can eliminate its inflation-bias problem that has been discussed in the literature in the context of rules versus discretion in monetary policy. This bias can stem from two sources—the desire to use monetary policy to overstimulate the economy in a cyclical context and incentives to monetize budget deficits and public debts. This kind of commitment was especially important for Argentina in the 1990s. However, on other grounds, Argentina was not a good candidate for linking to the US dollar.

Many governments lack the internal discipline and institutions that can provide for a firm domestic commitment to a monetary policy dedicated to price stability. By reviewing a country's history of inflation—in terms of mean and variability—we may gauge the extent of the domestic commitment to these problems.

Price stability for an anchor country translates into price stability for its clients only to the extent that relative prices do not vary significantly between them. That is, a country that joins a currency union receives the inflation rate of the anchor plus the change in the country's price level relative to that of the anchor. Hence, if the variability of relative prices is high, the benefit of importing monetary stability is lessened.

2.2.6 Political Proximity

The creation of a currency union is not only an economic decision; it is also a critical political decision of participating countries. The loss of a national currency is often regarded as loss of national sovereignty.[4] In reality, participation in a currency union requires the member country to delegate its monetary policy to the anchor country's central bank or a regional central bank. This delegation is bound to raise a number of delicate issues, such as provisions of seigniorage sharing and rules for central bank functions and operations. In this regard, political negotiation to form a currency union would necessitate great political and ideological affinity among participating countries, perhaps to a greater extent than that for other types of economic integration such as the formation of a free trade agreement (FTA).

Political proximity between potential members would help form a currency union by facilitating seigniorage sharing among members and, when necessary, fiscal transfers between members. Moreover, if political proximity reflects similar ideological preferences over economic policy objectives, they would be more willing to accept neighbors' policies.

The lack of political proximity would not necessarily be the ultimate barrier to the formation of a monetary union. In Europe, one appeal of economic integration was the promise of peace after World War II. Nevertheless, economic and political complexities in the process of monetary integration can be settled more harmoniously among politically aligned countries.

3 Which Currency Union for East Asia?

Typically, there are two types of currency unions. In the first, a client country adopts the money of an anchor country as its own currency. Examples are the use of the US dollar in the Bahamas, Bermuda, Panama, and Puerto Rico; the use of the Belgian franc by Luxembourg; the Swiss franc by Liechtenstein; and the Italian lira by San Marino. Recently. Ecuador and El Salvador have also adopted the US dollar as legal tender. In the second case, a group of countries creates a new currency and a new joint central bank. Examples are the European Monetary Union (EMU), Eastern Caribbean Currency Area (ECCA), and African French Franc zones (CFA). East Asia may either adopt an existing major currency, such as the US dollar, euro, or Japanese yen, or create a new regional currency.[5] In the latter case, East Asia could create a joint currency, and this new currency would float against the major world currencies.[6] The new joint central bank might then adopt a monetary policy to stabilize the regional average inflation rate at a low level (inflation targeting) or might also take into account the fluctuations of regional average gross domestic product (GDP).

It is important to evaluate the costs and benefits of joining a currency union from the perspective of a potential client country in East Asia. The OCA criteria discussed in the previous section imply that countries look more favorably on a currency union if they have: (i) substantial integration in trade and financial transactions with potential currency union members; (ii) an inclination to high inflation; (iii) high price and output co-movements with the other economies; (iv) high labor mobility between other currency union members; (v) fast adjustment to shocks; and (vi) relatively close political proximity to their potential partners.

In this chapter, empirical measures of trade integration, commitment to price stability, output and price co-movements, financial integration, and political proximity for East Asia are the main focus.[7] Data for European countries are presented for comparison.

3.1 Data for East Asia Monetary Union Analysis

Data on output are from *Penn World Tables* (PWT) 6.2, which provide a panel of yearly data for a large number of economies from 1958 to 2004. Output corresponds to purchasing power parity (PPP) per capita GDP in 2000 US dollars. Inflation is calculated as the continuously compounded (log-difference) growth rate of the GDP deflator from the World Bank's *World Development Indicators* (WDI). The concept of relative prices is a form of real exchange rate based on GDP deflators. The measure is the PPP for GDP, obtained from PWT, divided by the US dollar exchange rate. This variable determines the price level in country i relative to that of the US, $P_{it}/P_{US,t}$. The relative price between countries i and j is then computed by dividing the value for country i by that for country j.

Following the methodology of Alesina et al. (2002), a second-order auto-regression of relative per capita GDP was estimated using the annual time series for each country from 1958 to 2004. Then the root-mean-squared value of the estimated residual is used as the measure of co-movement of outputs or lack thereof; that is, the lower the root-mean-squared value, the greater the co-movement of outputs between countries i and j.[8] The co-movement of prices is computed in an analogous fashion by running a second-order auto-regression on annual data from 1958 to 2004 for relative prices and then constructing the root-mean-squared value of the estimated residual. Bilateral trade information comes from the International Monetary Fund (IMF)'s *Direction of Trade Statistics.* These data are expressed in US dollars.

The extent to which East Asian economies are financially integrated with the US, Europe, or Japan, or among themselves is measured by the size of bilateral international financial asset holdings. Data on cross-border holdings of international financial assets, including equity and debt securities, come from the Coordinated Portfolio Investment Survey (CPIS). The IMF conducted this survey for the first time in 1997, and annually since 2001. The first CPIS involved 20 economies and the CPIS 2001 expanded to some 75 source economies, including several offshore financial centers. In each case, the bilateral positions of the source economies in more than 220 destination economies/territories are reported.[9] The CPIS provides a breakdown of a country's stock of total portfolio investment assets by country of residence of the nonresident issuer. Problems of survey methods and underreporting of assets by participating countries are shortcomings of the CPIS data (Lane and Milesi-Ferretti, 2004). Nevertheless, the CPIS survey presents a unique opportunity for the examination of foreign equity and debt holdings of many participating countries.

Political proximity is measured by the extent to which two states have common foreign policy interests. Since the pioneering work of Bueno de

Mesquita (1975), the similarity of states' alliance policies is used as a measure. However, Signorino and Ritter (1999) point out that Bueno de Mesquita's measure of Kendall's τ_b is inappropriate in gauging the similarity of alliance policies and suggest an alternative measure. They also suggest that data other than alliance commitments, for example, United Nations (UN) votes, diplomatic missions, disputes, and trade may more accurately measure the similarity of foreign policy positions.

In this section, the measure of bilateral vote correlation at the UN General Assembly is used. The political proximity between two countries is the fraction of the votes that they cast on the same side in the UN General Assembly.[10] When the UN voting pattern of nations is similar, their foreign policy interests are better aligned.

3.1.1 Trade Openness

Table 2.1 lists the average ratio of exports plus imports to GDP for East Asian and European countries for the period 1990–2007 with four potential anchors for currency areas: the US, Europe, Japan, and East Asia (including Japan). The GDP value in the denominator of these ratios refers to the country paired with the potential anchor country or region.

The table shows that East Asia looks quite favorable for an OCA in terms of its substantial degree of intra-region trade. For 10 East Asian economies, including Japan, the average trade-to-GDP ratio with other East Asian partners is 31.8%. It reaches 86.4% in Hong Kong, China; 79.1% in Singapore; and 47.5% in Malaysia. These numbers are much higher than the corresponding figures for European countries. For 18 European economies, the intra-Europe trade-to-GDP ratio is 21.8% on average.[11] In East Asia, Japan has a very low trade-to-GDP ratio with other East Asian economies (3.7%), while it is one of the major trading partners for most of the other nine East Asian economies. It is notable that, even excluding Japan, for nine East Asian economies the average intra-region trade-to-GDP ratio is 26.1%, slightly higher than the average intra-region ratio for Europe, 21.8%.

While the share of intra-regional trade is quite high for East Asia, these countries also conduct substantial trade with the US and Europe. In fact, except for Japan, for the nine East Asian economies, on average the amount of trade is more or less equally dispersed across Europe and Japan and a little higher with the US: the trade-to-GDP ratio is 8.4% with Europe, 8.8% with Japan and 10.4% with the US. Hence, judging from their trade patterns, East Asian economies would benefit less from adopting any one major currency as an anchor than from forming a broad East Asian currency union.

3.1.2 Price Stability

Table 2.2 presents the average inflation rates, based on GDP deflators, for East Asian and European economies. The sample period is divided into

Table 2.1
Bilateral Trade-to-GDP Ratio for East Asia and Europe (percent), 1990–2007

Economy	Trade Partners				
	US	Europe	Japan	East Asia	World
China, People's Rep. of	3.2	3.3	3.5	10.4	22.1
Hong Kong, China	17.1	15.8	12.0	86.4	128.8
Indonesia	2.9	3.7	5.2	13.6	24.3
Japan	2.2	1.4	.	3.7	9.5
Korea, Rep. of	5.4	3.8	4.6	12.5	29.3
Malaysia	15.0	11.5	13.6	47.5	84.7
Philippines	8.6	5.1	6.8	19.9	38.0
Singapore	23.1	20.0	16.9	79.1	149.4
Taipei,China	8.4	5.7	7.5	21.8	42.8
Thailand	6.7	6.7	9.2	23.1	46.5
Average	*9.2*	*7.7*	*7.9*	*31.8*	*57.5*
Austria	1.3	24.8	0.6	1.3	32.7
Belgium	4.0	53.1	1.3	3.0	70.6
Denmark	1.4	19.5	0.7	1.9	27.5
Finland	1.7	17.1	0.8	2.1	27.6
France	1.4	13.3	0.4	1.2	20.5
Germany	2.0	15.6	0.8	2.1	25.0
Greece	0.5	8.0	0.4	1.0	12.7
Iceland	2.8	16.4	1.4	2.1	25.6
Ireland	7.5	34.0	1.9	4.1	52.2
Italy	1.2	11.6	0.4	1.1	19.0
Luxembourg	1.8	42.7	0.4	2.9	51.1
Netherlands	3.1	34.1	1.1	3.8	49.3
Norway	1.7	19.2	0.7	1.5	25.4
Portugal	1.0	19.9	0.4	0.8	25.8
Spain	0.9	12.7	0.4	1.1	18.6
Sweden	2.2	18.1	0.8	1.8	28.6
Switzerland	2.6	21.7	1.0	2.0	30.5
United Kingdom	2.5	11.0	0.7	1.7	20.3
Average	*2.2*	*21.8*	*0.8*	*2.0*	*31.3*
United States	.	1.9	1.0	3.0	9.4

. = not applicable.
Notes: Trade is the average of exports and imports. The GDP value in the denominator of these ratios refers to the economy paired with the potential anchor or region. East Asia refers to 10 East Asian economies including Japan.

Sources: IMF *Direction of Trade Statistics* (DOTS) and CEIC database.

Table 2.2
Mean and Standard Deviation of Annual Inflation Rates for East Asia and
Europe (percent)

Economy	1975–1989		1990–2007	
	Mean	Standard Deviation	Mean	Standard Deviation
China, People's Rep. of	3.8	3.9	5.8	5.9
Hong Kong, China	8.9	4.2	2.1	5.2
Indonesia	13.0	8.9	14.1	15.8
Japan	3.6	2.4	(0.2)	1.4
Korea, Rep. of	13.4	8.5	4.4	3.5
Malaysia	3.9	5.5	3.9	3.1
Philippines	13.3	11.7	7.5	3.3
Singapore	3.2	3.3	1.4	2.7
Taipei,China	4.9	4.8	1.1	2.0
Thailand	5.6	3.2	3.6	2.8
Average	*7.4*	*5.6*	*4.4*	*4.6*
Austria	4.4	1.6	1.9	1.1
Belgium	5.3	2.6	2.0	0.9
Denmark	7.4	2.9	2.0	0.8
Finland	8.6	2.8	1.9	1.6
France	8.3	3.5	1.7	0.7
Germany	3.3	1.3	1.5	1.5
Greece	18.1	3.9	7.7	6.0
Iceland	38.4	15.5	4.8	3.5
Ireland	11.0	6.0	3.2	1.9
Italy	13.4	5.2	3.6	1.9
Luxembourg	4.7	3.9	2.7	2.2
Netherlands	3.9	3.2	2.3	1.1
Norway	7.2	3.4	3.5	4.2
Portugal	18.9	5.2	5.0	3.4
Spain	13.0	5.2	4.2	1.4
Sweden	8.9	2.6	2.6	2.5
Switzerland	3.4	1.8	1.4	1.6
United Kingdom	10.6	6.6	3.1	1.6
Average	*10.5*	*4.3*	*3.1*	*2.1*
United States	5.6	2.6	2.4	0.7

( ) = negative.
Note: Data are GDP deflators

Source: World Bank *World Development Indicators* (WDI) database.

1975–1989 and 1990–2007, in consideration of the fact that in the 1990s European countries began to adopt currency arrangements, such as the European Monetary System (EMS), that contributed to reduced inflation. Our interest is to capture inflation rates that would occur in the absence of a nominal exchange rate anchor.

In the period 1975–1989, seven European countries—Greece, Iceland, Ireland, Italy, Portugal, Spain, and the United Kingdom—had double-digit inflation rates. However, in all European countries, average inflation rates fell significantly to lower levels in the 1990–2007 period. The average inflation rates were high for some East Asian economies, such as Indonesia, Korea, and the Philippines for the 1975–1989 period. While most East Asian economies maintained lower inflation rates in the second period, average inflation rates were still relatively high in Indonesia (14.1%) and the Philippines (7.5%).

Table 2.2 also shows inflation variability, gauged by standard deviations. The majority of European and East Asian economies have relatively low inflation variability. One exception is Indonesia, in which the variability of annual inflation rates over 1990–2007 was 15.8%, far above the regional average of 4.6%.

Since the majority of East Asian economies maintain relatively stable prices, gains from enhancing price stability by joining a currency union are not considered to be large, with the likely exception of Indonesia and the Philippines. Furthermore, when a country decides to join a currency union, it is not clear which currency would serve as a better nominal anchor. Over the 1990–2007 period, Japan recorded price deflation (–0.2%). The US had moderate inflation (2.4%), but not much different from the performance of Europe (3.1%). Compared to a currency union that adopts one major currency as an anchor, an East Asian currency union, particularly one that excludes Japan, would be less desirable in terms of enhancing price stability because the average inflation rate in East Asia is relatively high. Over the 1990–2007 period, the average inflation rates were 4.4% for the 10 East Asian economies and 4.9% for the nine economies when Japan is excluded.

Table 2.3 reports the measures of the co-movements of prices for selected countries with the US, Europe, Japan, and East Asia, for the 1975–1989 and 1990–2004 periods. Here a high number implies less co-movement in prices. The table shows that the co-movement of prices in East Asia is lower than in Europe. The average number for 10 East Asian economies is 0.097 in the 1975–1989 period and 0.121 in the 1990–2004 period, while it is 0.062 and 0.048 for Europe in the first and second periods, respectively. East Asian economies have a relatively lower degree of price co-movements with all potential anchor countries: the US (0.101), Europe (0.137), or Japan (0.104) in the 1990–2004 period. In particular, Indonesia shows the lowest co-movements of prices with all potential anchor countries. The high value of the co-movement measure for Indonesia is in part a reflection of higher inflation variability, as well as

Table 2.3
Co-Movements of Prices for East Asia and Europe, 1975–1989 and 1990–2004

Economy	1975–1989				1990–2004			
	US	Europe	Japan	East Asia	US	Europe	Japan	East Asia
China, People's Rep. of	0.103	0.132	0.155	0.104	0.125	0.174	0.152	0.165
Hong Kong, China	0.061	0.094	0.130	0.083	0.028	0.108	0.100	0.116
Indonesia	0.120	0.191	0.188	0.142	0.246	0.252	0.225	0.210
Japan	0.130	0.108	.	0.139	0.094	0.131	.	0.115
Korea, Rep. of	0.080	0.115	0.124	0.084	0.123	0.130	0.098	0.108
Malaysia	0.050	0.116	0.134	0.085	0.104	0.142	0.109	0.102
Philippines	0.070	0.125	0.154	0.087	0.109	0.133	0.103	0.105
Singapore	0.037	0.098	0.122	0.078	0.038	0.090	0.087	0.097
Taipei,China	0.080	0.109	0.127	0.090	0.060	0.107	0.076	0.092
Thailand	0.050	0.098	0.116	0.076	0.081	0.107	0.085	0.096
Average	*0.078*	*0.118*	*0.125*	*0.097*	*0.101*	*0.137*	*0.104*	*0.121*
Austria	0.116	0.051	0.090	0.126	0.103	0.040	0.121	0.132
Belgium	0.104	0.054	0.103	0.127	0.102	0.037	0.126	0.137
Denmark	0.103	0.052	0.095	0.122	0.103	0.037	0.128	0.136
Finland	0.076	0.064	0.111	0.102	0.119	0.063	0.146	0.154
France	0.109	0.055	0.113	0.128	0.095	0.039	0.130	0.134
Germany	0.106	0.050	0.095	0.123	0.098	0.041	0.121	0.131
Greece	0.087	0.077	0.121	0.101	0.101	0.042	0.133	0.133
Iceland	0.093	0.090	0.107	0.108	0.095	0.065	0.121	0.136
Ireland	0.109	0.056	0.111	0.119	0.096	0.048	0.134	0.138
Italy	0.113	0.059	0.105	0.122	0.108	0.059	0.154	0.149
Luxembourg	0.109	0.055	0.104	0.128	0.110	0.040	0.130	0.138
Netherlands	0.119	0.054	0.106	0.132	0.100	0.039	0.125	0.133
Norway	0.075	0.057	0.098	0.099	0.085	0.048	0.126	0.125
Portugal	0.095	0.069	0.117	0.117	0.110	0.048	0.136	0.142
Spain	0.113	0.071	0.128	0.124	0.112	0.044	0.139	0.146
Sweden	0.081	0.059	0.109	0.107	0.114	0.067	0.152	0.148
Switzerland	0.129	0.074	0.093	0.137	0.098	0.048	0.116	0.128
United Kingdom	0.104	0.073	0.130	0.113	0.078	0.069	0.123	0.132
Average	*0.102*	*0.062*	*0.107*	*0.118*	*0.101*	*0.048*	*0.131*	*0.137*
United States	.	0.102	0.130	0.078	.	0.102	0.094	0.101

. = not applicable.
Notes: The co-movement measure is the standard error of the residual for the AR-2 regression for the log of the real exchange rate using the sample of 1960–2004. The bilateral real exchange rate is constructed from the Penn World Tables v.6.2. A higher number implies less co-movement of prices. East Asia refers to 10 East Asian economies including Japan.

its unique industrial structure, which includes a reliance on oil production. A notable feature is that while all European countries have higher co-movements of prices with the other European countries than with the US, some East Asian economies—including Hong Kong, China; Singapore; and Taipei,China—have substantially higher co-movements of prices with the US than with Japan or the rest of East Asia. This pattern may reflect the effects of the existing exchange-rate systems on price co-movements.

In summary, based on average inflation rates and price co-movements, the benefit from joining currency unions is relatively low for East Asian economies. Since their average inflation rates are low and the degree of price co-movements is relatively small, East Asian economies, except for Indonesia and the Philippines, would not benefit much from the commitment to a currency union.

3.1.3 Co-Movement of Output

Table 2.4 shows measures of the co-movements of outputs (real per capita GDP). East Asia has a similar degree of output co-movements with any of the potential anchor countries: over the 1990–2005 period, the average number is 0.038 with the US, 0.034 with Japan, 0.042 with Europe, and 0.041 within East Asia. Compared to Europe, East Asia's co-movements of output with any of the potential anchors are relatively lower (a high number implies less co-movement of outputs): the average of output co-movements for Europe is 0.020 with the US, 0.023 with Japan, and 0.021 within Europe over the 1990–2005 period.

The business cycles of East Asian economies appear to be less associated with each other, compared to those of European countries. The average of the numbers of the intra-region output co-movement for East Asia (0.041) is higher than that for Europe (0.021). The co-movement of output with the rest of East Asia ranges from 0.033 (Malaysia) to 0.049 (the People's Republic of China [PRC]), while the degree of intra-region output co-movement for European countries ranges from 0.016 (France) to 0.032 (Finland). The degree of output co-movement within the region is often lower than that with the major anchor countries. For instance, PRC's business cycle is more associated with either the US (0.032) or Europe (0.033) than with the rest of East Asia (0.049). This pattern may reflect two forces—a high level of integration in trade with the US and Europe, particularly in the final goods, and the exchange-rate system that was in place.

Overall, based on the criterion of business cycle synchronization, it is not clear which currency would serve as a better nominal anchor for East Asia. There is not much difference in terms of the degree of output co-movements among the various choices of anchor. Compared to Europe, it could be potentially costly for East Asian economies to lose an independent monetary policy, because East Asia's business cycles are less associated with those of potential anchors.

Table 2.4
Co-Movements of Outputs for East Asia and Europe, 1975–1989 and 1990–2005

Economy	1975–1989				1990–2005			
	US	Europe	Japan	East Asia	US	Europe	Japan	East Asia
China, People's Rep. of	0.048	0.051	0.044	0.056	0.032	0.033	0.036	0.049
Hong Kong, China	0.035	0.041	0.042	0.041	0.042	0.046	0.035	0.038
Indonesia	0.030	0.045	0.046	0.044	0.045	0.048	0.039	0.040
Japan	0.027	0.027	.	0.041	0.022	0.023	.	0.038
Korea, Rep. of	0.031	0.044	0.039	0.046	0.053	0.053	0.046	0.041
Malaysia	0.032	0.033	0.034	0.040	0.028	0.035	0.030	0.033
Philippines	0.050	0.050	0.048	0.050	0.043	0.045	0.043	0.045
Singapore	0.043	0.042	0.043	0.045	0.052	0.057	0.050	0.044
Taipei,China	0.025	0.037	0.039	0.037	0.021	0.028	0.024	0.038
Thailand	0.039	0.042	0.033	0.045	0.046	0.048	0.039	0.041
Average	*0.036*	*0.041*	*0.037*	*0.044*	*0.038*	*0.042*	*0.034*	*0.041*
Austria	0.033	0.031	0.027	0.044	0.017	0.018	0.017	0.039
Belgium	0.027	0.025	0.022	0.037	0.017	0.017	0.019	0.037
Denmark	0.026	0.030	0.029	0.042	0.015	0.019	0.020	0.037
Finland	0.038	0.033	0.025	0.043	0.027	0.032	0.040	0.056
France	0.025	0.023	0.016	0.035	0.017	0.016	0.021	0.041
Germany	0.019	0.024	0.019	0.034	0.021	0.018	0.016	0.037
Greece	0.035	0.040	0.029	0.047	0.026	0.026	0.025	0.045
Iceland	0.043	0.043	0.043	0.050	0.025	0.030	0.030	0.050
Ireland	0.028	0.035	0.026	0.041	0.028	0.031	0.029	0.043
Italy	0.026	0.026	0.020	0.037	0.019	0.017	0.019	0.039
Luxembourg	0.039	0.041	0.046	0.046	0.030	0.031	0.036	0.045
Netherlands	0.020	0.025	0.022	0.036	0.016	0.017	0.020	0.039
Norway	0.029	0.031	0.026	0.041	0.018	0.020	0.016	0.036
Portugal	0.046	0.038	0.036	0.049	0.021	0.020	0.025	0.042
Spain	0.027	0.027	0.024	0.038	0.017	0.017	0.020	0.041
Sweden	0.029	0.030	0.020	0.040	0.019	0.020	0.025	0.043
Switzerland	0.035	0.033	0.031	0.044	0.017	0.019	0.020	0.041
United Kingdom	0.020	0.028	0.020	0.036	0.010	0.020	0.020	0.040
Average	*0.030*	*0.031*	*0.027*	*0.041*	*0.020*	*0.021*	*0.023*	*0.042*
United States	.	0.030	0.027	0.036	.	0.020	0.022	0.038

. = not applicable.
Notes: The co-movement measure is the standard error of the residual for the AR-2 regression for the log of the ratio of real per capita GDPs using the sample of 1960–2005. The real GDP data, adjusted by PPP are from the Penn World Tables v.6.2. A higher number implies less co-movement of outputs. East Asia refers to 10 East Asian economies including Japan.

3.1.4 Financial Integration

Tables 2.5 and 2.6 present the data on bilateral asset holdings for East Asia compared to that for Europe in 2006. Table 2.5 presents the ratio of gross portfolio asset holdings to GDP invested by East Asian and European economies (and the region's average) in each of four destinations that represent the potential anchor economy or region: the US, Europe, Japan, and East Asia (including Japan). The GDP value in these ratios refers to the East Asian or European economy paired with the potential anchor economy or region. In contrast, table 2.6 reports data for cross-border portfolio assets invested in East Asian or European economies by the potential anchor economy or region. Invested assets are expressed as a ratio to the GDP of each recipient East Asian or European economy. Observations for PRC and Taipei,China, are missing in table 2.5 because they are not in the sample of 75 source countries in the CPIS survey of IMF, whereas table 2.6 includes data for them, since they are listed among the destination economies in the CPIS survey.

According to table 2.5, small economies with financial and offshore centers have very high ratios of international portfolio asset holdings to GDP. For instance, Hong Kong, China; Ireland; Singapore; and Switzerland have worldwide asset holdings amounting to several times their own domestic output levels. The ratio of portfolio asset holdings amounts to 306% for Hong Kong, China and 190% for Singapore. In contrast, for a typical East Asian economy, such bilateral financial linkages are a relatively small fraction of GDP. While Japan has relatively larger cross-border portfolio asset holdings amounting to 54% of its GDP, other East Asian economies have very low ratios, ranging from 0.4% (Indonesia) to 9.4% (Korea). The average cross-border asset-to-GDP ratio for eight East Asian economies is 71.5%; in contrast, for 17 European countries, this average is 148.3%. The majority of East Asian economies, except Japan; Hong Kong, China; and Singapore, exhibit a relatively low degree of international financial integration, compared to the European economies.

The intra-region portfolio asset holding is also much lower in East Asia relative to Europe. The average of intra-East Asia asset holdings-to-GDP ratios for eight East Asian economies is 18.1%. The comparable average of intra-Europe asset holdings for 17 European countries amounts to 96.7%. East Asian economies are more integrated with global financial markets, including the US and Europe, than with each other. For the eight East Asian economies, the average asset-to-GDP ratio for the cross-border asset holdings is 20.8% in Europe and 10.6% in the US.[12] In particular, Japan has very low intra-region financial integration relative to its global integration. Japan's average asset holdings-to-GDP ratio is only 1.1% with East Asia, while it is 18.3% with the US and 20.5% with Europe.

In table 2.6, the general patterns from portfolio asset investment in East Asian or European economies by the potential anchor economy or region are

Table 2.5
International Portfolio Asset Holdings by Countries in East Asia and Europe in 2006 (percent of GDP)

Source Economy	Recipient Economy/Region				
	US	Europe	Japan	East Asia	World
China, People's Rep. of	...	...	...	...	...
Hong Kong, China	34.1	79.5	9.9	79.6	305.5
Indonesia	0.0	0.1	0.0	0.1	0.4
Japan	18.3	20.5	.	1.1	53.6
Korea, Rep. of	3.4	3.3	0.3	1.4	9.4
Malaysia	0.5	1.5	0.2	1.9	4.6
Philippines	2.6	1.4	0.0	1.1	6.1
Singapore	25.2	59.3	7.5	59.6	190.3
Taipei,China	...	...	...	...	...
Thailand	0.2	0.8	0.0	0.4	2.3
Average	*10.6*	*20.8*	*2.2*	*18.1*	*71.5*
Austria	8.4	79.2	0.9	1.9	109.4
Belgium	13.9	146.7	1.1	1.5	171.7
Denmark	18.4	57.9	4.0	6.9	95.0
Finland	7.8	84.2	1.8	3.1	102.5
France	11.3	81.0	3.8	4.8	109.2
Germany	9.3	60.8	1.1	1.8	78.1
Greece	2.3	17.8	0.0	0.1	28.7
Iceland	13.2	86.1	1.4	1.7	106.0
Ireland	179.8	432.5	25.9	43.4	736.0
Italy	5.6	47.7	0.8	1.1	61.6
Luxembourg	...	...	...	...	...
Netherlands	46.1	117.7	5.6	10.1	190.7
Norway	28.7	77.8	6.7	9.1	129.8
Portugal	4.8	62.0	0.1	0.2	82.3
Spain	4.3	40.2	0.2	0.2	54.4
Sweden	24.4	64.5	4.1	6.1	102.8
Switzerland	31.5	134.6	4.9	6.9	231.0
United Kingdom	35.1	53.7	9.5	16.1	132.1
Average	*26.2*	*96.7*	*4.2*	*6.8*	*148.3*
United States	.	22.8	4.4	8.0	45.4

... = data unavailable.
. = not applicable.
Notes: The amount of cross-border portfolio assets invested by each East Asian and European economy, as a ratio to the source economy's GDP. East Asia refers to 8 East Asian economies including Japan but excluding the People's Republic of China (PRC) and Taipei,China.

Source: IMF Coordinated Portfolio Investment Survey (CPIS) database.

Table 2.6
International Portfolio Assets Invested in Countries in East Asia and Europe in 2006 (percent of GDP)

Recipient Economy	Source Economy/Region				
	US	Europe	Japan	East Asia	World
China, People's Rep. of	2.8	2.7	0.4	4.5	10.4
Hong Kong, China	46.1	46.3	6.2	21.4	124.6
Indonesia	3.9	4.0	0.3	2.5	11.4
Japan	13.4	14.6	0.0	0.7	32.9
Korea, Rep. of	13.9	11.0	1.0	4.0	31.0
Malaysia	9.9	14.5	1.0	12.6	38.3
Philippines	9.3	13.0	1.4	3.3	26.8
Singapore	38.6	33.1	5.5	14.6	94.0
Taipei,China	20.3	15.7	0.7	2.8	40.5
Thailand	6.3	7.6	0.6	3.5	18.2
Average	*16.5*	*16.3*	*1.7*	*7.0*	*42.8*
Austria	8.3	85.1	4.4	4.9	108.5
Belgium	9.1	70.6	5.1	5.4	94.5
Denmark	12.3	51.7	4.2	5.2	74.8
Finland	28.5	77.0	3.7	4.4	118.6
France	17.7	60.1	6.3	7.2	96.2
Germany	10.0	57.1	6.0	6.7	88.9
Greece	5.2	72.8	2.3	2.4	83.3
Iceland	48.1	192.6	6.9	10.2	262.4
Ireland	54.7	321.7	18.1	24.6	440.8
Italy	5.7	67.1	3.6	3.8	80.2
Luxembourg	...	...	...	...	...
Netherlands	35.3	164.3	11.6	14.4	233.4
Norway	15.1	32.9	6.1	7.7	59.7
Portugal	3.3	86.3	1.1	1.5	94.8
Spain	9.1	76.4	2.7	2.9	92.5
Sweden	26.6	66.8	6.6	7.8	111.3
Switzerland	69.5	74.1	4.5	5.4	157.8
United Kingdom	45.2	59.5	6.1	11.3	134.8
Average	*23.7*	*95.1*	*5.8*	*7.4*	*137.2*
United States	.	23.6	6.1	7.1	48.5

... = data unavailable.
. = not applicable.
Notes: The amount of cross-border portfolio assets invested by source country or region, as a ratio to the source economy's GDP. East Asia refers to 10 East Asian economies including Japan.

Source: IMF Coordinated Portfolio Investment Survey (CPIS) database.

similar to those from table 2.5. Small economies with financial and offshore centers, including Hong Kong, China; and Singapore, still dominate the representation, by having higher asset-to-GDP ratios. East Asian economies, except Hong Kong, China; Singapore; and Japan, tend to have higher ratios for total international assets invested in their economies, compared to the ratios for their international asset holdings abroad. The likely explanation is that these East Asian economies are more restrictive in allowing cross-border portfolio investments by domestic residents, while permitting relatively free capital inflows by international investors. It can also reflect higher rates of return in East Asia.

Table 2.6 also shows that for a typical East Asian economy, the intra-region financial linkage is relatively low. The average of intra-East Asia asset holdings-to-GDP ratios for 10 East Asian economies is 7.0%, compared to 95.1% for the average intra-Europe asset holdings-to-GDP ratio for 17 European countries.

Overall, the data show that East Asian economies are far less financially integrated within the region than European economies. East Asian economies tend to be more closely financially linked with the US and Europe than with each other.

3.1.5 Political Proximity

Table 2.7 presents the measure of political proximity with potential anchor countries for East Asian economies over the 1985–1990 and 2000–2005 periods, and compares them with those for European countries. According to the UN vote correlation measure, the political affinities between the US and East Asian economies are relatively low. This pattern reflects, in part, the US tendency to vote contrary to the majority of UN member countries on resolutions such as those related to the Israel-Palestine conflicts. East Asia has a lower degree of political proximity with any potential anchor economy or region, compared to Europe. Over the 2000–2005 period, the average of political proximity for eight East Asian countries (not counting Hong Kong, China; and Taipei,China which are not UN members) is 0.166 with the US, 0.638 with Europe, 0.653 with Japan, and 0.775 within East Asia. In contrast, for 18 European countries, the average is 0.365 with the US, 0.922 within Europe, and 0.836 with Japan.

The degree of political proximity among East Asian countries is on average lower than that among European countries. In particular, Japan and Korea have the least political proximity with other East Asian countries, around 0.65. In contrast, PRC and Southeast Asian countries have a higher degree of political proximity, close to that among European countries. The relatively lower political proximity of Japan and Korea with the rest of East Asia reflects in part the stronger alliance they maintain with the US.[13] Japan and Korea have a higher degree of political proximity with the US than other East Asian countries.

Table 2.7
Political Proximity for East Asia and Europe, Average over 1985–1990 and 2000–2005

Country	1985–1990				2000–2005			
	US	Europe	Japan	East Asia	US	Europe	Japan	East Asia
China, People's Rep. of	0.150	0.487	0.489	0.791	0.106	0.532	0.591	0.787
Hong Kong, China	...	...	...	...	...	...	...	...
Indonesia	0.125	0.473	0.455	0.823	0.120	0.567	0.601	0.821
Japan	0.317	0.757	.	0.491	0.292	0.836	.	0.653
Korea, Rep. of	...	...	...	...	0.278	0.805	0.853	0.633
Malaysia	0.143	0.495	0.496	0.849	0.121	0.571	0.610	0.827
Philippines	0.142	0.513	0.488	0.835	0.142	0.587	0.626	0.828
Singapore	0.154	0.524	0.529	0.828	0.137	0.593	0.632	0.818
Taipei,China	...	...	...	...	...	...	...	...
Thailand	0.132	0.497	0.490	0.836	0.132	0.615	0.656	0.832
Average	*0.166*	*0.535*	*0.491*	*0.779*	*0.166*	*0.638*	*0.653*	*0.775*
Austria	0.223	0.737	0.713	0.634	0.346	0.928	0.856	0.665
Belgium	0.409	0.796	0.793	0.473	0.362	0.939	0.840	0.636
Denmark	0.300	0.806	0.800	0.564	0.369	0.944	0.861	0.649
Finland	0.225	0.738	0.718	0.623	0.353	0.935	0.862	0.653
France	0.466	0.713	0.685	0.414	0.413	0.858	0.742	0.560
Germany	0.429	0.764	0.756	0.439	0.369	0.933	0.832	0.630
Greece	0.220	0.698	0.723	0.664	0.357	0.937	0.842	0.655
Iceland	0.292	0.792	0.793	0.552	0.365	0.942	0.856	0.641
Ireland	0.249	0.773	0.753	0.613	0.323	0.900	0.844	0.675
Italy	0.395	0.798	0.800	0.496	0.368	0.933	0.837	0.647
Luxembourg	0.390	0.789	0.783	0.476	0.365	0.942	0.847	0.643
Netherlands	0.404	0.796	0.792	0.481	0.365	0.942	0.850	0.643
Norway	0.300	0.802	0.792	0.565	0.367	0.936	0.854	0.645
Portugal	0.388	0.793	0.816	0.505	0.364	0.924	0.841	0.654
Spain	0.275	0.742	0.787	0.591	0.360	0.921	0.838	0.647
Sweden	0.237	0.748	0.726	0.633	0.337	0.907	0.864	0.659
Switzerland	...	...	...	...	0.331	0.930	0.841	0.653
United Kingdom	0.562	0.674	0.642	0.377	0.464	0.849	0.749	0.548
Average	*0.339*	*0.762*	*0.757*	*0.535*	*0.365*	*0.922*	*0.836*	*0.639*
United States	.	0.339	0.317	0.166	.	0.367	0.292	0.166

... = data unavailable.
. = not applicable.
Notes: Political proximity is the fraction of times out of all votes that countries voted alongside in the UN General Assembly along with each other. East Asia includes 7 economies except Hong Kong, China; Korea; and Taipei,China for 1985–1990, and 8 economies including Korea for 2000–2005.

The lower political proximity among East Asian countries may imply that it would be difficult for them to rally their political wills toward formation of a monetary union. In particular, the low political proximity between Japan and other East Asian economies may impede Japan's leadership for the creation of an East Asian currency union. A currency union for a subgroup of Southeast Asia and PRC seems to be more feasible from the standpoint of current geopolitical conditions. Figure 2.1 shows that the political proximity between PRC and Association of Southeast Asian Nations (ASEAN) members, such as Malaysia and Singapore, is quite high.

However, the degree of political proximity among East Asian economies, particularly between Japan and other East Asian economies, has been increasing over time, from 0.491 in 1985–1990 to 0.653 in 2000–2005 (see table 2.7). The average of intra-region political proximity for East Asia in 2000–2005 (0.775) is comparable to that for Europe in 1985–1990 (0.762). The political proximity among European countries has continued to increase over time,[14] which may reflect the continuous efforts of European countries toward integration. The political proximity among East Asian economies would also tend to increase over time if they continue to conduct policy dialogue for deeper trade and financial integration.

3.2 Is East Asia an OCA?

In the previous section, various OCA criteria for forming a currency union in East Asia were evaluated. Overall, it is unclear whether the region is suitable for a currency union. A favorable factor is the substantial degree of intra-region trade. Less favorable elements, particularly compared to Europe, involve the degree of financial integration and business-cycle synchronization. East Asian economies are far less financially integrated with anchor countries or with each other, compared to Europe. Losing independent monetary policy could potentially be costly for East Asian economies, because East Asia's business cycles are less associated with those of potential anchors.

Another issue is whether East Asian economies have sufficient political proximity to form a currency union. The degree of political proximity within East Asia is lower than that within Europe. In particular, the low political proximity between Japan and other East Asian economies would impede Japan's leadership in the creation of an East Asian currency union. However, political proximity among East Asian economies, particularly if Japan is omitted, appears reasonably strong. Notably, today's levels of political proximity for East Asia are similar to those for Europe in the past. When we consider that the political affinity between Japan and the other regional economies has been rising over time (Figure 2.1), East Asia would likely be able to achieve political cooperation sufficient to advance a currency union in the region.

It is not clear, however, which currency East Asian economies should choose as an anchor. While these economies can benefit the most from

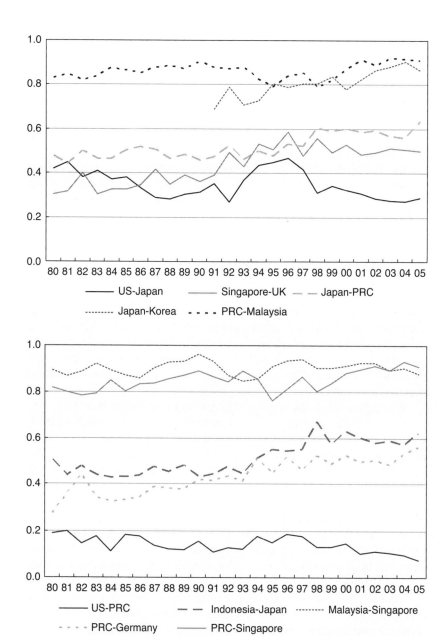

Figure 2.1 Political Proximity for Selected Country-Pairs, 1980–2005

Note: Political proximity is the fraction of times out of all votes that countries voted alongside in the UN General Assembly along with each other.

forming a broad East Asian currency union, a currency union that adopts any major currency as an anchor might also be beneficial. Although intra-region trade in East Asia has been rapidly expanding, the business cycles of East Asian economies tend to be more associated with the US and Europe than with each other. East Asian economies also tend to be more closely linked financially with the US and Europe than with each other.

Overall, at the current stage of economic and political development, East Asia does not appear to be an optimum currency area. More appropriate criteria for a successful currency union, however, involve the pattern of trade and financial integration that would be shaped after the setup of a currency union. Frankel and Rose (1998) point out that country characteristics affecting OCA conditions can be endogenously determined. For example, once a group of economies forms a currency union, the degree of intra-region trade and investment and the degree of symmetry of economic shocks can be increased. The endogeneity of OCA criteria implies that a country's decision to join a monetary union should not just consider the situation that applies *ex ante*, but also allow for the conditions that would apply *ex post*, that is, allow for the economic effects of a currency union.

There is some evidence that joining a currency union leads to increased trade among member countries, further strengthening the formation of the currency union. In his seminal paper, Rose (2000) reports that bilateral trade between countries that use the same currency is, controlling for other effects, over 200% larger than otherwise. Most subsequent research confirmed a significantly positive effect of a currency union on trade, though smaller than 200%.

Reduced currency risk among currency union members is also likely to enhance financial integration among member countries. Fratzscher (2001) provides evidence that the introduction of the euro has increased the degree of integration among European stock markets. Spiegel (2004) shows that Portugal's accession to the EMU has led to a substantial increase in bilateral borrowing from EMU members.

There is more uncertainty in predicting whether endogenous adjustments of output movements after forming a currency union will act for or against the union. Frankel and Rose (1998) argue that increased trade by a currency union can help business cycles to be more synchronized between countries. However, as argued by Eichengreen (1992) and Krugman (1993), an increase in trade linkages may encourage greater specialization of production, resulting in less synchronization of business cycles. Rose and Engle (2002) show that business cycles are more synchronized across currency union member countries than across countries with sovereign monies. In contrast to the findings of Rose and Engle, however, Tenreyro and Barro (2007) demonstrate that by adopting an instrumental-variable (IV) approach, currency unions decrease output co-movement.

Joining a currency union can also have an impact on the degree of political proximity among member countries. Currency union can help increase mutual economic and political dependence among member countries and limit the use of military force in interstate relations (see discussion in the next section). Thus, it can enhance political proximity among member countries. On the other hand, a currency union can amplify internal conflicts between domestic interest groups and disputes among members over the implementation of common monetary policy and seigniorage revenue sharing, and this can lead to a decrease in political proximity among member countries.

4 Welfare Effects of East Asian Currency Unions

This section discusses welfare effects of East Asian currency unions, focusing on a dollar bloc and a new regional currency bloc for 10 East Asian economies. We compare the potential benefits of joining a currency union with the potential costs. In terms of the benefits, we focus on the effects from additional trade between countries that adopt the common currency in East Asia. Increased trade leads to an increase in output and consumption, thereby raising welfare. Currency unions would also assist in providing a credible nominal anchor for monetary policy. However, as discussed in the previous section, the benefits from enhancing price stability by joining a currency union would not be significant for the majority of East Asian economies, because they already tend to keep prices relatively stable under present arrangements.

In terms of costs, the major downside from joining a currency union involves the loss of an independent monetary policy. The loss of monetary policy independence can lead to increasing output and consumption fluctuations, which would incur welfare loss for risk-averse consumers. In conventional models, the costs of business cycle fluctuations tend to be small relative to the benefits from increasing growth rates. Lucas (1987, 2003) finds small welfare costs of output fluctuations at business cycle frequencies based on a representative agent framework in which output is assumed to revert quickly to a deterministic trend. Subsequent studies propose different models and assumptions, yielding a wide range of estimates of the welfare cost of business cycles. For instance, Imrohoroglu (1989) and Krusell and Smith (1999) introduce heterogeneous agents and uninsurable individual risk and find a larger welfare cost of business cycle fluctuations. Obstfeld (1994) and Barro (2006b) suggest that the welfare cost of consumption volatility is significantly higher than in Lucas's calculations when the consumption process contains a stochastic trend, so that shocks have permanent effects.

In this section, we discuss the welfare effects from the implementation of various types of East Asian currency unions. These effects work mainly through changes in consumption growth rates and consumption volatility.

4.1 The Effects of Currency Unions on Growth and Volatility

This section discusses how a currency union can affect consumption growth rates and consumption volatility. The quantitative assessment unavoidably calls for a number of simplifying assumptions.

A currency union can generate welfare gains from the additional trade with countries belonging to the same currency union, thereby stimulating an increase in consumption growth rates. The increase of trade (as a ratio to GDP) as a result of joining a currency union, ΔTR_i^j, can be measured by $\Delta TR_i^j = \frac{trade_{i,j}}{GDP_i}\alpha$. In this equation, $\frac{trade_{i,j}}{GDP_i}$ denotes country i's total trade (exports plus imports) with a potential anchor country j, expressed as a ratio to country i's GDP, and α is the parameter capturing the marginal effect of joining a currency union on trade. Existing studies report a wide range of estimates of α. The seminal paper of Rose (2000) reports an estimate of 2.0. Subsequently, there have been a vast number of studies made to check the robustness of his finding. Rose and Stanley (2005) summarize 34 studies that yield 754 point estimates of common-currency trade effects, ranging between −0.7 and 7.1 based on different samples and techniques. They use meta-regression analysis to combine these disparate estimates and conclude that the true effects range between 0.3 and 0.9.[15] They also control for publication bias, that is, selection favoring the reporting of significantly positive trade effects, and report the "meta-estimate" for the currency union trade effect to be 0.47. For our benchmark calibration, we use the estimate $\alpha = 0.5$. This estimate implies, for given GDPs, that joining a currency union increases bilateral trade volume between members by 50%. The trade volume would rise by more than 50% if the induced increase in output due to trade expansion were considered.

The increased trade tends to raise the growth rates of output and consumption in country i. Let ψ be the parameter that captures the marginal effect of a one-unit increase in the trade-to-GDP ratio on the growth rate. Then the increase in the growth rate is given by

$$\Delta \gamma_i = \Delta TR_i^j \cdot \psi = \frac{trade_{i,j}}{GDP_i} \cdot \alpha \cdot \psi.$$

With more countries, we would add up the trade volumes for all the js belonging to the currency union to get the total effect on country i's growth rate.

Barro and Sala-i-Martin (2003) and De Gregorio and Lee (2005) show that, using a five-year panel data set for a broad number of countries, ψ is around 0.01. In a different framework, Frankel and Rose (2002) estimate that an increase in the trade-to-GDP ratio by x leads to a proportionate increase in per capita GDP by $x/3$ over 20 years, thereby implying an increase of about $0.015 \cdot x$ per year. For the benchmark calibration, we assume $\psi = 0.01$. Therefore, a currency union for 10 East Asian economies would increase the average trade-to-GDP ratio from its initial value, 0.30 to 0.45, and then the average GDP growth rate by 0.0015 per year ($0.30 \times 0.50 \times 0.01$).

To quantify the impact of joining a currency union on the welfare cost of business cycles involves several critical assumptions. First, the nature of the shocks must be defined. Unlike Lucas, but in line with Obstfeld and Barro, we assume that consumption is a random walk with drift, so that shocks have permanent effects. Empirical studies found that output and consumption tend to have a stochastic trend (Cogley, 1990). In particular, the evidence conflicts with rapid reversion to a fixed trend line. The welfare cost from the loss of an independent monetary policy is magnified because shocks have permanent effects on consumption.

Second, the exact role of independent monetary policy in stabilizing output and consumption fluctuations needs to be assessed. It is hard to gauge exactly how much the cyclical variability can be eliminated by monetary policy in East Asia. It may not be feasible for the monetary authority to remove the systematic cyclical variability originating from technological shocks. Not all monetary authorities in East Asia have the institutional capabilities to conduct monetary policy to minimize business fluctuations. Lucas (2003) summarizes previous research and suggests that nominal shocks have accounted for something less than 30% of output variability in the postwar US. We assume that monetary policy can stabilize a constant fraction, χ, of shocks to output and consumption. For the benchmark simulation, $\chi = 0.3$ is assumed, implying that independent monetary policy can stabilize 30% of normal disturbance volatility, $0.3 \cdot \sigma^2$.[16]

Under a currency union, country i can no longer use its own monetary policy for stabilization. When it adopts an anchor country j's currency, country i's monetary policy is administrated by the monetary authority in the anchor country. It is assumed that the monetary authority of anchor country j uses its monetary policy to stabilize its own consumption as much as possible.

Since the anchor country reacts only to its own economic disturbances, country i's shocks cannot be stabilized as much as in the case of monetary policy independence under a floating exchange rate regime, but it is accommodated to the extent that country i's shock moves along with country j's. That is, when country i adopts country j's currency, the volatility of consumption of country i increases by $\chi \cdot Var(\varepsilon_t^i - \varepsilon_t^j)$.

If a group of countries creates a new currency and a new joint central bank, the new monetary authority would adopt the monetary policy that stabilizes the fluctuation of the regional average output and thereby eliminate the systematic part of regional consumption volatility. Hence, when country i forms a currency union with the other countries in East Asia, the volatility of consumption of country i increases by $\chi \cdot Var(\varepsilon_t^i - \frac{1}{N} \sum_{j=1}^{N} \varepsilon_t^j)$.[17]

Table 2.8 presents statistics for the mean and standard deviation of per capita consumption growth rates over the period from 1960 to 1997 for

Table 2.8

Mean and Standard Deviation of Annual Per Capita Real Consumption Growth over the Period of 1960–1997

Country	Mean Growth Rate	Std. Dev. of Growth Rate Shocks	Std. Dev. of Growth Rate Shocks after a Currency Union	
			US dollar	East Asia10
China, People's Rep. of	0.0367	0.0532	0.0614	0.0603
Hong Kong, China	0.0569	0.0462	0.0525	0.0527
Indonesia	0.0359	0.0593	0.0687	0.0680
Japan	0.0458	0.0322	0.0378	0.0372
Korea, Rep. of	0.0495	0.0367	0.0433	0.0410
Malaysia	0.0326	0.0441	0.0532	0.0497
Philippines	0.0139	0.0338	0.0405	0.0379
Singapore	0.0480	0.0381	0.0432	0.0428
Taipei,China	0.0628	0.0319	0.0371	0.0365
Thailand	0.0411	0.0360	0.0420	0.0406
Average	*0.0423*	*0.0410*	*0.0478*	*0.0465*

Notes: The consumption fluctuation of country i, after adopting a currency of anchor country j or joining a currency union involving a group of 10 East Asian countries including country i, is assumed to increase by $\chi \cdot Var(\varepsilon_t^i - \varepsilon_t^j)$ or $\chi \cdot Var(\varepsilon_t^i - \frac{1}{10}\sum_{j=1}^{10} \varepsilon_t^j)$. The parameter χ measures a constant fraction of shocks to output and consumption that can be stabilized by the monetary policy and is assumed to be 0.3. Data for Singapore is from 1966 to 1997.

East Asian economies. The last two columns of table 2.8 report the estimates of the increased consumption volatility for individual East Asian economies that join a currency union. For the average East Asian economy, adopting the US dollar as an anchor currency increases the annual standard deviation of consumption by 0.007, from 0.041 to 0.048, while joining a currency union involving 10 East Asian economies increases the standard deviation by the smaller amount 0.005.

By assuming that all shocks have a permanent effect on welfare, this analysis may be considered to give the upper-bound estimate of the welfare cost from increasing volatility caused by the loss of independent monetary policy. If the increased volatility due to the loss of an independent monetary policy were transitory, the welfare cost would be small.[18] It is also assumed that other policy arrangements such as cooperative fiscal policy between member countries would not offset the loss of monetary policy independence and, thereby, lessen the overall welfare cost.

The analysis does not take into account the welfare effects from increasing financial integration among the member countries joining a currency union. Integration of financial markets can provide greater risk-sharing within member countries. However, it is not clear whether increased financial integration can promote or hamper financial market stability. In addition, we do not consider whether a currency union can cause loss of seigniorage revenue, or whether a new seigniorage sharing mechanism can compensate partially for the loss.

4.2 Rare Disasters and Currency Unions

Recent models such as Reitz (1988) and Barro (2006a) allow for a small probability of a large drop in consumption. In an economy where big disasters such as wars or financial crises can occur, the uncertainty implies large welfare costs, compared to that from normal disturbances.

In order to gauge the probability and size of disaster, we follow the approach of Barro (2006a), which assesses disaster events from long-term time-series data on real per capita GDP. Table 2.9 reports major economic contractions, defined as a decline of 10% or more in real per capita GDP, which took place in 10 East Asian economies over the period 1915–2004. There were 14 major disasters—four associated with the Great Depression, seven with World War II, and three with major financial crises. Reliable GDP data for Hong Kong, China and Singapore, both former British colonies, and for Thailand are unavailable until after World War II. Based on the frequency of 14 events for the available country-year observations over 1915–2004, the probability of experiencing a major economic contraction for 10 East Asian economies is approximately 1.8% per year. The average contraction size is 0.29.[19]

The loss of monetary policy independence may have an impact on consumption fluctuations due to rare disasters. Monetary policy is often alleged to play a central role in major economic crises. For example, during the emerging market financial crises in the 1990s a major issue was the role played by monetary policy being tightened at the beginning of the crisis in order to avoid excessive currency depreciation (De Gregorio and Lee, 2005). A key unresolved question is to what extent an independent monetary policy influences the probability or size of major economic contractions.

Joining a currency union might lower the probabilities or sizes of disasters such as wars and financial crises. One of the fundamental benefits of joining a currency union is that it can eliminate the possibility of a currency crisis, although its impact on the likelihood and magnitude of banking crises is rather ambiguous. A complete elimination of exchange rate movement is the ultimate solution for currency crises. However, the adoption of a perfect floating exchange rate regime or credible pegs with sound macroeconomic policies, combined with sufficient international reserves, can also offer safeguards against speculative attacks. Therefore, the net welfare effect of a currency union

Table 2.9
Declines of 10% or More in Real Per Capita GDP in East Asia

Event	Country*	Years	% Fall in Real Per Capita GDP
Great Depression	China, People's Rep. of	1932–1934	10
	Indonesia	1929–1935	14
	Malaysia	1929–1932	17
	Taipei,China	1928–1931	12
World War II	China, People's Rep. of[1]	1936–1950	18
	Indonesia[2]	1941–1949	36
	Japan	1943–1945	52
	Korea, Rep. of	1937–1945	58
	Malaysia[3]	1942–1947	36
	Philippines[4]	1939–1946	60
	Taipei,China	1942–1945	51
Financial Crises	Indonesia	1997–1999	12
	Philippines	1982–1986	17
	Thailand	1997–1998	12
Mean for 14 contractions			29

Notes: Data are compiled from Maddison (2003) for 7 East Asia countries for 1915–1955, and the Penn World Tables for 10 East Asian economies for 1955–2004. Satisfactory data for Hong Kong, China; Singapore; and Thailand are unavailable until after World War II.
*Current nomenclature is used instead of historical name.
[1] No data available for 1939–1949.
[2] No data available for 1942–1948.
[3] No data available for 1941–1945.
[4] No data available for 1943–1946.

must depend on the country characteristics that determine the probability of financial crises.

Currency unions (or more generally, economic and political unions) can help to increase political as well as economic interdependence among member countries and this in turn will limit the incentive to use military force in interstate relations. The "liberal" view in political science, which can be traced back to Montesquieu, Kant, and Angell, emphasizes the degree of mutual economic interdependence as a condition of peace. In this regard, an increase in interstate economic dependence by sharing a common currency can help to lower the likelihood of bilateral military conflicts. In Europe, the impetus for forming the European Union and adopting the euro was the desire for peace, in particular between France and Germany, after World War II.

Recent empirical studies find that an increase in bilateral trade interdependence significantly decreases the probability of military conflict between countries (see Glick and Taylor, 2005; Martin et al., 2008; and Lee and

Pyun, 2009). They also suggest that greater bilateral trade interdependence brings about considerably greater peace-promotion efforts for neighboring countries that are likely to have more conflicts.

An increase in trade integration due to a currency union can have a significant impact on the probability or size of interstate conflicts. Using a logit estimation based on a large panel data set of country-pair observations from 1950 to 2000, Lee and Pyun (2009) find that an increase in the bilateral trade ratio by 10% (starting from the sample mean) decreases the probability of bilateral military conflict by about 0.1% with other variables held constant.[20] It also finds that the peace-promotion effect of bilateral trade integration is significantly higher for contiguous countries; the probability of military conflict decreases by about 1.9% with an increase in the bilateral trade ratio of 10%. This estimate indicates that increased trade integration due to an East Asia currency union can substantially reduce the probability of military conflict among the neighboring countries. An increase in the bilateral trade-to-GDP ratio by 50% from 0.30 to 0.45 for an average East Asian country due to currency union membership can lead to a decrease in the probability of military conflict by about 20% among the neighboring East Asian countries, which amounts to about 0.0010 reduction in the probability of conflict from its sample mean of 0.0055 for all dyad-year observations.[21]

Since the average bilateral trade-to-GDP ratio with the US is smaller (0.092, compared to 0.318 with the East Asia region) and the estimated peace-promotion effect of trade is smaller among non-neighboring states, joining a US dollar bloc would lead to a comparatively small reduction of the probability of military conflict for an individual East Asian country (about one-tenth of the impact from the East Asia currency union). However, this estimate does not take into consideration the fact that the US is a major power and more likely to be engaged in interstate militarized conflict. In addition, joining a US dollar bloc can also lower the probability of militarized conflict against the states that are already in the dollar bloc.

Joining a currency union may have a significant impact, independently from bilateral trade creation, on the probability or size of interstate conflicts. A currency union is often considered as a final stage of economic cooperation and thus may have a direct impact on reducing the likelihood of interstate conflicts. It is also important to note that while a currency union might lower the probability of war, it may deprive independent monetary policy of the role of mitigating the output loss during a disaster. Also it may be noted that there is the possibility that conflicts over fiscal policy or differences in desired monetary policy might lead to a greater probability of conflict.

4.3 Estimation of Welfare Effects of East Asian Currency Unions: An Illustration

We use calibrations of a representative consumer model to estimate the welfare effects from the implementation of various types of East Asian currency unions. Consider a representative consumer with a conventional constant relative risk aversion (CRRA) utility function.

$$U_t = E_t \sum_{i=0}^{\infty} [e^{-\rho i} \cdot (C_{t+i}^{1-\theta} - 1)/(1 - \theta)], \tag{1}$$

where $\rho \geq 0$ denotes the rate of time preference and $\theta > 0$ measures the magnitude of relative risk aversion.

We assumed that the consumer is endowed with a stochastic consumption stream as follows:

$$C_t = C_{t-1} e^{\gamma} \varepsilon_t e^{V_t}, \tag{2}$$

where two stochastic terms ε_t and v_t are included. The random term ε_t is assumed to be independent and identically distributed (i.i.d.) log-normal, $\ln(\varepsilon_t) \sim N(0, \sigma^2)$. This term reflects "normal" economic fluctuations, such as those analyzed in Lucas (1987, 2003). The random term v_t reflects low-probability disasters, such as the Great Depression and World War, described in Barro (2006a). The probability of a disaster is the known amount $p \geq 0$ per unit of time, where p is a constant. If a disaster occurs, consumption contracts proportionately by the fraction b. The probability of disaster in a period is small but b is large. The distribution of v_t is given by

$$\text{probability } e^{-p} : v_t = 0,$$

$$\text{probability } 1 - e^{-p} : v_t = log(1 - b)^3.$$

In the format of equation (2), volatility shocks from both normal disturbances and disasters are considered to have a permanent effect.

Using equations (1) and (2), expected utility calculated as of period t is expressed by

$$U_t = (C_t)^{1-\theta}/(1-\theta) \cdot \sum_{i=0}^{\infty} e^{[-\rho-(\theta-1)\gamma+(1/2)(\theta-1)^2\sigma^2+p[(1-b)^{1-\theta}-1]i]} \tag{3}$$

As the arbitrary period length approaches zero, equation (3) is rewritten as[22]

$$U_t = V \cdot (C_t)^{1-\theta}/(1 - \theta), \tag{4}$$

$$1/V = \rho + (\theta - 1) \cdot \gamma - (1/2) \cdot (\theta - 1)^2 \cdot \sigma^2 - p \cdot [(1 - b)^{1-\theta} - 1]. \tag{5}$$

The risk-averse consumer would prefer a less risky (σ^*) to a risky ($\sigma > \sigma^*$) path. This difference in consumer welfare can be quantified by multiplying the less risky path by the constant factor $1 + \lambda$ ($\lambda < 0$) in all dates and states and choosing λ so that the consumer is indifferent between the two cases:

$$V_{(\sigma)} \cdot (C_t)^{1-\theta} = V_{(\sigma^*)}^* \cdot [(1 + \lambda)C_t]^{1-\theta} \tag{6}$$

The parameter λ measures the proportional decrease in initial consumption (C_t) compensating for a fall in σ. That is, the consumer would be willing to give up λ of consumption each year to have lower volatility of consumption. The compensation parameter λ is calculated by

$$\lambda_{(\sigma*)} = [V_{(\sigma)}/V^*_{(\sigma*)}]^{1/(1-\theta)} - 1. \tag{7}$$

The parameter compensating for the change in $p, b,$ or γ can be also constructed in a similar way.

We can also consider the welfare effects of eliminating all consumption risk from normal disturbances, σ. This exercise corresponds to setting $\sigma* = 0$ in equation (7). The formula V in equation (5) implies for this case

$$1/V^*_{(\sigma*=0)} = 1/V_{(\sigma)} + (1/2) \cdot (\theta - 1)^2 \cdot \sigma^2.$$

Substituting into equation (7) yields

$$\lambda_{(\sigma*=0)} = [1 + V_{(\sigma)} \cdot (1/2) \cdot (\theta - 1)^2 \cdot \sigma^2]^{1/(1-\theta)} - 1. \tag{8}$$

In a similar way, the welfare effects of eliminating all consumption risk from the disasters can be constructed by setting p or b to zero

$$\lambda_{(p*,b*=0)} = [1 + V_{(p,b)} \cdot p \cdot ((1 - b)^{1-\theta} - 1)]^{1/(1-\theta)} - 1. \tag{9}$$

For the benchmark calibration exercise, we assume a rate of time preference of $\rho = 0.03$ per year, and the relative risk aversion coefficient $\theta = 4$. According to the statistics in table 2.8, the mean of per capita consumption growth rates, γ, ranges from 0.063 (Taipei,China) to 0.014 (the Philippines), and its standard deviation ranges from 0.032 (Japan) to 0.059 (Indonesia). For 10 East Asia economies, the average growth rate, γ, is 0.042 and the standard deviation, σ, is 0.041. By combining these parameters with the disaster probability, p, of 0.018 and the average contraction size, b, of 0.29,[23] we can calculate welfare effects of changes from various shocks. The assumed parameters yield $V = 8.6$ in equation (5).[24]

With the parameters assumed, the proportional decrease in initial consumption required to compensate for elimination of σ turns out to be 2.1%. That is, the economy would be willing to give up about 2.1% of consumption each year to eliminate all of the normal economic fluctuations represented by σ. The compensation parameter for eliminating disaster shocks turns out to be 7.9%. When both normal and disaster shocks are eliminated, the compensating proportional decrease in initial consumption turns out to be 9.4%.[25]

Table 2.10 presents the estimation results of the welfare effects of various currency unions such as a dollar bloc and a new regional currency bloc for 10 East Asian economies. This benchmark calibration exercise assumes that the trade creation effect of a currency union, α, is 0.50 and the growth effect of an increase in trade-to-GDP ratio, ψ, is 0.01. The fraction of output volatility that monetary policy stabilizes, χ, is assumed to be 0.30.

Since the simulation hinges critically on the assumptions of parameter values, the estimation results should be considered only as illustrative.

Table 2.10
Welfare Effects of Currency Unions in East Asia: A Benchmark Simulation

A. Welfare Effect from US Dollar Currency Union

Country	Trade Creation (A)	Volatility Increase (B)	Total Effect (C=A+B)	Total Effect with Lower Disaster Probability (D)
China, People's Rep. of	0.20	(1.54)	(1.32)	(0.03)
Hong Kong, China	0.40	(0.60)	(0.19)	0.56
Indonesia	0.18	(2.11)	(1.91)	(0.51)
Japan	0.08	(0.46)	(0.38)	0.54
Korea, Rep. of	0.20	(0.58)	(0.38)	0.48
Malaysia	0.87	(1.58)	(0.66)	0.72
Philippines	1.36	(2.29)	(0.80)	2.57
Singapore	0.81	(0.47)	0.36	1.22
Taipei,China	0.31	(0.30)	0.01	0.66
Thailand	0.29	(0.61)	(0.32)	0.71
Average	*0.39*	*(0.79)*	*(0.38)*	*0.63*

B. Welfare Effect from Currency Union of 10 East Asian Economies

Country	Trade Creation (A)	Volatility Increase (B)	Total Effect (C=A+B)	Total Effect with Lower Disaster Probability (D)
China, People's Rep. of	0.69	(1.30)	(0.58)	0.68
Hong Kong, China	1.93	(0.61)	1.36	2.06
Indonesia	0.81	(1.92)	(1.05)	0.30
Japan	0.12	(0.40)	(0.28)	0.63
Korea, Rep. of	0.41	(0.36)	0.05	0.89
Malaysia	2.77	(0.92)	1.94	3.19
Philippines	2.80	(1.34)	1.61	4.68
Singapore	2.53	(0.42)	2.15	2.95
Taipei,China	0.69	(0.26)	0.44	1.08
Thailand	0.91	(0.46)	0.46	1.46
Average	*1.23*	*(0.63)*	*0.64*	*1.61*

( ) = negative.
Notes: The welfare effect corresponds to a proportional change in initial consumption per year caused by joining a currency union in East Asia. The welfare effect for an US dollar currency union is derived by assuming that each East Asian economy adopts the corresponding anchor currency as a national currency independently. The simulation is based on the model and specific parameter values discussed in the paper. It is assumed that trade creation effect of a currency union (α) is 0.5, and growth effect of an increase in trade-to-GDP ratio (ψ) is 0.01. The fraction of output volatility that monetary policy can stabilize (χ) is assumed to be 0.3. The total effect in Column D includes additional welfare gain from lowering the disaster probability from 0.018 to 0.016, by assuming that an East Asian currency union (or a US dollar union) can reduce the probability of a war or a financial crisis in East Asia decreases by about 10%.

For example, with the parameters assumed here, the lower value of the coefficient of relative risk aversion (θ) leads to a lower value of V, which increases the welfare gain from a higher growth rate, while decreasing the welfare cost from higher volatility. Hence, the welfare gain from a currency union increases. If monetary policy can stabilize a larger fraction of output volatility (χ), the loss of independent monetary policy would be more costly. The higher value of the parameter for trade creation effect ($\alpha \cdot \psi$) would make currency unions more favorable to East Asian economies.

The main results from the benchmark simulation results in table 2.10 are summarized as follows:

1. The welfare gain from increasing growth rate due to trade creation is estimated to be substantial (Column A). The gain is larger for more open economies such as Hong Kong, China; Malaysia; and Singapore. The Philippines also gets a substantial welfare benefit from trade creation since the marginal welfare effect of an increased growth rate is larger for a lower-growth economy. The welfare gain is comparably smaller for the larger countries in East Asia—PRC, Indonesia, Japan, and Korea—which are relatively less open. The broader the membership a currency union has, the more beneficial it can be to the members. Because of their substantial degree of intra-region trade, the East Asia countries would benefit most from forming a larger currency union involving all East Asian economies, compared to a dollar bloc.[26] The net welfare benefit from increased growth rate due to a currency union involving all 10 East Asian economies is estimated to range from 0.1% (Japan) to 2.8% (Malaysia and the Philippines) in terms of their initial consumption per year.

2. The potential welfare cost of increasing volatility due to the loss of an independent monetary policy is also substantial (Column B). This relatively larger cost of increasing volatility is attributed to our assumption that consumption has a stochastic trend. The welfare cost from the loss of an independent monetary policy amounts to approximately 2.0% of initial consumption for PRC, Indonesia, and the Philippines when they adopt the US dollar. In contrast, the welfare cost of increasing volatility is smaller than 0.5% of initial consumption for Japan, Singapore, and Taipei,China. The potential welfare cost of increasing volatility becomes smaller when an economy joins a broad East Asian currency bloc, compared to a dollar bloc. This is because regional monetary policy can play a role of offsetting a part of country-specific shocks. The welfare cost of increasing volatility from joining a currency union involving all 10 East Asian economies is estimated to range from 0.3% (Taipei,China) to 1.9% (Indonesia) of initial consumption.

3. A dollar bloc would not be welfare-improving for most East Asian economies because the potential welfare loss from increasing volatility

dominates the potential benefit of increasing growth rates (Column C). An exception is Singapore, where adopting the US dollar as an anchor currency would result in net welfare gain. However, the majority of economies in East Asia would benefit most from forming a currency union involving all their economies. Hong Kong, China; Malaysia; the Philippines; and Singapore turn out to benefit most from joining an East Asia-wide currency union, with a net welfare gain of between 1.4% and 2.2% of initial consumption. On the other hand, PRC, Indonesia, and Japan lose from joining such a currency union. This is mainly because the welfare gain from increasing trade creation is smaller for these economies, since they begin with smaller bilateral trade shares with other East Asian economies.

4. The welfare consequences of a currency union likely involve the influence it would have on the probability and size of disasters such as wars and financial crises in East Asia. Column D considers the case that the disaster probability decreases by about 10% from 0.018 to 0.016, by assuming that an East Asian currency union can substantially lower the likelihood of a war or a financial crisis in the region. The lower probability of disaster shocks generates a substantial welfare gain. It shows that with the baseline parameter values, all the East Asian economies would obtain net positive welfare gain with an East Asia-wide currency union, ranging from 0.3% to 4.7%. In contrast, for a US dollar bloc, it turns out that a few countries, including PRC and Indonesia, still have net welfare loss.

5 Conclusion

Judging from OCA criteria, it is not clear that East Asia is ready to form a currency union. While the degree of intra-region trade is high, the degree of output co-movement is relatively low. Overall, these forces make the net welfare gain from a currency union small. The low trade intensity and political proximity between Japan and other East Asian economies raise the leadership issue for an East Asian currency union. The calibration results show that most countries in East Asia would obtain a net welfare gain by forming a currency union involving a broad group of economies there. The gain will be larger if a currency union contributes to a lessened frequency and size of disasters such as wars and financial crises in the region.

The prospect for an East Asian currency union will hinge on future developments of economic and political conditions, rather than current environments. In East Asia, since the 1997–1998 financial crisis there has been intensified interest in regional financial and monetary cooperation, and substantial progress has been made in several areas, such as information coordination and surveillance, reserve pooling, and a regional bond market. Eventually, increasing economic cooperation will assist these economies in satisfying more OCA criteria. It would also enhance political cooperation among them if intensified economic interdependence in the region were to provide impetus to foster cooperation.

Despite potential gains, an East Asia-wide monetary union, such as one involving ASEAN+3 countries, is not likely to emerge in the immediate future. The creation of a monetary union is the outcome of a long-term process of financial cooperation and monetary integration. In Europe it took many decades to achieve economic integration of the region. It started with the European Coal and Steel Community in 1952, followed by the Werner Plan in 1969, which eventually evolved into the European Monetary Union. We note that the institutional inefficiencies and governance problems are more significant in East Asia than in Europe because of the lack of institutional experience and leadership. Therefore it could be much harder to build an effective mechanism to help minimize inefficiencies from the political decision-making process in the integration of East Asian economies. Nevertheless, the discussion of a currency union in East Asia at the present time is not premature. Given the uncertain outlook created by the global financial crisis and economic recession, it may be the moment for East Asian countries to intensify their collaboration to build effective institutional frameworks that can foster greater regional economic integration.[27]

East Asian economies need to improve exchange rate coordination. The most important step for an East Asian currency union is to maintain exchange rate stability of national currencies in the region. In recent years, there have been suggestions for various exchange rate regimes that East Asia can adopt to increase intra-region rate stability. They include the adoption of the G3 currency basket system based on the US dollar, the euro, and the Japanese yen; the introduction of an Asian Currency Unit (ACU); the use of a parallel currency based on an ACU and national currencies; and adoption of an "Asian Exchange Rate Mechanism." The assessments of the benefits and costs of these alternative regimes for East Asian economies during transition to an Asian monetary union is an important research topic.

Notes

1. Prior to the crisis, the Hong Kong dollar and the yuan were fixed to the dollar. The Thai baht and the Malaysian ringgit were similarly stable against the dollar, although these monetary authorities officially adopted a multiple currency basket system. Singapore, Korea, and the Philippines also targeted their currencies to the dollar, though with some discretion. Indonesia was on a de facto crawling peg to the US dollar by sliding the rupiah to offset the inflation gap between home and abroad.
2. See Wyplosz (2004) for the discussion of potential benefits of the AMS. In recent years, the idea of an ACU has been widely discussed by Asian scholars. See, for instance, Kawai (2007). In May 2006, finance ministers of 13 East Asian nations including ASEAN+3 (PRC, Japan, and Korea) agreed to launch a research

project on the ACU. Eichengreen (2006) argues that the circulation of the ACU as a parallel currency alongside national currencies would be advantageous for East Asian economies.

3. For example, consider an Asian country whose output fluctuations are closely correlated with those of Japan, but its variance of output is much larger than that of Japan. In this case, the Japanese yen would not be a very attractive anchor for the country, despite the high correlation of outputs. The countercyclical monetary policy chosen by the Japanese central bank would be of insufficient amplitude (because of the different variances in their outputs) to serve the interests of the potential client.

4. Helleiner (2003) claims that the construction of national currencies, which emerged for the first time in the nineteenth century along with the emergence of nation-states, was an outcome of an intensively political process to foster national identities.

5. It is unlikely that either the euro or Japanese yen would be adopted as an anchor currency by East Asian economies, since the US dollar plays a more important role in trade and financial transactions in East Asia. Dornbusch and Park (1999) suggested that pegging to the Japanese yen is not appropriate for East Asian economies because it is an unreliable anchor. In addition, the PRC would not join a yen bloc because of its rivalry for Asian leadership with Japan. A Chinese renminbi bloc is not considered as an anchor because the currency has only very limited international convertibility and the country's record of political and economic stability necessary to be an international anchor currency is not yet sufficiently established. Nevertheless, when considering the PRC's continuing economic growth and international integration, the renminbi will eventually emerge, though slowly, as a major international currency. See Chinn and Frankel (2005) for an empirical investigation of the determinants of international reserve currency status.

6. Although it is rare, countries can have a joint currency and then tie it to a major currency. For example, the CFA franc zone in Africa has a common currency, the CFA franc, tied to the French franc (to the euro from 1 January 1999). However, the CFA franc has been adjusted twice relative to the French franc. The member countries receive seigniorage. France has made some commitments for support in emergencies.

7. Regarding other conditions such as labor mobility and speed of adjustment to shocks, East Asia is considered to have fairly favorable conditions, at least comparable to those in Europe. See Goto and Hamada (1994) and Athukorala (2006) for the issue of labor mobility in East Asia, and Eichengreen and Bayoumi (1999) and Baek and Song (2002) for the issue of speed of adjustment.

8. The root-mean-squared (RMS) value is inversely related to the correlation of outputs, and positively to the individual variances of outputs. As discussed in section 2, the measure of output co-movement not only involves the correlation of outputs, but also the variance of relative outputs.

9. Refer to the IMF web site at http://www.imf.org/external/np/sta/pi/cpis.htm for details.

10. UN roll-call voting data on resolutions in the General Assembly are available online at http://unbisnet.un.org. The variable that measures the political proximity of two countries is the fraction of times that they voted identically (either both voting yes, both voting no, or both voting abstention or not-voting)

in all General Assembly plenary votes in a given year. Barro and Lee (2005) used this measure to investigate the influence of the US and major Western European countries on the IMF's lending decisions. UN voting variables have also been used by Alesina and Dollar (2000) to explain foreign-aid patterns. Because of lack of available information, the vote correlation measure does not take into account the different degree of importance attached to each vote by different countries.

11. The number changes little when the 12 European countries that adopted the euro are used.

12. See Kim et al. (2007) for a discussion of the factors contributing to the limited regional integration of East Asian financial markets.

13. Katzenstein (2005) points out that East Asia and Europe in the early postwar years went through different experiences. The US assembled an anti-Communism alliance by creating multilateral institutions such as NATO in Europe, while setting up bilateral defense treaties with Japan, Korea, and the Philippines in East Asia. He argues that pervasive identification of the US with Europe in terms of religion, democratic values, and perhaps race contributed to the different military-strategic approaches for two regions.

14. The averages of political proximity for 18 European countries have increased continuously from 0.727 in 1980–1984, to 0.762 in 1985–1990, 0.875 in 1991–1994, 0.904 in 1995–1999, and 0.922 in 2000–2005.

15. Recent studies such as Tenreyro and Barro (2007) attempt to get around the endogeneity issue by developing a new instrumental-variable (IV) technique. The instrumental-variable approach reveals a significantly larger effect of a currency union on trade. Other approaches based on matching techniques show slightly smaller estimates than those from Rose-type regressions. See Baldwin (2006) for a survey of the literature on the trade effects of currency union.

16. Alternatively, the central bank may stabilize the part of transitory fluctuations that it considers to be a deviation from trend. We construct the transitory movement of consumption around its trend by using the widely used Hodrick-Prescott filter. Then monetary stabilization policy can be designed to mitigate the transitory part of fluctuations. We find this type of experiment can generate simulation results similar to those reported in subsection 4.3. These results are available upon request from the authors.

17. For simplicity, we assume that the shocks of 10 East Asian economies are equally weighted in the monetary policy objective of the regional central bank.

18. Business fluctuations would have long-term consequences if they affected investment rates and growth rates (Ramey and Ramey, 1995; and Barlevy, 2004). When people live in an economy that is subject to a higher volatility, they may be more willing to adopt risk-avoiding technology, and accept reduced average growth rates. Fluctuations may lower the level of investment in growth-enhancing activities.

19. The size of contraction is measured by the cumulative decline in per capita GDP during each disaster, corresponding to the measure of the probability, which is the number of disasters (rather than fraction of years) during the period 1915–2004.

20. Lee and Pyun (2009) define bilateral trade interdependence by the geometric average of bilateral trade flows over GDP of the two countries. The measure of militarized conflicts, which is constructed from the database of the "Correlates

Of War (COW)" project, includes all militarized interstate disputes (MID) with a level of hostility ranging from 2 to 5 (2 = Threat to use force, 3 = Display of force, 4 = Use of force, 5 = War).

21. The mean probability of bilateral military conflict of 0.46% in Lee and Pyun (2009) implies 58.6% $[1-(1-0.0055)^{160}]$ for the probability of interstate war for an individual country against any state out of a total of 160 countries in the world. This high estimate comes from the fact that the measure of military conflict includes not only major wars but all militarized interstate disputes.

22. We assume that the transversality condition is satisfied to guarantee that expected utility U_t, is finite. The transversality condition requires that the expected rate of return on risky assets exceeds the growth rate of real GDP. See Alvarez and Jermann (2004) and Barro (2006b) for the discussion of the link between business cycle costs and asset prices.

23. For simplicity, we treat the contraction proportion b as a constant of 0.29, which is the mean value for 10 East Asian economies over the 1915–2004 period. The welfare effect can be generated from the empirically observed distribution of b. See Barro (2006a, 2006b) for further discussion.

24. The estimated value of V is low, compared to around 20 for cases considered in Barro (2006b). This is because the average growth rate parameter $\gamma = 0.042$ is relatively high for 10 East Asian economies. When a lower value of long-term growth rate parameter (0.025) is assumed, the qualitative result of the benchmark simulation does not change.

25. Lucas (1987, 2003) suggests a negligible welfare gain from eliminating normal consumption fluctuations by considering that the impact of a shock on output and consumption is purely transitory. In our framework, if all the shocks—both normal disturbances and disasters—are assumed to be transitory, the volatility shocks occurred at period t can have an effect on output and consumption at period t, but do not have any persistent effect to output and consumption path. The expected utility in equation (3) is changed:

$$U_t = (C_t)^{1-\theta}/(1-\theta) \cdot e^{[(1/2)(\theta-1)^2\sigma^2 + p[(1-b)^{1-\theta}-1]}\sum_{i=0}^{\infty} e^{(-\rho-(\theta-1)\gamma)i}$$

The compensation parameter for eliminating consumption risk due to the random shock ε_t is $\lambda^*_{(\sigma^*=0)} \cong \frac{1}{2}(\theta-1)\sigma^2$. With the parameters assumed here, the compensation parameter is 0.0025, implying that the proportional increase in initial consumption required to compensate for elimination of σ is 0.25% per year. The compensation parameter for eliminating disaster shocks, v_t, is calculated by $\lambda^*_{(p^*=0)} \cong p[(1-b)^{1-\theta}-1]/(\theta-1)$. Thus, the proportional increase in initial consumption compensating for elimination of disaster shocks, if transitory, turns out to be 1.1%.

26. The trade creation effect is evaluated for the case that an East Asian economy adopts the US dollar as an anchor currency, independent from the other East Asian economies. If a dollar bloc is formed by involving all East Asian economies, the trade-creation effect would increase as the effect from adopting the US dollar is added to that from joining an East Asia-wide currency union. For example, for Korea, the welfare gain from trade creation increases from 0.2% of initial consumption when it adopts the US dollar as an anchor currency by itself to 0.6% when the other nine East Asian economies also join a US dollar currency union.

27. There have been efforts by the 10 members of ASEAN, along with the PRC, Japan, and Korea—or ASEAN+3—to build closer cooperation in the area of bond market development (Asian Bond Markets Initiative) and reserve swap arrangement (Chiang Mai Initiative). In May 2009, for example, the ASEAN+3 finance ministers reached an agreement on the details of the so-called Chiang Mai Initiative Multilateralization (CMIM), a reserve pooling arrangement totaling $120 billion. They also agreed to establish an independent surveillance unit to promote objective economic monitoring.

References

Alvarez, F., and U. J. Jermann. 2004. Using Asset Prices to Measure the Cost of Business Cycles. *Journal of Political Economy*. 112(6). pp. 1223–1256.

Alesina, A., and R. J. Barro. 2002. Currency Unions. *Quarterly Journal of Economics*. 117(2). pp. 409–436.

Alesina, A., R. J. Barro, and S. Tenreyro. 2002. Optimal Currency Areas. *NBER Macroeconomics Annual.*

Alesina, A., and D. Dollar. 2000. Who Gives Foreign Aid to Whom and Why? *Journal of Economic Growth*. 5. pp. 33–64.

Athukorala, P-C. 2006. International Labour Migration in East Asia: Trends, Patterns and Policy Issues. *Asian-Pacific Economic Literature*. 20. pp. 18–39.

Baek, S-G., and C-Y. Song. 2002. Is Currency Union a Feasible Option in East Asia? In H. G. Choo, and Y. Wang, eds. *Currency Union in East Asia*. Korea Institute for International Economic Policy. pp. 107–146.

Baldwin, R. 2006. The Euro's Trade Effects. *European Central Bank Working Paper* 594.

Barro, R. J. 2004. Currency Unions for the World. In Asian Development Bank, ed. *Monetary and Financial Integration in East Asia: The Way Ahead*. Volume 2. Basingstoke: Palgrave MacMillan.

Barro, R. J. 2006a. Rare Disasters and Asset Markets in the Twentieth Century. *Quarterly Journal of Economics*. 121. pp. 823–866.

Barro, R. J. 2006b. On the Welfare Costs of Consumption Uncertainty. *NBER Working Paper* 12763.

Barro, R. J., and J-W. Lee. 2005. IMF Programs: Who Is Chosen and What Are the Effects. *Journal of Monetary Economics*. 52. pp. 1245–1269.

Barro, R. J., and X. Sala-i-Martin. 2003. Economic Growth. Second edition. Cambridge, MA: MIT Press.

Barlevy, G. 2004. The Cost of Business Cycles Under Endogenous Growth. *American Economic Review*. 94. pp. 964–990.

Bueno de Mesquita, B. 1975. Measuring Systemic Polarity. *Journal of Conflict Resolution*. 19(2). pp. 187–216.

Calvo, G., and C. Reinhart. 2002. Fear of Floating. *Quarterly Journal of Economics*. 117(2). pp. 379–408.

Chinn, M., and J. Frankel. 2005. Will the Euro Eventually Surpass the Dollar as Leading International Reserve Currency? *NBER Working Paper* 11510.

Cogley, T. 1990. International Evidence on the Size of the Random Walk in Output. *Journal of Political Economy*. 98. pp. 501–518.

De Gregorio, J., and J-W. Lee. 2005. Growth and Adjustment in East Asia and Latin America. *Economia.* 5(1). pp. 69–134.

Dooley, M., D. Folkerts-Landau, and P. Garber. 2003. An Essay on the Revived Bretton Woods System. *NBER Working Paper* 9971.

Dornbusch, R., and Y. Park. 1999. Flexibility or Nominal Anchors? In S. Collignon, J. Pisani-Ferry, and Y. Park, eds. *Exchange Rate Policies in Emerging Asian Countries.* London: Routledge. pp. 3–34.

Eichengreen, B. 1992. Should the Maastricht Treaty Be Saved? *Princeton Studies in International Finance.* 74. International Finance Section. Princeton University.

Eichengreen, B. 2006. The Parallel Currency Approach to Asian Monetary Integration. *American Economic Review. Papers and Proceedings.* 96(2). pp. 432–436.

Eichengreen, B., and T. Bayoumi. 1999. Is Asia an Optimum Currency Area? Can It Become One? Regional, Global and Historical Perspectives on Asian Monetary Relations. In S. Collignon, J. Pisani-Ferry, and Y. Park, eds. *Exchange Rate Policies in Emerging Asian Countries.* London: Routledge. pp. 347–366.

Frankel, J. 2004. Lessons from Exchange Rate Regimes. In Asian Development Bank, ed. *Monetary and Financial Integration in East Asia: The Way Ahead.* Volume 2. Basingstoke: Palgrave MacMillan.

Frankel, J., and A. Rose. 1998. The Endogeneity of the Optimum Currency Area Criteria. *Economic Journal.* 108. pp. 1009–1025.

Frankel, J., and A. Rose. 2002. An Estimate of the Effect of Currency Unions on Trade and Income. *Quarterly Journal of Economics.* 117. pp. 437–466.

Fratzscher, M. 2001. Financial Market Integration in Europe: On the Effects of EMU on Stock Markets. *European Central Bank Working Paper* 48.

Glick, R., and A. M. Taylor. 2005. Collateral Damage: Trade Disruption and the Economic Impact of War. *NBER Working Paper* 11565.

Goto, J., and K. Hamada. 1994. Economic Preconditions for Asian Regional Integration. In T. Ito, and A. Krueger, eds. *Macroeconomic Linkage.* Chicago: Chicago University Press. pp. 359–385.

Helleiner, E. 2003. *The Making of National Money: Territorial Currencies in Historical Perspective.* Ithaca and London: Cornell University Press.

Imbs, J. 2004. Trade, Finance, Specialization and Synchronization. *The Review of Economics and Statistics.* 86(3). pp. 723–734.

Imrohoroglu, A. 1989. Cost of Business Cycles with Indivisibilities and Liquidity Constraints. *Journal of Political Economy.* 97. pp. 1364–1383.

Kalemli-Ozcam, S., B. Sorensen, and O. Yosha. 2001. Economic Integration, Industrial Specialization and the Asymmetry of Macroeconomic Fluctuations. *Journal of International Economics.* 33. pp. 107–137.

Katzenstein, P. J. 2005. *A World of Regions: Asia and Europe in the American Imperium.* Ithaca: Cornell University Press.

Kawai, M. 2007. Toward a Regional Exchange Rate Regime in East Asia. *Asian Development Bank Institute (ADBI) Discussion Paper* 68.

Kawai, M., and T. Motonishi. 2005. Is East Asia an Optimum Currency Area? Unpublished paper.

Kim, S-Y., J-W. Lee, and K. Shin. 2007. Regional and Global Financial Integration in East Asia. In B. Eichengreen, C. Wyplosz, and Y. C. Park, eds. *China, Asia and the New World Economy.* Oxford: Oxford University Press.

Krugman, P. 1993. Lessons of Massachusetts for EMU. In F. Giavazzi, and F. Torres, eds. *The Transition to Economic and Monetary Union in Europe*. New York: Cambridge University Press. pp. 241–261.

Krusell, P., and A. A. Smith Jr. 1999. On the Welfare Effects of Eliminating Business Cycles. *Review of Economic Dynamics*. 2. pp. 245–272.

Kwan, C. H. 1998. The Theory of Optimum Currency Areas and the Possibility of Forming a Yen Bloc in Asia. *Journal of Asian Economics*. 9(4). pp. 555–580.

Lane, P., and G. M. Milesi-Ferretti. 2004. International Investment Patterns. *Centre for Economic and Policy Research (CEPR) Discussion Paper* 4745.

Lee, J-W., Y. Park, and K. Shin. 2004. A Currency Union in East Asia. In Asian Development Bank, ed. *Monetary and Financial Integration in East Asia: The Way Ahead*. Volume 2. Basingstoke: Palgrave MacMillan.

Lee, J-W., and J. Pyun. 2009. Does Trade Integration Contribute to Peace? *ADB Working Papers on Regional Economic Integration* 24.

Lucas, R. 1987. *Models of Business Cycles*. New York: Basil Blackwell.

Lucas, R. 2003. Macroeconomic Priorities. *American Economic Review*. 93. pp. 1–14.

Maddison, A. 2003. *The World Economy: Historical Statistics*. Paris: OECD.

Martin, P., T. Mayer, and M. Thoenig. 2008. Make Trade not War? *Review of Economic Studies*. 75. pp. 865–900.

McKinnon, R. 1963. Optimum Currency Areas. *American Economic Review*. 53. pp. 717–724.

McKinnon, R. 1999. The East Asian Dollar Standard. Life after Death? *Working Paper*. Stanford University.

Mundell, R. 1961. A Theory of Optimum Currency Area. *American Economic Review*. 60. pp. 657–665.

Obstfeld, M. 1994. Evaluating Risky Consumption Paths. *European Economic Review*. 38(7). pp. 1471–1486.

Ogawa, E., and T. Ito. 2002. On the Desirability of a Regional Currency Basket Arrangement. *Journal of the Japanese and International Economics*. 16. pp. 317–334.

Ramey, G., and V. Ramey. 1995. Cross-Country Evidence on the Link Between Volatility and Growth. *American Economic Review*. 85. pp. 1138–1151.

Rietz, T. A. 1988. The Equity Risk Premium: A Solution. *Journal of Monetary Economics*. 22. pp. 117–131.

Rose, A. 2000. One Money One Market: Estimating the Effect of Common Currencies on Trade. *Economic Policy*. 30. pp. 7–46.

Rose, A. and C. Engle. 2002. Currency Unions and International Integration. *Journal of Money. Credit and Banking*. 34. pp. 804–826.

Rose, A. and T. D. Stanley. 2005. A Meta-Analysis of the Effect of Common Currencies on International Trade. *Journal of Economic Survey*. 19(3). pp. 347–365.

Roubini, N. 2007. Asia is Learning the Wrong Lessons from Its 1997–98 Financial Crisis: The Rising Risks of a New and Different Type of Financial Crisis in Asia. *Roubini Global Economics*. Available: http://www.rgemonitor.com.

Signorino, C., and J. Ritter. 1999. Tau-b or Not Tau-b: Measuring the Similarity of Foreign Policy Positions. *International Studies Quarterly*. 43. pp. 115–144.

Spiegel, M. M. 2004. Monetary and Financial Integration: Evidence from Portuguese Borrowing Patterns. *Federal Reserve Bank of San Francisco Working Paper* 2004–07.

Tenreyro, S., and R. J. Barro. 2007. Economic Effects of Currency Unions. *Economic Inquiry.* 45(1). pp. 1–23.

Williamson, J. 1999. The Case for a Common Basket Peg for East Asian Currencies. In S. Collignon, J. Pisani-Ferry, and Y. Park, eds. *Exchange Rate Policies in Emerging Asian Countries.* London: Routledge.

Wyplosz, C. 2004. Regional Exchange Rate Arrangements: Lessons from Europe for East Asia. In Asian Development Bank, ed. *Monetary and Financial Integration in East Asia: The Way Ahead.* Volume 2. Basingstoke: Palgrave MacMillan.

3

Asian Financial Integration: Trends and Interruptions

Eduardo Borensztein and Prakash Loungani

We thank Robert Barro, David Cook, Hans Genberg, Warwick McKibbin, Jong-Wha Lee, and other participants at the Asian Development Bank and Hong Kong Institute for Monetary Research (ADB-HKIMR) workshop "Quantifying the Costs and Benefits of Regional Economic Integration in Asia" for very useful comments on the first draft of this chapter. We thank Ioannis Tokatlidis, Jair Rodriguez, and Hites Ahir for numerous discussions on this topic and excellent research assistance. We are also grateful for data and advice from Gianni De Niccolo, Ayhan Kose, Akito Matsumoto, Martin Schindler, Ken Singleton, Bent Sorenson, and Christian Thimann. Andrew Rose's web site was also a source for the data used in this study. The views expressed in this chapter should not be attributed to either the International Monetary Fund (IMF) or the Inter-American Development Bank (IDB).

1 Introduction

Financial integration has been prominent on the agenda of Asian policy makers over the last decade "as a platform for regional development" and "as a safeguard against the vagaries of the global market" (Asian Development Bank [ADB], 2008). This chapter provides a selective survey and some new evidence on the extent of regional financial integration in Asia and compares it with the extent of Asian countries' global financial integration.

The drive toward regional financial integration in Asia was in large measure motivated by the financial crisis of 1997–1998. The fact that a large share of corporate and bank liabilities were denominated in a foreign currency has been recognized as a major factor that contributed to the vulnerability of financial positions throughout Asian economies. A local bond market would be the natural environment to develop long-term, local-currency denominated debt instruments that would provide a more stable and reliable financing framework. Many Asian economists and policy makers have argued that an integrated Asian bond market would be valuable in achieving such a liability structure (see Ito and Park, 2004).

An integrated Asian bond market could bring about a number of benefits. It would help to increase the scale and liquidity of markets, reducing costs and improving the value of price signals, which would be especially valuable for the smaller economies in the region. It is not obvious, however, whether a regional market would provide the same strong support for local currency instruments that domestic markets do. In other words, would Asian investors reveal a consistent preference for Asian assets similar to the preference for domestic assets that domestic investors tend to show? The latter tendency has been termed "home bias" in the economic literature. Would there be an equivalent "regional bias" with the proper regional market infrastructure in place?

In this paper we investigate the degree of financial market integration in Asia, both equity and debt, and the strength of home and regional bias tendencies of Asian investors. In section 2, we look at the degree of integration of equity and bond markets as gauged by the convergence in equity premia and in interest rates across different countries. Standard economic theories suggest that as a group of countries becomes more financially integrated, dispersion in asset returns across countries should get smaller, cross-border flows should increase, and home bias in investments should get smaller. The broad trends in cross-country dispersion suggest a fairly rapid progress toward convergence in Asian equity markets, broadly similar to that among Eastern European markets and more pronounced than trends toward convergence among Latin American markets. In the case of interest rates, convergence among Asian markets was already pretty high, but other regional groups have now caught up.

In section 3 we take a direct look at international investors' preferences by examining data for 2001 to 2007 from the Coordinated Portfolio Investment Survey (CPIS) that estimates international portfolio holdings by investors from 75 countries. We perform several tests of the extent of home bias and regional bias and benchmark tendencies in Asia with comparable evidence for Latin America and Eastern Europe as well as for a group of industrialized countries. Broadly speaking, Asia as a region appears slightly more "home biased" than other regions as concerns equity holdings, although this may be related to home bias in the individual countries toward their domestic stock markets rather than a preference for assets from the region.

Of course, financial integration is not an end in itself but is sought because it can confer benefits in the form of increased risk sharing and greater financial stability. In section 4, we show the extent of cross-country dispersion of consumption expenditures and gross domestic product (GDP), which provides an indirect measure of the extent of market integration and risk sharing. If financial markets were fully integrated, and consumers across the world shared risks in an optimal way, economic theory would predict lower dispersion in consumption over time. The evidence suggests that while dispersion in consumption has declined, so has the cross-country dispersion in output.

In the Asian context, the case for greater regional integration is sometimes made by claiming that local investors provide a more stable basis for funds than investors outside the region. Hence, in section 4 of the chapter, we also review studies of recent crisis episodes that have tried to establish the extent to which local—and regional—investors have in fact been less prone to financial panics and a source of stability in markets. We also examine the recent experience in one country, Brazil, which has had considerable success in shifting its finance sources to domestic markets, where foreign investors have filled the gap when local savings are insufficient. In recent months, the global financial crisis is testing the resilience of this model of financing based on local currency instruments issued in the home markets.

2 Convergence in Interest Rates and Equity Premia

The typical approach to testing for integration in equity markets is to compute the pairwise correlations between stock indices for different countries and see if those correlations have increased over time (see ADB, 2008). Solnik and Roulet (2000) showed that the evolution of the cross-country dispersion of equity premia is inversely related to the pairwise correlations. Furthermore, as discussed in Adjaoute and Danthine (2004), convergence in equity premia is directly associated with convergence in the cost of capital.

Following De Nicolo and Ivaschenko (2008), we construct $\sigma(t)$, the cross-country standard deviation (or dispersion) of equity premia, using monthly data on equity prices and the yield on short-term government securities for the countries listed in table 3.1.[1] The equity premium is defined as the annualized rate of change in the equity prices minus the annualized yield on government securities at maturities ranging from one to three months, depending on the availability of data. The period covered is January 1984 to March 2009, though as indicated in figures 3.1 and 3.2 some countries enter the sample at different points over this period.

The top panel of figure 3.1 shows the evolution of $\sigma(t)$ when available observations for all countries in the sample are used in computing the dispersion. Over the period as a whole dispersion in equity premia has averaged about 75%, albeit with sharp spikes. While there is no discernible linear downward trend overall, there was a marked decrease in dispersion during the period 2002 to mid-2007 that was dramatically reversed by the onset of the current financial crisis.

Table 3.1
List of Countries Used in the Various Sections of the Paper
(except where indicated otherwise by a 'x')

	Section 2		Section 3	Section 4
	Government Interest Rates	Equity Premium	CPIS	Consumption GDP
Asia				
China, People's Republic of			x	
Hong Kong, China				x
India				
Indonesia				
Japan				
Korea, Republic of				
Malaysia				
Pakistan				
Philippines				
Singapore				x
Sri Lanka	x	x	x	
Taipei,China			x	x
Thailand				
Industrialized				
Australia				
Austria				
Belgium				
Canada				
Denmark				
Finland				
France				
Germany				
Greece				
Iceland	x	x		x
Ireland			x	
Italy				
Luxembourg	x	x	x	x
Netherlands				
New Zealand				
Norway				
Portugal				
Spain				
Sweden				
Switzerland				
United Kingdom				
United States				

Continued

Table 3.1
continued

	Section 2		Section 3	Section 4
	Government Interest Rates	Equity Premium	CPIS	Consumption GDP
Latin America				
Argentina				
Barbados	x	x		x
Bermuda	x	x	x	x
Bolivia	x	x	x	
Brazil	x			
Cayman Islands	x	x	x	x
Chile				
Colombia				
Costa Rica	x	x		
Ecuador	x	x	x	
El Salvador	x	x	x	
Guatemala	x	x	x	
Honduras	x	x	x	
Mexico				
Nicaragua	x	x	x	
Panama	x	x	x	x
Paraguay	x	x	x	
Peru			x	
Uruguay	x	x		
Venezuela	x	x		
Eastern Europe				
Bulgaria				x
Croatia			x	x
Czech Republic				x
Estonia				x
Hungary				x
Kazakhstan	x	x		x
Latvia				x
Lithuania			x	x
Poland				x
Romania				x
Russian Federation				x
Slovak Republic				x
Slovenia			x	x
Ukraine	x	x		x

Continued

Table 3.1
continued

	Section 2		Section 3	Section 4
	Government Interest Rates	Equity Premium	CPIS	Consumption GDP
Other				
Bahrain	x	x		x
Cyprus	x	x		x
Egypt	x	x		
Israel	x	x		
Kuwait	x	x		x
Lebanon	x	x		x
Malta	x	x		x
Mauritius	x	x		
South Africa	x	x		
Turkey				

The other panels of figure 3.1 show the evolution of $\sigma(t)$ for specific country groups: Asia, industrialized countries, Latin America, and Eastern Europe. The impression from these panels is that though convergence in equity premia may be taking place within these groups, the process is often interrupted by periods of unusual volatility, during which within-group dispersion increases. After the Asian crisis of the late 1990s, the pace of regional convergence within Asia has been almost as fast as that for any other region. Overall, though, the Eastern European economies have converged to each other faster than any other group. Nevertheless, the present crisis has disrupted once again the convergence process within and across all regions.

Similarly, figure 3.2 shows the cross-country dispersion in government interest rates. In the top panel, where we take into account available observations for all the economies in the sample, the dispersion in interest rates averaged 5% over the decade 1984–1994, was elevated during the following years of the emerging market financial crises, and since 2002 has declined to below its pre-crisis average. Among the industrialized countries, dispersion has declined from an average of about 5% to about 1%. Among the Asian economies, dispersion has averaged about 4%, well below the heights observed during the time of crises in the 1990s. Since 2002, dispersion in Asia declined to about 2%, before rising again during the present financial crisis. Latin America and Eastern Europe display a qualitatively similar pattern: dispersion has fallen from very high levels in the mid-1990s to much lower levels in recent years. In the case of Latin America, the decline has been from about 16% to 4%;

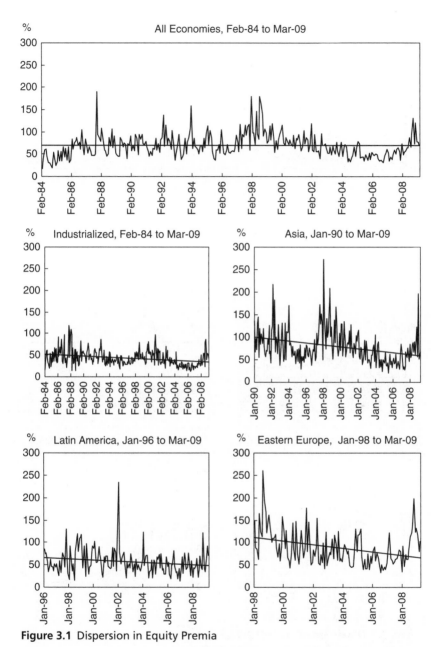

Figure 3.1 Dispersion in Equity Premia

Notes: In each panel we show the cross-country standard deviation in equity premia across the economies in the group, in percent, and a linear trendline.

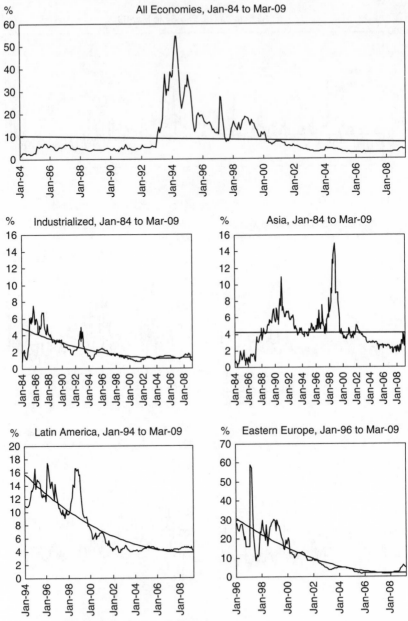

Figure 3.2 Dispersion of Interest Rates

Notes: In each panel we show the standard deviation in government interest rates across the economies in the group, in percent. For the group of all economies and Asia we also show a linear trendline. For the other groups we show a quadratic trendline.

for Eastern Europe, the decline has been more dramatic—from 35% to 1.5%, before increasing again with the onset of the crisis.

Tables 3.2 and 3.3 confirm the visual impression given by these figures. We estimate regressions along the lines of equation (1) for the dispersion in equity premia in table 3.2, and for the dispersion in interest rates in table 3.3:

$$\sigma(t) = A_0 + A_1\sigma(t-1) + A_2\sigma(t-2) + A_3Z(t) + A_4 TREND, \quad (1)$$

$Z(t)$ is a vector of controls to be described below. Convergence in equity premia or in interest rates occurs if A_4 is negative.

We include in the vector of controls $Z(t)$ two indicators to reflect periods of unusual volatility. The first indicator is *VIX*, a measure of the implied volatility of Standard & Poor's (S&P) 500 index options.[2] The second, *CRISIS*, is an indicator of the number of banking, currency, and sovereign debt crises that occurred throughout the world in a given year, taken from Laeven and Valencia (2008). A third control is the cross-section *MEAN* of either the equity premia or the interest rates, depending on the dependent variable of the regression.

The regression results for dispersion in equity premia are given in table 3.2. *VIX* is crucial in accounting for the dispersion in equity premia for the group of all countries, as well as for all four individual country groups: periods of higher volatility are associated with higher cross-section dispersion. On the other hand, the *MEAN equity premium* is not significant in any of the regressions. *CRISIS* is significant in the All Countries sample or Asia (columns 1 and 3, respectively), but not for the other groups. Notice that the estimated *TREND* in dispersion is faster in Eastern Europe (column 5), then Asia (column 3), the Industrialized Countries (column 2), and, finally, Latin America (column 4). *TREND* decline would be even faster in the case of Eastern Europe, but for the effects of the ongoing financial crisis.[3]

The regression results for dispersion in interest rates are given in table 3.3. In contrast to the results for dispersion in equity premia, *VIX* is significant only for the Asian and East European country groups, whereas the *MEAN interest rate* is very significant in all regressions. In this case, a *quadratic TREND* provided a better fit than a *linear TREND*. The results suggest a drop in dispersion in Asia and Eastern Europe (columns 4 and 5) over the last decade. In the case of industrialized countries and for Latin America, despite the visual impression conveyed by figure 3.2, it appears that there is no decline in dispersion, once we control for the shift in the cross-section *MEAN of interest rates*.

3 Portfolio Holdings and Home Bias

3.1 Portfolio Holdings: Summary Statistics

We follow Kim, Lee, and Shin (2006) in using the CPIS to study the cross-border portfolio holdings among countries. The CPIS provides information

Table 3.2
Convergence in Equity Premia

	Dependent Variable: Log of Dispersion in Equity Premia				
	All Countries (1)	Industrialized (2)	Asia (3)	Latin America (4)	Eastern Europe (5)
Log *Dispersion in* EqPrem(t-1)	0.186***	0.153**	0.194**	0.0875	0.122
	(0.058)	(0.059)	(0.081)	(0.080)	(0.079)
Log *Dispersion in* EqPrem(t-2)	0.105*	0.0635	0.0669	0.0295	0.0681
	(0.057)	(0.057)	(0.080)	(0.080)	(0.079)
VIX	0.0116***	0.0182***	0.0162***	0.0131**	0.0173***
	(0.0025)	(0.0033)	(0.0042)	(0.0050)	(0.0049)
Cross-section MEAN Equity Premium	-0.000462	-0.000296	0.000197	-0.0000949	0.0000346
	(0.00028)	(0.00039)	(0.00044)	(0.00063)	(0.00042)
CRISIS	0.0242***	-0.00518	0.0371**	0.00724	-0.0297*
	(0.0052)	(0.024)	(0.015)	(0.019)	(0.017)
Time TREND	-0.0000806	-0.00162***	-0.00231***	-0.00148*	-0.00278***
	(0.00022)	(0.00028)	(0.00080)	(0.00084)	(0.00076)
Constant	2.620***	2.742***	2.912***	3.301***	3.469***
	(0.27)	(0.27)	(0.41)	(0.43)	(0.45)
Observations	279	279	159	159	159
R-squared	0.41	0.39	0.44	0.11	0.27
Sample Period	Jan 1986 to Mar 2009	Jan 1986 to Mar 2009	Jan 1996 to Mar 2009	Jan 1996 to Mar 2009	Jan 1996 to Mar 2009

Notes: *, ** and *** indicate significance at, or below the 10%, 5% and 1% levels respectively. Robust standard errors are reported in parentheses.

Table 3.3
Convergence in Interest Rates

	Dependent Variable: Log of *Dispersion in Interest Rates*				
	All Countries (1)	Industrialized (2)	Asia (3)	Latin America (4)	Eastern Europe (5)
Log *Dispersion in Int Rates* $(t-1)$	0.992***	0.842***	0.347***	0.823***	0.612***
	(0.060)	(0.060)	(0.069)	(0.080)	(0.076)
Log *Dispersion in Int Rates* $(t-2)$	−0.120**	0.0823	0.250***	0.0510	0.0205
	(0.057)	(0.060)	(0.063)	(0.081)	(0.068)
VIX	0.00153	−0.000891	0.00572***	0.000787	0.0109***
	(0.00095)	(0.00062)	(0.0013)	(0.00099)	(0.0018)
Cross-section MEAN Interest Rate	0.0383***	0.0150***	0.101***	0.00992**	0.0410***
	(0.0058)	(0.0045)	(0.011)	(0.0045)	(0.0049)
CRISIS	−0.00465***	−0.0187***	−0.0173***	0.00229	−0.00694
	(0.0017)	(0.0064)	(0.0064)	(0.0048)	(0.0077)
Time TREND	0.00126**	0.000123	0.00650***	0.00107	0.0118***
	(0.00050)	(0.00056)	(0.0013)	(0.0011)	(0.0024)
Time TREND squared	−0.00000328*	0.0000000826	−0.0000349***	−0.00000622	−0.0000716***
	(0.0000019)	(0.0000014)	(0.0000068)	(0.0000054)	(0.000012)
Constant	−0.159***	−0.0484	−0.353***	0.0999	−0.401**
	(0.050)	(0.077)	(0.100)	(0.11)	(0.17)
Observations	279	279	159	159	159
R-squared	0.97	0.98	0.94	0.95	0.98
Sample Period	Jan 1986 to Mar 2009	Jan 1986 to Mar 2009	Jan 1996 to Mar 2009	Jan 1996 to Mar 2009	Jan 1996 to Mar 2009

Notes: *, **, and *** indicate significance at, or below the 10%, 5% and 1% levels respectively. Robust standard errors are reported in parentheses.

on a country's portfolio holdings of foreign equity securities and debt securities, valued at market prices, classified by the economy of residence of the issuer of the securities. Participation in the CPIS is voluntary, and some 75 economies currently participate in the survey. Though the CPIS was initiated in 1997, it was expanded significantly in 2001 and data are available annually since that year. The data used in this paper are from 2001 to 2007, the latest year available.[4]

Table 3.4 provides summary statistics on the pattern of cross-border flows from each of the 10 Asian economies in our sample for year-end 2007. Each row shows the share of the holdings accounted for by the four major groups of economies that we have used thus far in this study, that is, industrialized, Asia, Latin America, and Eastern Europe, and by a fifth group of other countries, which are mostly emerging markets. Also shown, in the last column of the table, is the total year-end holding in millions of US dollars.

The size of the holdings varies enormously across the Asian countries, ranging from roughly $500 billion for Japan to $5 million for Pakistan. There is also considerable heterogeneity in the distribution of holdings across country groups. Several countries—such as Singapore, Malaysia, and the Republic of Korea (Korea)—are making significant equity investments within Asia.[5] The simple (equally weighted) average shows that nearly 40% of investments are within Asia, but the average drops to just over 20% if each country's numbers are weighted by the size of its holdings. This is higher than the corresponding figures for Latin America and Eastern Europe; as shown in the table, on a weighted basis the respective figures are about 12% for Latin America and 14% for Eastern Europe. Of course, all three regional groups differ considerably from the pattern for the Industrialized countries, where on a weighted basis 75% of the investments are within that group of countries. In this sense, all three regions have a fair distance to go before they approach the industrialized country benchmark.

Table 3.5 presents a similar set of summary statistics for cross-border debt holdings. As with equity, several Asian countries hold a significant share of their overall debt portfolios in the form of within-region investments; Singapore, for instance, holds 30% of international debt in within-Asia investments. The simple average of within-Asia investments is 15%. On a weighted basis, however, the average drops to less than 7% because Japan's $1.4 trillion investments are largely held outside of Asia. The weighted average is in the ballpark of the corresponding figures for Eastern Europe and Latin America but much lower than the industrialized country benchmark.

To summarize, the extent of regional financial integration within Asia, using cross-border portfolio investments as an indicator, is broadly similar to that in other regional groups but far below the industrialized country average.

Table 3.6 shows the relative shares of United States (US) and Japanese assets at year-end 2007 in equity and debt holdings of Asian countries. It is evident that the US looms large in the portfolio allocation of Asian countries (including that of Japan itself) relative to Japan. For equity holdings, only

Table 3.4
Equity Securities Holdings: Summary Statistics, 2007

Investor Economy	Issuer Economy Group					Total
	Industrialized	Asia	Latin America	Eastern Europe	Other	
	(As a Ratio of the Total Invested by the Investor Economy)					($ million)
Asia						
Hong Kong, China	0.7751	0.2231	0.0002	0.0003	0.0012	105,047.0
India	0.3036	0.5187	0.0572	0.0156	0.1051	236.7
Indonesia	0.0343	0.9656	0.0001	0.0000	0.0000	507.4
Japan	0.8889	0.0821	0.0146	0.0096	0.0049	479,145.3
Korea, Republic of	0.4077	0.5170	0.0534	0.0127	0.0092	79,073.8
Malaysia	0.2600	0.7291	0.0023	0.0002	0.0084	7,150.8
Pakistan	0.9788	0.0000	0.0000	0.0000	0.0212	5.0
Philippines	0.9546	0.0454	0.0000	0.0000	0.0000	115.4
Singapore	0.3992	0.5825	0.0088	0.0045	0.0051	92,625.6
Thailand	0.8189	0.1811	0.0000	0.0000	0.0000	2,209.7
Average	0.5821	0.3845	0.0136	0.0043	0.0155	
Weighted average	0.7576	0.2139	0.0158	0.0079	0.0049	
Latin America						
Average	0.9034	0.0107	0.0841	0.0005	0.0014	
Weighted average	0.8604	0.0123	0.1258	0.0006	0.0007	
Eastern Europe						
Average	0.7687	0.0155	0.0021	0.1838	0.0299	
Weighted average	0.7819	0.0168	0.0005	0.1415	0.0592	
Industrialized Countries						
Average	0.8529	0.0957	0.0155	0.0218	0.0141	
Weighted average	0.7508	0.1737	0.0379	0.0195	0.0181	

Hong Kong, China; Singapore; and Korea have a share of greater than 5% of their portfolios in Japanese assets, while for debt only Hong Kong, China's holdings exceed 5%. Some countries such as the Philippines display a very marked tilt toward US assets.

3.2 Portfolio Holdings: Gravity Model Estimates

To investigate further these trends in regional vs. global integration, we next estimate a gravity model using these data.[6] The dependent variable is the

Table 3.5
Debt Securities Holdings: Summary Statistics, 2007

Investor Economy	Issuer Economy Group					Total
	Industrialized	Asia	Latin America	Eastern Europe	Other	
	(As a Ratio of the Total Invested by the Investor Economy)					($ million)
Asia						
Hong Kong, China	0.7799	0.2101	0.0018	0.0019	0.0062	205,591.0
India	1.0000	0.0000	0.0000	0.0000	0.0000	5.7
Indonesia	0.6563	0.2368	0.0000	0.0000	0.1069	1,350.0
Japan	0.9706	0.0140	0.0067	0.0061	0.0026	1,363,105.9
Korea, Republic of	0.9048	0.0710	0.0111	0.0113	0.0018	45,986.6
Malaysia	0.5741	0.3778	0.0000	0.0011	0.0470	2,006.7
Pakistan	0.9996	0.0004	0.0000	0.0000	0.0000	214.7
Philippines	0.7977	0.2023	0.0000	0.0000	0.0000	4,880.9
Singapore	0.6946	0.3003	0.0017	0.0015	0.0020	168,745.9
Thailand	0.8807	0.0938	0.0073	0.0034	0.0148	10,659.2
Average	0.8258	0.1506	0.0029	0.0025	0.0181	
Weighted average	0.9197	0.0662	0.0058	0.0053	0.0031	
Latin America						
Average	0.8631	0.0519	0.0844	0.0001	0.0005	
Weighted average	0.8961	0.0678	0.0358	0.0000	0.0002	
Eastern Europe						
Average	0.8640	0.0091	0.0050	0.0962	0.0257	
Weighted average	0.9003	0.0206	0.0019	0.0523	0.0249	
Industrialized Countries						
Average	0.9390	0.0285	0.0113	0.0143	0.0068	
Weighted average	0.9372	0.0291	0.0130	0.0131	0.0075	

bilateral investment holding between countries in our sample. Following Kim, Lee, and Shin (2006), we pool the data for all years from 2001 to 2007. The independent variables are a mix of time-varying and time-invariant ones. The former set comprises the *Product of Real GDP* and the *Product of Real per Capita GDP* of the investor and issuer countries. The latter set was taken from Rose (2005) and includes: (a) the *Distance* between countries; (b) three (0,1) dummy variables to indicate whether they share a *Common Language,* if one of them is an *Island,* and if they have a *Regional Trade Agreement;* and (c) the *Bilateral Trade* between them in 1998.

Table 3.6

Equity and Debt Securities Holdings toward the US and Japan in 2007

Investor Economy	Equity Securities		Debt Securities	
	US	Japan	US	Japan
	(As a Ratio of the Total Invested by the Investor Economy)			
Asia				
Hong Kong, China	0.1745	0.0851	0.2540	0.0597
India	0.2037	0.0000	1.0000	0.0000
Indonesia	0.0139	0.0008	0.1890	0.0148
Japan	0.4631	0.0000	0.4339	0.0000
Korea, Republic of	0.3175	0.0555	0.6010	0.0107
Malaysia	0.1325	0.0280	0.2295	0.0098
Pakistan	0.0000	0.0000	0.0000	0.0000
Philippines	0.7682	0.0019	0.4671	0.0170
Singapore	0.1800	0.0620	0.1393	0.0159
Thailand	0.3445	0.0077	0.0564	0.0043
Average	0.2598	0.0241	0.3370	0.0132
Weighted average	0.3705	0.0252	0.3875	0.0087
Latin America				
Average	0.7507	0.0047	0.6492	0.0095
Weighted average	0.7741	0.0071	0.6346	0.0185
Eastern Europe				
Average	0.1011	0.0111	0.1903	0.0068
Weighted average	0.1292	0.0142	0.3466	0.0194
Industrialized countries				
Average	0.2689	0.0545	0.2215	0.0220
Weighted average	0.1695	0.0955	0.1959	0.0188

In addition to these standard determinants, we follow Fidora et al. (2007) in including the *Real Exchange Rate Volatility* as an additional variable. From the point of view of a domestic investor, real exchange rate volatility adds to the volatility of the return of foreign assets, and reduces their appeal. Fidora et al. expect this effect to be stronger for bonds than stocks because bond returns are normally less volatile than stock returns and thus the increase in volatility coming from the exchange rate would be relatively more important.

Columns 1 and 3 in table 3.7 present the results from estimating the gravity model for cross-border bilateral equity and debt holdings. As in several previous studies, the estimates have the expected sign and nearly all

Table 3.7
Determinants of Bilateral Equity and Debt Holdings, 2001–2007

	Dependent Variable			
	Log of *Equity Holdings*		Log of *Bond Holdings*	
	(1)	(2)	(3)	(4)
Product of GDPs (log)	0.488***	0.490***	0.462***	0.430***
	(0.11)	(0.11)	(0.083)	(0.091)
Product of per capita GDP (log)	0.904***	0.772***	0.679***	0.517***
	(0.11)	(0.14)	(0.072)	(0.11)
Distance (log)	−0.187	0.146	−0.379***	−0.256*
	(0.17)	(0.15)	(0.12)	(0.13)
Common Language	0.909***	0.894***	0.0506	0.0888
	(0.33)	(0.28)	(0.21)	(0.24)
Island	0.564*	0.487	0.802***	0.968***
	(0.33)	(0.31)	(0.22)	(0.31)
Regional Trade Agreement	0.537	0.683**	1.095***	0.591**
	(0.39)	(0.32)	(0.28)	(0.25)
Bilateral Trade (log)	0.510***	0.504***	0.328***	0.377***
	(0.099)	(0.10)	(0.072)	(0.071)
Real Exchange Rate Volatility (log)	−0.661**	−0.294	−0.890***	−0.891***
	(0.30)	(0.27)	(0.22)	(0.21)
Asia_Single		−0.584		−0.442
		(0.42)		(0.37)
Asia_Pair		0.0347		0.122
		(0.78)		(0.58)
Industrialized_Single		0.211		0.211
		(0.50)		(0.39)
Industrialized_Pair		0.761*		0.979**
		(0.44)		(0.43)
LatAm_Single		−1.523***		0.0608
		(0.55)		(0.40)
LatAm_Pair		−0.370		−0.107
		(1.36)		(0.58)
EEurope_Single		−0.136		0.0330
		(0.52)		(0.37)
EEurope_Pair		1.557**		0.330
		(0.78)		(0.50)
Constant	−16.05***	−16.51***	−9.968***	−10.99***
	(2.40)	(2.61)	(1.71)	(1.86)
Observations	10,815	10,815	11,545	11,545
R-square overall	0.571	0.597	0.596	0.607
Year Fixed Effects	Yes	Yes	Yes	Yes

Notes: *, ** and *** indicate significance at, or below the 10%, 5% and 1% levels respectively. Robust standard errors corrected for clustering by the investor economy are reported in parentheses.

are statistically significant. Bilateral holdings rise with the *Product of GDPs*, the *Product of per Capita GDP* and the strength of trading links between the countries. *Real Exchange Rate Volatility* lowers holdings, as conjectured by Fidora et al. One interesting finding is that *Distance* appears to matter far more for debt holdings than for equity.[7]

To investigate regional financial integration among Asian countries, and to compare it to trends outside Asia, we follow an empirical strategy suggested by Kim, Lee, and Shin (2006). This consists of adding to the basic gravity model specification some dummy variables that are defined as follows: the (0,1) variable *Asia_Single* takes the value 1 if either the investor or issuer country belongs to Asia, whereas the (0,1) variable *Asia_Pair* takes on the value 1 if both countries belong to Asia. The difference in the estimated coefficients of these two dummies can measure the difference between the level of integration of these economies among themselves relative to their level of integration with the rest of the world. Furthermore, constructing dummy variables for the other groupings in a similar manner, we examine how Asia compares in this respect to the other regions.[8]

As shown in column 2, neither *Asia_Single* nor *Asia_Pair* is significant in the equity holdings equation. This is in contrast to the Industrialized or Eastern European economies' case, where the corresponding *Pair dummy* has a large and significantly positive coefficient. In other words, we fail to detect, according to this test, a preference among Asian economies for each other's equity holdings that is above the sample average, unlike what may be happening in other regions. A similar result for debt holdings is shown in column 4. Here again, the coefficients for the Asia dummies, *Single* or *Pair*, are insignificant whereas the coefficient for the *Industrialized_Pair* is positive and very significant.[9]

We also looked for regional differences by estimating the gravity model separately for groups of countries classified by the investor economy. Table 3.8 presents the results for equity holdings, and table 3.9 presents the results for bond holdings. With the loss in cross-country variation that comes with estimating the regression for smaller subsamples, variables that remain consistently significant are the *Product of per Capita GDPs* (with the exception of the debt holdings regression for Eastern Europe) and the extent of *Bilateral Trade* (with the exception of the debt holdings regression for Latin America). The last decade has been marked by a strong increase in the number of regional trade agreements in the Asia-Pacific region. While the impact of regional trade agreements on both cross-border Asian equity and debt holdings is positive, it is not precisely measured.[10]

The results suggest that there is scope in future work to look for specific determinants that may matter for individual country groups. In the case of Asia, the role of foreign direct investment, the effects of the presence of financial centers, the impact of People's Republic of China's (PRC) gravitational pull, and the role played by the overseas Chinese community may be worth investigating.

Table 3.8
Determinants of Bilateral Equity Holding by Group, 2001–2007 (Based on the Investor Economy)

	Dependent Variable: Log of *Bilateral Equity Holdings*			
	Asia (1)	Industrialized (2)	Latin America (3)	Eastern Europe (4)
Product of GDPs (log)	0.149	0.642***	0.628*	0.269
	(0.22)	(0.089)	(0.33)	(0.21)
Product of per	1.027***	0.847***	0.406*	0.413*
capita GDP (log)	(0.14)	(0.078)	(0.23)	(0.23)
Distance (log)	−0.664***	0.0246	−0.440	−0.312
	(0.25)	(0.14)	(0.62)	(0.20)
Common Language	0.453	0.681***	−0.434	
	(0.37)	(0.22)	(1.28)	
Island	0.730*	0.0897	−1.002*	−0.276
	(0.44)	(0.18)	(0.56)	(0.69)
Regional Trade	0.802	−0.0502	1.109	
Agreement	(0.61)	(0.34)	(1.12)	
Bilateral Trade (log)	0.651***	0.622***	0.540**	0.352*
	(0.24)	(0.12)	(0.26)	(0.20)
Real Exchange Rate	−0.647	−0.218*	−0.953	−0.216
Volatility (log)	(0.60)	(0.12)	(0.96)	(0.44)
Constant	−11.55***	−17.10***	−15.51**	−8.474***
	(3.80)	(1.74)	(6.19)	(1.72)
Observations	1,504	5,729	912	1,416
R-square overall	0.603	0.709	0.423	0.302
Year Fixed Effects	Yes	Yes	Yes	Yes

Notes: *, ** and *** indicate significance at, or below the 10%, 5% and 1% levels respectively. Robust standard errors corrected for clustering by the investor economy are reported in parentheses.

3.3 Home Bias

There is a large literature on the determinants of home bias in cross-border financial flows; see Fidora et al. (2007) for a recent example. The determinants tend to fall into two clusters: (i) variables that capture the barriers to flows imposed by geography and by information frictions (e.g., distance; lack of a common language); (ii) variables that capture barriers imposed by policies and institutions (e.g., capital controls; transparency; political risk). In our work thus far in this chapter we have focused mainly on the first set of variables,

Table 3.9
Determinants of Bilateral Debt Holding by Group, 2001–2007 (Based on the Investor Economy)

	Dependent Variable: Log of *Bilateral Bond Holdings*			
	Asia	Industrialized	Latin America	Eastern Europe
	(1)	(2)	(3)	(4)
Product of GDPs (log)	0.242	0.760***	0.283**	0.349***
	(0.19)	(0.10)	(0.12)	(0.12)
Product of per	0.810***	0.597***	0.754***	0.140
capita GDP (log)	(0.18)	(0.11)	(0.21)	(0.19)
Distance (log)	−0.0673	−0.626***	−0.839***	−0.334*
	(0.41)	(0.14)	(0.24)	(0.20)
Common Language	0.0691	−0.169	0.337	
	(0.42)	(0.28)	(0.49)	
Island	0.981**	0.123	−0.583	0.473***
	(0.40)	(0.34)	(0.46)	(0.16)
Regional Trade	0.381	1.101***	0.758	
Agreement	(0.72)	(0.30)	(0.73)	
Bilateral Trade (log)	0.499***	0.281**	0.170	0.242**
	(0.19)	(0.12)	(0.11)	(0.094)
Real Exchange Rate	−0.463	−0.199	−1.570**	−1.102***
Volatility (log)	(0.34)	(0.16)	(0.69)	(0.29)
Constant	−11.39**	−6.792***	−5.042	−8.025***
	(5.02)	(1.91)	(3.72)	(1.79)
Observations	1,662	5,770	1,150	1,492
R-square overall	0.607	0.677	0.312	0.314
Year Fixed Effects	Yes	Yes	Yes	Yes

Notes: *, ** and *** indicate significance at, or below the 10%, 5% and 1% levels respectively. Robust standard errors corrected for clustering by the investor economy are reported in parentheses.

though studies have found the second set to be important as well and hence they should be included in a fuller investigation.[11]

Following Fidora et al. (2007) and others in the literature, we compute home bias by comparing actual portfolio allocations to those predicted by a simple benchmark, that is, the share of a country's market capitalization in the world market. Hence, home bias "measures the degree to which investors in a given country are overweight in domestic assets and underweight in international assets, as compared to the benchmark portfolio that would weigh home and foreign assets, according to the respective shares in the global financial market" (Fidora et al., 2007, p. 635).

Let w_i^* denote the market weight of the rest of the world seen from the perspective of country i, and w_i denote the share of international assets in the country's portfolio. Then, home bias is given by:

$$HB_i = 1 - (w_i/w_i^*). \tag{2}$$

Similarly, bilateral home bias can be computed by comparing w_{ij}, the actual allocation of financial assets of country i vis-à-vis country j with the benchmark weight:

$$HB_{ij} = 1 - (w_{ij}/w_j^*). \tag{3}$$

With full international diversification, w_{ij} equals w_j^* and home bias is zero; if investors from country i do not hold any of country j's assets, home bias against that country is 1.

Table 3.10 provides summary statistics on the home bias indices for the Asian economies in our sample, and the regional groups. In particular, for each investor economy in Asia, the table shows the 2001–2007 average home bias toward the five regional groups. Regarding bias in equities holdings (panel A), the Asian economies seem very home-biased toward the industrialized group, with the exception of Singapore and the Philippines. With the exception of Japan and the Philippines, they tend to be slightly less home-biased toward other Asian economies than they are toward the industrialized ones. When we compare the Asian regional average to that of the other groups, Asia shows a lower regional home bias than Latin America (0.841 vs. 0.907) but not as low as that of Eastern Europe (0.755) or the industrialized countries (0.617).

Panel B of table 3.10 presents the corresponding set of statistics for home bias in bond holdings. In general, home bias in bonds tends to be below home bias in equities. Most numbers in this panel are lower than the corresponding entries in panel A. Notice again, that some Asian economies, such as Hong Kong, China; Indonesia; or the Philippines, are significantly less home-biased in bond holdings than other Asian economies, toward either the industrialized, or the Asian group. With respect to the regional averages at the bottom of the panel, Asia is the second less home-biased region in bond holdings (0.791), after the Industrialized (0.512), but before Latin America (0.851) or Eastern Europe (0.879).

In table 3.11, we examine the determinants of the 2001–2007 average bilateral home bias in our sample. Looking across the columns of the table, the standard gravity variables come in with the expected signs and are statistically significant in most cases. In addition, as in Fidora et al. (2007), *Real Exchange Rate Volatility* raises home bias, and the effect is larger for bonds than for equities. Then, in columns 2 and 4, we add to the basic specifications the *Regional Dummies* that we discussed before. As shown in column 2, bilateral equity home bias is higher, if either, or both, the investor and issuer economies are in Asia, in contrast to the industrialized group. In the case of the average bilateral home bias in bond holdings, in column 4, we detect, *ceteris paribus*,

Table 3.10
Summary Statistics of Equity and Bond Investment Home Bias, Average
2001–2007

Investor Economy	Issuer Economy Group				
	Industrialized	Asia	Latin America	Eastern Europe	Other
Panel A: Equity					
Hong Kong, China	0.933	0.896	1.000	1.000	1.000
India	1.000	1.000	0.999	1.000	1.000
Indonesia	0.960	0.903	1.000	1.000	0.648
Japan	0.951	0.994	0.999	1.000	1.000
Korea, Republic of	0.966	0.938	0.995	0.998	0.999
Malaysia	0.973	0.829	0.999	1.000	0.994
Pakistan	0.915				0.928
Philippines	0.857	0.978			
Singapore	0.754	0.100	0.952	0.977	0.926
Thailand	0.949	0.931	1.000	1.000	0.998
Asia Average	0.926	0.841	0.993	0.997	0.943
Industrialized Average	0.617	0.782	0.963	0.950	0.941
Latin America Average	0.781	0.853	0.907	0.970	0.909
Eastern Europe Average	0.628	0.865	0.881	0.755	0.872
Other Countries Average	0.774	0.894	0.833	0.921	0.795
Panel B: Debt					
Hong Kong, China*	0.613	0.347	0.884	0.828	0.779
India	0.998	1.000			1.000
Indonesia	0.524	0.633	0.691	0.996	1.000
Japan	0.959	0.999	0.999	1.000	1.000
Korea, Republic of	0.926	0.982	0.998	0.999	1.000
Malaysia	0.789	0.895	0.985	0.993	0.972
Pakistan	0.923	0.982			0.976
Philippines	0.501	0.421	0.841	0.545	0.882
Singapore*	0.649	0.918	0.982	0.965	0.888
Thailand	0.799	0.730	0.988	0.996	0.947
Asia Average*	0.768	0.791	0.921	0.915	0.944
Industrialized Average	0.512	0.956	0.965	0.958	0.984
Eastern Europe Average	0.677	0.939	0.895	0.879	0.963
Other Countries Average	0.836	0.658	0.688	0.742	0.916

Notes: * in Panel B, due to data limitations, we report the average 2001–2006 rather than 2001–2007 for Hong Kong, China; and Singapore. Consequently the Asia Average takes into account of these 2001–2006 values for these two countries, but relies on the 2001–2007 values reported for the rest of the group.

Table 3.11
Determinants of Average Bilateral Home Bias for Equities and Bonds

	Dependent Variable: Average over 2001–2007 of			
	Bilateral Home Bias in Equities		Bilateral Home Bias in Bonds	
	(1)	(2)	(3)	(4)
Product of GDPs (log)	0.0341***	0.0297***	0.0781***	0.0605***
	(0.010)	(0.011)	(0.013)	(0.013)
Product of per	−0.0669***	−0.0547***	−0.0829***	−0.0877***
capita GDP (log)	(0.0072)	(0.0089)	(0.0092)	(0.012)
Distance (log)	0.0865***	0.0647***	0.0766***	0.0306
	(0.015)	(0.020)	(0.020)	(0.024)
Common Language	−0.0757**	−0.111***	−0.0874**	−0.0661
	(0.034)	(0.037)	(0.042)	(0.045)
Island	−0.0724***	−0.130***	−0.125***	−0.168***
	(0.024)	(0.025)	(0.029)	(0.031)
Regional Trade	−0.0153	0.0268	−0.0392	−0.0267
Agreement	(0.058)	(0.067)	(0.063)	(0.073)
Bilateral Trade (log)	−0.0293***	−0.0400***	−0.0452***	−0.0481***
	(0.0090)	(0.0097)	(0.012)	(0.013)
Real Exchange Rate	0.0902***	0.118***	0.136***	0.218***
Volatility (log)	(0.022)	(0.026)	(0.027)	(0.031)
Asia_Single		0.0853***		0.193***
		(0.033)		(0.041)
Asia_Pair		0.138**		−0.0658
		(0.057)		(0.086)
Industrialized_Single		−0.00255		0.0437
		(0.029)		(0.042)
Industrialized_Pair		−0.0824		0.125**
		(0.054)		(0.060)
LatAm_Single		−0.0835**		−0.0363
		(0.034)		(0.044)
LatAm_Pair		0.0167		−0.262**
		(0.081)		(0.11)
EEurope_Single		−0.0563*		0.0128
		(0.030)		(0.039)
EEurope_Pair		−0.204***		−0.257***
		(0.077)		(0.092)
Constant	0.704***	1.167***	0.682***	1.517***
	(0.17)	(0.21)	(0.22)	(0.26)
Observations	2,840	2,840	2,871	2,871
F-Statistics (Prob>F)	50.74 (.000)	29.30 (.000)	64.45 (.000)	38.18 (.000)

Notes: *, ** and *** indicate significance at, or below the 10%, 5% and 1% levels respectively. Robust standard errors are reported in parentheses.

an increased home bias when one of the economies in the pair, investor or issuer, is in Asia, but not both. In contrast, pairs of Latin American or Eastern European economies seem less (bilaterally) home biased in bond holdings than the rest.[12]

4 Risk Sharing and Financial Stability

4.1 Risk Sharing

Standard theory predicts that financial integration should be reflected in higher cross-country correlations in consumption and lower cross-country correlations in output (Backus et al., 1994; Lewis, 1999). It should also lower correlations between domestic saving and domestic investment (Feldstein and Horioka, 1980).

Imbs (2006) presents empirical evidence for a large panel of countries that financial integration (which he measures using CPIS data for 2001) does raise cross-country consumption correlations, indicating increased risk sharing. However, puzzlingly from the perspective of the theory, financial integration also raises cross-country output correlations. Kose et al. (2009) argue that any increase in international risk sharing is modest and well below the levels suggested by theory; moreover, the gains in risk sharing thus far have accrued largely to industrialized countries. Bekaert et al. (2006) find that financial liberalization is associated with lower consumption growth volatility, but that the effect is weaker for emerging market countries. For the Asian economies, the thrust of this evidence raises some doubts about whether financial integration is conferring some of the ultimate benefits that it is expected to confer. The Asia-specific literature on this issue delivers somewhat mixed results (see Kim and Lee, 2008; Kim, Kim and Wang, 2006; Kim et al., 2005).

Following our approach in section 2, we rely on cross-country dispersions of output and consumption growth to provide some evidence on the degree of risk sharing in Asia, compared to other regional groups. Figure 3.3, indicating a decline in the dispersion of consumption growth, shows that there is some evidence for increased risk sharing among countries. However, consistent with the literature review, there is also a decline in dispersion in output growth.

Then, in table 3.12, we show that regressions of the kind presented earlier for the dispersion in equity premia and interest rates confirm the visual impression of figure 3.3. In panel A, the dependent variable is the standard deviation of real GDP growth across the economies in the respective samples, and in panel B, it is the corresponding dispersions of consumption growth. In each case, the other regressors are a *Lagged Dependent* variable, the cross-country *Mean GDP (or Consumption), Growth,* the *CRISIS* indicator used earlier, and a *Time TREND*. While the performance of the other variables is mixed, the *Time TREND* is very significant in all cases.[13]

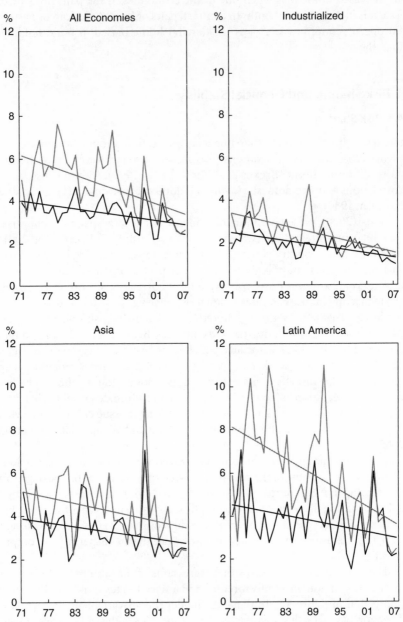

Figure 3.3 Cross-Country Dispersion in Output and Consumption Growth, 1971–2007

Notes: In each panel we show in black the standard deviation of GDP growth across the economies in the group and the associated linear trendline. We show in grey the standard deviation of consumption growth and the corresponding linear trendline.

Table 3.12
Determinants of Dispersion in GDP and Consumption Growth

	All Countries (1)	Industrialized (2)	Asia (3)	Latin America (4)
Panel A: Standard Deviation of GDP Growth				
Standard Deviation	0.106	0.303*	0.162	−0.101
of GDP Growth (t-1)	(0.17)	(0.16)	(0.15)	(0.15)
Per Capita World	−0.0602	−0.120	0.0822	0.0843
GDP Growth	(0.10)	(0.084)	(0.19)	(0.24)
CRISIS	0.0776**	0.0403	0.280	0.141
	(0.034)	(0.096)	(0.20)	(0.086)
Time TREND	−0.0236***	−0.0282***	−0.0294**	−0.0317*
	(0.0085)	(0.0079)	(0.014)	(0.018)
Constant	3.216***	2.050***	2.973***	4.107***
	(0.66)	(0.46)	(0.72)	(0.97)
Observations	37	37	37	37
R-squared	0.40	0.59	0.32	0.20
Panel B: Standard Deviation of Consumption Growth				
Standard Deviation of	−0.0543	0.00715	0.0732	0.213
Consum. Growth (t-1)	(0.20)	(0.15)	(0.11)	(0.16)
Per Capita World	−0.318**	0.0589	−0.333	−0.705**
Consumption Growth	(0.13)	(0.14)	(0.23)	(0.29)
CRISIS	0.0693	0.336**	0.357	0.0336
	(0.043)	(0.14)	(0.33)	(0.11)
Time TREND	−0.0453***	−0.0469***	−0.0395*	−0.0553**
	(0.012)	(0.012)	(0.021)	(0.024)
Constant	5.469***	2.940***	5.143***	5.835***
	(0.80)	(0.49)	(0.64)	(1.03)
Observations	35	35	35	35
R-squared	0.38	0.50	0.20	0.34

Notes: *, ** and *** indicate significance at, or below the 10%, 5% and 1% levels respectively. Robust standard errors are reported in parentheses.

4.2 Financial Integration and Crises

There is broad agreement on a number of benefits that would follow from a fuller development of local financial markets. Prominent among these would be the achievement of higher scale, which makes markets more liquid and prices more meaningful, and provides firms with a richer choice of instruments to manage their capital structure, including bond debt and equity; and enhancement of the ability to issue long-term, local currency-denominated debt, which improves the firms' ability to manage debt more efficiently. These issues, as they pertain to the development of Asian bond markets, have been studied extensively in the context of the Asian Bond Markets initiative (see ADB, 2008).

There is weaker consensus, however, on whether the development of local Asian regional financial markets can contribute to reducing the likelihood of financial crises. The discussion in Ito and Park (2004) sets out the arguments for and against this important potential benefit. On the one hand, it is argued that Asian investors will probably display a "regional bias" in their portfolio choices, given their familiarity with Asian companies and assets and a more favorable perception of risk, which would make them less likely to fall into a panic-driven sale of assets. On the other hand, it is replied that nontransparent corporate governance and accounting in Asia make any informational advantage less reliable and that there is no solid evidence that Asian investors would have a stronger preference for Asian financial assets than global investors. Further, the fact that Asian investors have a vested interest in the regional economies would not affect their portfolio decisions. Nevertheless, the development of financial markets in the Asian region would provide a better set of instruments (more long-term, local currency debt, for example) which would make it less crisis-prone even if investors themselves are equally fickle. That point was also disputed, as the structure of financial portfolios is probably related to deeper reasons, such as risk diversification and macroeconomic fundamentals, and was not believed to change even with better market infrastructure and liquidity in the region's markets.

One direction in which an integrated Asian market could help lower costs of borrowing and enhance market stability would be through the creation of a single currency market. This seems to have been a lesson from the experience of European bond markets. After the introduction of the euro, borrowing costs fell sharply for the countries that had higher yield spreads before the introduction of the common currency. Of course, the introduction of the euro had multiple effects, including gaining confidence in the future strength of the exchange rate compared to the traditionally less stable currencies of Europe, such as the Italian lira. Furthermore, the Maastricht Treaty imposed fiscal targets and limits that helped to boost the credibility of the public finances in many of the member countries. Nevertheless, there were also factors that were more directly linked to the change in the market structure, in particular the gains in liquidity and broadening of the investor base that was facilitated by the larger scope of a market denominated in a major currency like the euro, instead of the smaller, fragmented bond markets. Investors perceived bonds issued by countries in the euro group as belonging to the same asset class. Thus, the creation of a much larger asset class of euro-denominated bonds helped achieve more favorable borrowing conditions and a deeper, more stable market. This suggests that benefits from Asian financial integration would be enhanced in the presence of a currency union, even if the institutional framework on which the currency union is based were not as extensive as in the case of the European Union.[14]

It would seem that the key factor in this debate is whether global hedge funds, or non-Asian investors more generally, are more prone to panic and freeze funding on a broad scale than local investors, and by extension, regional investors. It is true that international capital flows, particularly in the 1990s, followed cycles of surges in inflows and "sudden stop" episodes. Is there evidence, however, that domestic investors have a different temperament with regard to mood changes toward domestic assets and currencies? More to the point, do we know if regional investors behave differently from more distant international investors?

In the remainder of this chapter, we review studies that have investigated these questions during recent financial crises in Mexico and Asian economies, and we note developments in recent months in the context of the global financial distress that followed the subprime mortgage crisis. We focus on the case of Brazil, which has gone a long way in recent years in developing local markets in domestic currency, and has relaxed the rules that regulate the participation of foreign investors, attracting significant amounts of foreign investment into the local securities markets. As the events are still unfolding, this discussion is obviously only a preliminary analysis of the impact on the Brazilian capital markets of the current financial crisis, and the extent to which a structure of capital flows that emphasizes local currency instruments has had a beneficial effect.

4.3 Local vs. Foreign Investors: Recent Studies

We can divide the issue in two parts. Are local investors a more stable investor base that provide resilience against financial panics and, if the answer is in the affirmative, do these benefits extend to regional foreign investors as well?

It is true that some groups of local investors—heavily regulated domestic institutions like banks and pension funds, in particular—are in many cases a "captive audience" in domestic securities markets (Borensztein et al., 2007). Pension funds, for example, are often required by law to maintain a large proportion of their portfolios in domestic assets, and sometimes specifically in government debt instruments. Likewise, commercial banks frequently must hold reserve requirements in some form of government liability, and sometimes are subject to "moral suasion" to hold even more. Nevertheless, these requirements usually do not apply to holdings of regional securities beyond the national borders. If regional financial integration resulted in the creation of a single market, as in Europe, then regional institutional investors would be subject to the same rules that now apply to home investors, and this may enhance market stability, particularly in smaller economies.

Alternatively, it may be possible that, by being better informed than global investors about domestic developments, local (or regional) investors would be less likely to fall into panics and liquidate positions in a wholesale manner, at times of economic or financial distress. While this conjecture has some intuitive appeal, and does enjoy some popularity, evidence from recent financial events—albeit essentially anecdotal and fragmented—does not suggest a clear-cut injunction of fickle international investors. The case against global investors gained popularity in the wake of the speculative attacks on the Hong Kong dollar in October 1997. The alleged scheme was that a number of global investors would short the Hong Kong currency "a little" and short the Hong Kong stock market "a lot." The pressure on the currency would cause a large increase in domestic interest rates through the mechanical operation of the currency board, which in turn triggered a sharp fall in the stock market. Although it is true that many global hedge funds had short positions on the Hong Kong stock market at the time, some observers have cast a skeptical view on the story, because of the practical difficulties of implementing the scheme and by tracking the short positions of foreign investors in the Hang Seng index (see International Monetary Fund [IMF], 1998).

Regarding the Mexican peso crisis of December 1994, Frankel and Schmukler (1996) find evidence that Mexican investors turned pessimistic on the sustainability of the exchange rate before international investors. They compare the prices of equity "country funds" traded in New York with their net asset values, namely the value of the constituent shares that are traded and determined in Mexico City. They find that net asset values declined sharply relative to the value of country funds two weeks before the devaluation. This is in line with the view expressed at the time by the IMF's *Global Financial Stability Report* and *The Economist*. In fact, applying a similar approach, Frankel and Schmukler (1998) find that the domestic investors lead market trends over foreign investors in similar ways in a study of 61 country (and multi-country) funds based in New York City.

In the Asian context, a detailed study of the behavior of international investors in the Korean stock market during the currency crisis period did not find support for the view that global investors exerted a major destabilizing influence. Choe et al. (1999) took a detailed look at daily trades of foreign investors in the Korean stock market throughout 1997. They found that, although foreign investors tended to follow "positive feedback strategies," in the sense of selling stocks that fell in price and buying those that had appreciated, there was no evidence that their trades had a lasting impact on market prices, particularly during the last three months of 1997.

Borensztein and Gelos (2003) studied the behavior of international mutual funds that invest in emerging markets over the period 1996 to 1999, particularly around the currency crises episodes in various countries. They found that, although these funds have a tendency to "herd," that is, to be concentrated on one side of the transactions, the extent of herding is actually small. Although herding is statistically significant, it is unlikely to exert a major influence on prices. On average, international mutual funds were 7% more concentrated on one side of the market (either buying or selling).

Furthermore, by examining the behavior of mutual funds around crisis episodes, they found that funds tended to cut their exposure in the month before the crisis, but again that the extent of their sales was relatively modest. Similarly, Bekaert et al. (2006) studied countries that liberalized their equity markets to international investment, and did not find evidence of increased market instability after the liberalization.

There are few studies and little information regarding the behavior of regional foreign investors. One special case is a study of lending patterns by banks from seven Organisation for Economic Co-operation and Development (OECD) economies during the Asian crises (Siregar and Choy, 2010). The study reports that Japanese banks reduced their loan exposure to East Asian markets by about 30% in 1998–1999, whereas United Kingdom (UK) and US banks cut back by only 13% and 17%, respectively. Moreover, loans by Japanese banks failed to recover to levels anywhere close to pre-crisis values as late as nearly 10 years after the Asian crisis. The econometric analysis suggests that a higher sensitivity to financial risk (an index including variables such as external debt and international reserves) seems to explain this behavior by Japanese banks.

4.4 Investor Behavior during the Subprime Crisis: Evidence from Brazil

The financial crisis that hit global markets in 2008 provides a new and important opportunity to assess the impact of global financial stress on domestic markets in the presence of foreign investors. While at the time of this writing—early 2009—it is too soon to form a well-defined account of the impact of the crisis, some developments are surfacing that are informative. Global financial markets have changed a lot since the Asian crisis, and more so since more recent events. The pattern of capital flows and asset positions of domestic firms and banks, as well as foreign investors have significantly evolved. We take the case of Brazil as the subject of study. It has a rich set of financial relations with the global markets and good availability of data, but we think that the pattern must be broadly similar in other emerging economies with a similar degree of financial development.

The presence of foreign investors in the local Brazilian securities markets started to change dramatically since 2005, as a result of changes in global investors' risk appetite, the liberalization of rules, and the lowering of taxes on inflows into the Brazilian markets. The net asset value of the total holdings of local securities by foreign investors, which hovered below $50 billion during the previous decade, started to grow sharply. They surpassed $250 billion by mid-2008. These figures are reported by the Securities Commission of the Brazilian government, and are broadly consistent with the figures collected from the investor side through the CPIS used in previous sections.

Notice that two factors may contribute to the sharp increase in foreign holdings of local securities: the capital inflows themselves and the asset value

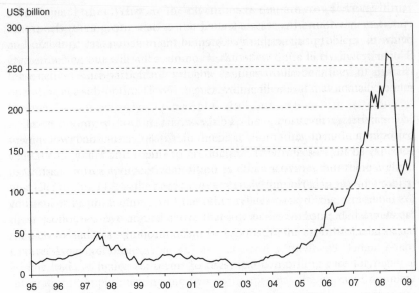

US$ billion

Figure 3.4 Total Asset Holdings of Foreign Investors in Brazil, January 1995 to May 2009

appreciation. The latter was largely driven by the booming stock market and the appreciating exchange rate of the real.For example, during 2007, net inflows amounted only to less than $34 billion, but the asset holdings of foreign investors increased by over $112 billion. The rise in the stock market (that gained over 40% in the year) and the strengthening of the real (that appreciated by 16% in the year) help explain this divergence. International investors' holdings comprised mostly stocks, which accounted for around 80% of the total asset value in 2007. Naturally, although the appreciation acts mechanically on the value of the holding, it was the investors' choice to increase the size of their Brazilian asset holdings by effectively reinvesting those capital gains in Brazilian securities.

Similarly, the large contraction in the net asset holdings of foreign investors since September 2008 was mostly the result of the large drop in asset prices. While outflows predominated, net outflows in September–November amounted to about $13 billion, which contrasts with the decline of over $116 billion in asset holdings. The stock market collapse and the sharp real depreciation resulted in a compound loss of 55% of the value of the stock market index (the Bovespa) in US dollar terms, which explains this large drop in the value of international investors' asset position. It is noteworthy that, despite the relatively large outflows by international investors, the situation did not suggest a stampede by foreign investors, as gross flows ran in both directions. In fact, gross inflows amounted to about $25 billion during the September–November period.

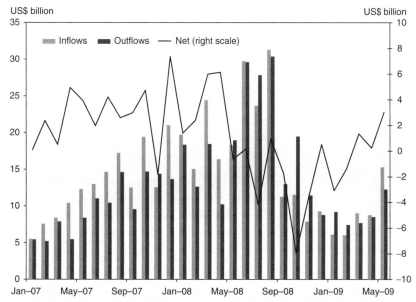

Figure 3.5 Portfolio Foreign Investment in Brazil, January 2007 to May 2009

These developments highlight the fact that the change in the structure of liabilities to international investors relative to the "original sin" structure that predominated in the 1990s has involved an important change in the impact of the financial crisis on solvency and liquidity factors. The new liability structure implies improvements in solvency but possibly an increase in liquidity problems. In the previous "original sin" period, most liabilities were foreign currency–denominated debt issued in international markets. In the event of a sudden stop, governments—and usually the private sector as well— were unable to roll over these instruments, and the shortage of international finance resulted in large exchange-rate depreciations that increased the burden of the foreign currency debt. With the new liability structure, where a large part of the debt liabilities are denominated in local currency and local equity positions are also a large fraction of foreign investors' portfolios, a sudden stop that results in a depreciation of the local currency in fact spreads the losses to foreign investors and reduces the dollar value of the liabilities. This bolsters the financial solvency of the government, as well as firms and banks that have debts in local currency. But the other side of the coin is that liquidity pressures can be stronger. Global investors can sell their securities immediately and put pressure on the exchange rate as they repatriate their positions.[15] In the "original sin" world, the liquidity crunch was limited to the rollover needs; attempts to liquidate positions remained within the international investors' realm and did not have a direct effect on the foreign exchange market of the country. With the current financial structure, the potential sell-off of the domestic currency is the total investment position in domestic markets, albeit devalued by the crash in asset prices that is likely to take place.

Available data suggest that outflows by Brazilian investors and firms amounted to just under $6 billion in the September–November period. This is a relatively modest outflow but it does not include the foreign currency facilities and currency swaps that the central bank of Brazil made available to local banks and firms that were facing financing pressure in their foreign currency debts. For example, there were some notorious cases of losses suffered by some Brazilian firms, which had entered derivative contracts as a protection against an appreciation of the real. These trades were originally designed for exporting firms that are vulnerable to a currency appreciation. However, they also included a multiple liability for the case of a depreciation of the real beyond a certain level that ultimately caused the heavy losses. While it is certainly premature to draw definitive lessons, the Brazilian case does not suggest a clear-cut distinction between foreign and local investors in terms of their impact on local financial markets.

5 Conclusions

Using Kim, Lee, and Shin (2006) and ADB (2008) as a guide, we have surveyed the empirical terrain used in past studies to assess the extent of regional financial integration in Asia. We have provided updates of the evidence by using recent data (e.g., using data on equity premia through March 2009 and the CPIS data to 2007), in some cases by looking at the evidence from a different angle, and by providing a comparison of Asia with other country groups. Our conclusions from this selective survey are as follows:

1. There is a process of convergence in equity premia and interest rates among Asian countries, particularly over the period 2000–2006 (see section 2, tables 3.2 and 3.3, and figures 3.1 and 3.2). However, with some exceptions, much the same process has occurred in Latin America and Eastern Europe. Convergence has tended to be faster in the Eastern European case than in Asia. In all regions, crises interrupt the process of convergence;

2. Cross-border holdings among Asian countries are significant in many cases and have increased over the last decade. But their pattern is not strikingly different from that in other regional groups (Latin America and Eastern Europe) and not near industrialized country benchmarks (section 3.1, tables 3.4 and 3.5). US assets continue to play a dominant role relative to Japanese assets in the portfolio allocations of Asian countries (table 3.6);

3. The gravity model, not surprisingly, continues to describe successfully cross-border equity and bond holdings. We were unable to find evidence that financial integration in Asia has reached such a point that it can counter the effects of the gravity variables (section 3.1, tables 3.7 to 3.9);

4. Several Asian economies display departures from regional home bias comparable to that in Latin American countries but lower than that in Eastern Europe or industrialized countries (section 3.2, table 3.10). A gravity model works well for explaining home bias, with real exchange rate volatility an important addition to the standard model. There is again little evidence to suggest that Asia no longer conforms to the standard model (section 3.2, table 3.11);

5. The trends in prices (equity premia and interest rates) and quantities (cross-border equity and bond holdings) are also reflected in convergence in consumption growth rates among Asian countries (section 4.1, figure 3.3 and table 3.12). However, we do not find evidence that the increased risk sharing within Asia, a presumed great benefit of deeper regional financial integration, is occurring at a faster rate than in other country groups. Puzzlingly from the perspective of standard economic theory, but consistent with the evidence from previous studies, we find that there is convergence not just in consumption growth but also in GDP growth; and

6. In the Asian context, the stability of a local investor base is put forward, often, as one of the benefits of regional financial integration (section 4.2). However, our survey of the evidence invites some caution about this claim (section 4.3). Our case study of Brazil's experience to date with the ongoing financial crisis does not point to a clear distinction between foreign and local investors in terms of their impact on local financial markets (section 4.4, figures 3.4 and 3.5).

Our bottom-line assessment is that though Asian regional financial integration is clearly increasing, at least in tranquil times, the Asian economies remain more integrated with global financial markets than with their regional neighbors. As far as economic considerations are concerned, this is not necessarily undesirable: as shown by Imbs and Mauro (2007), the gains from global diversification may be higher than those achievable solely through regional integration.

Notes

1. Table 3.1 provides the list of economies that we were able to include, based on data availability and quality, in the sequence of empirical exercises we have undertaken in the sections of this chapter.
2. We use the new series of *VIX* from 1990 onward and the older *VXO* series for 1986 through 1989.
3. If the sample period is truncated in December 2006, the coefficient on the *TREND* for Eastern Europe is −0.00364 compared with the −0.00278 reported in column 5 and the −0.00231 estimate for Asia in Column 3.
4. Data for 5 countries—Bermuda, the Cayman Islands, Ireland, Luxembourg, and Panama—represent huge outliers relative to the rest of the sample and are excluded from the regressions that follow. In addition, some of the 2007

bond holdings data for Hong Kong, China; and Singapore also are huge outliers relative to their 2001 to 2006 data. As indicated where appropriate in the rest of the paper, for the bond holdings and bond home bias indices for these two economies we used data for 2001–2006.

5. The inclusion of Bermuda heavily biases the figures on Asian investment in Latin America upward.

6. The standard errors reported in tables 3.7, 3.8, and 3.9 take into account clustering by the investor economy. The main conclusions presented in those tables are not sensitive to this choice. Also, estimating separate regressions for each year, rather than pooling the data, does not affect the thrust of the results.

7. See Portes and Rey (2005) and Loungani et al. (2007) for a discussion of the importance of distance in gravity models for trade, financial assets, and FDI.

8. Two global financial markets, the US and the UK, loom large in these data. In order to examine the extent to which Asia relies on these global markets relative to regional markets, Kim, Lee, and Shin (2006) suggest constructing a set of dummy variables as follows: The (0,1) variable *Global* takes the value 1, if the issuer is either the US or the UK. The (0,1) variable *Asia_Global* takes the value 1, if the investor country is in Asia and the issuer country is either the US or the UK, and similarly for the other regional groups. The coefficient variable *Global* is very significant, showing the importance of the US and UK in cross-border financial flows. However, the other interactions were not generally significant, and adding them did not change our conclusions about the sign or significance of the other variables.

9. We also implemented a variant of the empirical strategy suggested by Kim, Lee, and Shin (2006) by interacting the variables of the basic gravity model with *Asia_Pair* to examine whether regional integration in Asia has modified the effects of the gravity variables. However, the magnitude, signs, and significance of the gravity variables did not change appreciably, while the interaction terms, by and large, were not significant.

10. See Tumbarello (2007). Also, Fernald et al. (1999) and Ahearne et al. (2006) discuss the growing trade linkages among Asian countries.

11. We investigated the effect of capital controls on cross-border asset holdings and home bias using a new and comprehensive data set on controls (Schindler, 2009). For equities and bonds separately, we constructed a measure of capital controls by summing, for every investor-issuer pair of countries in our sample, the 1995–2005 average of the index of restrictions on outflows by the investor country and the 1995–2005 average of the index of restrictions on inflows by the issuer country. We did not find any systematic or significant effect of controls on asset holdings using the regressions discussed above. The results were somewhat clearer in the home bias regressions: while there was no effect on equities, capital controls increased home bias in the regressions for bond holdings in the all-countries sample and in the country-group regressions for the industrialized countries, Latin America, and Eastern Europe (but not Asia).

12. We also estimated the home bias regressions for the different country groups. The *Product of per Capita GDPs* reduces home bias across all country groups and for both equities and bonds, but the performance of the other gravity variables is mixed. *Real Exchange Rate Volatility* raises home bias, but the effect is not significant for industrialized countries for both equities and bonds and for Asian countries in the case of bonds.

13. Flood et al. (2009) suggest that risk sharing should be thought of as a long-term phenomenon, "driven perhaps by output-growth-rate convergence related to trade in ideas and technologies and to diffusion of institutions." Their measure shows that risk sharing has improved over time as industrial countries' consumption growth rates have converged dramatically since the 1960s and consumption growth rates for emerging markets started converging in the 1990s.

14. Of course, countries can always issue debt denominated in a major international currency—and they often do—but in this case, they are shifting the currency risk from investors to themselves rather than eliminating it.

15. However, one can argue that the foreign investors' urge to flee the domestic markets and the sharp depreciation of the real caused the crash in the Bovespa in the first place. Thus, gains in reducing solvency risk may be offset by increased market volatility in the post-original sin world.

References

Adjaoute, K., and J-P. Danthine. 2004. Equity Returns and Integration: Is Europe Changing? *Oxford Review of Economic Policy.* 20(4). pp. 555–570.

Ahearne, A., J. Fernald, P. Loungani, and J. Schindler. 2006. Flying Geese or Sitting Ducks? China's Impact on the Trading Fortunes of Other Asian Economies. *Federal Reserve Board International Finance Discussion Paper 887.*

Asian Development Bank. 2008. *Emerging Asian Regionalism: A Partnership for Shared Prosperity.* Manila: Asian Development Bank.

Backus, D., P. Kehoe, and F. Kydland. 1994. Dynamics of the Trade Balance and the Terms of Trade: The J-Curve? *American Economic Review.* 84(1). pp. 84–103.

Bekaert, G., C. R. Harvey, and C. Lundblad. 2006. Growth Volatility and Financial Liberalization. *Journal of International Money and Finance.* 25(3). pp. 370–403.

Borensztein, E., E. Levy Yeyati, and U. Panizza. 2007. *Living with Debt: How to Limit the Risks of Sovereign Finance.* Inter-American Development Bank Report on Economic and Social Progress in Latin America. Cambridge, MA: Harvard University Press.

Borensztein, E., and R. G. Gelos. 2003. A Panic-Prone Pack? The Behavior of Emerging Market Mutual Funds. *IMF Staff Papers.* 50(1). pp. 43–63.

Choe, H., B-C. Kho, and R. Stulz. 1999. Do Foreign Investors Destabilize Stock Markets? The Korean Experience in 1997. *Journal of Financial Economics.* 54(2). pp. 227–264.

De Nicolo, G., and I. Ivaschenko. 2008. Financial Integration and Risk-Adjusted Growth Opportunities. *IMF Working Paper 08/126.*

Feldstein, M., and C. Horioka. 1980. Domestic Saving and International Capital Flows. *The Economic Journal.* 90(358). pp. 314–329.

Fernald, J., H. Edison, and P. Loungani. 1999. Was China the First Domino? Assessing Links Between China and Other Asian Economies. *Journal of International Money and Finance.* 18(4). pp. 515–535.

Fidora, M., M. Fratzcher, and C. Thimann. 2007. Home Bias in Global Bonds and Equity Markets: The Role of Real Exchange Rate Volatility. *Journal of International Money and Finance.* 26(4). pp. 631–655.

Flood, R., N. Marion, and A. Matsumoto. 2009. International Risk Sharing During the Globalization Era. *IMF Working Paper 09/209.*

Frankel, J., and S. Schmukler. 1996. Country Fund Discounts and the Mexican Crisis of December 1994: Did Local Residents Turn Pessimistic before International Investors? *Board of Governor of the Federal Reserve System International Finance Discussion Paper* 563.

Frankel, J., and S. Schmukler. 1998. Country Funds and Asymmetric Information. *World Bank Policy Research Working Paper* 1886.

Imbs, J. 2006. The Real Effects of Financial Integration. *Journal of International Economics.* 68(2). pp. 296–324.

Imbs, J., and P. Mauro. 2007. Pooling Risk among Countries. *IMF Working Paper* 07/132.

International Monetary Fund. 1998. *World Economic Outlook. Financial Crises: Causes and Indicators.* Washington DC: IMF.

Ito, T., and Y. C. Park. 2004. Overview: Challenges and Strategies. In T. Ito, and Y. C. Park, eds. *Developing Asian Bondmarkets.* Canberra: Asia Pacific Press.

Kim, S., S. Kim, and Y. Wang. 2006. Financial Integration and Consumption Risk Sharing in East Asia. *Japan and the World Economy.* 18(2). pp. 143–157.

Kim, S., and J-W. Lee. 2008. Real and Financial Integration in East Asia. *ADB Working Paper Series on Regional Economic Integration* 17.

Kim, S., J-W. Lee, and K. Shin. 2006. Regional and Global Financial Integration in East Asia. *MPRA Paper* 695. Available online at http://mpra.ub.uni-muenchen.de/695.

Kim, H., K-Y. Oh, and C-W. Jeong. 2005. Panel Cointegration Results on Capital Mobility in Asian Economies. *Journal of International Money and Finance.* 24(1). pp. 71–82.

Kose, M. A., E. Prasad, and M. Terrones. 2009. Does Financial Globalization Promote Risk Sharing? *Journal of Development Economics.* 89(2). pp. 258–270.

Laeven, L., and F. Valencia. 2008. Systemic Banking Crises: A New Database. *IMF Working Paper* 08/224.

Lewis, K. 1999. Trying to Explain Home Bias in Equities and Consumption. *Journal of Economic Literature.* 37(2). pp. 571–608.

Loungani, P., A. Mody, and A. Razin. 2007. The Global Disconnect: The Role of Transactional Distance and Scale Economies in Gravity Equations. In A. Mody, ed. *Foreign Direct Investment and the World Economy.* London: Routledge.

Portes, R., and H. Rey. 2005. The Determinants of Cross-Border Equity Flows. *Journal of International Economics.* 65(2). pp. 269–296.

Rose, A. 2005. Which International Institutions Promote International Trade? *Review of International Economics.* 13(4). pp. 682–698.

Schindler, M. 2009. Measuring Financial Integration: A New Data Set. *IMF Staff Papers.* 56(1). pp. 222–238.

Siregar, R., and K. M. Choy. 2010. Determinants of International Bank Lending from the Developed World to East Asia. *IMF Staff Papers.* 57(2). pp.484–516.

Solnik, B., and J. Roulet. 2000. Dispersion as Cross-Sectional Correlation. *Financial Analysts Journal.* 56(1). pp. 54–61.

Tumbarello, P. 2007. Are Regional Trade Agreements in Asia Stumbling or Building Blocks? Some Implications for the Mekong-3 Countries. *IMF Working Paper* 07/53.

4

Understanding Business Cycle Synchronization: Is Inflation Targeting Paving the Way to Asian Monetary Union?

Andrew K. Rose

I thank Ayhan Kose and Chris Candelaria for discussions and data assistance, and Kwanho Shin, Pol Antras, Robert Barro, Robert Flood, Hans Genberg, Jong-Wha Lee, Prakash Loungani, Warwick McKibbin, Jayant Menon, Hans-Joachim Voth, Shang-Jin Wei, conference participants at the Asian Development Bank and Hong Kong Institute for Monetary Research (ADB-HKIMR), and seminar participants at the ADB for comments.

1 Motivation and Introduction

This chapter is concerned with why business cycles are synchronized across countries. Understanding the degree of business cycle synchronization (BCS) is key to understanding a number of phenomena, such as international policy coordination and the transmission of shocks across countries. Perhaps most importantly, a country is more willing to relinquish monetary sovereignty and join a currency union if the other members of the union have business cycles that are highly correlated with its own. This logic was first laid out clearly by Mundell (1961), and has been studied rigorously of late by Alesina and Barro (2002). I am particularly interested in understanding the degree of BCS among East Asian countries, since a high degree of Asian BCS would enhance the case for Asian monetary union (AMU).

What drives BCS? Frankel and Rose (1998) first discussed this issue, and focused on international trade linkages. They showed that the extent of international trade between a pair of countries has, in theory, an ambiguous effect on their BCS. If trade is mostly driven by factor-proportions and if industry-specific shocks play an important role in business cycles, then reduced trade barriers that deepen trade will lower BCS by encouraging specialization and inducing more asynchronous cycles. On the other hand, if trade is mostly intra-industry in nature and aggregate demand shocks are important in business cycles, then enhanced trade can be expected to raise BCS. Empirically, Frankel and Rose found the linkage between trade and BCS to be positive.

In this chapter, I build on the work of Frankel and Rose. I begin by reviewing the literature that analyzes the links between trade and BCS. I estimate the size of the effect, and provide some data that allow one to gauge the potential size of the effect in the Asian context.

I then expand the scope of the analysis of BCS. I am particularly interested in two phenomena. The first is "decoupling," the idea that business cycles are becoming more independent and less synchronized between countries. This phenomenon has been much discussed of late in Asia and throughout the developing world. It is of particular interest during the current financial crisis, which originated in Western countries but seems to have spread quickly, casting doubt on the notion of decoupling. Of more direct relevance for this study, if BCS is low, then monetary union is both less desirable and unlikely. Thus, the second phenomenon of interest is the effect of the monetary regime on BCS. I examine what the effects of monetary regimes like fixed exchange rates and monetary unions are for BCS, using graphical, parametric, and semi-parametric techniques.

Of special interest for Asia is inflation targeting (IT), a recent policy that allows the monetary authority to focus on domestic inflation. IT has been recently adopted by a number of Asian countries (Indonesia, Republic of Korea [Korea], the Philippines, and Thailand), as well as some related Pacific countries (Australia and New Zealand). One of the oft-cited advantages of IT is the fact that it provides insulation from foreign shocks. In this chapter, I empirically investigate whether the advent of inflation targeting can be linked to BCS, and thus decoupling. I find that it cannot, for two reasons. First, decoupling simply does not seem to be present in the data. Second, IT does not, in fact, seem to result in less cross-country synchronization of business cycles. Indeed, countries that target inflation have somewhat higher levels of BCS (as do countries that fix their exchange rates together or collaborate through a monetary union). This suggests that IT might be a good monetary regime above and beyond its intrinsic merits, since it may raise BCS and thus help ease the way to any future AMU.

2 The Effect of Trade on Business Cycle Synchronization

The most commonly considered determinant of the degree of business cycle synchronization between a pair of countries is the amount of trade between them. This linkage has been studied extensively in the literature; in this section of the chapter, I provide an estimate of its effect, with special reference to Asia.

A number of studies have already estimated the effect of trade on the cross-country synchronization of business cycles. These studies have typically followed Frankel and Rose (1998) and run regressions of the form:

$$BCS_{i,j,\tau} = \theta \, Trade_{i,j,\tau} + Controls + \epsilon_{i,j,\tau}, \tag{1}$$

where $BCS_{i,j,\tau}$ is a measure of business cycle synchronization between countries i and j over some period of time τ, typically measured as the correlation coefficient between detrended real output of the two countries (more on this below); θ is the coefficient of interest; $Trade$ denotes a measure of bilateral trade shared by the same countries over the same period of time; $Controls$ denotes extra regressors (usually some combination of fixed or random time-, country-, or country-pair specific effects); and ε represents the host of other factors affecting BCS, which are omitted from (and hopefully orthogonal to) the equation. Frankel and Rose (1998) show that θ cannot be unambiguously signed in theory.[1]

Rather than provide yet another estimate, I provide a brief quantitative survey of the literature instead, using meta-analysis to provide an aggregate estimate of the effect. Meta-analysis is a set of quantitative techniques for evaluating and combining empirical results from different studies. Essentially, one treats different point estimates of a given coefficient (in this case, θ) as individual observations, one from each underlying study. One can then use this vector to estimate the underlying coefficient of interest, test the hypothesis that the coefficient is zero, and link the estimates to features of the underlying studies. Since there are currently a number of studies that have provided estimates of the effect of trade on BCS, meta-analysis seems an appropriate way to summarize the current state of the literature. Stanley (2001) provides a review of meta-analytic techniques for economists, and further references.

One begins meta-analysis by collecting as many estimates of a common effect as possible. To my knowledge, there are 21 papers that provide estimates of the effect of bilateral trade on BCS.[2] These articles are tabulated in table 4.1. I also present each study's preferred estimate, along with its standard error. In each case, I present the estimate of θ that seems to be most preferred or representative (if a preferred estimate is not available) by the author(s) of the study. I weigh each estimate equally, simply because there is no easily defensible alternative weighting scheme.[3]

The most basic piece of meta-analysis is a test of the null hypothesis that the effect is zero when the 21 point estimates (and their standard errors) are pooled across studies. This classic test is due originally to Fisher and uses the p-values from each of the (21) underlying θ estimates. Under the null hypothesis that each of the p-values is independently and randomly drawn

Table 4.1
Estimates of Impact of Trade on Business Cycle Synchronization from Literature

Authors	θ Estimate	Std.Err. of θ
Baxter and Kouparitsas	0.134	0.032
Bower and Guillenmineau	0.021	0.005
Calder	0.013	0.004
Calderon, Chong and Stein	0.015	0.003
Choe	0.027	0.008
Clark and Wincoop	0.090	0.030
Crosby	0.048	0.063
Fidrmuc	0.021	0.045
Fiess	0.123	0.062
Frankel and Rose	0.086	0.015
Gruben, Koo and Mills	0.059	0.017
Imbs	0.031	0.020
Imbs	0.074	0.022
Inklaar. Jong-a-Pin and de Haan	0.115	0.041
Kalemli-Ozcan, Papaioannou and Peydro	−0.034	0.020
Kose and Yi	0.091	0.022
Kose, Prasad and Terrones	0.011	0.005
Kumakura	0.058	0.035
Kumakura	0.056	0.012
Otto, Voss and Willard	0.046	0.090
Shin and Wang	0.077	0.077

from a normal [0, 1] distribution, minus twice the sum of the logs of the p-values is drawn from a chi-square. The hypothesis can be rejected at any standard significance level, since under the null hypothesis the test-statistic of 277 is drawn from chi-squared (42).

I tabulate meta-estimates of the currency union effect on trade in table 4.2. I provide both "fixed effect" and "random effect" meta-estimates that are common in the area. The former are based on the assumption that a single fixed effect underlies every study, so that, in principle, if every study were infinitely large, every study would yield an identical result. This is the same as assuming there is no heterogeneity across studies. By way of contrast, the random effects estimator assumes that the studies are estimating different treatment effects, drawn from a distribution whose mean is of interest.[4]

Table 4.2
Meta-Analysis of Impact of Trade on Business Cycle Synchronization

Estimator	Pooled Estimate of θ	Lower Bound of 95%	Upper Bound of 95%
Fixed	0.019	0.016	0.023
Random	0.040	0.028	0.051

Manifestly, there is considerable heterogeneity; the fixed and random effect estimators differ by a factor of two. However, both estimates are economically substantial. The smaller fixed effect estimate indicates that 1% more trade raises the synchronization (read "correlation coefficient") of business cycles between a pair of countries by about 0.02, while the random effect estimate is twice as large. It seems wiser to act conservatively and I accordingly take 0.02 as my default estimate.[5]

Rising trade tends to increase business cycle synchronization. Accordingly, BCS should be expected to rise in Asia if trade rises. Table 4.3 presents some time series data on Asian trade patterns since 1990. As is well-known, trade is rising relative to gross domestic product (GDP) for almost all Asian countries. It is also becoming increasingly Asian-focused over time, again for almost all countries (People's Republic of China [PRC] being the exception here).

If Asian countries were to consummate a monetary union, their trade could be expected to rise further still, since currency unions eliminate the monetary barrier to trade and expand trade accordingly. The size of this effect is much disputed. In Rose (2008), I used meta-analysis to survey 26 recent studies that use European Economic and Monetary Union (EMU) data and find that currency union has already raised trade within EMU by at least 8%, even though Europe was well integrated before EMU, and EMU is a relatively young currency union. Rose and Stanley (2005) use similar techniques to summarize 34 studies that analyze the same effect, using data from mostly poor and/or small currency union members, and find that currency union increases trade by at least 33%. So, above and beyond any positive long-term trends that seem to be raising both trade relative to GDP and Asian trade relative to common trade, monetary union can be expected to increase the trade of its members still further.

I conclude that Asian business cycle synchronization is likely to grow. Even without monetary union, Asian trade seems likely to continue to rise relative to GDP as transportation costs shrink and supply chains become ever more complex and integrated. Much of the growth in this trade will occur between Asian countries; AMU might expand this trade further.

I now begin to look beyond trade as a determinant of BCS. While my focus is on the monetary regime, I pay special attention to inflation targeting because of its dramatic expansion in Asia and abroad.

Table 4.3
Trade Patterns in Asia

Country	Trade/GDP (%)			Intra-Asian Trade		
	1990	2007	Growth Rate (%)	1990	2007	Growth Rate (%)
Australia	32.6	42.1	1.4	0.38	0.54	2.30
Bangladesh	19.7	50.8	3.6	0.49	0.58	1.00
China, People's Rep. of	34.8	72.0	3.2	0.51	0.43	−0.90
Hong Kong, China	252.6	404.1	2.2	0.68	0.77	0.70
India	15.7	45.8	3.9	0.20	0.34	3.90
Indonesia	49.1	54.7	0.6	0.49	0.62	1.50
Japan	10.0	15.2	2.0	0.31	0.45	2.50
Korea, Rep. of	57.0	90.4	2.2	0.37	0.49	1.80
Malaysia	147.0	210.0	1.8	0.55	0.62	0.70
New Zealand	53.4	58.6	0.5	0.45	0.62	2.10
Pakistan	38.9	36.2	−0.4	0.32	0.38	1.00
Papua New Guinea	89.6	146.7	2.4	0.80	0.91	0.80
Philippines	60.8	92.3	2.0	0.43	0.56	1.70
Singapore	226.0	433.0	2.8	0.50	0.55	0.60
Thailand	75.8	132.5	2.5	0.55	0.59	0.40
Viet Nam	81.3	159.3	2.9	0.34	0.71	6.00

Sources: Intra-Asian trade data from IMF's *Direction of Trade Statistics*; Trade/GDP data from World Bank's *World Development Indicators*. 2006 data used for Trade/GDP for: Australia, PRC, Papua New Guinea. OECD data used for Japan.

3 Inflation Targeting and Business Cycle Synchronization: Theory and Literature

There are many theoretical reasons to believe that IT should be associated with a lower synchronization of business cycles. The basic theory is laid out in chapter 18 of Mundell's classic (1968) textbook; a modern version is provided by Céspedes et al. (2004). For alternative theoretical models that deliver similar results, see Svensson (2000) and Dehejia and Rowe (2000).

Mundell first formally explored the logic of the insulation value of floating exchange rates in his famous textbook *International Economics* (1968). While he is best known for his presentation of the small open economy comparison of fixed and flexible exchange rates with perfect capital mobility, Mundell also presents a two-country model in an appendix to chapter 18. He shows that under fixed exchange rates, monetary shocks lead to positive BCS, while the effect of real shocks is theoretically ambiguous. By way of contrast, with flexible exchange rates, real shocks are associated with positive spillovers and BCS for very large countries, while a monetary shock leads to opposite effects in the domestic and foreign economies. He states explicitly, "It cannot, therefore, be asserted that a country is automatically immunized by its flexible exchange rate from business cycle disturbances originating abroad." His reasoning is that a positive domestic real shock raises the domestic interest rate, attracting foreign capital and appreciating the exchange rate. Similarly, with fixed rates, business cycles caused by real shocks of large countries may or may not be transmitted abroad. Still, he leaves little doubt that BCS would ordinarily be expected to be much higher for fixed exchange rates.

Turnovsky (1976) shows that foreign price shocks have a greater impact on domestic income under fixed as opposed to flexible exchange rates; business cycle correlations should be larger under fixed exchange rates. Indeed, Turnovsky writes (p. 42) "the domestic economy is fully insulated from foreign price fluctuations" with flexible exchange rates. He concludes (p. 45) "output will always be more stable under flexible rates if the stochastic disturbances are either in foreign trade (say exports) or in foreign output prices." Such models have been criticized by many recently, since regime optimality is made in terms of ad hoc combinations of variances rather than utility; see, for example, Devereux and Engel (1999, 2003). Devereux and Engel instead use dynamic stochastic general equilibrium models to investigate regime choice. However, their models do not easily lend themselves to the questions at hand here for a number of reasons (e.g., the models are restrictive, there are a very limited number of shocks, and the focus is on welfare and thus consumption rather than GDP). Still, such analysis usually retains the celebrated "insulation" effect in that floating exchange rates protect the domestic economy from foreign monetary shocks.

Mundell's work has been perhaps most recently analyzed by Céspedes et al. (2004), an explicit defense of the insulating role of flexible exchange rates. They begin their paper, "Any economics undergraduate worthy of a B learns this key policy implication of the Mundell-Fleming model: if any economy is predominantly hit by foreign real shocks, flexible exchange rates dominate fixed rates." However, the underlying logic for this goes back at least to Friedman's (1953) celebrated case for floating exchange rates. Friedman states (p. 200): "In effect, flexible exchange rates are a means of combining interdependence among countries through trade with a maximum of internal monetary independence; they are a means of permitting each country to seek for monetary stability according to its own lights, without either imposing its mistakes on its neighbors or having their mistakes imposed on it."

Countries with foreign-oriented monetary regimes (e.g., monetary unions or fixed exchange rates) should be expected to have more correlated business cycles than countries with purely domestically oriented monetary policy. But in almost all theoretical exercises, the monetary regime (e.g., a fixed exchange rate) is chosen endogenously, typically as a function of the types and importance of different shocks that hit the economy (among other things).

That is, causality flows both ways. Thus it will be important to allow for the endogeneity of the monetary regime in empirical analysis.

There is relatively little empirical literature of relevance. Wyplosz (2001) examines correlations of shocks to GDP across Asian countries, but with essentially no structure. Eichengreen and Bayoumi (1996) provide more structural analysis using an identified vector autoregression (VAR) approach to disentangle aggregate demand and supply shocks for Asia to construct an "optimum currency area" index. This analysis is now sorely dated by the Asian crisis and the resulting switching in Asian monetary regimes. Fortunately, the analysis has been updated by Ahn et al. (2006), though again in a relatively astructural way; they find that the cross-country correlation of shocks suggest that AMU may be feasible. Such work—see also Ling and Yuen (2001), Kwack (2004), and Sato and Zhang (2006)—assumes that the structure of the economies and shocks will remain invariant to monetary regimes and other phenomena. This assumption has been questioned in general by Frankel and Rose (1998) and in the context of East Asia by Lee et al. (2003) in particular. Finally, another recent paper of interest is Kose et al. (2008), who use a factor model to analyze the interdependence of business cycles. They cover more countries than I do here, but at the annual frequency. My empirical model is consistent with most of their findings, but is focused differently. The emphasis here is on linking BCS to economic determinants, rather than characterizing its univariate properties.

4 The Data Set

I am interested in what determines the coherence of business cycles across countries, especially the effect of monetary regimes like inflation targeting. Accordingly, I choose a data set which spans a large number of countries with different monetary regimes and a number of business cycles at an appropriate frequency.[6]

Since New Zealand began to target inflation in early 1990, 26 other countries have adopted formal inflation targeting regimes.[7] I include all IT countries in my sample. To provide a comparison group, I also include all countries that are at least as large as the smallest (Iceland) and as rich as the poorest IT country (the Philippines), as long as they have reasonable data on aggregate output. IT only began in 1990, and reliable quarterly data ends for most countries in 2007; I begin my data set in 1974. This coincides with the beginning of the post-Bretton Woods era, and almost exactly doubles the span of data over time. I choose the quarterly frequency so as to be able to measure business cycle movements with aggregate output series.

I end up with a set of 64 countries that have reliable GDP data, though many are missing observations for some of the sample. The list of countries in the sample is tabulated in table 4.A1, along with the date of IT adoption (if appropriate). I note in passing that this sample of countries includes a large number of observations for countries that have either fixed exchange rates or relinquished monetary sovereignty in a currency union (the latter are almost all members of EMU but also include Ecuador, a recent "dollarizer"). Nine of the countries are East Asian (PRC; Hong Kong, China; Indonesia; Japan; Korea; Macau, China; the Philippines; Singapore; and Thailand); limiting the sample to strictly Asian countries would restrict the data set dramatically.

At the core of my measure of business cycle synchronization lies aggregate real output. I take seasonally adjusted GDP data from three different sources: the International Monetary Fund's (IMF) *International Financial Statistics* and *World Economic Outlook* data sets, and the Organisation for Economic Co-operation and Development (OECD). I have checked these data extensively for mistakes.[8] Table 4.A1 also includes the date of the earliest reliable data on output.

Since my focus in this study is on (the cross-country coherence of) business cycle deviations from trend, it is necessary to detrend the output series. Since there is no universally accepted method, I use four different techniques to create trends. First, I use the well-known Hodrick-Prescott (HP) filter.[9] Second, I use the more recent Baxter-King (BK) band-pass filter.[10] Third, I construct the fourth difference, thus creating annual growth rates from quarterly data. Finally and perhaps least plausibly, I construct trends by regressing output on linear and quadratic time trends as well as quarterly dummies. I refer to these four methods of detrending as HP, BK, Growth, and Linear respectively:

$$y_{i,t}^{HP} \equiv y_{i,t} - \hat{y}_{i,t}^{HP}, \tag{2}$$

$$y_{i,t}^{BK} \equiv y_{i,t} - \hat{y}_{i,t}^{BK}, \tag{3}$$

$$y_{i,t}^{Growth} \equiv y_{i,t} - y_{i,t-4}, \tag{4}$$

$$y_{i,t}^{Linear} \equiv y_{i,t} - (\hat{\alpha} + \hat{\beta}t + \hat{y}t^2 + \hat{\delta}_1 D_{1,t} + \hat{\delta}_2 D_{2,t} + \hat{\delta}_3 D_{3,t}) \tag{5}$$

where: $y_{i,t}$ is the natural logarithm of real GDP at time t; $\hat{y}_{i,t}^{HP}$ is its underlying HP trend; $\hat{y}_{i,t}^{BK}$ is its BK filtered level; and the coefficients for the linear regression are estimated over the whole sample period on time, the square of time, and three quarterly dummy variables $\{D_{j,t}\}$.

Having created business cycle deviations for all my countries, I then compute measures of cross-country coherences of business cycles. I do this by creating conventional sample Pearson correlation coefficients, as is now common practice in the literature (e.g., Baxter and Kouparitsas, 2005, and Imbs, 2006).[11] The correlation coefficients are created using 20 quarterly observations (five years) of data (though in statistical work I typically only use every twentieth observation), and are defined as

$$\hat{\rho}_{i,j,\tau}^{d} \equiv \frac{1}{T-1} \sum_{t=1}^{\tau} \left(\frac{y_{i,t}^{d} - y_{i,\tau}^{d}}{\sigma_{i,\tau}^{d}} \right) \left(\frac{y_{j,t}^{d} - y_{j,\tau}^{d}}{\sigma_{j,\tau}^{d}} \right), \tag{6}$$

where: $\hat{\rho}^d_{i,j,\tau}$ is the sample correlation coefficient estimated between output for countries i and j over the 20 (T) quarters preceding through time τ; the natural logarithm for real GDP (y) has been detrended with method d (d = HP, BK, Linear, and Growth); and $\bar{y}$ and σ denote the corresponding sample mean and standard deviation, respectively. This statistic, computed between a pair of countries over time, constitutes my key measure of business cycle synchronization (BCS). Note that this measure is not constrained to be constant across time for a dyad, consistent with the findings of Kose et al. (2008), who find considerable time-variation in business cycle synchronization.

Decoupling is sometimes considered to refer to the linkages between a particular developing country and a composite of industrial countries (not simple random pairs of countries). Accordingly, I construct analogous measures for both the G3 (Germany, Japan, and the United States [US]) and G7 (the G3 plus Canada, France, Italy, and the United Kingdom [UK]), as well as comparable measures of BCS between countries and the G3 and G7.[12]

I am interested in understanding the determinants of business cycle synchronization, especially the role of the monetary regime. Accordingly, I add dummy variables to the data set to account for whether either or both of the countries engaged in inflation targeting. I also include comparable dummies for countries that were in a monetary union (such as EMU) or a fixed exchange rate regime (such as Hong Kong, China's currency board).[13]

There are a number of other potential determinants of BCS, above and beyond any possible effect of the monetary regime; the effects of trade have already been discussed. Baxter and Kouparitsas (2005) have recently examined a host of potential determinants of BCS. They conclude that only four variables have a robust effect on it: (i) the degree of bilateral trade between the two countries; (ii) a dummy variable when both countries are industrialized countries; (iii) a dummy when both countries are developing countries; and (iv) a variable that measures the distance between the two countries. Accordingly, I add data for all four of these variables.[14] As already mentioned, the first effect—that of trade on BCS—is the most important. Below, I provide an estimate of this coefficient from the literature.

I also add one final variable, not considered by Baxter and Kouparitsas: the degree of financial integration between a pair of countries. Imbs (2006) uses the recently developed Coordinated Portfolio Investment Survey (CPIS) data set, and finds that a country-pair with closer financial ties tend to have more synchronized business cycles. He uses the first cross-section of CPIS data for 2001, and measures financial integration in a manner analogous to the Baxter-Kouparitsas trade measure. I follow his lead, but include data for the 2002 through 2006 CPIS data sets, as well as that for 2001. Unfortunately, this results in a very short data set; Kalemli-Ozcan et al. (2008) use a proprietary data set available for a longer span.

5 Decoupling

I begin by examining the stylized facts concerning decoupling. I am particularly interested in any trends in BCS over time.

Figure 4.1 presents a first look at the BCS measures. It contains time series plots of BCS, averaged across all feasible country-pairs at a point in time. There are four graphs, one for each of the four detrending techniques (Hodrick-Prescott, Baxter-King, deterministic linear/quadratic regression, and growth rate). In each case, the average value of the BCS correlation coefficient, and a confidence interval of ± two-standard deviation (of the mean) are portrayed.[15]

The single most striking thing about the trends portrayed in figure 4.1 is that there are no obvious trends. The average level of BCS varies some over time, but it is typically around 0.25 or so. There is, however, no evidence that the average correlation coefficient is significantly lower (in either economic or statistical terms) toward the end of the sample period. That is, there is little *prima facie* evidence of decoupling. If anything, there is a slight tendency for business cycles to be slightly more correlated across countries in 2007 compared to, say, 2000.[16] This is consistent with the (more narrowly based) findings of Doyle and Faust (2002) and Stock and Watson (2003), neither of whom finds significant changes in business cycle synchronization between the G7 countries.[17]

Figure 4.1 considers bilateral measures of BCS; all possible pairs of countries are considered (there are over 2,000 of these dyads). Figure 4.2 is an analogue

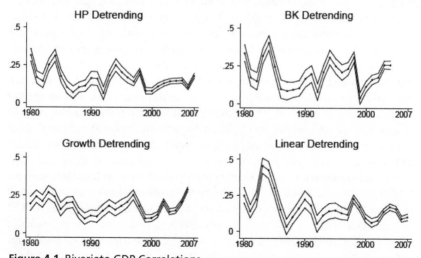

Figure 4.1 Bivariate GDP Correlations

Note: The upper and lower bands refer to ± two-standard deviation of mean.

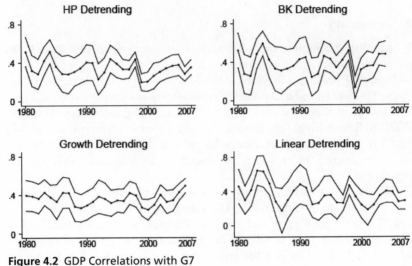

Figure 4.2 GDP Correlations with G7

Note: The upper and lower bands refer to ± two-standard deviation of mean.

that considers BCS between a given country and an index for the business cycle of the G7 industrial countries. In this more multilateral sense, there is still no evidence that business cycles are becoming more isolated from one another.[18]

Some think of decoupling as referring to a shrinking relationship between the business cycles of industrial and developing countries. This is of special importance to Asia, where most countries are developing. Accordingly, figure 4.3 is an analogue to figure 4.1; it considers only pairs of countries in which one is industrial and the other is developing. Again, no dramatic declines in the degree of business cycle synchronization are apparent; instead, the correlations seem to fluctuate around an approximately constant mean. The same description characterizes figure 4.4, which is an analogue to figure 4.2; it considers only BCS between developing countries and the G7 aggregate. Finally, figure 4.5 is an analogue that restricts attention to pairs of countries where at least one is in Asia; again, no conclusions are changed. That is, decoupling does not seem to be a phenomenon that works at the regional level.[19]

Of course, there are many ways that one can divide up the data, so these findings cannot be taken as definitive. Further, this analysis is unconditional; no other factors have been taken into account that might possibly affect BCS. Still, I conclude that there seems to be remarkably little *prima facie* evidence of decoupling in the aggregate output data. National business cycles do not in fact seem to be moving more asynchronously over time; if anything, the opposite is true.

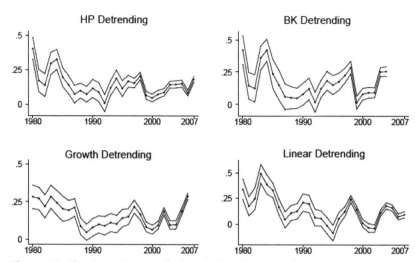

Figure 4.3 Bivariate GDP Correlations, Industrial-LDC Pairs
Notes: LDC refers to less developed countries. The upper and lower bands refer to ±
two-standard deviation of mean.

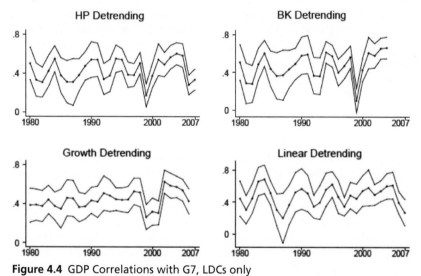

Figure 4.4 GDP Correlations with G7, LDCs only
Notes: LDC refers to less developed countries. The upper and lower bands refer to ±
two-standard deviation of mean.

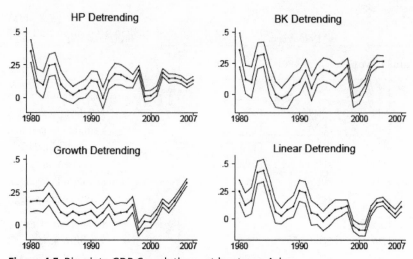

Figure 4.5 Bivariate GDP Correlations, at least one Asian
Note: The upper and lower bands refer to ± two-standard deviation of mean.

6 Business Cycle Synchronization and Inflation Targeting

What about the impact of inflation targeting on BCS? The easiest way to start is to consider countries that have been targeting inflation for a considerable period of time. Figure 4.6 is a set of four time-series plots (again, one for each method of detrending) that portray BCS between New Zealand (the first country to adopt IT) and the G7. The introduction of inflation targeting is marked with a vertical line, and the average levels of BCS before and after its introduction are also depicted.[20]

Somewhat surprisingly, there is no evidence that New Zealand's business cycle has become systematically less synchronized with that of the main industrial countries since IT was introduced. If anything, there has been a slight increase in BCS, though it is insignificant compared with the considerable volatility in BCS over time.

Figure 4.7 contains the analogue for Korea, the first of the Asians to enter a formal IT regime (in 1998). There is also no clear-cut sign that BCS fell dramatically after Korea introduced inflation targeting.

The evidence of figures 4.6 and 4.7 is narrow, since they only include data for the relationships between New Zealand and Korea vis-à-vis the major industrial countries. Figure 4.8 broadens the sample considerably and provides evidence for a large number of country-pairs around the time of IT entry. All dyads are portrayed when either country in the pair enters an IT regime. The graphs begin seven and a half years before entry and end ten years after entry into IT, data allowing. The mean value of the correlation coefficient is shown on the y-axis, along with a confidence interval extending ± two-standard

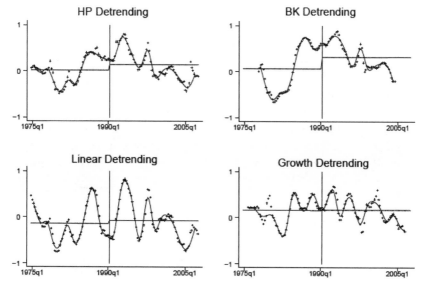

Figure 4.6 Business Cycle Synchronization: New Zealand
Note: Each point represents a 5-year moving average correlation with G7 and is connected by a non-parametric smoother.

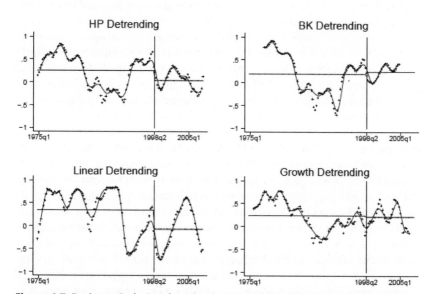

Figure 4.7 Business Cycle Synchronization: Republic of Korea
Note: Each point represents a 5-year moving average correlation with G7 and is connected by a non-parametric smoother.

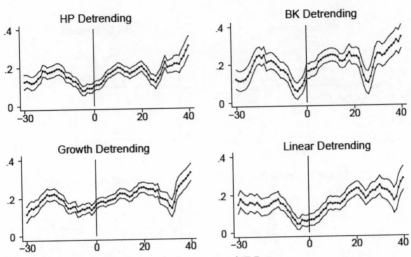

Figure 4.8 Bivariate GDP Correlations around IT Entry

Notes: The upper and lower bands refer to ± two-standard deviation of mean. The x-axis shows the quarters before and after entry into IT.

deviation on either side; the x-axis shows the quarters before and after entry into IT.[21]

The event studies of figure 4.8 show little evidence that inflation targeting is systematically associated with a decline in business cycle synchronization across countries. While there is considerable variation over time in BCS, it still seems to be somewhat higher in the years after one of the countries has adopted IT. Differences across detrending techniques tend to be small. Figure 4.9 is an analogue that portrays the relationships between countries entering IT and the G7 business cycle; it also shows a slight increase in BCS following the adoption of inflation targeting.

For the purpose of comparison, figure 4.10 is an event study that considers an alternative monetary regime of interest, namely entry into a fixed exchange rate.[22] Countries fixing exchange rates against each other seem to have systematically more synchronized business cycles within five or ten years after the event. Since theory generally leads one to expect that a common monetary policy should be associated with more synchronized business cycles, these intuitive findings encourage one to think that the data have power enough to speak.

Thus the overview of the data ends on a double note of puzzlement. First, it seems that there is little evidence that business cycles have actually become less synchronized across countries of late; decoupling is hard to see in the data. Second, entry by a country into an inflation targeting regime does not seem to be associated with a decline in business cycle synchronization; if anything, BCS seems to rise.

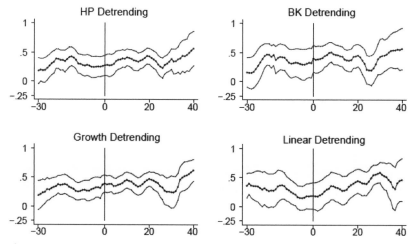

Figure 4.9 Bivariate GDP Correlations with G7 around IT Entry

Notes: The upper and lower bands refer to ± two-standard deviation of mean. The x-axis shows the quarters before and after entry into IT.

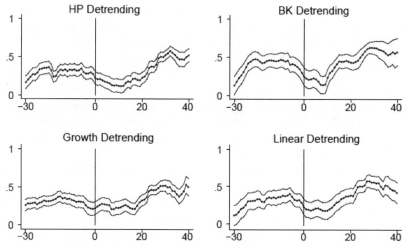

Figure 4.10 Bivariate GDP Correlations around Entry into Fixed Exchange Rate

Notes: The upper and lower bands refer to ± two-standard deviation of mean. The x-axis shows the quarters before and after entry into IT.

7 Regression Analysis

The event studies discussed above are intrinsically bivariate in that they do not control for other potential reasons why BCS might have varied across countries and/or time. Further, they use a limited amount of data. In this section, I attempt to remedy both problems, using standard regression techniques.

I run regressions of the form:

$$\hat{\rho}^d_{i,j,\tau} = \beta_1 IT(1)_{i,j,\tau} + \beta_2 IT(2)_{i,j,\tau} + \gamma_{Fix,1} Fix(1)_{i,j,\tau}$$
$$+ \gamma_{Fix,2} Fix(2)_{i,j,\tau} + \gamma_{MU,1} MU(1)_{i,j,\tau} + \gamma_{MU,2} MU(2)_{i,j,\tau}$$
$$+ \theta_T Trade_{i,j,\tau} + \theta_D Dist_{i,j} + \theta_I Ind_{i,j} + \theta_L LDC_{i,j}$$
$$+ \{\delta_{i,j}\} + \{\delta_\tau\} + \epsilon^d_{i,j,\tau}, \tag{7}$$

where: $IT(1)$ and $IT(2)$ are dummy variables that are unity if one or both of the countries are inflation targeters during the period; Fix and MU represent comparable dummies for fixed exchange rates and monetary unions, respectively; $Trade$ denotes the Baxter-Kouparitsas measure of bilateral trade shared by the countries; $Dist$ denotes the natural logarithm of great-circle distance between the countries; Ind and LDC are dummy variables for both countries being industrialized or developing countries, respectively; $\{\gamma\}$ and $\{\theta\}$ are nuisance coefficients, $\{\delta\}$ are fixed-effects for either country-pair dyads or time periods; and ε represents the host of other factors affecting BCS which are omitted from (and hopefully orthogonal to) the equation.[23] The coefficients of interest are $\{\beta\}$. The theoretical reasons discussed above indicate that IT should reduce business cycle synchronization, that is, $\beta < 0$.

Estimates for the key coefficients are reported in table 4.4. There are two panels; the top panel excludes the Baxter-Kouparitsas control variables (so that $\{\theta\} = 0$), while the bottom panel includes these controls.[24] For the sake of comparison, I also tabulate $\gamma_{Fix,2}$ and $\gamma_{MU,2}$, the effects of countries sharing a fixed exchange rate regime or currency. Robust standard errors are reported in parentheses; coefficients that are significantly different from zero at the 0.05 level are marked with one asterisk; at the 0.01 level, with two.

I estimate the model using two variants of least squares. To the left of the table, I report results estimated with time effects (setting $\{\delta_{i,j}\} = 0$), retaining a comprehensive set of time effects to account for shocks that are common across countries. On the right I include both time and a comprehensive set of time-invariant dyadic effects that will pick up any effect that is common to a pair of countries. To avoid serial correlation induced by overlapping observations, I estimate this equation with quarterly data sampled every twentieth observation.[25]

The estimates of the impact of inflation targeting on business cycle synchronization in table 4.4 are weak, in the sense that most estimates are economically small and statistically indistinguishable from zero. Of the 32 coefficients ($= 4$ detrending techniques $\times$ 2 sets of fixed effects $\times$ with/without controls $\times$ one/both countries in IT), only two are significantly negative at the 5% level (none are significantly negative at the 1% level). On the other hand, three-quarters of the coefficients have positive point estimates, and five of them are significantly so at the 5% level (one of these at the 1% level).

Table 4.4
Regression Analysis: Monetary Regimes and Business Cycle Synchronization

Detrending Method	Time Fixed Effects				Time and Dyads Fixed Effects			
	One IT	Both IT	Fixed ER	Monetary Union	One IT	Both IT	Fixed ER	Monetary Union
Without Controls								
HP	0.03	0.05*	0.27**	0.41**	0.03	−0.04	0.14**	0.08
	(0.02)	(0.02)	(0.05)	(0.03)	(0.02)	(0.03)	(0.05)	(0.05)
BK	0.02	0.06	0.21	0.59**	0.03	0.02	0.04	0.11*
	(0.04)	(0.04)	(0.12)	(0.01)	(0.04)	(0.06)	(0.07)	(0.05)
Linear	0.05*	0.07	0.34**	0.55	0.14**	0.01	0.24**	0.18**
	(0.02)	(0.04)	(0.07)	(0.22)	(0.03)	(0.05)	(0.07)	(0.06)
Growth	0.03	0.01	0.20*	0.23**	0	−0.10*	0.10*	−0.02
	(0.02)	(0.05)	(0.07)	(0.01)	(0.03)	(0.04)	(0.05)	(0.05)
With Controls								
HP	0.03	0.05	0.22**	0.29**	0.03	−0.03	0.14**	0.11*
	(0.02)	(0.02)	(0.05)	(0.03)	(0.02)	(0.03)	(0.05)	(0.05)
BK	0.04	0.07	0.09	0.40**	0.03	0.02	0.01	0.15**
	(0.02)	(0.03)	(0.10)	(0.03)	(0.04)	(0.06)	(0.09)	(0.05)
Linear	0.06**	0.07	0.28**	0.41	0.14**	0.02	0.26**	0.22**
	(0.01)	(0.04)	(0.05)	(0.18)	(0.03)	(0.05)	(0.07)	(0.06)
Growth	0.02	0.01	0.12	0.06*	0.01	−0.10*	0.07	−0.03
	(0.02)	(0.05)	(0.06)	(0.02)	(0.03)	(0.04)	(0.05)	(0.06)

Notes: Using least squares estimation, regressand is bilateral correlation coefficient for detrended GDP between countries, computed with 20 observations. Robust standard errors in parentheses; coefficients that are significantly different from zero at the 0.05 level are marked with one asterisk (*); at the 0.01 level, with two (**). Quinquennial data, computed from quarterly observations between Q4 1974 and Q4 2007 for up to 64 countries (with gaps). Controls included but not reported include: one country with fixed exchange rate, and one country in monetary union. Bottom panel adds controls: bilateral trade, log distance, and dummies for both industrial and developing countries.

The results do not seem to depend very much on which detrending technique is used, nor whether dyadic fixed effects or extra controls are included.

By way of comparison, we expect positive coefficients for the effects of both fixed exchange rates and monetary union on BCS, and we mostly find them. Eleven of the 32 coefficients are significantly positive at the 1% level and five more at the 5% level. Only two of the coefficients are negative, neither significantly so. So the data set seems able to reveal the effect of the monetary regime, if they are there.[26]

Table 4.5 is an analogue to table 4.4, but deals with linkages between countries and the G7 instead of between pairs of countries. Table 4.6 is an analogue to table 4.4 that excludes all non-Asian dyads, so that each observation contains at least one Asian country. For both tables 4.5 and 4.6, results are weak, just as in table 4.4.[27]

I conclude that there is little evidence based on these regressions that targeting inflation appreciably lowers BCS by any significant amount.

8 Estimating Treatment Effects via Matching

The regression analysis of tables 4.3 through 4.5 can be criticized on a number of grounds. Most importantly, countries do not choose their monetary regimes randomly. Rather, they choose to link their exchange rates or currencies through monetary regimes deliberately, perhaps in order to desynchronize their business cycles further. Similarly, countries that choose to target inflation might do so deliberately in order to isolate themselves from foreign shocks that they might otherwise import. In such cases, it would be inappropriate to treat the monetary regime as exogenous. Countries that choose to target inflation may not be a random sample of all countries. Rather, they may possess special features that the regression analysis does not adequately model. The usual solution to this is to find a plausible set of instrumental variables, but it is not easy to find variables that are reasonably correlated with the monetary regime, let alone instrumental variables that do not otherwise drive BCS. These issues may be further complicated if the relationship between the monetary regime and BCS is not linear. Also, there may be breaks in the process linking business cycles across both countries and time, as emphasized by Doyle and Faust (2005).

For these reasons, I now use a matching technique to estimate the linkage between the monetary regime and business cycle synchronization. The essential idea is to use a strategy akin to that generally used in medicine of conducting a controlled randomized experiment. I use a common technique, matching together individual "treatment" observations (each consisting of a country-pair at a point in time that includes an inflation targeting country) to "control" observations that are similar but do not include an inflation targeter.

I implement my technique by using the well-known propensity score of Rosenbaum and Rubin (1983), the conditional probability of assignment

Table 4.5
Determinants of Synchronization with G7

Detrending Method	Time Fixed Effects			Time and Dyads Fixed Effects		
	IT	Fix	MU	IT	Fix	MU
Without Controls						
HP	0.11	0.03	0.15	−0.02	0.03	−0.04
	(0.07)	(0.05)	(0.19)	(0.11)	(0.10)	(0.14)
BK	0.16	0.05	0.44**	0.00	0.23*	0.27*
	(0.09)	(0.10)	(0.02)	(0.13)	(0.11)	(0.12)
Linear	0.14	0.13	0.37	0.08	0.20	0.27*
	(0.07)	(0.12)	(0.19)	(0.13)	(0.10)	(0.12)
Growth	0.04	0.04	0.21*	−0.09	0.10	−0.03
	(0.09)	(0.05)	(0.08)	(0.10)	(0.10)	(0.14)
With Controls						
HP	0.07	0.01	0.02	0.01	0.07	−0.03
	(0.05)	(0.03)	(0.15)	(0.11)	(0.10)	(0.14)
BK	0.12	0.03	0.20**	0.05	0.27*	0.29*
	(0.07)	(0.10)	(0.04)	(0.13)	(0.11)	(0.14)
Linear	0.09	0.13	0.20	0.13	0.26**	0.28*
	(0.06)	(0.10)	(0.12)	(0.12)	(0.10)	(0.12)
Growth	0.00	0.02	0.00	−0.07	0.13	−0.03
	(0.07)	(0.04)	(0.06)	(0.11)	(0.10)	(0.14)

Notes: Using least squares estimation, regressand is bilateral correlation coefficient for detrended GDP between countries, computed with 20 observations. Robust standard errors in parentheses; coefficients that are significantly different from zero at the 0.05 level are marked with one asterisk (*); at the 0.01 level, with two (**). Quinquennial data, computed from quarterly observations between Q4 1974 and Q4 2007 for up to 64 countries (with gaps). Controls included but not reported include: one country with fixed exchange rate, and one country in monetary union. Bottom panel adds controls: bilateral trade and dummy for both industrial countries.

to a treatment given a vector of observed covariates. Conditional on these variables, BCS is expected to be similar for treatment and control observations, ignoring any possible effect of the monetary regime. Since I construct $\hat{\rho}^d_{i,j,\tau}$ from 20 periods of quarterly data, I only use one observation of $\hat{\rho}^d_{i,j,\tau}$ every five years. For the covariates of the propensity score, I choose the four variables shown by Baxter and Kouparitsas (2005) to have a robust effect on BCS: bilateral trade, distance, and dummies for pairs of industrialized and developing countries.[28] As a sensitivity check, I also augment this model by using a measure of financial integration. I begin with the popular "nearest neighbor" matching technique, comparing each treatment observation to its five closest neighbors from the control group.

Table 4.6
Regression Analysis Excluding Non-Asian Country Pairs

Detrending Method	Time Fixed Effects			Time and Dyads Fixed Effects		
	One IT	Both IT	Fixed ER	One IT	Both IT	Fixed ER
Without Controls						
HP	−0.02	−0.09	0.10	−0.01	−0.07	0.28
	(0.04)	(0.05)	(0.13)	(0.04)	(0.05)	(0.44)
BK	0.01	0.02	−0.05	0.05	0.01	0.48
	(0.04)	(0.02)	(0.10)	(0.07)	(0.12)	(0.34)
Linear	0.00	−0.03	−0.05	0.05	−0.06	0.53**
	(0.05)	(0.03)	(0.15)	(0.05)	(0.08)	(0.16)
Growth	−0.06	−0.12	0.15	−0.06	−0.15*	0.28
	(0.05)	(0.07)	(0.06)	(0.04)	(0.08)	(0.22)
With Controls						
HP	−0.02	−0.08	0.10	−0.01	−0.07	0.27
	(0.04)	(0.05)	(0.11)	(0.04)	(0.05)	(0.44)
BK	0.02	0.03	0.03	0.04	0.01	0.47
	(0.04)	(0.02)	(0.12)	(0.07)	(0.12)	(0.34)
Linear	0.01	−0.03	−0.05	0.05	−0.06	0.52**
	(0.05)	(0.03)	(0.16)	(0.05)	(0.08)	(0.16)
Growth	−0.05	−0.12	0.11	−0.05	−0.15*	0.29
	(0.05)	(0.07)	(0.08)	(0.04)	(0.08)	(0.22)

Notes: Using least squares estimation, regressand is bilateral correlation coefficient for detrended GDP between countries, computed with 20 observations. Robust standard errors in parentheses; coefficients that are significantly different from zero at the 0.05 level are marked with one asterisk (*); at the 0.01 level, with two (**). Quinquennial data, computed from quarterly observations between Q4 1974 and Q4 2007 for up to 64 countries (with gaps). Controls included but not reported include: one country with fixed exchange rate, and one country in monetary union. Bottom panel adds controls: bilateral trade, log distance, and dummies for both industrial and developing countries.

Table 4.7 contains matching estimates, one for each of the four different detrending techniques. I begin considering as "treatment" observations any pair of countries where one country is an inflation targeter; the other country can have any monetary regime (other than IT). As controls, I consider all observations since 1990 that are not inflation targeters.[29] I am left with 1,041 treatment observations and 5,038 controls.

The default estimates are tabulated at the left side of the table. All four of the point estimates are not only positive, but significantly so at the 1% significance level. The exact size of the effect varies a little, depending on the precise method used to detrend the data, but the cross-country correlation of

Table 4.7
Matching Estimates of Effect of Monetary Regime on Cycle Synchronization

Monetary Regimes, Treatment Pair	IT, any	IT, any	IT, any	IT, any	IT, any	IT, any	IT, Fix/MU
Number	1,041	30	1,041	1,041	1,041	1,041	276
Monetary Regimes, Control Pair	Any	G7	Fix or MU	Fix	Fix or MU †	No fix or MU	Fix or MU
Number	5,038	532	469	267	3,185	1,853	478
Detrending Method							
HP	0.08**	0.08	−0.03	−0.08	0.09**	0.06**	0.08*
	(0.01)	(0.07)	(0.05)	(0.06)	(0.02)	(0.02)	(0.04)
BK	0.14**	0.11	0.03	−0.04	0.15**	0.12**	0.17**
	(0.03)	(0.10)	(0.07)	(0.08)	(0.03)	(0.03)	(0.06)
Linear	0.10**	0.07	0.02	−0.02	0.12**	0.08**	0.01
	(0.02)	(0.09)	(0.07)	(0.08)	(0.02)	(0.02)	(0.06)
Growth	0.13**	0.14*	0.03	−0.06	0.15**	0.11**	0.11**
	(0.02)	(0.06)	(0.05)	(0.06)	(0.02)	(0.02)	(0.04)

Notes: Coefficients reported are sample average of treatment effect on BCS; standard errors in parentheses. Coefficients that are significantly different from zero at the 0.05 level are marked with one asterisk (*); at the 0.01 level, with two (**). Propensity score model used for matching includes: bilateral trade, log distance, and dummies for both industrialized and developing countries. Estimates from nearest neighbor matching, with five matches per treatment. Quinquennial data, computed from quarterly observations between Q1 1990 and Q4 2007 for up to 64 countries (with gaps). † indicates both countries must be in fixed exchange rate regime or monetary union but not necessarily vis-à-vis each other.

business cycles seems to rise by around 0.1. Since the average value of $\hat{\rho}^d_{i,j,\tau}$ for this sample is around 0.15, an increase of 0.1 represents an economically significant increase in business cycle synchronization.

Do these results depend very sensitively on the exact methodology? Perhaps, for instance, the results depend on the exact definition of treatment and control groups. I explore this idea in the remaining columns of table 4.7, which consider seven alternative sets of treatment and/or control groups. Of course, as one varies either the treatment or control group, one is comparing different groups and thus implicitly asking different questions.

The first robustness check compares business cycle synchronization between countries with IT to that of the entire G7. This dramatically reduces the sample size and thus increases the standard errors considerably. However, none of the point estimates are dramatically changed; all stay positive, and one remains statistically significant.

While inflation targeting is a well-defined monetary regime, the absence of inflation targeting is not. It is thus natural and interesting to compare IT with well-defined alternatives such as fixed exchange rates or monetary unions. Accordingly, I vary the control group in a number of different ways, considering first: (i) country-pairs that maintain either fixed exchange rates or are in a currency union vis-à-vis each other; and (ii) country-pairs that fix exchange rates against one another. These groups are of special interest, since IT can theoretically be expected to deliver monetary sovereignty when compared directly to either fixing or currency union. However, in practice, IT is associated with only statistically insignificant differences in BCS compared with either group; any differences also tend to be economically small. This is a striking result, to which I will return later.

I next consider for my control group pairs of countries that maintain either fixed exchange rate policies or participate in monetary unions, but not vis-à-vis each other (so that, e.g., Hong Kong, China–France would qualify in 2005). However, this does not lead to substantively different results from those of the default; IT has a significantly positive effect on cross-country business cycle coherence. The same is true when I exclude from the control group countries that either fix exchange rates or are in a currency union.

Finally, for my treatment group I consider pairs of countries where one targets inflation and the other participates in either a fixed exchange rate regime or a monetary union. I compare these to a control group where both countries share a monetary policy either directly through a currency or indirectly through a fixed exchange rate regime. Yet even here, all four of the coefficients are positive, three of them significantly so.[30]

Table 4.8 checks the sensitivity of the default results further by examining a number of different estimators. At the far left data column, I retabulate the default nearest neighbor results, estimated with five control matches per treatment observation. I then provide results for five different estimation techniques. First, I reduce the number of control group observations matched from five to one. Next, I augment the propensity score model by adding a

Table 4.8
Different Matching Estimators

Detrending Method	Nearest Neighbor (5 matches)	Nearest Neighbor (1 match)	Nearest Neighbor (5 matches)	Stratification	Kernel	Radius
HP	0.08**	0.08**	0.07**	0.06**	0.07**	0.08**
	(0.01)	(0.02)	(0.02)	(0.01)	(0.02)	(0.01)
BK	0.14**	0.12**	0.16**	0.08**	0.10**	0.12**
	(0.03)	(0.03)	(0.04)	(0.02)	(0.02)	(0.02)
Linear	0.10**	0.10**	0.12**	0.11**	0.11**	0.12**
	(0.02)	(0.03)	(0.03)	(0.02)	(0.02)	(0.02)
Growth	0.13**	0.13**	0.17**	0.13**	0.13**	0.13**
	(0.02)	(0.02)	(0.02)	(0.01)	(0.01)	(0.01)
Propensity Score Model	Standard	Standard	Augmented	Standard	Standard	Standard
Effect on	Average	Average	Average	Treated	Treated	Treated

Notes: Coefficients reported are sample treatment effects on average/treated on BCS; standard errors in parentheses. Coefficients that are significantly different from zero at the 0.05 level are marked with one asterisk (*); at the 0.01 level, with two (**). Standard errors for stratification and kernel estimated with (50) bootstrap replications. Standard model for propensity score used for matching includes: bilateral trade, log distance, and dummies for both industrialized and developing countries. Augmented propensity score model adds financial integration. Treatment dyad includes one IT country and one non-IT country; control dyads include any non-IT countries. Quinquennial data, computed from quarterly observations between Q1 1990 and Q4 2007 for up to 64 countries (with gaps).

measure of cross-country financial integration to the other four variables. Finally, I move away from the nearest neighbor technique and perform my matching using three different estimators: (i) stratification matching; (ii) kernel matching; and (iii) radius matching (further details on these techniques are available from Becker and Ichino, 2002).[31] However, none of these results substantially change the estimated treatment effects; all are positive and both economically and statistically significant, averaging around 0.1. It seems that the treatment effects delivered by matching techniques are even more puzzling than the regression results, showing that inflation targeting actually seems to increase the synchronization of business cycles.

Table 4.9 is an analogue to table 4.7, but restricts the data set to pairs of countries that include at least one in Asia. This reduces the sample size considerably, so there is far less precision in the estimates. However, as can be seen in the first data column at the far left of the table, IT is still associated with an increase in BCS compared with a randomly chosen pair of otherwise similar countries. One does not want to stress this result too much, since this effect is only statistically significant for two of the four detrending techniques;

Table 4.9
Matching Estimates for Asian Data

Monetary Regimes, Treatment Pair	IT, any	IT, any	IT, any	IT, any
Number	1,041	1,041	1,041	1,041
Monetary Regimes, Control Pair	Any	Fix or MU	Fix or MU [†]	No fix or MU
Number	5,038	469	3,185	1,853
Detrending Method				
HP	0.04	−0.01	0.06	0.00
	(0.03)	(0.17)	(0.03)	(0.03)
BK	0.11*	0.28	0.18**	0.03
	(0.05)	(0.16)	(0.05)	(0.05)
Linear	0.05	0.18	0.10**	−0.01
	(0.04)	(0.22)	(0.04)	(0.04)
Growth	0.09**	−0.03	0.13**	0.03
	(0.03)	(0.14)	(0.03)	(0.03)

Notes: Coefficients reported are sample average of treatment effect on BCS; standard errors in parentheses. Coefficients that are significantly different from zero at the 0.05 level are marked with one asterisk (*); at the 0.01 level, with two (**). Propensity score model used for matching includes: bilateral trade, log distance, dummies for both industrial/developing countries, and product of the countries' standard deviations. Estimates from nearest neighbor matching, with five matches per treatment. Quinquennial data, computed from quarterly observations between Q1 1990 and Q4 2007 for up to 64 countries (with gaps). [†] indicates both countries must be in fixed exchange rate regime or monetary union but not necessarily vis-à-vis each other.

other results are also weaker than the full-sample results of table 4.7. Still, there is no evidence that BCS is substantially lower for countries that target inflation, even if one considers only a sample focused on Asia.

9 Why?

Why do countries that target inflation not have business cycles that are less synchronized with foreign business cycles? Perhaps there are just fewer common shocks that hit a large number of countries during the recent era of inflation targeting. This would be consistent with the results of Stock and Watson (2003), who conclude that fewer common international shocks between the G7 countries are a large part of the reason that American business cycle volatility fell after the 1970s. Given that this study relies on a wide panel of data, the solution to this problem in a regression context would be to include a full set of common time effects. Unfortunately, the results above indicate that including time effects does not induce a negative effect of inflation targeting on BCS; the temporal pattern of common shocks does not seem to explain the results.

An alternative explanation would stress the decline in output volatility that occurred late in the period (though before 2008). Figure 4.11 is an event study that is analogous in many ways to figure 4.8. Like the latter, it is focused on the periods of time before, during, and after a country enters a regime of inflation targeting. But where figure 4.8 examines the bilateral synchronization of business cycles across countries, figure 4.11 looks at the univariate volatility of real GDP. In particular, it portrays the

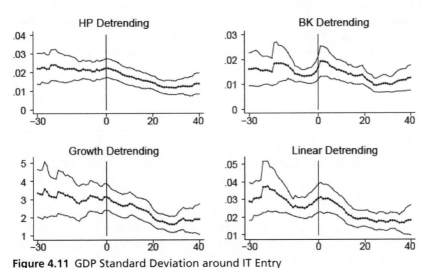

Figure 4.11 GDP Standard Deviation around IT Entry

Notes: The upper and lower bands refer to ± two-standard deviation of mean. The x-axis shows the quarters before and after entry into IT.

standard deviation of GDP detrended in four different ways, along with a ± two-standard deviation confidence interval. There is evidence that output volatility falls after a country adopts inflation, sometimes by a significant amount.[32] Since output volatility enters the denominator of the measure of BCS, $\hat{\rho}^d_{i,j,\tau}$, this might be expected to mechanically raise the measured degree of business cycle synchronization. On the other hand, table 4.10 is an analogue to table 4.7, but matches covariances instead of correlation coefficients.[33] It shows evidence that the numerator of the correlation coefficient which I use to measure BCS has also risen after inflation targeting, sometimes significantly. That is, BCS has not fallen simply because of a decline in macroeconomic volatility following entry into inflation targeting.

I am left with a mystery; there is no obvious explanation why inflation targeting is associated with an increase in business cycle synchronization.[34] Unsatisfactory explanations exist: countries may not choose their monetary regimes optimally, or countries may have been surprised by the shocks that have hit their economies. Still, for whatever reason, it seems reasonably clear that inflation targeting has not resulted in a generalized and significant decline in business cycle synchronization. The analysis undertaken here is exploratory and relies on reduced-form techniques. The next step in the research program is verifying and understanding this result more deeply. The obvious way forward in analyzing the insulation effect of different monetary regimes is to pursue more structural analysis that isolates (possibly different types of) domestic and foreign shocks.

10 Summary and Conclusion

Countries that adopt inflation targeting do not seem to increase their monetary independence in the sense of having business cycles that are significantly less correlated with those of their neighbors. Instead, the degree of business cycle synchronization seems if anything to rise when a country adopts an inflation target. I have shown this for a number of different measures of business cycle synchronization and a number of different graphical and statistical techniques. Indeed, entering an inflation target seems to raise business cycle synchronization about as much as fixing the exchange rate or entering a monetary union.

A high degree of business cycle synchronization is desirable for countries about to enter a monetary union. Inflation targeting is an intrinsically desirable monetary regime from a variety of different purely domestic perspectives, as shown already by a variety of countries in Asia and elsewhere. But the attraction of inflation targeting increases further if IT also leads to a rise in business cycle synchronization, and thus provides a convenient starting point for any deeper monetary integration. Still, it is appropriate to be cautious in dispensing any policy advice, since I have been unable as yet to come up with a convincing reason why inflation targeting seems to be so associated with

Table 4.10

Matching Estimates of Effect of Monetary Regime on Covariances instead of Correlation Coefficients

Monetary Regimes, Treatment Pair	IT, any	IT, any	IT, any	IT, any	IT, any	IT, Fix/MU
Number	1,041	1,041	1,041	1,041	1,041	276
Monetary Regimes, Control Pair	Any	Fix or MU	Fix	Fix or MU [†]	No fix or MU	Fix or MU
Number	5,038	469	267	3,185	1,853	478
Detrending Method						
HP	−0.00000	−0.00001	−0.00002	0.00001	−0.00002	0.00001
	(0.00001)	(0.00001)	(0.00001)	(0.00001)	(0.00001)	(0.00001)
BK	0.00003**	0.00001	0.00000	0.00003**	0.00003**	0.00002
	(0.00001)	(0.00001)	(0.00001)	(0.00001)	(0.00001)	(0.00001)
Linear	0.00008**	−0.00002	−0.00004	0.00006**	0.00009**	−0.00003
	(0.00002)	(0.00003)	(0.00004)	(0.00002)	(0.00003)	(0.00003)
Growth	0.53**	0.23	−0.10	0.58**	0.45	0.24
	(0.19000)	(0.24000)	(0.29000)	(0.15000)	(0.23000)	(0.15000)

Notes: Coefficients reported are sample average of treatment effect; standard errors in parentheses. Coefficients that are significantly different from zero at the 0.05 level are marked with one asterisk (*); at the 0.01 level, with two (**). Propensity score model used for matching includes: bilateral trade, log distance, dummies for both industrialized and developing countries, and product of output standard deviations for both countries. Estimates from nearest neighbor matching, with five matches per treatment. Quinquennial data, computed from quarterly observations between Q1 1990 and Q4 2007 for up to 64 countries (with gaps). [†] indicates both countries must be in fixed exchange rate regime or monetary union but not necessarily vis-à-vis each other.

greater business cycle synchronization. This study is better viewed as one that seeks to establish a new stylized fact—a fact that should be verified and understood more deeply before any serious policy recommendations can be made.

Any reasonable observer thinks that AMU is a long way away; European monetary union took a huge international effort spread over decades, an effort that seems unlikely to be repeated any time soon in Asia. Asians are far more diverse than Europeans, and they are more wary of political integration and more suspicious of supranational institutions. Even regional trade liberalization has proved to be a serious challenge in Asia. So any serious thinking about AMU should assume that it is far from inevitable. Inflation targeting in the region is a reasonable monetary regime from a purely domestic viewpoint, and may have the added benefit of making AMU more feasible. I conclude that the case for inflation targeting in Asia remains strong.

Notes

1. The nature of the linkage between trade and business cycle synchronization depends on the nature of the trade (whether it is driven by factor proportions, a love of varieties, vertical specialization, and so forth) and the nature of the shocks that are striking the economies. Thus the coefficient need not be constant across time or country-groupings. Exploring this link further is intrinsically interesting, but not directly relevant for this study.
2. Since different studies often have samples that overlap in part, the different estimates should not be viewed as independent as those from, for example, medicine that rely on completely different patients.
3. I try to avoid publication bias by including all papers that, to the best of my knowledge, have estimated the relationship; a number have not been published.
4. http://www.cochrane-net.org/openlearning/HTML/mod13.htm. To elaborate: the fixed effect assumption is that differences across studies are only due to within-study variation. By way of contrast, random effects models consider both between-study and within-study variability and assume that the studies are a random sample from the universe of all possible studies.
5. For purposes of comparison, the mean values of BCS vary in the sample I use below, between 0.16 and 0.22, depending on the exact detrending method used.
6. I focus on countries rather than more aggregated groupings like regions because business cycles typically have a highly national flavor (in part because countries typically retain monetary and fiscal sovereignty). Throughout this chapter, "country" should be taken to mean territory, and does not necessarily imply sovereignty.
7. I follow the definition of Mishkin (2004), who lists five components to an inflation targeting regime: (i) the public announcement of medium-term numerical targets for inflation; (ii) an institutional commitment to price stability as the primary goal of monetary policy; (iii) an information-inclusive strategy to set policy instruments; (iv) increased transparency of the monetary policy strategy; and (v) increased accountability of central bank for attaining its inflation objectives. For more discussion of this and the dates when inflation targeting began, see Rose (2007).

8. I was unsuccessful in my attempt to construct feasible series for employment and unemployment. I also note in passing that some series had to be seasonally adjusted, which I performed via the X-12 filter.

9. I use a smoothing parameter of 1600, as is standard for quarterly data.

10. I focus on cycles of between 6 and 32 quarters in length, and follow the Baxter-King recommendation of using, and therefore losing, 12 quarters of data for leads/lags.

11. Gouveia and Correia (2008) provide further references to BCS determination in the context of EMU. I note in passing that the bivariate correlation coefficient for detrended output is not the only choice as a measure of BCS; one could also use the method proposed by Alesina et al. (2002). I follow the literature in using the correlation coefficient, but in practice the ABT measure typically delivers similar results; see, for instance, Darvas et al. (2007).

12. I construct weights for the G3 and G7 by comparing sample-averages for real PPP-adjusted GDP for the countries from the *Penn World Table 6.2*. For the G3, this results in weights of: 0.1551266 (Germany); 0.2179533 (Japan); and 0.6269201 (US). For the G7, the weights are: 0.0398185 (Canada); 0.0791699 (France); 0.1135938 (Germany); 0.071953 (Italy); 0.1598016 (Japan); 0.0759468 (UK); and 0.4597164 (US).

13. I use the updated Reinhart-Rogoff "coarse" measure of fixed exchange rate regimes; details and the data set are available at http://www.wam.umd.edu/~creinhar/Papers.html. The coarse measure includes: (i) no separate legal tender; (ii) pre-announced peg or currency board arrangement; (iii) pre-announced horizontal band that is narrower than or equal to $\pm 2\%$; and (iv) de facto peg.

14. I follow Baxter and Kouparitsas (2005) and use their preferred "BT1" measure, thus defining bilateral trade between a pair of countries (i and j) as the sum of all four bilateral trade flows (exports from i to j, imports into j from i, exports from j to i, and imports into i from j), divided by the corresponding multilateral sums (i's exports, j's exports, i's imports, and j's imports). Annual bilateral trade data on free on board (FOB) exports; and cost, insurance, and freight (CIF) exports are drawn from the IMF's *Direction of Trade Statistics* data set; values are the same for all quarter in a given year (the same is true of my measure of financial integration). I follow the IMF in defining a country as industrial if its IFS country code is less than 200. I also use the natural logarithm of bilateral distance, where a country's location in longitude and latitude is given by the Central Intelligence Agency's (CIA) *World Factbook* location. I note in passing that Baxter and Kouparitsas used data at two points of time (1970 and 1995), and did not consider fixed exchange rate, inflation targeting, or EMU regimes. They did not find a robust effect of developing country currency unions on BCS.

15. Since the correlation coefficients are computed with 20 observations each, they are highly dependent over time.

16. "Decoupling" is not typically defined carefully, but is usually considered to refer to divergences in short-term aggregate fluctuations across countries. For instance, in their May 23, 2007, Global Economics Report, *Global Decoupling: A Marathon, Not a Sprint*, Merrill Lynch seems to refer to a chart entitled "Chart 1: Yes, decoupling" with divergent growth between the US and the rest of the world since 2004. On page 2 of the same report, they refer to this divergence taking place in 2000, though their chart 2 focuses on divergence beginning in early 2006. Perhaps most revealingly, on page 20 Merrill Lynch writes "the arguments

and evidence in favor of decoupling appear stronger than ever. We still think a US slowdown—even a mild US recession—would have a modest impact on Asian growth." It is hard to think of decoupling as referring to longer-term growth, since substantial differences in growth rates across countries are the norm.

17. In my sample, there is a very small negative correlation between (country x quarter) observations of business-cycle volatility and the incidence of inflation targeting; the average (across the different detrenders) is around -0.04.

18. Figure 4.2 includes the observations of the individual G7 countries with the G7 aggregate. No conclusions change if these observations are dropped.

19. Results are similarly weak when one restricts the sample to pairs of Asian countries.

20. The correlation coefficients are individually marked and connected with a nonparametric data smoother.

21. The correlation coefficients are highly dependent, both across time (for a given dyad) and across dyads (at a given point in time), so the standard errors should be taken with a large grain of salt.

22. In contrast to the events portrayed in figures 4.6–4.9, the events of figure 4.10 are intrinsically dyadic; in the latter, both countries must begin to fix exchange rates vis-à-vis each other simultaneously to count as an event, whereas in the former, precisely one of the two countries in the dyad must adopt IT to count as an event.

23. Note that $Fix(2)$ is only unity if both countries are fixed vis-à-vis each other; similarly, $MU(2)$ is unity if both countries are in the same currency union. Thus, for example, $MU(2) = 0$ in 2002 for Ecuador and France; both were in currency unions at the time though they did not share a common currency.

24. Only time-varying effects can be estimated when dyadic fixed effects are included in the regressions.

25. The exact choice of which quarter is included does not seem to affect any conclusions.

26. Table 4.A2 adds financial integration to the list of controls, as suggested by Imbs (2006). This additional regressor reduces the sample size considerably, but does not induce substantively negative IT effects. Only five of the 12 coefficients are significantly different from zero, and all are positive.

27. It is unsurprising that the monetary union coefficient is often positive, since both Ecuador and the EMU countries share currencies with other members of the G7.

28. One can test the suitability of the propensity score model in part by determining whether it delivers "balanced" characteristics independent of treatment/control status, so that the treatment/control status is random for a given value of the propensity score. In practice, the propensity score model consisting of the four Baxter-Kouparitsas variables essentially never satisfies the balancing property. Adding interactions and second-order terms to the model does not allow the balancing property to be satisfied. This throws doubt on the matching estimates.

29. In addition, for computation reasons, I restrict control group observations to first-quarter observations. For my default measure, I am also forced for computational reasons to draw my control group observations from even years. However, the latter restriction is not necessary when I consider more restricted control groups, which thus also include odd years.

30. The sample is much smaller when I restrict attention to just fixed exchange rate regimes instead of either fixes or monetary union. In this case, none of the effects is significantly different from zero, though three of the four are positive.
31. The latter three estimates are of the treatment effect on the treated, not the average treatment effect.
32. Some or all of this decline may be coincidental, since the "Great Moderation" that occurred late in the sample coincided with the adoption of inflation targets by a number of countries.
33. I add the product of the countries' standard deviations to the propensity score model.
34. Hans Genberg has worked out a simple example that shows that if (i) inflation targeting countries care much more about stabilizing inflation that non-IT countries, and (ii) shocks that are common across countries play an important role in driving inflation, then BCS will be higher for IT than non-IT countries. I plan to pursue this suggestion in future work; it is closely linked to ongoing research I am pursuing with Robert Flood.

References

Ahn, C., H-B. Kim, and D. Chang. 2006. Is East Asia Fit for an Optimum Currency Area? *The Developing Economies*. 44(3). pp. 288–305.

Alesina, A., and R. J. Barro. 2002. Currency Unions. *Quarterly Journal of Economics*. 107(2). pp. 409–436.

Alesina, A., R. J. Barro, and S. Tenreyro. 2002. Optimal Currency Areas. In M. Gertler and K. Rogoff, eds. *NBER Macroeconomics Annual*. Cambridge: MIT Press.

Baxter, M., and M. A. Kouparitsas. 2005. Determinants of Business Cycle Comovement: A Robust Analysis. *Journal of Monetary Economics*. 52(1). pp. 113–157.

Becker, S. O., and A. Ichino. 2002. Estimation of Average Treatment Effects Based on Propensity Scores. *The Stata Journal*. 2–4. pp. 358–377.

Bower, U., and C. Guillenmineau. 2006. Determinants of Business Cycle Synchronisation Across Euro Area Countries. *European Central Bank Working Paper* 587.

Calder, C. 2007. Trade, Specialization and Cycle Synchronization. World Bank. Unpublished.

Calderon, C., A. Chong, and E. Stein. 2007. Trade Intensity and Business Cycle Synchronization: Are Developing Countries Any Different? *Journal of International Economics*. 71. pp. 2–21.

Céspedes, L. F., R. Chang, and A. Velasco. 2004. Balance Sheets and Exchange Rate Policy. *American Economic Review*. 94(4). pp. 1183–1193.

Choe, J-I. 2001. An Impact of Economic Integration through Trade. *Journal of Asian Economics*. 12. pp. 569–586.

Clark, T., and E. Wincoop. 2001. Borders and Business Cycles. *Journal of International Economics*. 55. pp. 59–85.

Crosby, M. 2003. Business Cycle Correlations in Asia-Pacific. *Hong Kong Institute for Monetary Research (HKIMR) Working Paper* 4/2003.

Darvas, Z., A. Rose, and G. Szapáry. 2007. Fiscal Divergence and Business Cycle Synchronization: Irresponsibility is Idiosyncratic. In J. Frankel and C. Pissarides, eds. *International Seminar on Macroeconomics*. Cambridge, MA: MIT Press.

Dehejia, V. H., and N. Rowe. 2000. Macroeconomic Stabilization: Fixed Exchange Rates vs. Inflation Targeting vs. Price Level Targeting. *Center for Economic and Policy Research (CEPR) Discussion Paper* 2460.

Devereux, M., and C. Engel. 1999. The Optimal Choice of Exchange-Rate Regime. *NBER Working Paper* 6992.

Devereux, M., and C. Engel. 2003. Monetary Policy in the Open Economy Revisited: Price Setting and Exchange Rate Flexibility. *Review of Economic Studies.* 70. pp. 765–784.

Doyle, B., and J. Faust. 2002. An Investigation of Co-Movements among the Growth Rates of the G7 Countries. *Federal Reserve Bulletin.* October.

Doyle, B., and J. Faust. 2005. Breaks in the Variability and Co-Movement of G7 Economic Growth. *The Review of Economics and Statistics.* 87(4). pp. 721–740.

Eichengreen, B., and T. Bayoumi. 1996. Is Asia an Optimum Currency Area? Can It Become One? Regional, Global and Historical Perspectives on Asian Monetary Relations. *Center for International and Development Economics Research (CIDER) Working Paper* C96–81.

Fidrmuc, J. 2004. The Endogeneity of the Optimum Currency Area Criteria, Intra-Industry Trade, and EMU Enlargement. *Contemporary Economic Policy.* 22(1). pp. 1–12.

Fiess, N. 2007. Business Cycle Synchronization and Regional Integration: A Case Study for Central America. *World Bank Economic Review.* 21(1). pp. 49–72.

Frankel, J., and A. Rose. 1998. The Endogeneity of the Optimum Currency Area Criteria. *Economic Journal.* 108(449). pp. 1009–1025.

Friedman, M. 1953. The Case for Flexible Exchange Rates. *Essays in Positive Economics.* Chicago: The University of Chicago Press.

Gouveia, S., and L. Correia. 2008. Business Cycle Synchronization in the Euro Area. *International Economics and Economic Policy.* 5(1). pp. 103–122.

Gruben, W., J. Koo, and E. Mills. 2002. How Much Does International Trade Affect Business Cycle Synchronization? *Federal Reserve Bank of Dallas Working Paper* 203.

Imbs, J. 2003. Co-Fluctuations. Unpublished.

Imbs, J. 2004. Trade, Finance, Specialization and Synchronization. *Review of Economics and Statistics.* 86(3). pp. 723–734.

Imbs, J. 2006. The Real Effects of Financial Integration. *Journal of International Economics.* 68(2). pp. 296–324.

Inklaar, R., R. Jong-a-Pin, and J. de Haa. 2005. Trade and Business Cycle Synchronization in OECD Countries—A Re-examination. *CESIfo Working Paper* 1546.

Kalemli-Ozcan, S., E. Papaioannou, and J. L. Peydro. 2008. Financial Integration, Synchronization, and Volatility. Unpublished.

Kose, M. A., and K-M. Yi. 2005. Can the Standard International Business Cycle Model Explain the Relation between Trade and Comovement? *Federal Reserve Bank of Philadelphia Working Paper* 05–03.

Kose, M. A., E. Prasad, and M. Terrones. 2003. Volatility and Comovement in a Globalized World Economy: An Empirical Exploration. *IMF Working Paper* 03/246.

Kose, M. A., C. Otrok, and E. Prasad. 2008. Global Business Cycles: Convergence or Decoupling? *Institute for the Study of Labor (IZA) Discussion Papers* 3442.

Kumakura, M. 2006. Trade and Business Cycle Co-Movements in Asia-Pacific. *Journal of Asian Economics.* 17(4). pp. 622–645.

Kumakura, M. 2009. Trade, Production and International Business Cycle Co-Movement. *International Journal of Applied Economics.* 6(1). pp. 11–40.

Kwack, S. Y. 2004. An Optimum Currency Area in East Asia. *Journal of Asian Economics.* 15(1). pp. 153–169.

Lee, J-W., Y. Park, and K. Shin. 2003. A Currency Union in East Asia. *Institute of Social and Economic Research (ISER) Discussion Paper* 571.

Ling, P., and H. Yuen. 2001. Optimum Currency Areas in East Asia: A Structural VAR Approach. *Asean Economic Bulletin.* 18(2). pp. 206–217.

Mishkin, F. S. 2004. Can Inflation Targeting Work in Emerging Market Countries? *NBER Working Paper* 10646.

Mundell, R. 1961. A Theory of Optimum Currency Areas. *American Economic Review.* 51(4). pp. 657–665.

Mundell, R. 1968. *International Economics.* New York: Macmillan.

Otto, G., G. Voss, and L. Willard. 2001. Understanding OECD Output Correlations. *Reserve Bank of Australia Discussion Paper* 2001–5.

Rose, A. K. 2007. A Stable International Monetary System Emerges: Inflation Targeting is Bretton Woods, Reversed. *Journal of International Money and Finance.* 26(5). pp. 663–681.

Rose, A. K. 2008. EMU, Trade and Business Cycle Synchronization. *Towards the First Decade of Economic and Monetary Union.* 36. Volkswirtschaftliche Tagung 2008.

Rose, A. K., and T. Stanley. 2005. A Meta-Analysis of the Effect of Common Currencies on International Trade. *Journal of Economic Surveys.* 19(3). pp. 347–365.

Rosenbaum, P., and D. Rubin. 1983. The Central Role of the Propensity Score in Observational Studies for Causal Effects. *Biometrika.* 70(1). pp. 41–55.

Sato, K., and Z. Zhang. 2006. Real Output Co-Movements in East Asia. *World Economy.* 29(12). pp. 1671–1689.

Shin, K., and Y. Wang. 2004. Trade Integration and Business Cycle Synchronization in East Asia. *Asian Economic Papers.* 2(3). pp. 1–20.

Stanley, T. D. 2001. Wheat from Chaff: Meta-Analysis as Quantitative Literature Review. *Journal of Economic Perspectives.* 15(3). pp. 131–150.

Stock, J., and M. Watson. 2003. Has the Business Cycle Changed? Evidence and Explanations. Paper presented at the Monetary Policy and Uncertainty: Adapting to a Changing Economy Symposium. Federal Reserve Bank Kansas City. August 28–30.

Svensson, L. 2000. Open-Economy Inflation Targeting. *Journal of International Economics.* 50(1). pp. 155–183.

Turnovsky, S. 1976. The Relative Stability of Alternative Exchange Rate Systems in the Presence of Random Disturbances. *Journal of Money, Credit, and Banking.* 8(1). pp. 29–50.

Wyplosz, C. 2001. A Monetary Union in Asia? Some European Lessons. In D. Gruen and J. Simon, eds. *Future Directions for Monetary Policies in East Asia.* Sydney: Reserve Bank of Australia.

Appendix

Table A.1
Sample of Countries

Country	IT	Data	Country	IT	Data
Argentina		1994	Japan		1974
Australia	1993	1974	Korea, Rep. of	1998	1974
Austria		1974	Latvia		1996
Belarus		1996	Lithuania		1997
Belgium		1974	Luxembourg		1999
Brazil	1999	1995	Macau, China		2002
Bulgaria		2002	Malta		1974
Canada	1991	1974	Mauritius		2003
Chile	1991	1984	Mexico	1999	1997
China, People's Rep. of		1998	Morocco		2002
Colombia	1999	1998	Netherlands		1974
Costa Rica		2004	New Zealand	1990	1974
Croatia		1997	Norway	2001	1974
Cyprus		1999	Peru	2002	1983
Czech Republic	1998	1998	Philippines	2002	1985
Denmark		1974	Poland	1998	1999
Ecuador		1995	Portugal		1974
Estonia		1997	Romania	2005	2002
Finland	1993	1974	Russian Federation		1995
France		1974	Singapore		1987
Georgia		2000	Slovakia	2005	1997
Germany		1974	Slovenia		1996
Greece		1974	South Africa	2000	1994
Hong Kong, China		1977	Spain	1995	1974
Hungary	2001	1999	Sweden	1993	1974
Iceland	2001	2001	Switzerland	2000	1974
Indonesia	2005	1997	Thailand	2000	1997
Iran		1999	Tunisia		2004
Ireland		1974	Turkey	2006	1991
Israel	1992	1984	United States		1974
Italy		1974	United Kingdom	1992	1974
Jamaica		2000	Venezuela		2001

Note: Dates indicate year of entry into inflation targeting, and year of earliest reliable output data.

Table A.2
Adding Financial Integration to Business Cycle Synchronization Determination

Detrending Method	Time Fixed Effects				Time and Dyad Fixed Effects			
	One IT	Both IT	Fixed ER	Monetary Union	One IT	Both IT	Fixed ER	Monetary Union
HP	0.07*	0.02	0.25	0.29*	0.19**	0.06	−0.39**	n/a
	(0.01)	(0.02)	(0.07)	(0.01)	(0.06)	(0.07)	(0.05)	
BK	n/a	n/a	n/a	n/a	n/a	n/a	n/a	n/a
Linear	0.11*	0.05	0.26	0.39	0.40**	0.19	−0.22**	n/a
	(0.00)	(0.04)	(0.02)	(0.17)	(0.06)	(0.12)	(0.06)	
Growth	0.02	−0.02	0.07	0.05	0.23**	−0.01	−0.14	n/a
	(0.05)	(0.09)	(0.03)	(0.04)	(0.07)	(0.13)	(0.15)	

Notes: Using least squares estimation, regressand is bilateral correlation coefficient for detrended GDP between countries, computed with 20 observations. Robust standard errors in parentheses; coefficients that are significantly different from zero at the 0.05 level are marked with one asterisk (*); at the 0.01 level, with two (**). Quinquennial data, computed from quarterly observations between Q4 1974 and Q4 2007 for up to 64 countries (with gaps). Controls included but not reported include: one country with fixed exchange rate; one country in monetary union; bilateral financial integration, bilateral trade, log distance, and dummies for both industrial/developing countries.

5

Trading Silver for Gold: Nineteenth-Century Asian Exports and the Political Economy of Currency Unions

Kris James Mitchener and Hans-Joachim Voth

We are grateful to Andrew Rose, our discussant at the Asian Development Bank and Hong Kong Institute for Monetary Research (ADB-HKIMR) workshop "Quantifying the Costs and Benefits of Regional Economic Integration in Asia," Hong Kong, China, January 19–20, 2009, for his feedback and advice. Conference participants, in particular Pol Antras, Robert Barro, Jong-Wha Lee, and Warwick McKibbin, helped us with their comments.

1 Introduction

Should Asian countries follow Europe's lead and adopt a common currency standard? Following the devastating financial crisis in 1997–1998, prospects for an Asian monetary union have become a matter of intense debate.[1] We examine Asia's historical experience with a shared monetary standard—silver—in the nineteenth century, and ask what lessons can be drawn from it. We focus on the trade effects of the silver standard and the political economy of switching from one currency regime to another.

As a result of custom, history, and law, Asian countries shared a silver standard in the nineteenth century. As European countries moved to gold (and demonetized silver) after 1870, Asian economies found themselves using a monetary standard that was quickly becoming marginalized. In addition, they saw their currencies depreciate. Eventually, the majority of Asian countries stabilized their currencies vis-à-vis gold, mainly through adopting gold-exchange standards (van der Eng, 1999).

Overall, trade grew markedly in the late nineteenth century, both to overseas destinations and within Asia. As Asian countries increasingly found themselves on a silver standard that they did not share with the rest of the world (after 1880), intra-Asian trade growth outpaced Asia's trade with the rest of the world. Once stabilization vis-à-vis gold standard currency had been imposed—more often than not by the imperial center—intra-Asian trade declined in relative importance.

In this chapter, we use evidence from the Asian silver standard during the nineteenth century to examine whether common currencies boosted trade and whether leaving the Asian silver bloc (often by fiat of a colonial power) reduced trade. We do so by using a new, comprehensive data set on bilateral trade volumes in the nineteenth century. We focus on trade within Asia as well as Asia's trade with the rest of the world. While many authors have investigated the effects of common currencies (Rose, 2001; Glick and Rose, 2002; Rose and Engel, 2002; Yeyati, 2003; Rose, 2007), and of the gold standard (Estevadeordal et al., 2003; López-Córdova and Meissner, 2003), the effects of the silver standard on Asian trade are relatively underexplored.[2]

We argue that countries that started on silver traded intensively with each other, largely as a result of historical legacy and the tyranny of distance. However, it appears, *ex post,* that staying on the silver standard was less attractive than moving to gold. Hence, as countries switched from silver to gold, their total trading volumes rose quickly. Remarkably, even bilateral trading volumes with partner countries that stayed on the silver standard increased significantly: being on silver was good for trade, but leaving silver for gold was even better. We interpret this as a consequence of the nature of trading relationships in the nineteenth century, when easier access to the capital goods and intermediate products of Europe was crucial in fostering development.

In many Asian countries, the decision to change currency arrangements in the late nineteenth century was largely taken by (and in the interest of) colonial powers (Kemmerer, 1916; van der Eng, 1999). Where Asian countries retained some degree of control over their currency arrangements, the decision to abandon silver for gold was not taken lightly. Countries on silver, where a switch to gold was under discussion, often saw vocal opposition from exporters and other interest groups that had benefited from silver's depreciation relative to gold (through 1895). Nonetheless, our evidence suggests that overall exports grew markedly faster in countries that switched to gold. This implies that imperial intervention may have been beneficial in overcoming entrenched interests of existing trading companies.[3] In cases where countries had the ability to make decisions independently, the voice of exporters mattered more. We examine the determined internal opposition to the adoption of the gold standard in the late nineteenth century as well as the political means by which it was overcome.

In addition to numerous papers that investigate the effects of common currencies on trading volumes (Persson, 2001; Ritschl and Wolf, 2003;

Tenreyro and Barro, 2003; Yeyati, 2003; Melitz et al., 2004), our study also contributes to the literature on optimum currency areas. Mundell's (1961) classic contribution to this literature emphasized the importance of labor market integration, price and wage flexibility, synchronous business cycles, and diversified production structures. Alesina and Barro (2002) extended his analysis by adding the trade-enhancing effects of currency unions, and the benefits of monetary unions as a commitment device to price stability. Nominal rigidities were not an important feature of nineteenth-century economies, and importing inflation-fighting credentials did not feature prominently in discussions of optimum currency arrangements. Consequently, synchronization of business cycles mattered less as a criterion for currency union membership, while the reductions in trade costs should have received relatively greater weight. We examine to what extent these specific differences between nineteenth- and twentieth-century economic conditions undermined the benefits of the Asian silver standard, while increasing the relative benefits from gold.

We proceed as follows. We first discuss the history and context of the rise and fall of the silver standard in Asia. Next, in section 3, we introduce a new, comprehensive database on Asian trade compiled from contemporary data sources. This source allows one to provide a detailed analysis of the evolution of Asian trade during the classical gold standard era—something that has not been possible with earlier data sets because they did not include a sufficient number of country pairs with less prominent roles in the world economy. The larger size of this new database also enables us to estimate the effects of currency unions with much greater precision. Our methodology and main results are presented in section 4. In section 5, we use a novel way to pin down the causal effect of gold standard adoption, with military success as the source of identifying variation. Next, we discuss the political economy of currency arrangements in section 6, using the case of Japan, which is particularly instructive, to illustrate key issues. Section 7 concludes.

2 Historical Background and Context

In this section, we summarize Asia's position in nineteenth-century world trade and describe the history of currency arrangements in the Far East, with special emphasis on the period after 1870. We summarize the structure and coherence of the "silver bloc" in the region, and examine its decline under the influence of colonial powers and the growing attractions of gold.

The nineteenth century probably marked a nadir in terms of Asia's role in world trade. By 1870, Asia's share had declined to an unusually low level. Table 5.1 provides an overview. Despite accounting for over a third of world gross domestic product (GDP), Asia's exports were less than 15% of the total. A century later, in 1998, when its share of world GDP was identical to the 1870 value, Asia accounted for 27% of exports—almost twice as much. Remarkably,

Table 5.1
World Trade by Region, 1870

Region	Percent of World GDP	Percent of World Merchandise Exports	Merchandise Exports as % of GDP	Annual Growth in Volume of Merchandise Exports, 1870–1913
Europe	33.6	64.4	8.8	3.2
Western Offshoots*	10.2	7.5	4.7	4.7
Asia (incl. Japan)	38.3	13.9	1.7	2.8
Latin America	2.5	5.4	9.7	3.3
Eastern Europe	11.7	4.2	1.6	3.4
Africa	3.7	4.6	5.8	4.4

Note: * Canada, United States, Australia, New Zealand.

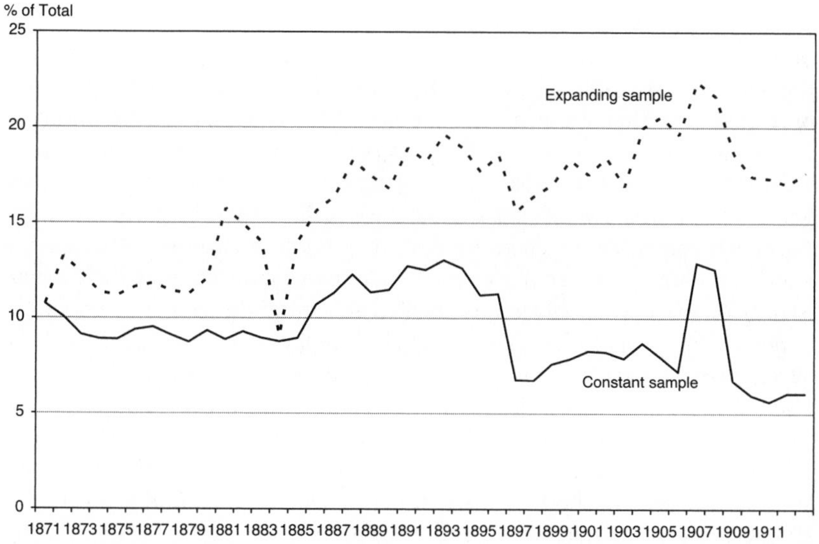

Figure 5.1 Intra-Asian Trade, 1871–1913

Source: Authors' calculations based on data described in text.

despite having one of the lowest export-GDP ratios in 1870, growth in Asian exports between 1870 and 1913 was also the slowest of any region.

Overall, Asia's trading volume was low. Intra-Asian trade did not rise as the global economy further integrated. As shown in figure 5.1, if we look at a constant set of trading partners we see that the rising percentage for intra-Asian trade in the expanding sample is a result of more and more trade within

Asia being captured in our database; trade within Asia for the constant sample declined from a little over 10% of total trade to 6% between 1870 and 1913. The main engine of growth for Asian trade came from exchanging goods with the rest of the world, principally Europe. For example, trade with the United Kingdom (UK) grew more than 5% per year for Asian countries during the period—twice as fast as Asian trade overall and almost three times faster than inter-Asian trade (which grew by 1.9% per year).

Trade with the rest of the world, as well as within Asia, was low by 1870. It increased in absolute terms after that date, but not enough to halt a further decline relative to rapidly growing trade outside the region. Long before the start of our sample period, Asian countries had been using silver as the standard currency of choice. As European countries and areas of recent European settlement increasingly switched to gold in the nineteenth century, Asia found itself on a currency standard different from the one used by the rest of the world. How did this divergence in currency arrangements occur?

Starting with the Age of Discovery, Europeans often exchanged silver for Far Eastern goods. After the discovery of America—and especially after the rich silver mines of Potosí came on stream—Europe received substantial inflows of silver. Between 1500 and 1800, Europe imported 72,000 tons of silver from the Americas (Maddison, 2001). The value of silver in terms of goods fell only gradually after 1500 (despite the use of the term "price revolution" in the academic literature describing this period). Silver was relatively more valuable in Asia.[4] It was also useful as means of exchange, given that most goods were markedly cheaper in silver terms there than in Europe.[5] As the European companies reached the East, they found a currency system based almost entirely on silver. Between the Arabian Peninsula and the furthest islands of the Pacific, silver was used as the standard means of exchange, almost without exception. The Mughal currency system in India used the silver rupee as a means of exchange and a unit of account. Gold coins were also minted, but remained largely out of circulation. Only in southern India, in the areas of the former Hindu kingdoms, was gold the main currency in use. In Persia and in Yemen, the dominant currency was silver. Farther East, only silver was in use. In the Indonesian islands, agents of the European trading companies used Spanish silver dollars as a means of payment (Chaudhuri, 2006).

Because Europeans in the sixteenth century had few goods to offer that Far Eastern customers wanted (except firearms, gold, and silver), they exchanged specie for a steady stream of tea, pepper, nutmeg, and clove (Andaya, 1999). Between 1600 and 1780 alone, it has been estimated that Europe exported 29,000 tons of silver, 10,000 tons of which went to the Far East. Most silver was bought in London and Amsterdam as bullion, often in the form of Mexican dollars. British and Dutch importers then exchanged these for Asian goods. Western trading companies were not the only ones whose economic interests were directly tied to currency arrangements and the exchange of Asian goods for European silver. Hao (1986) emphasizes the importance of the use of silver by local traders, for both intra-Asian and long-distance trade.

Until the late nineteenth century, China coined no silver money.[6] Instead, foreign coins such as the Mexican dollar circulated side by side with bullion. To complicate matters yet further, units of exchange were traded in the form of ingots. These varied from area to area, so that the Shanghai tael (515.4 grains of fine silver), the Kuping tael, and the Haikwan tael all had different weight and fineness (Leavens, 1939). The system was not without complications, and many contemporaries noted the high transactions costs that it caused.

Mexican dollars were prized for their purity and exact weight, but other silver currencies were also imported throughout Asia. Some of these were recoined, but in many cases they circulated alongside the national currencies. In Hong Kong, the Mexican silver dollar circulated as legal tender after 1863. In 1867, the British authorities introduced a Hong Kong dollar equal in size and weight to the Mexican silver dollar, though the experiment was quickly abandoned. In 1895, the British colonial administration tried again, using spare capacity at the Indian mint. This time, the experiment met with greater success (Andrew, 1904). From 1903, the Straits Settlement (Singapore) also issued its own silver currency.[7] In the nineteenth century, Malaya operated on a silver basis. In spite of the earlier political link with India, under whose government the Straits Settlement and Panang fell (until 1867), these settlements and the whole Malayan peninsula mainly used the (Mexican) silver dollar rather than the silver rupee.[8] This undoubtedly reflected close trade links with China.

In India, "standard" rupees of the East India Company were the main means of payment after 1835, but other silver rupees circulated alongside them (van der Eng, 1999). In 1852, following the depreciation of gold vis-à-vis silver, gold was effectively taken out of circulation by the East India Company. De facto, silver was the sole legal tender (Leavens, 1939). In Ceylon, the monetary system originally introduced by the Dutch was replaced entirely by the rupee system of British India (Muhleman, 1895).

Throughout the nineteenth century, contemporaries spoke of a "silver shortage" in much of East Asia. Silver coins, imported from Mexico or elsewhere, often found their way to Asia. In a bid to resolve the issue, colonial powers employed different strategies. The British introduced the Indian rupee in the Straits Settlements, and the Dutch in Indonesia issued currency certificates (van der Eng, 2004). In Hong Kong, bank notes issued and authorized by the Chartered Bank of India in 1853 and the Hong Kong and Shanghai Bank in 1866 were circulating widely, and often traded at a premium to silver coins (Muhleman, 1895). Other countries imported silver currency outright, often from Mexico. The French introduced a silver piaster in Indochina, based on the Mexican dollar (Muhleman, 1895), while the Dutch rix dollar was used in parts of Asia under Dutch control.

While legal tender was often limited to the currency issued by the government, silver coins from many countries circulated side by side with the official currency. Thus, the Asian "silver standard" used mainly two currencies—the Indian silver rupee (in use in India, Ceylon, the Maldives, and some British colonies in East Africa) and the Mexican silver dollar (circulating widely in the Far East, especially in areas trading extensively with China). Transactions costs were thus minimized, in a way that is similar, but not identical to that in full-fledged currency unions. Imports could be paid for with the same coin obtained in domestic sales, and both the risk and the transactions costs of dealing in foreign currencies were substantially reduced.

Following the Franco-Prussian War, Germany used the French war indemnity to adopt the gold standard. Following this switch, an increasing number of countries adopted the gold standard. While only 35% of countries were on gold in 1870, the figure had reached 90% in 1913 (Estevadeordal et al., 2003). After 1870, the price of silver relative to gold came under increasing pressure. This was driven by silver discoveries and by the demonetization of silver in countries switching to gold. Between 1870 and 1890, world stocks of mined silver rose by 170%; gold stocks rose by only 13%. Large silver deposits were discovered in Broken Hill in Australia, Pulacayo in Bolivia, and Colorado in Mexico (Schmitz, 1979). These discoveries increasingly depressed the value of silver, giving a cost advantage to exporters in countries that remained on silver (Nugent, 1973). At the same time, the volatility of exchange rates increased.

As more and more countries switched to gold, silver was demonetized. Silver coins were melted down, and existing stocks of precious metal no longer used for coinage were sold on the world market. This added to pressure on the gold-silver price ratio. Holland was among the European countries that felt the greatest pressure to switch to gold, since much of its trade was with Germany. By 1875, silver coinage was restricted, and the country switched in all but name to the gold standard. This had the potential to lead to complications in its trade with Indonesia, which was on a silver standard (van der Eng, 1999). Some two years after the switch to gold in Europe, the Java Bank in Dutch Indonesia started to guarantee the value of silver guilders in terms of gold. Intrinsic and face value of the silver guilder started to diverge. Until the 1870s, many Asian countries traded goods for Dutch guilders from Indonesia, which was more advantageous than obtaining silver from London, but this pattern of trade ceased once silver guilders became overvalued. Increasingly, other Asian nations began to send their goods elsewhere.

There are a number of factors that led to the switch from silver to gold in Asia. For some colonies, as in Indonesia, the use of the same currency in the colony and the metropole made rapid adaptation inevitable. In other colonies, such as India, the peg with sterling was only introduced in 1898. After a series of attempts at halting the slide of silver through international conferences had come to naught, the colonial administration decided to act unilaterally. In part, this was done so as to stabilize the cost of administering and defending India, which was incurred in terms of gold. Once India had switched standards, other countries followed suit. Ceylon, using the Indian

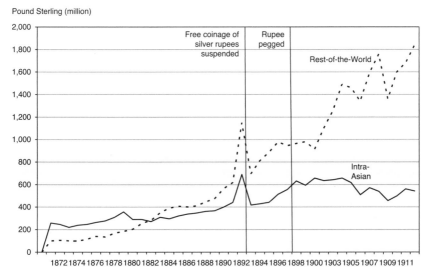

Pound Sterling (million)

Figure 5.2 India's Trade Patterns, 1871–1913

rupee, followed automatically. Figure 5.2 illustrates the declining role of India's intra-Asian trade. Until the rupee's stabilization, trade with the rest of Asia already grew more slowly than trade with the rest of the world. However, after 1898 intra-Asian trade fell behind decisively, while total trading volumes with Europe surged. In 1906, the Straits Settlement—which would eventually become Singapore—followed the Indian lead and pegged the Straits dollar relative to sterling. In 1908, Siam decided to do the same relative to gold, having abandoned the silver standard in 1902 (Brown, 1978). In Indochina, on the other hand, the French colonial authorities did not peg the piaster to the French franc until 1930.

As an independent country, Japan's adoption of gold sheds additional light on Asia's transition from silver to gold. After grappling with high inflation in the late 1870s and early 1880s, Japan formally adopted the silver standard in May 1885. By the early 1890s, however, as more countries moved onto gold, Japanese policy makers began to consider alternatives to silver—bimetallism and gold. A formal committee was convened in 1893 to study which metallic standard would be most advantageous for Japan. Its final summary report in 1895 recorded seven members voting to remain on silver, six suggesting that Japan go onto gold at some point in the future, and two favoring a bimetallic standard. Under the direction of Finance Minister (and later Prime Minister) Count Masayoshi Matsukata, the ruling party nevertheless began to engineer Japan's shift to gold. Using the sterling-denominated war indemnity paid by China in 1895, Matsukata acquired the necessary gold for backing the currency. As described in more detail below, Matsukata then shrewdly engineered passage of the gold standard act by forming a political alliance with a key opposition party to ensure a majority at both the committee and chamber levels of the Diet (Japanese parliament). Japan formally adopted gold in September 1897.

In terms of Asian countries, rather than colonies, China was the stalwart, staying on silver throughout our sample period.

3 Data

We use a new, large database of Asian-based annual bilateral export trade based on Mitchener and Weidenmier (2008a) that draws extensively on a consistent set of British statistical sources published by the Board of Trade. The information is hand-collected from the *Statistical Abstract for the United Kingdom,* the *Statistical Abstract for the Several British Self-governing Dominions, Colonies, Possessions, and Protectorates,* and the *Statistical Abstract for the Principal and other Foreign Countries* for the period 1870 to 1913. Some additional data for French colonies is from the *Tableau général du commerce extérieur.* Overall, the data consist of more than 17,526 bilateral observations on exports for 347 distinct country pairs or dyads.[9] We include all intra-Asian trade, the exports of Asian countries to non-Asian countries, and exports of non-Asian countries to Asia.

Export data were collected from British Board of Trade publications and converted into current pounds using annual exchange rates from the *Global Financial Database* and Ferguson and Schularick (2004). We then deflated the data using the UK producer price index (PPI) and expressed the figures in £2,000 to obtain our estimates of trade volume. Although using GDP to measure "mass" would have been useful in estimating gravity models, reliable annual estimates for a wide range of non-OECD countries prior to 1914 (including smaller colonies) are scarce. In our data analysis, we therefore use population to capture mass. Total railroad miles capture a country's transportation network. It serves as a proxy for internal transport costs that might affect bilateral trade flows. These data series (as well as population) are from Banks (1976) and the aforementioned Board of Trade publications. Data on the natural log of distance in miles are from Rose (2002) and an online distance calculator that employs United States (US) Geographical Survey information.[10] Data on periods when countries were on gold and silver standards are from Flandreau and Muriel (2001), Bae and Bailey (2003), Ferguson and Schularick (2004), Meissner (2005), and Officer (2004). Empires include only formal empires and only those with more than one dependency, which rules out Sweden-Norway. Otherwise Mitchener and Weidenmier's data contain codings for all empires that existed during this period and for which trade data existed.[11] Information on empire affiliation is from the *Correlates of War Database* (COW) described in Sarkees (2000), Olson (1991), O'Brien (1991), and the online historical encyclopedia available at http://regiments.org/nations/index.htm.

The Mitchener and Weidenmier (2008a) database significantly improves upon the trade data used in earlier studies of the first era of globalization and allows us to better test the impact of different monetary standards during this era. The reason is its sheer size. Their database is roughly 20 times larger than previous data sets.[12] Even the Asia-based trade sample used in this study is considerably larger than earlier global trade databases for the classical gold standard period. It contains a very large portion of non-European, non-US, and colonial bilateral trade flows in Asia.

4 Method and Results

Does a shared monetary standard promote trade? Since Rose's (2000) claim that currency unions increase trade by 200% or more, scholars have debated the robustness and implications of this result.

The experience of Asia in the nineteenth and early twentieth centuries is relevant to the broader debate over measuring the effects of currency unions on trade for a number of reasons. First, much of the evidence in favor of the initial Rose result came from cross-sectional variation. As Persson (2001) and Ritschl and Wolf (2003) *inter alia* argue, omitted variable issues potentially loom large. Other factors, such as colonial origin, common language, shared legal standards, and so on, may facilitate the adoption of a common currency while simultaneously increasing trade. The use of panel data (Frankel and Rose, 2000; Glick and Rose, 2002) has the potential to resolve some of these issues; however, since the dissolution of currency unions is often associated with the end of colonial status, selection bias may remain. The experience of Asia in the nineteenth century offers a way to solve some of these estimation issues. As colonial powers moved to gold, their Asian colonies initially remained on silver (Indochina, India, Indonesia, Straits Settlement). Colony and imperial center were on different monetary standards while still sharing the benefits of a related legal system, imperial control, and a common language. Estimating the effect of currency unions based on these episodes is useful since the identifying variation comes from the time-series, and because it does not coincide with the dissolution of colonial ties.

Second, the breaking of a common standard as a result of the move by European powers and Japan to gold is reasonably exogenous to conditions in the colonies themselves. The adoption of gold was largely driven by trade relations between developed countries (López-Córdova and Meissner, 2003) and was accelerated by historical accident (war indemnities paid to Germany and Japan which enabled them to acquire sufficient gold to move to this standard). Third, there is a good deal of variation, even within Asia itself. Dutch Indonesia switched to a gold-exchange standard in 1873, while French Indochina only stabilized its currency relative to gold in the interwar period. Fourth, analogies between historical specie standards and currency unions are not without challenges. As Rose noted in his critique of Ritschl and Wolf

(2003), coding gold standard membership as a currency union implies that New Zealand and Germany shared a common means of exchange. It is at least arguable that adopting the gold standard was closer to fixing exchange rates (though with a greater degree of implied permanence, at least before 1914). Because of the way the silver standard operated, however, with coins from different countries circulating freely side by side throughout Asia (and especially east of India), it is much closer to the preferred definition of Glick and Rose (2002): "By 'currency union' we mean essentially that money was interchangeable between the two countries at a 1:1 par for an extended period of time, so that there was no need to convert prices when trading between a pair of countries."[13]

We begin by examining how the silver standard affected exports by estimating pooled ordinary least square (OLS) regressions of the following form:

$$\ln(Exports_{ijt}) = \beta_0 + \beta_D(Dist_{ijt}) + \beta_P \ln(Pop_{it}Pop_{jt}) + \beta_L Landl_{ijt}$$
$$+ \beta_E Empire_{ijt} + \beta_R \ln(Rail_{it}Rail_{jt}) + \beta_G Gold_{ijt}$$
$$+ \beta_S Silver_{ijt} + \gamma \mathbf{X} + \varepsilon_{ijt} \tag{1}$$

where $Exports_{ijt}$ are exports from country i to country j at time t, and $Dist$ is the distance between them. We use unidirectional flow data on exports. This avoids the "silver medal" mistake of averaging exports and imports for the dependent variable when estimating the gravity model (Baldwin and Taglioni, 2006).[14] Comparing our specification to that most commonly used in comparable studies (Estevadeordal et al., 2003), we are estimating without the income variable. We control for size using the natural log of the product of populations in country i and j at time t because of data constraints for smaller countries.[15] $Landl$ is equal to unity if the country is landlocked and $Empire$ is equal to unity if trading partners are both members of the same colonial empire. Infrastructure development ($Rail$) is measured by the (natural) log product of the length of railway lines in countries i and j. $Gold$ is equal to unity if both countries are on the gold standard, and $Silver$ is equal to unity if both countries are on the silver standard. $\mathbf{X}$ is a vector of additional controls, used in some of our specifications, mainly a full set of currency arrangements variables that are defined in our tables of regression results.

For most variables, our results, shown in table 5.2, are similar to earlier contributions in the literature. They confirm the usefulness of the gravity equation for the nineteenth century. The effect of economic "mass" is smaller than in present-day models, and the overall explanatory power, while satisfactory, is lower than is typically the case in the twentieth century (Bergstrand, 1985). We find that distance reduced trade. So did being landlocked. Membership in the same empire had a positive effect on trading volumes, and longer railway lines were helpful in boosting trade. The gold standard's trade-increasing effect is substantial: it raised trading volume in

Table 5.2
Pooled OLS Results—Currency Standards and Exports

	(1)	(2)	(3)	(4)
Distance	−0.700***	−0.688***	−0.660***	−0.643***
	(−34.51)	(−34.13)	(−32.78)	(−30.62)
Ln *(pop)*	0.285***	0.314***	0.305***	0.316***
	(43.55)	(41.29)	(39.41)	(39.51)
Landlocked	−0.394***	−0.556***	−0.547***	−0.578***
	(−3.63)	(−5.04)	(−5.05)	(−5.34)
Empire	0.540***	0.343***	0.330***	0.358***
	(11.76)	(7.58)	(7.30)	(7.66)
Ln *(rail)*	0.125***	0.0724***	0.0851***	0.0733***
	(23.35)	(11.43)	(13.25)	(10.55)
Gold standard		0.437***	0.458***	0.474***
		(11.76)	(12.31)	(10.87)
Silver standard			0.394***	0.339***
			(5.69)	(4.81)
Paper-bimetallic				−0.142
				(−1.15)
Bimetallic-silver				−1.045***
				(−4.17)
Bimetallic-gold				−2.077***
				(−4.82)
Paper-silver				−0.688***
				(−7.29)
Paper-gold				0.265***
				(4.48)
Paper standard				−0.0761
				(−1.12)
Constant	14.91***	14.99***	14.70***	14.53***
	(77.12)	(75.29)	(74.93)	(70.52)
N	15,599	14,517	14,517	14,517
Adj. R^2	0.290	0.311	0.313	0.319

Notes: Our sample includes all available exports from Asian countries to other countries, whether in Asia or not, as well as exports from non-Asian countries to Asia. The excluded category for currency arrangement is gold-silver. *t*-statistics in parentheses. *$p < 0.10$; **$p < 0.05$; and ***$p < 0.01$.

our set of country pairs by at least 54% $[(e^{0.43}-1) \times 100]$ relative to the average for "all other" currency arrangements.

Being on the silver standard also had positive effects on trading volumes. These appear to have been similar in magnitude to the benefits from gold. In column 4 of table 5.2, the excluded category is gold-silver. The regression coefficient suggests that when both countries of a trading pair were on silver, on average, they traded roughly 35-45% more than dyads on a combination of silver and gold. Currency combinations involving bimetallism were generally associated with much lower levels of bilateral trade. Paper-silver and paper-paper were also combinations that saw low trade volumes, while paper-gold was a relatively dynamic combination.

Since we are using pooled OLS, there is no way of knowing if the results reflect omitted variable bias—with unobserved factors jointly determining trade volume and exchange regime status—or a causal effect. For this reason, numerous authors have noted the advantages of estimating the effects of currency unions using fixed-effects regressions. Table 5.3 therefore presents estimates of dyad, fixed-effects regressions.

Many of the results are similar to those obtained with pooled OLS. Bimetallism was generally not good for trade. Countries that switched to gold saw higher trade volumes. This effect is large and significant, except in the final specification where we control for year effects. This suggests that much of the gain in trade volume among nations switching to gold coincided with a period of generally growing trade volumes. One important difference when compared with the OLS results is that we now find a negative effect for countries that are jointly on silver. The result is highly statistically significant, and large. It implies a reduction in trading volume by almost 24%. We interpret the difference in results across specifications as follows: Pair-specific unobserved factors made it more likely for trading partners to be on a joint silver standard. These include a long history of commercial exchange, the presence of groups from similar ethnic backgrounds involved in trade, and broader cultural similarities. All the identifying variation in the fixed effects model comes from countries that decided to switch from silver to gold, and from silver to a stabilized exchange rate vis-à-vis gold. The negative coefficient implies that, as countries left the silver standard during the late nineteenth and early twentieth century, on average, they saw their export volumes rise—even if they now traded on a mix of currency standards, with one country on gold and the other on silver.

4.1 Multilateral Resistance

Trade costs were falling rapidly after 1870, and the effective barriers to trade between countries changed over time. This is a classic problem of time-varying multilateral resistance (Anderson and Van Wincoop, 2003). Dealing with it in a panel setting is not trivial. Column 1 of table 5.4 presents the results when we include time dummies, in addition to the dyad fixed effects. The benefits of the gold standard itself are no longer apparent, indicating that there was

Table 5.3
Fixed Effects Regressions—Currency Standards and Exports

	(1)	(2)	(3)	(4)
Ln *(pop)*	0.512***	0.452***	0.456***	0.453***
	(24.08)	(21.15)	(21.35)	(21.44)
Empire	0.687***	0.576***	0.534***	0.677***
	(7.19)	(6.40)	(5.92)	(7.56)
Ln *(rail)*	0.131***	0.106***	0.100***	0.0893***
	(26.20)	(21.28)	(19.72)	(17.66)
Gold standard		0.395***	0.377***	0.296***
		(16.77)	(15.84)	(10.69)
Silver standard			−0.210***	−0.272***
			(−5.16)	(−6.69)
Paper-bimetallic				−0.364***
				(−3.02)
Bimetallic-silver				−1.419***
				(−15.95)
Bimetallic-gold				−2.141***
				(−10.63)
Paper-silver				−0.369***
				(−6.26)
Paper-gold				−0.0279
				(−0.65)
Paper standard				−0.222**
				(−2.40)
Constant	4.985***	6.344***	6.395***	6.626***
	(14.87)	(18.84)	(19.00)	(19.86)
Year Dummies	N	N	N	N
Fixed Effects	Y	Y	Y	Y
N	15,601	14,519	14,519	14,519
Adj. R^2	0.154	0.169	0.170	0.192

Notes: Our sample includes all available exports from Asian countries to other countries, whether in Asia or not, as well as exports from non-Asian countries to Asia. The excluded category for currency arrangement in Column 4 is gold-silver. t-statistics in parentheses. *$p < 0.10$; **$p < 0.05$; and ***$p < 0.01$.

Table 5.4
Fixed Effects Regressions—Time Dummies and Time-Varying
Country Dummies

	(1)	(2)
Ln *(pop)*	0.187***	0.294***
	(7.61)	(8.59)
Empire	0.631***	0.596***
	(7.17)	(6.01)
Ln *(rail)*	0.0113*	0.00207
	(1.74)	(0.23)
Gold standard	−0.0108	0.0419
	(−0.35)	(1.08)
Silver standard	−0.112***	−0.237***
	(−2.73)	(−4.87)
Paper-bimetallic	−0.159	−0.210
	(−1.33)	(−0.96)
Bimetallic-silver	−1.068***	−1.212***
	(−11.81)	(−10.49)
Bimetallic-gold	−2.217***	−2.409***
	(−11.10)	(−11.63)
Paper-silver	−0.189***	−0.183***
	(−3.21)	(−2.73)
Paper-gold	−0.136***	0.00575
	(−3.18)	(0.11)
Paper standard	−0.104	0.117
	(−1.13)	(1.06)
Constant	11.69***	9.198***
	(27.99)	(13.95)
N	14,519	14,519
Adj. R^2	0.221	0.314

Notes: Our sample includes all available exports from Asian countries to other countries, whether in Asia or not, as well as exports from non-Asian countries to Asia. The excluded category for currency arrangement is gold-silver. t-statistics in parentheses. $*p < 0.10$; $**p < 0.05$; and $***p < 0.01$.

no gain from two trading partners being jointly on gold as compared to the excluded category, gold-silver. The negative result for silver, however, remains highly significant, but is now somewhat less.

In column 2, we include dyad fixed effects and time dummies, as well as time-varying country dummies. This effectively controls for country-specific time-effects, so that the remaining identifying variation is only at the *ijt* level. This is intended to deal with changes in multilateral resistance to trade over time—the effects of Baldwin and Taglioni's (2006) "non-constant." Estimation is computationally intensive, requiring 16,676 dummy variables. As the results show, our substantive conclusions are not affected by this more advanced estimation technique. In particular, the key results for silver continue to hold. In comparison to the results in column 1 with only time dummies and dyad fixed effects, the fully interacted model shown in column 2 produces a gold standard effect that is positive, but not statistically significant. As for silver, the estimated effect becomes more negative, and remains highly significant.

4.2 Results for Subperiods

What is behind the strikingly negative results for the silver standard? We next examine the stability of our results for subperiods. Until the 1890s, with the exception of Dutch Indonesia, the majority of Asian colonies continued to use silver—the legacy monetary standard. It is only with the move toward stabilized exchange rates vis-à-vis sterling in India that more and more countries and colonies switched to gold-exchange standards. The movement to stabilize relative to gold gathered pace after 1898, when India pegged the rupee to the pound; the Straits Settlement and Siam followed suit in 1906 and 1908, respectively. To capture the changing nature of currency arrangements and their effects on trade in Asia, we split our sample in 1895, and examine the stability of our results.

Table 5.5 broadly confirms the positive coefficient of gold in the two subsamples. The pooled OLS estimator shows that countries on gold before 1895 traded markedly more with each other. The size of the coefficient drops after 1895, and becomes statistically indistinguishable from zero. Silver countries also trade more with each other before 1895, but in contrast to the result for gold, the coefficient is larger thereafter; however, the silver standard is not statistically different from zero in either subperiod. In the final two columns, we use fixed effects estimation for each of the two separate subperiods. Many estimation results are stable across periods. In the fixed effects regressions, the gold standard significantly boosted trade in both periods. By contrast, the negative and statistically significant sign on the silver standard coefficient in column 3 suggests that the silver standard reduced trade before 1895. The negative effect of the silver standard disappears after 1895, suggesting that most of the gains from switching from silver to other currencies were realized by the early adopters.

4.3 Discussion

How are we to interpret the seemingly negative effect of the silver standard in the fixed-effects regressions? One possible interpretation is that the lower transactions costs and reduced volatility of a joint currency standard produced

Table 5.5
Results Before and After 1895

	(1) <1895	(2) ≥ 1895	(3) <1895	(4) ≥1895
Distance	−0.486***	−0.859***		
	(−3.22)	(−5.28)		
Ln *(pop)*	0.410***	0.259***	0.430***	0.435***
	(6.96)	(4.64)	(11.58)	(15.25)
Landlocked	−0.386	−0.529		
	(−1.08)	(−0.81)		
Empire	0.746**	0.135	0.843***	0.794***
	(2.04)	(0.44)	(5.92)	(5.73)
Ln *(rail)*	−0.00640	0.184***	0.0903***	0.156***
	(−0.17)	(3.13)	(11.62)	(14.40)
Gold standard	1.324***	−0.122	0.684***	0.199***
	(3.96)	(−0.48)	(8.35)	(6.97)
Silver standard	0.120	0.746	−0.685***	0.0493
	(0.28)	(1.37)	(−7.47)	(1.01)
Paper-bimetallic	0.142	0	−0.381***	0
	(0.35)	.	(−2.96)	.
Bimetallic-silver	−1.041	0	−1.199***	0
	(−1.23)	.	(−12.37)	.
Bimetallic-gold	−1.681**	0	−1.700***	0
	(−2.42)	.	(−8.22)	.
Paper-silver	−0.563	−1.012	−0.385***	−0.110
	(−0.99)	(−1.36)	(−4.20)	(−1.22)
Paper-gold	1.022***	−0.592*	−0.0949	0.0856
	(2.77)	(−1.75)	(−1.23)	(1.51)
Paper standard	0.173	−0.252	−0.0980	0.221
	(0.56)	(−0.65)	(−0.85)	(1.34)
Constant	12.34***	15.97***	7.103***	5.634***
	(7.49)	(10.56)	(12.69)	(11.30)
Year dummies	N	N	N	N
Dyad fixed effects	N	N	Y	Y
N	7,177	7,340	7,179	7,340
Adj. R^2	0.346	0.333	0.168	0.084

Notes: Our sample includes all available exports from Asian countries to other countries, whether in Asia or not, as well as exports from non-Asian countries to Asia. The excluded category for currency arrangement is gold-silver. t-statistics in parentheses. $^*p < 0.10$; $^{**}p < 0.05$; and $^{***}p < 0.01$.

a certain amount of "lock-in" in trading patterns. As countries left one currency arrangement and adopted another, these preexisting trade patterns began to dissolve. According to our findings in table 5.5, countries that remained on silver after 1895 appear to have had particularly strong ties to other silver standard countries. Countries in question include China and Hong Kong (for the entire sample period), Siam (until 1908), the Straits Settlement (until 1906), Japan (until 1897), and India plus the countries on a rupee standard (until 1898). Hence they stayed on silver for much longer, in a world that was rapidly switching to gold. As the pooled OLS results suggest, bilateral trade was not markedly higher for silver standard countries before 1895; it is only afterward that we find a positive coefficient. The fixed effects models suggest that as countries exited silver, their trade volume overall grew rapidly. Exports surged particularly strongly for those countries that left silver before 1895. Late switchers, on the other hand, did not see their exports increase.

5 Identifying the Effects of Currency Choice

It could be argued that the effects estimated in tables 5.3–5.5 are reasonably exogenous. Since the identifying variation in the fixed-effects models comes from changes over time, and most currency arrangements in Asia were decided by colonial powers, the normal issues relating to endogeneity should not arise. However, it can be argued that colonial powers ignore the interests of their overseas possessions at their peril. Britain, for example, waited for almost half a century after it took direct control of India to push for the adoption of the gold standard. The debate that proceeded revolved largely around the interests of the Indian economy. To the extent that currency arrangements are changed in response to expected benefits, we cannot treat the effects estimated in table 5.3 as causal.[16]

In this section, we present estimates using a new instrument derived from a close reading of the historical record of currency adoption. Switching to gold happened under a variety of circumstances. One of most frequent determinants of adopting gold after 1850 was success on the battlefield—states that won wars often used indemnities imposed on the vanquished to fund the acquisition of specie required. Two of the most prominent cases are Germany's adoption of the gold standard in 1875, and Japan's in 1897 (Flandreau, 1996; Mitchener et al., 2010). In both cases, these changes in currency arrangement followed hot on the heels of victory—against the French in the case of Germany, and against China in the case of Japan. Conversely, the failure to adopt gold appears correlated with defeat, such as in the case of Spain (beaten by the US in 1898, and one of the very few European powers not to adopt gold permanently).[17]

In our sample, countries that lost a war (within a ten-year interval) had a 23% chance of being on gold in any one year. If they neither won nor lost, the probability rose to 47% and for victors to 54%. Of course, it is very likely that countries on gold were structurally different from those that were not—they were, on average, richer, more industrialized, and more likely to possess an efficient war machine. Hence, we will simply exploit the time-series dimension of war success. In the relevant thought experiment, a range of countries may possess the characteristics that make being on gold and winning a war possible. Then, due to a set of historically contingent events, a war breaks out, and the winner adopts gold. The exclusion restriction is therefore the following: the variation in gold-standard adoption driven by the time-series dimension of victory at war will not directly affect trade volume.

Table 5.6 presents our instrumental variables (IV) estimates. The first two columns are estimated without currency dummies other than gold-gold; the third and fourth columns contain estimates where we include all possible currency pairs except gold-silver, the excluded category. In all cases, the results show a strong and significant effect of gold standard adoption on trade volumes. These are stronger than in the main specification. Measurement issues are unlikely to be responsible. We surmise that the much larger coefficient could reflect the timing of trade increases. Those countries that adopted gold because of sudden wartime success would not have adopted the gold standard for many years under normal circumstances. The sudden reduction in trading costs probably led to a sharper increase in trading volume than would otherwise have occurred.

6 The Political Economy of Currency Arrangements

If one were to ignore the evidence on trade flows, it is not clear why Asian economies abandoned silver for gold. The long historical dominance of silver in the region, the declining price of silver relative to gold, and the cost advantages of trading with neighbors might seem like sufficient conditions to significantly delay adoption at least until World War I. As we noted earlier, however, all but China, Hong Kong, and French Indochina had switched to gold by this time.

What is particularly interesting is that, according to our findings shown above, the decision to abandon silver turned out to be advantageous in terms of increasing trade flows. So, were policy makers prescient? Did they realize that the large decline in the price of silver, relative to gold, had run its course by 1895 and exporters would no longer benefit from this, that non-Asian trade would grow faster than Asian trade, and that trade based on Ricardian principles with Europe and the Americas would be large enough in magnitude to offset the cost advantages of intra-Asian trade? The historical record suggests that the abandonment of silver in Asia was largely driven by politics rather than economic considerations. There is little evidence that policy makers expressed concern over potentially higher transactions costs if the switch from silver to gold in the region was partial or slow. Rather, the historical record suggests that two political factors dominated the decision to adopt gold. First, colonies

Table 5.6
Instrumental Variables Estimates

	(1)	(2)	(3)	(4)
Gold standard	1.689***	3.857*	1.602***	1.984*
	(7.86)	(1.69)	(5.48)	(1.67)
Ln *(pop)*	0.246***	0.363***	0.317***	0.315***
	(5.97)	(2.72)	(8.43)	(3.90)
Empire	0.215*	−0.122	0.450***	0.390**
	(1.87)	(−0.29)	(4.18)	(2.24)
Ln *(rail)*	0.0650***	0.139*	0.0665***	0.0646**
	(7.55)	(1.73)	(9.00)	(1.99)
Silver standard			0.124	0.0619
			(1.26)	(0.55)
Paper-gold			0.988***	1.208
			(4.28)	(1.51)
Bimetallic-gold			−0.930***	−0.424
			(−2.70)	(−0.39)
Paper standard			0.639***	0.716
			(2.96)	(1.44)
Paper-silver			0.479**	0.588
			(2.40)	(1.26)
Paper-bimetallic			0.416*	0.605
			(1.93)	(1.28)
Bimetallic-silver			−0.803***	−0.628**
			(−4.82)	(−2.24)
Constant	12.30***	10.42***	10.76***	10.68***
	(12.36)	(5.40)	(12.44)	(7.63)
Year dummies	N	Y	N	Y
Dyad fixed effects	Y	Y	Y	Y
N	14,519	14,519	14,519	14,519
Adj. R^2	0.834	0.690	0.846	0.835

Notes: Our sample includes all available exports from Asian countries to other countries, whether in Asia or not, as well as exports from non-Asian countries to Asia. The excluded category for currency arrangement in Columns 3 and 4 is gold-silver. t-statistics in parentheses. $^*p < 0.10$; $^{**}p < 0.05$; and $^{***}p < 0.01$.

had little or no say in the matter. For example, the Herschell Committee was appointed to decide on the future of Indian currency. It met in London from 1892 to 1893 and heard 28 witnesses. Only one was Indian. Manufacturers, bankers, and tea planters in India favored staying on silver, while British textile exporters favored gold. In the end, the fact that the gold value of remittances for home charges (effectively a British tax on India) had been declining decided the matter (Leavens, 1939). The committee's decision was facilitated by over 1,700 submissions from officials in the Indian civil service, army, and so on, who complained about the declining value of their earnings in silver when sent back to Britain. On the whole, it appears that currency arrangements were decreed by imperial metropoles with little or no regard for the interests of the colonized. Much of Asia's decision to switch was taken out of the realm of domestic considerations, including interest-group politics. Nonetheless, and despite the heavy-handed nature of the decision to change colonies' monetary standards, it appears to have been economically efficient in that it increased trade flows.[18]

In contrast to the Straits Settlement, India, Indochina, Dutch East Indies, Indochina, and other Asian colonies, Japan's decision to switch was entirely based on domestic politics.[19] In introducing the legislation to the Diet, Prime Minister and Finance Minister Matsukata argued that trade would be one of the chief benefits as a result of gold standard adoption. "First, fluctuations of prices will be smaller under the gold standard than under the silver standard. Second, the introduction of the gold standard will promote trade, especially with other gold standard countries. Third, the introduction of the gold standard will reduce exchange rate risk with gold standard currencies."[20]

Before becoming law, the legislation had first to clear a vote at the committee level and then before the entire Diet, and while the proponents of going onto the gold standard had the powerful backing of the ruling party, many other legislators believed that adopting the gold standard would hurt the Japanese economy and that the timing was not propitious. They noted that the majority opinion of the 1895 report had concluded that recent fluctuations in the gold-silver price (while Japan was on the silver standard) had increased the volume of exports, reduced the burdens of debtors and fixed taxpayers, created a boom in agriculture, and led to prosperity in commerce and industry. As Eiichi Shibusawa, one member of the 1895 committee and a prominent business leader wrote: "The exports to gold standard countries increased by more than 260% from 1878 to 1893 while the imports from these countries only increased by 70% over the same period. This is because the price of exports has fallen while the price of imports has risen. This has promoted the development of industries, technical progress, and growth in the demand for labor. These benefits exceed the costs of being a silver standard country."[21]

The business community was largely in favor of remaining on the silver standard as export-producing sectors of the economy had benefited from the depreciation of silver. In 1898, economist Garrett Droppers wrote in the *Quarterly Journal of Economics* the following about the business community's view on Japan's monetary standard: "From 1886 to 1897, a period of over a decade, it is doubtful whether there was the slightest demand for return to the gold standard. On the contrary, every so-called decline of silver was hailed with general satisfaction by those engaged in industrial and commercial pursuits."[22]

Opposition from the business community to the gold standard was, in part, a function of the more unified voice of exporters. Based on data from the 1890s, Japan's exports were concentrated in a few key commodities and industries. Silk products accounted for 41% of Japanese exports, and 27% were tea, rice, and matches.[23] The value added of these commodities was almost entirely domestic, and Japanese producers of these goods had gained the most from the depreciation of the silver yen against gold-standard currencies. In contrast to exports, there was no single item that accounted for a large portion of total imports. Raw cotton accounted for 19%, sugar for 10%, machinery for 9%, and petroleum for 4%. Given that imports were used as inputs into a variety of products or were final goods sold to consumers, it proved more difficult for policy makers to drum up support from the business community to jettison the silver standard, since no one industry was experiencing a disproportionate rise in input prices due to the depreciation of silver.

Despite this opposition, Matsukata and his allies prevailed by forging a strategic alliance with a key opposition party, the Progressive Party. In particular, when Matsukata formed the cabinet in September 1896, and as a condition of his acceptance of the post of prime minister, he offered the post of foreign minister to Shigenobu Okuma, the leader of the Progressive Party (another large political party in Japan).[24] Indeed, the ruling government found itself in a crisis of leadership after the resignation of Prime Minister Ito in 1896, and commentators believed that the "Matsukata-Okuma coalition seems the only appropriate outcome of the crisis."[25] The press quipped that the Progressive Party (which had previously spearheaded opposition to the government) now signaled their alliance with the Matsukata cabinet by "issuing a singularly tactless manifesto, in which they arranged for themselves the position of austere mentors."[26] The Progressive Party was a key player in the Diet and one of two parties that, along with the Liberals, often voted to block the legislation of the ruling party.[27] More importantly, the Progressive Party was well represented on the House of Representatives Special Committee on Monetary System to which the legislation was referred. Matsukata also bought off some Liberal Party members.[28]

When the voting record and composition of the committee is examined more carefully, it is apparent that without the support of Progressives (who held the committee chair and made up 8 of the 26 voting members), the legislation would have stalled at the committee level. With the support of the Progressives and some of the Liberals, the legislation narrowly passed, 14 to 12.[29]

This coalition again proved sustainable when the debate moved out of committee and to the full Diet. Count Mutsu, secretary for the Japanese legation in Washington, commented in American newspapers that the debate seemed to have already been won by the coalition in support of adoption: "In many instances the discussion [in the Diet] proceeded upon lines as far removed as well could be from the real point at issue."[30] The bill cleared the House of Representatives and the House of Lords and was proclaimed law on March 29; the new currency act took effect on October 1, 1897.

China's experience stands in contrast to that of the rest of Asia. Neither the heavy hand of the European empire nor the strong arm of domestic politicians guided it onto the gold standard. China did not vote against adopting gold, rather it simply stayed on silver, unable to form any consensus about what type of currency system would be optimal. Both external and civil wars took their toll on Chinese politics, and little support emerged for abandoning the status quo. As a consequence, it experienced lower trade as a result of its staying on silver and being the last to do so.

7 Conclusion

Large parts of Asia shared a common currency in the nineteenth century— silver. Country pairs with particularly extensive bilateral trade remained on silver longer. This reflected a reluctance to break with the traditional currency arrangements, as well as the vocal opposition of exporters who feared losing the competitive advantage that rapid devaluation of silver offered. In our case study of Japan, we saw that overcoming this opposition depended on a confluence of political factors that were not easy to achieve, and that contained a considerable element of chance. In general, switching to the currency of the largest trading network was easier where the imperial center, rather than a national government, had control over policy. Starting with Dutch Indonesia in 1873, European powers prevailed on their Asian dependencies to stabilize their currencies relative to gold as the nineteenth century wore on. While the aim of imperial authorities was mainly to facilitate exports from the mother country, de facto gold standard membership offered large advantages that more than amply compensated for leaving silver.

By using a new data set on bilateral annual trading volume between Asian countries and the rest of the world, 1870–1913, we document the silver standard's impact on exports. Its effect was not uniformly positive. We find evidence that countries on silver traded more with each other than one would have expected, given their distance apart, empire membership, and population sizes. After abandoning their ties to silver, how did Asian countries fare on gold? It is with respect to this monetary standard that we find qualified support for the hypothesis that common currencies boosted trade in Asia. We obtain mainly positive coefficients for gold standard membership, and strongly negative coefficients for silver standard membership in fixed effects regressions. The latter result at first glance appears to contrast sharply with the documented effects of currency unions in the twentieth century, as well as under the gold standard. In fact, what it shows is that countries that left silver and joined gold saw large increases in their exports.

Since identification in our fixed effects models comes from time-series variation and the switch from silver to gold in Asia was in most cases the result of a decision made by the imperial power, our estimate of a positive gold standard effect should be free of concerns of reverse causality. Nevertheless, we offer a novel way of identifying exogenous variation in gold standard adoption so that causal inferences in our results are clearer. Using the effects of military success on currency adoption as an instrumental variable, we show that the gold standard indeed had strong, positive effects on bilateral trade volumes.

As the nineteenth century drew to a close, one by one, Asian countries and colonies left a currency arrangement that had served them well for centuries. Instead of continuing to share the silver standard with their immediate neighbors, they joined the gold standard—and struck out to develop more extensive trading relationships with partners located thousands of miles away. Alesina and Barro (2002) argue that members of a currency union should ideally be formed by adjacent countries, with synchronous business cycles, already engaged in extensive trade with each other. In contrast, we find that exiting a currency union with immediate neighboring countries can be beneficial, even for trade with member states of the abandoned currency union.

We argue that the peculiar gains from leaving silver reflect the nature of trade in the nineteenth century. The gold standard was a much larger and more dynamic currency union after most European countries had switched to it. By 1914, almost 90% of world trade took place between countries on the gold standard, or on a gold-exchange standard—up from 35% four decades earlier. Total world trade was booming—it increased by 320% between 1870 and 1913 (Maddison, 2001). As earlier authors have noted (O'Rourke and Williamson, 1994) trade before 1900 can in good measure be explained in terms of technological differences and factor endowments.[31] This is very different from trade today, where a large proportion is intra-industry trade of the "North-North" type.[32] On the whole, Asian countries exported raw materials and traditional finished goods in exchange for industrial products and capital equipment. While goods flowed from East to West geographically, trade was largely of the "North-South" variety, rather than intra-industry.[33] Since Ricardian trade based on differences in technology was important, and the greatest differential for Asian countries was vis-à-vis developed nations at the other end of the globe, the benefits from using the same currency as neighboring countries (with relatively similar factor endowments and technology) were limited. Because gold standard membership for Asian countries offered easier trade with the countries that had the largest potential for North-South trade, its adoption boosted trading volumes to a considerable degree. Even breaking ancient trading arrangements that were shared with neighboring countries could be beneficial in such circumstances. Countries that left silver and adopted gold began to import more capital goods from European countries and the US as a result of lower transactions costs. Growing exports facilitated trade financing and capital imports, and thus allowed further export expansion—a virtuous circle. These factors boosted trade with silver and gold bloc countries alike. In this sense, our finding of a negative silver effect may reflect positive spillover effects from adopting gold—spillovers that were so strong that they dominated the increased uncertainty and higher direct trade costs that came from using different currencies.

Asian trading volumes in the late nineteenth century were low relative to the region's population size and GDP. Sharing a common currency arrangement over a long period had not prevented this decline in numerous cases. In addition, vocal opposition of exporters prevented some Asian countries from joining the dominant currency arrangement of the day—gold—for an extended period. When the switch occurred, its benefits were large, but not enough to reverse the unusual decline of Asia's share in world trade.

For modern-day discussions of currency arrangements in Asia, our findings offer some tentative implications. Nineteenth-century exporters opposed leaving the silver standard since many of them had benefited from the enormous decline in the price of silver relative to gold. The cost advantages of a depreciating currency were too good to give up—much as exporters in European soft-currency countries felt in the 1990s. In retrospect, the misgivings of Asian exporters turned out to be shortsighted—joining gold was good for overall trading volumes, even vis-à-vis silver countries.

The prospects for an Asian currency union face similar challenges today.[34] The current development model in many Asian countries is based on exports to the US and Europe. Such policies have a long history. Governments used active exchange rate policies (Japan in the immediate postwar period, the Republic of Korea in the 1960s, and the People's Republic of China in the 1990s and 2000s) to create conditions favorable for their growth of exports. Exchange rates are still often fixed at levels that can be seen as undervalued. In the case of the European Monetary Union (EMU), the possible gains from importing the credibility of the Bundesbank were enough to overcome initial skepticism (Eichengreen, 2002). European monetary integration was also widely seen as the crowning achievement of a political process. Neither prospect is likely or appealing in the case of Asia today, where a pan-Asian vision is, at best, still in its infancy. In the nineteenth century, colonial powers—or the strong-arm tactics of politicians such as Count Matsukata—solved the issue of political feasibility. Based on the historical record, it is hard to see what external factors or force could help to achieve a similar outcome in the region today.[35]

Notes

1. In 1999, the Association of Southeast Asian Nations (ASEAN) plus People's Republic of China, Japan, and Republic of Korea (ASEAN+3) summit in Manila launched a number of initiatives that broadened financial cooperation. In 2004, the ADB lent its support to Japanese plans for a five-stage plan to adopt a common currency (Eichengreen, 2004). Alesina et al. (2002) investigate the economic feasibility of a "yen bloc."
2. Nugent (1973) provides some evidence of the effects of silver depreciation on exports. A recent working paper by Mitchener and Weidenmier (2008b)

provides quantitative estimates on the overall effects of silver standards on global trade, but does not focus on Asia's experience in particular, which formed the core of the nineteenth-century silver bloc and is the focus of this paper.

3. The overall effects of empire on trade are examined in Mitchener and Weidenmier (2008a). The benefits of empire for bond financing are emphasized in Ferguson and Schularick (2008).

4. Isaac Newton already noted the fact that the exchange ratio between gold and silver was 1:9 or 1:10 in the Far East, but closer to 1:15 in Europe (Chaudhuri, 2006).

5. Broadberry and Gupta (2005).

6. The only exception was provincial coinage in Foochow and Amoy (Leavens, 1939).

7. Andrew (1904).

8. The Straits Settlement had used rupees, but in 1867, the Legal Tender Act repealed legal tender status of the rupee and other Indian subsidiary coins. Silver coins including Mexican, Hong Kong, Spanish, Peruvian, and Bolivian would be legal tender instead (Lee, 1990).

9. The colonies included in the sample are Aden, Algeria, Australia (New South Wales, Western Australia, Queensland, South Australia, Tasmania, Victoria), Bahamas, Barbados, Belgian Congo, Bermuda, British Guiana, British Honduras, Brunei, Canada, Ceylon, Cuba, Cyprus, Djibouti, Dutch Guiana, Egypt, Falkland Islands, Fiji, French Guiana, French Indochina, Gambia, German East Africa, German South West Africa, German West Africa, Gibraltar, Gold Coast, Guadeloupe, Hawaii, Hong Kong, India, Jamaica, Labuan, Lagos, Madagascar, Maldives, Malta, Martinique, Mauritius, Morocco, Netherlands East Indies, New Caledonia, New Hebrides, New Zealand, Newfoundland, Nyasa, Philippines, Portonovo, Portuguese West Africa, Puerto Rico, Réunion, Sarawak, Senegal, Seychelles, Sierra Leone, Somalia, South Africa (Natal Province, Cape Province, and Transvaal), Southern Nigeria, St. Helena, St. Pierre/Miquelon, Straits Settlement, Togo, Trinidad and Tobago, Tunis, Uganda, British East Africa, and Zanzibar.

10. We use information from www.wcrl.ars.usda.gov/cec/java to calculate great circle distance.

11. Belgium, Italy, Japan, Portugal, and Russia also had colonial empires during this period. We have very limited bilateral trade data for the Belgian, Italian, Japanese, and Portuguese colonial empires and no bilateral trade data for members of the Russian Empire. As a result, we could not consider these empires in the empirical analysis.

12. López-Cordova and Meissner (2003); and Barbieri (2002).

13. This is not to say that the silver standard worked without transactions costs.

14. In a methodological critique of the currency union literature, Cheng and Wall (2005) also use exports as a dependent variable.

15. In his comments on our paper, Rose examined the effect of changing the specification of the standard gravity model in this way. In present-day data, he found that the coefficient of interest (currency union) is not affected when one uses population instead of GDP as a control for size (Rose, 2009).

16. We thank Andy Rose for pushing our thinking on this point.

17. The potential endogeneity of currency choice has been recognized before. López-Córdova and Meissner (2003) used the stock of gold reserves relative to notes

in circulation as an instrument. Since changes to gold stocks are normally part of the process that leads to the adoption of gold, it is difficult to see how this identifies a source of exogenous variation.

18. A possible exception is the case of the Straits Settlement, where local interests favored the introduction of gold after Japan had adopted it in 1898 (Leavens, 1939).

19. The case of Siam is more complex. While generally portrayed as a de facto dependency of Britain by many, there is some evidence that British financial advisors wielded less influence than commonly thought (Brown, 1978).

20. Speech of Finance Minister Count Masayoshi Matsukata. Ministry of Finance (1905, pp. 182–183). Matsukata suggested that the way the gold standard would increase exports was by reducing price fluctuations and making commercial transactions more convenient (Matsukata's speech cited in *The Oregonian* [1897]). Matsukata may have also believed that adopting gold would increase the prestige and standing of Japan, and that it was broadly consistent with the national goals of modernizing Japan's economy and military.

21. Committee on the Monetary System (1895, p. 945).

22. Droppers (1898. p. 164).

23. Figures are average shares of exports based on data from 1893–1897.

24. *London Times* (1896).

25. Ibid.

26. *London Times* (1897).

27. During his first term as prime minister (1891–1892), Matsukata failed to get the support of Progressives and Liberals for the budget, which included finances for the building of warships. The failure of the budget resulted in his resignation (Masumi, 1966. pp. 202–209 and 233–239).

28. A contemporary reported that some 40 members from the Liberal Party were bought off by Matsukata's allies (Masumi, 1966. p. 281).

29. See Mitchener et al. (2009) for a detailed, empirical analysis of the vote on gold standard adoption.

30. *Salt Lake Tribune* (1897).

31. Work on the case of Japan's opening up to trade after 1868 documents the size of welfare gains (Bernhofen and Brown, 2004 and 2005).

32. Krugman (1981).

33. For models of North-South trade, see Flam and Helpman (1987), Grossman and Helpman (1991a and 1991b), Matsuyama (2000), and Dinopoulos and Segerstrom (2006).

34. In addition, there is evidence to suggest that a "yen bloc" would not be an optimum currency area (Alesina et al., 2002).

35. For a related argument about the key differences in terms of political culture and institutions, cf. Eichengreen (2007).

References

Alesina, A., and R. Barro. 2002. Currency Unions. *Quarterly Journal of Economics.* 107(2). pp. 409–436.

Alesina, A., R. J. Barro, and S. Tenreyro. 2002. Optimal Currency Areas. *NBER Macroeconomics Annual.* 17. pp. 301–345.

Andaya, L. 1999. Interactions with the Outside World and Adaptation in Southeast Asian Society, 1500–1800. In N. Rarling, ed. *The Cambridge History of Southeast Asia.* Cambridge: Cambridge University Press.

Anderson, J., and E. Van Wincoop. 2003. Gravity without Gravitas: A Solution to the Border Puzzle. *American Economic Review.* 93(1). pp. 170–192.

Andrew, A. P. 1904. The End of the Mexican Dollar. *Quarterly Journal of Economics.* 18(3). pp. 321–356.

Bae, K-H., and W. Bailey. 2003. The Latin Monetary Union: Some Evidence on Europe's Failed Common Currency. Cornell University. *Mimeo.*

Baldwin, R., and D. Taglioni. 2006. Gravity for Dummies and Dummies for Gravity Equations. *NBER Working Paper Series* 12516.

Banks, A. 1976. Cross-National Time Series: 1815–1973. Computer file. Inter-University Consortium for Political and Social Research, Ann Arbor, MI.

Barbieri, K. 2002. *The Liberal Illusion: Does Trade Promote Peace?* Ann Arbor: University of Michigan Press.

Bergstrand, J. H. 1985. The Gravity Equation in International Trade: Some Microeconomic Foundations and Empirical Evidence. *Review of Economics and Statistics.* 67(3). pp. 474–481.

Bernhofen, D. M., and J. C. Brown. 2004. A Direct Test of the Theory of Comparative Advantage: The Case of Japan. *Journal of Political Economy.* 112(1). pp. 48–67.

Bernhofen, D. M., and J. C. Brown. 2005. An Empirical Assessment of the Comparative Advantage Gains from Trade: Evidence from Japan. *American Economic Review.* 95(1). pp. 208–225.

Broadberry, S. N., and B. Gupta. 2005. The Early Modern Great Divergence: Wages, Prices and Economic Development in Europe and Asia, 1500–1800. *Centre for Economic Policy Research (CEPR) Discussion Paper Series* 4947.

Brown, I. 1978. British Financial Advisers in Siam in the Reign of King Chulalongkorn. *Modern Asian Studies.* 122. pp. 193–215.

Chaudhuri, K. N. 2006. *The Trading World of Asia and the English East India Company, 1660–1760.* Cambridge, UK: Cambridge University Press.

Cheng, I. H., and H. J. Wall. 2005. Controlling for Heterogeneity in Gravity Models of Trade and Integration. *Federal Reserve Bank of St. Louis Review.* 87(1). pp. 49–63.

Committee on the Monetary System. 1895. Final Report. (Reprinted in Bank of Japan. 1957. Nihon Kin'yu Shi Shiryo: Meiji/Taisho Hen [Materials of Japan's Financial History: Meiji/Taisho Edition]). 16. pp. 571–957. Tokyo: Ministry of Finance, Printing Bureau.

Dinopoulos, E., and P. Segerstrom. 2006. North-South Trade and Economic Growth. *Centre for Economic Policy Research (CEPR) Discussion Paper Series* 5887.

Droppers, G. 1898. Monetary Changes in Japan. *Quarterly Journal of Economics.* 12(2). pp. 153–185.

Eichengreen, B. J. 2002. Lessons of the Euro for the Rest of the World. Paper delivered under the auspices of the Austrian Marshall Plan Foundation, Vienna. 4 December.

Eichengreen, B. J. 2004. Real and Pseudo Preconditions for an Asian Monetary Union. *Asian Development Bank High-Level Conference on Asia's Economic Cooperation and Integration.* Manila.

Eichengreen, B. J. 2007. European Integration: What Lessons for Asia? University of California, Berkeley. *Mimeo.*

Estevadeordal, A., B. Frantz, and A. Taylor. 2003. The Rise and Fall of World Trade. *Quarterly Journal of Economics.* 118(2). pp. 359–407.

Ferguson, N., and M. Schularick. 2004. The Empire Effect: The Determinants of Country Risk in the First Age of Globalization, 1880–1913. *Journal of Economic History.* 66(2). pp. 283–312.

Ferguson, N., and M. Schularick. 2008. The Thin Film of Gold: Monetary Rules and Policy Credibility in Developing Countries. *NBER Working Paper Series* 13918.

Flam, H., and E. Helpman. 1987. Vertical Product Differentiation and North-South Trade. *American Economic Review.* 77(5). pp. 810–822.

Flandreau, M. 1996. The French Crime of 1873: An Essay on the Emergence of the International Gold Standard, 1870–1880. *Journal of Economic History.* 56(4). pp. 862–897.

Flandreau, M., and M. Muriel. 2001. Monetary Union, Trade Integration, and Business Cycles in 19th Century Europe: Just Do It. *Centre for Economic Policy Research (CEPR) Discussion Paper Series* 3087.

Frankel, J., and A. Rose. 2000. Estimating the Effect of Currency Unions on Trade and Output. *NBER Working Paper Series* 7857.

Glick, R., and A. K. Rose. 2002. Does a Currency Union Affect Trade? The Time-Series Evidence. *European Economic Review.* 46(6). pp. 1125–1151.

Grossman, G. M., and E. Helpman. 1991a. Endogenous Product Cycles. *Economic Journal.* 101(408). pp. 1214–1229.

Grossman, G. M., and E. Helpman. 1991b. Quality Ladders and Product Cycles. *Quarterly Journal of Economics.* 106(2). pp. 557–586.

Hao, Y-P. 1986. *The Commercial Revolution in Nineteenth-Century China: The Rise of Sino-Western Mercantile Capitalism.* Berkeley: University of California Press.

Kemmerer, E. W. 1916. *Modern Currency Reforms: A History and Discussion of Recent Currency Reforms in India, Porto Rico, Philippine Islands, Straits Settlements and Mexico.* New York: The Macmillan Company.

Krugman, P. R. 1981. Intra-Industry Specialization and the Gains from Trade. *Journal of Political Economy.* 89(5). pp. 959–973.

Leavens, D. 1939. *Silver Money.* Bloomington, Indiana: Principia.

Lee, S. Y. 1990. *The Monetary and Banking Development of Singapore and Malaysia.* Singapore: Singapore University Press.

London Times. 1896. Japanese Politics. 4 December. p. 8.

London Times. 1897. Ministerial Changes in Japan. 22 November. p. 6.

López-Córdova, J. E., and C. Meissner. 2003. Exchange-Rate Regimes and International Trade: Evidence from the Classical Gold Standard Era. *American Economic Review.* 93(1). pp. 344–353.

Maddison, A. 2001. *The World Economy: A Millennial Perspective.* Paris: OECD.

Masumi, J. 1966. Nihon Seito-Shi Ron [A Thesis on the History of Japanese Political Party System]. Vol. 2. Tokyo: University of Tokyo Press.

Matsuyama, K. 2000. A Ricardian Model with a Continuum of Goods under Non-Homothetic Preferences: Demand Complementarities, Income Distribution, and North-South Trade. *Journal of Political Economy.* 108(6). pp. 1093–1120.

Meissner, C. 2005. A New World Order: Explaining the Emergence of the Classical Gold Standard. *Journal of International Economics.* 66. pp. 385–406.

Melitz, J., V. Alexander, and G. von Furstenberg. 2004. Geography, Trade, and Currency Union. In J. Melitz, V. Alexander, and G. von Furstenberg, eds.

Monetary Unions and Hard Pegs: Effects on Trade, Financial Development, and Stability. New York and Oxford: Oxford University Press. pp. 69–87.

Mitchener, K. J., and M. D. Weidenmier. 2008a. Trade and Empire. *Economic Journal.* 118(533). pp. 1805–1834.

Mitchener, K. J., and M. D. Weidenmier. 2008b. The Value of Silver in an Age of Gold. *Santa Clara University Working Paper.*

Mitchener, K. J., M. Shizume, and M. Weidenmier. 2010. Why Did Countries Adopt the Gold Standard? Lessons from Japan. *Journal of Economic History.* 70(1). pp. 27–56.

Muhleman, M. L. 1895. *Monetary Systems of the World: A Study of Present Currency Systems and Statistical Information Relative to the Volume of the World's Money.* New York: C. H. Nicoll.

Mundell, R. A. 1961. A Theory of Optimum Currency Areas. *American Economic Review.* 51. pp. 657–664.

Nugent, J. B. 1973. Exchange-Rate Movements and Economic Development in the Late Nineteenth-Century. *Journal of Political Economy.* 81(5). pp. 1110–1135.

O'Brien, P. K. 1991. *Oxford Atlas of World History.* New York: Oxford University Press.

Olson, J. S. 1991. *Historical Dictionary of European Imperialism.* New York: Greenwood Press.

O'Rourke, K., and J. G. Williamson. 1994. Late Nineteenth-Century Anglo-American Factor-Price Convergence: Were Heckscher and Ohlin Right? *Journal of Economic History.* 54(4). pp. 892–916.

Officer, L. 2004. The Gold Standard. from http://www.eh.net/encyclopedia/?article= officer.gold.standard.

Persson, T. 2001. Currency Unions and Trade: How Large Is the Treatment Effect? *Economic Policy: A European Forum.* 33. pp. 433–448.

Ritschl, A., and N. Wolf. 2003. Endogeneity of Currency Areas and Trade Blocs: Evidence from the Inter-War Period. *Centre for Economic Policy Research (CEPR) Discussion Papers* 4112.

Rose, A. K. 2000. One Money, One Market: The Effect of Common Currencies on Trade. *Economic Policy.* 15. pp. 7–33.

Rose, A. K. 2001. Currency Unions and Trade: The Effect Is Large. *Economic Policy: A European Forum.* 33. pp. 449–457.

Rose, A. K. 2002. Do We Really Know That the WTO Increases Trade? *NBER Working Paper Series* 9273.

Rose, A. K. 2007. Checking Out: Exits from Currency Unions. *Journal of Financial Transformation.* 19. pp. 121–128.

Rose, A. K. 2009. Comment on Mitchener and Voth. ADB-HKIMR Workshop, Quantifying the Costs and Benefits of Regional Economic Integration, Hong Kong, China. January 19–20.

Rose, A. K., and C. Engel 2002. Currency Unions and International Integration. *Journal of Money, Credit, and Banking.* 34(4). pp. 1067–1089.

Salt Lake Tribune. 1897. Japan's Gold Standard Law. September 14.

Sarkees, M. R. 2000. The Correlates of War Data on War: An Update to 1997. *Conflict Management and Peace Science.* 18(1). pp. 123–144.

Schmitz, C. 1979. *World Non-Ferrous Metal Production and Prices, 1700–1976.* London: Frank Cas.

Tenreyro, S., and R. J. Barro. 2003. Economic Effects of Currency Unions. *NBER Working Paper Series* 9435.

The Oregonian, 1897. The Gold Standard. August 7.

van der Eng, P. 1999. The Silver Standard and Asia's Integration into the World Economy, 1850–1914. *Review of Asian and Pacific Studies*. 18. pp. 59–85.

van der Eng, P. 2004. Coinage and Currency. In K. Gin Oi, ed. *Southeast Asia: A Historical Encyclopedia*. Santa Barbara: ABC-Clio.

Yeyati, E. L. 2003. On the Impact of a Common Currency on Bilateral Trade. *Economics Letters*. 79(1). pp. 125–129.

6

The ASEAN Free Trade Agreement: Impact on Trade Flows and External Trade Barriers

Hector Calvo-Pardo, Caroline Freund, and Emanuel Ornelas

We are grateful to the Asian Development Bank (ADB) for very helpful assistance in obtaining the data on ASEAN preferential liberalization employed in this chapter, and to Matias David Horenstein and Nathan Converse for excellent research assistance. We thank Fukunari Kimura (our discussant), Robert Barro, Jong-Wha Lee, and the other participants of ADB and Hong Kong Institute for Monetary Research (HKIMR) workshop "Quantifying the Costs and Benefits of Regional Economic Integration" for helpful comments. This chapter reflects the views of the authors and does not necessarily reflect the views of the World Bank or ADB.

1 Introduction

Regional integration has become the main form of trade liberalization since the early 1990s. Since the conclusion of the Uruguay Round in 1994, no significant progress has been made at multilateral liberalization. By contrast, a new regional trade agreement (RTA) is announced almost every month. According to the World Trade Organization (WTO), more than 300 RTAs are currently in force and all but one (Mongolia) of its 153 members participate in at least one of those arrangements. Given the rising prominence of bilateral and regional trade liberalization, it is important that we understand their implications for world trade.

This is even more important because, unlike multilateral liberalization, which most economists believe to be largely beneficial for both liberalizing countries and bystanders, preferential liberalization is controversial.

The reason comes from its inherent discriminatory nature: when forming an RTA, members agree to lower trade barriers to each other but their tariffs on imports from outsiders remain unconstrained by the RTA.[1] This can induce members to substitute inefficiently produced imports from bloc members for imports previously sourced efficiently from nonmember countries. Such trade diversion harms the nonmembers through lost markets, as well as the members through reduced tariff revenue. However, like broader trade liberalization, the RTA is also likely to enhance trade of the goods that are efficiently sourced within the bloc. This trade creation will enhance welfare. These two forces suggest that preferential liberalization can in principle be either welfare-enhancing or welfare-reducing. Ultimately, the verdict must be empirical, and may be different for different trading blocs. Trade creation forces may prevail over trade diverting ones in some cases, but the reverse could be true in others.

In this chapter, we assess the consequences of the Association of Southeast Asian Nations (ASEAN) Free Trade Agreement (AFTA) on trade and external tariffs. AFTA's negotiations were concluded in 1992 and the agreement was implemented in 1993. It was originally composed by Brunei Darussalam, Indonesia, Malaysia, the Philippines, Singapore, and Thailand. In the second half of the 1990s, AFTA expanded to incorporate Viet Nam, Lao People's Democratic Republic (PDR), Myanmar, and Cambodia. Internal trade liberalization within the bloc has not been as abrupt as in some other trading blocs, for instance, the North American Free Trade Agreement (NAFTA). Instead, liberalization has evolved gradually, though steadily. Furthermore, there are significant differences in the speed and size of tariff reductions between countries and across products. This variation helps us assess how preferential liberalization has affected trade and tariffs.

We first examine trade effects. We find that the formation of the trade bloc has had a meaningful positive impact on the trade flows among members. Interestingly, this does not seem to have happened at the expense of trade with outsiders. Growth of imports from nonmembers did not falter after the formation and the enlargements of AFTA. Nor is growth in imports from nonmembers significantly different from growth in imports from members subsequent to AFTA.

To examine the effect of AFTA on trade in more detail, we focus on the impact of preferential and multilateral tariff changes on intra-bloc import growth and import growth from excluded countries. For the analysis, we rely on detailed data on preferential- and MFN (most favored nation)-applied tariffs at the product level for all ASEAN members, since the bloc was created in 1993 through 2007. This allows us to use a large set of fixed effects that control for a wide range of unobserved shocks. We find strong evidence that reductions in MFN tariffs have stimulated trade with nonmembers, but no evidence that preferential tariff reduction has reduced trade with nonmembers.

Next, we examine the effect of preferential tariff reduction on external tariffs. It is possible that preferential and MFN tariffs are related, and that governments respond to changes in the preferential tariffs by adjusting MFN tariffs. We therefore proceed to analyze the reaction of the bloc members' trade policies vis-à-vis outsiders. Specifically, we ask: Has the reduction of tariffs on within-ASEAN trade led its members to change their barriers on imports from excluded countries? If so, have they gone up or down as a result of ASEAN, and by how much?

Several theoretical forces have been advanced suggesting that the formation of a free trade agreement such as AFTA should induce changes in external tariffs. But just as in the trade creation/trade diversion debate, there are reasons supporting changes in either direction. Once again, the resolution of the debate must be empirical.

Our data set provides enough variation to allow us to obtain very precise estimates on whether products with relatively large preferences have been liberalized or protected to the same extent as other products. It is also helpful that the ASEAN members generally set their applied MFN tariffs well below their bound rates at the WTO, so we do not need to worry about this potential institutional constraint.

In line with recent analyses of regionalism in developing countries, our results imply that AFTA is a "building bloc" to free trade. There is strong evidence that preferences induce a faster decline in external tariffs than otherwise would occur. The results are both statistically and economically significant. For example, in a country where imports of a certain product from outsiders faced a 10% MFN tariff but were granted duty free access if stemming from other ASEAN members, the member would subsequently tend to reduce its MFN tariff on that product by between 2.5 and 4.5 percentage points.

While the correlation between changes in external and preferential tariffs is unquestionable, determining causality is trickier. For example, it may be that some products are easier to liberalize than others, and trade in those products tends to be liberalized both regionally and multilaterally. We use three main distinct strategies to determine if this is a causal effect and find evidence that it is. First, evidence of "tariff complementarity" remains strong if we use lagged changes in preferential tariffs (or preferential margins) as our main regressor. Second, we look for differential effects precisely where either the theory or the practice tells us we should find them. Specifically, no tariff complementarity arises when the margin of preferences is too small to be meaningful for exporters. Furthermore, stronger tariff complementarity is obtained in sectors where the margin of preferences is meaningful and the share of intra-bloc imports is higher, as theory suggests. Third, we employ an instrumental variables (IV) approach that takes advantage of a unique feature of our data set: the agreed speed and depth of internal liberalization of the six original members in their 1992 negotiations. As it turns out, observed changes in preferences have not corresponded to the planned ones in 1992. Numerous reasons may have caused this discrepancy. For us, this is especially valuable because the planned internal liberalization can serve as an instrument for the actual one. While they are strongly correlated, the negotiated preferences should not have an independent effect on the incentives of countries to alter their external tariffs. To strengthen this rationale, in the IV regressions we restrict the sample to the post-Asian crisis period, during which trade policies were significantly affected. Interestingly, the qualitative results of our IV and ordinary least squares (OLS) estimations are very similar, and quantitatively, they are higher under the IV procedure. Replacing the actual with the planned preferential tariffs in the OLS estimation also delivers similar results.

Taking all of our results together, we conclude that AFTA has promoted trade within the bloc without hurting trade with outsiders. An important reason for this is the unilateral reductions in external tariffs that ASEAN members implemented as a result of their liberalization vis-à-vis each other. These reductions suggest that AFTA provides an important contribution to the global process of multilateral liberalization.

The remainder of this chapter is organized as follows: In the next section we discuss the related theoretical literature and the empirical findings. We provide a general view of ASEAN and discuss the data in section 3. In section 4, we examine the impact of tariffs on trade. In section 5, we develop the empirical analysis on the effects of AFTA on external tariffs. Section 6 concludes.

2 Trade Creation, Trade Diversion, and Import Barriers on Outsiders

We know since Viner (1950) that the formation of a free trade agreement (FTA) can lead to trade creation and/or trade diversion. The former arises when the FTA promotes trade among the members without disrupting trade with nonmembers, and tends to be efficiency-enhancing. In contrast, trade diversion arises when the FTA promotes trade among members at the expense of trade with bloc outsiders, and tends to be efficiency-reducing.

There have been attempts to pin down theoretically the characteristics that make FTAs more trade-creating or more trade-diverting. Frankel (1997) develops the "natural trading partners" hypothesis, which states broadly that agreements between countries that already trade significantly (in particular, geographically close countries and those that share cultural characteristics, such as language, that reduce transaction costs) are the ones most likely to be trade-creating. Although theoretically this does not need to always hold, as Bhagwati and Panagariya (1999) point out, Frankel (1997) finds evidence consistent with the natural trade partners hypothesis in a number of regression analyses based on the gravity equation with country-level trade flows.

Lee and Shin (2006) extend the approach of Frankel (1997) and estimate a gravity model with year dummies and with both random and fixed effects to assess trade creation and trade diversion in 175 countries, using data from 1948 to 1999. The key trade creation variable is a dummy that is set equal to one if both countries are members of a common RTA, and the key trade diversion variable is a dummy that is set equal to one if one country belongs to an RTA and the other does not belong to that RTA. Lee and Shin allow these dummy variables to interact with geographical and common language variables to identify whether trade creation and trade diversion are different for "natural" trade patterns.

In most specifications, Lee and Shin (2006) confirm that RTAs increase bilateral trade between members. The magnitudes are around 50%, but if the countries share a common border this effect increases to up to 200%. Similarly, the closer the countries are to each other, the larger the trade creation. On the other hand, RTAs are never found to reduce trade between members and nonmembers significantly. In fact, in most specifications, RTAs are estimated to increase trade between members and nonmembers from 6% to 15%. Trade with nonmembers grows more for RTAs with a smaller average distance between their members and when more members of the RTA have common borders or share a common language. Having the trade-creation and trade-diversion estimates in hand, Lee and Shin then predict the average trade impact of several proposed RTAs in Asia. They find in particular that the trade effects of AFTA are significantly positive.[2]

Clausing (2001) develops a detailed (at the product-level) analysis of the Canada–United States Free Trade Agreement (CUSTA) of 1988. She also finds that trade creation tends to be the rule, and trade diversion the exception, in most sectors.[3] A somewhat different picture is presented by Chang and Winters (2002), who find evidence that the formation of the Southern Common Market (*Mercado Común del Sur* [MERCOSUR]) hurt outsiders. However, MERCOSUR is distinct from CUSTA, NAFTA, and all the Asian RTAs, as it is a customs union (CU), rather than a free trade agreement.[4]

Now, while structural characteristics of FTA members can make the bloc more or less prone to be trade creating/diverting, it is perhaps even more critical to understand the members' trade policy reactions to the formation of the bloc, in particular their incentives to alter their trade taxes on the imports from outsiders. This follows from two simple observations. First, the country's external tariffs can be altered unilaterally, provided they are within the bounds established at the WTO. Second, the higher the difference between a member's preferential tariffs and its external tariffs, the greater is the discrimination and the scope for trade diversion. Thus, if the formation of a preferential trading bloc is accompanied by reductions in external tariffs, the arrangement is more likely to enhance aggregate world welfare without harming excluded countries. In contrast, if the trading bloc raises trade barriers against excluded countries (or fails to reduce them), diversion of external trade to bloc members is more likely, harming outsiders and possibly countries in the bloc as well. Therefore, the trade, as well as the welfare consequences of an RTA, depends critically on the member countries' tariff response. But if the original choice of MFN tariffs resulted from economic and political considerations by the government, those motives would lead to different outcomes when constrained by the presence of preferential rates. Accordingly, we should indeed expect the external tariffs to change after the formation of a trading bloc.

There is a sizable theoretical literature that explores the optimal external tariff response of countries following the formation of FTAs. In a standard model, with a welfare-maximizing government, optimal external tariffs are likely to fall in a free trade area precisely to limit the welfare costs of trade diversion (Bagwell and Staiger, 1999; Freund, 2000; Bond et al., 2004). The intuition is that the welfare cost of trade diversion induces governments to lower external tariffs to recapture tariff revenue and improve economic efficiency.

When political-economy motives are incorporated, the results are ambiguous. For example, Richardson (1993) and Ornelas (2005a, 2005b) find that, upon the formation of a free trade area, lobbying will decline and external tariffs will fall, as the import-competing sector contracts and becomes weaker politically. The greater the share of imports stemming from the bloc partners, the more important will be this force. However, in a different model, Panagariya and Findlay (1996) find that countries in a free trade area will raise protection against outsiders because lobbying in favor of tariffs against FTA partners will be diverted to lobbying for a greater external tariff. Furthermore, it is not just existing trade blocs that matter. As Bagwell and Staiger (2004) show, the mere potential for a future trade agreement may affect the extent of current tariff reduction that can be negotiated multilaterally. The threat of "bilateral opportunism" reduces the extent of multilateral tariff reduction because current global trade agreements can be later diluted by bilateral preferences.

In contrast, the empirical literature on the effect of RTA formation on external tariffs is still in its infancy. Bohara et al. (2004) examine tariff adjustments in Argentina following the formation of MERCOSUR, finding some support for the hypothesis that the decline of industries driven by the formation of a trading bloc leads to lower external tariffs. Similarly, Estevadeordal et al. (2008) examine the direct impact of changes in preferential tariffs on changes in MFN tariffs in 10 Latin American countries and 100 industries over 12 years. Using a number of empirical techniques to extract causality, they find that preferences in free trade areas lead to a decline in external tariffs, whereas the effects are negligible in customs unions. In contrast, Limão (2006) finds that the United States (US) was more reluctant to lower tariffs in the Uruguay Round for products where preferences were granted. His results imply that trade preferences lead to less multilateral tariff reduction. Karacaovali and Limão (2008) find similar results for the European Union (EU).

Recently, Lendle (2007) has developed the first analysis of the trade policy reactions to regionalism in Asia. Specifically, Lendle evaluates whether products receiving preferential treatment in Indonesia, Malaysia, the Philippines, and Thailand under the ASEAN Free Trade Agreement underwent greater reduction in MFN tariffs during the late 1990s and early 2000s than goods that did not receive preferential treatment. The approach resembles that of Limão (2006), in that he estimates the change in the MFN tariff from the mid-1990s to the early 2000s (the precise years vary according to the country in analysis due to data availability) on a dummy that represents whether the country offered preferential treatment under AFTA. Lendle finds evidence of tariff complementarity for Indonesia, the Philippines, and Thailand, where the MFN tariffs of preferential products were reduced by more (between one and five percentage points) than for nonpreferential products. In contrast, the results for Malaysia, which has the lowest average MFN among the four countries studied, are somewhat mixed, varying according to the specification. While Lendle's study is very instructive about the developments in internal and external liberalization in ASEAN, it does not take into account the variations in the extent and the speed of intra-bloc liberalization, which are significant.

3 The ASEAN Free Trade Agreement

The ASEAN Free Trade Agreement was signed by Brunei Darussalam, Indonesia, Malaysia, the Philippines, Singapore, and Thailand in 1992, and entered into force in 1993. It consisted of a schedule of preferential tariff reductions for goods in the Inclusion List, to be implemented progressively until 2008 (later postponed to 2010). Goods were divided in five categories: Inclusion List-Fast Track (IL-FT); Inclusion List-Normal (IL-N); Temporary Exclusion List (TEL); Sensitive List (SL); and General Exceptions (GE). The group titles reveal their meanings quite accurately. IL-FT goods were expected to have preferential tariffs reduced to 0–5% by 2000, while IL-N products had until 2003 to reach that level. TEL items were expected to be phased into the Inclusion List by 2000 for most manufactured products, and by 2003 for unprocessed agricultural products. SL goods corresponded mainly to unprocessed agricultural products that were granted a more flexible arrangement for phasing into the Inclusion List. Finally, GE products were permanently excluded from the agreement. In the second half of the 1990s, four other countries (Cambodia, Lao PDR, Myanmar, and Viet Nam) joined the group. They were incorporated into the existing scheme for preferential liberalization, although with more flexibility both with respect to the products added to the Inclusion List and with respect to the timing of liberalization.

Overall, AFTA has proved to be a "deep" free trade agreement, at least relative to other arrangements among developing countries (probably second only to MERCOSUR in this respect). There are several reasons for that. First, AFTA's coverage is comprehensive (over 90% of product classifications were in the Inclusion List from the outset of the liberalization program). Second, the liberalization program is very ambitious, ultimately requiring free/near-free trade within the area for the large majority of products. Third, and most importantly, AFTA members have indeed—unlike members of many other developing-country trading blocs—largely stuck to their announced goal of reaching near free intra-bloc trade.

AFTA's successful implementation does not imply, however, that the 1992 original preference-granting schedule has been followed strictly by its signatories. In fact, there have been numerous updates and amendments to the schedule.[5] It is not uncommon for members to move slower than the schedule originally specified, and sometimes they actually move faster. This implies that actual liberalization, while correlated, is not fully dictated by the previously negotiated tariffs. This feature of AFTA turns out to be very useful for our identification strategy of the effects of preferences on countries' choices of MFN tariffs, as we discuss in section 5. Other features of the AFTA liberalization process are useful for our analysis as well. First, the speed and degree of intra-bloc liberalization vary across products and across member countries, as well as over time, generating significant variation in our data set. Second, there were important changes in the liberalization process provoked by the Asian crisis of 1997–1998, a crisis that arose independently of AFTA and therefore can be treated as exogenous to AFTA.[6] Third, as in any free trade agreement (but unlike in customs unions), bloc members are fully independent to define their external (MFN) tariffs.[7]

In parallel to the broader tariff negotiations under AFTA, other specific, sectoral liberalization programs (such as in information technology products and in automobiles) were also implemented by ASEAN members in the early 2000s, accelerating the liberalization process within the bloc. To the extent that these sectoral agreements affected the tariffs of the ASEAN members, their impact is incorporated in our analysis. Other institutional elements that are likely to affect our relationships include nontariff barriers (NTBs) and schemes like the members' duty drawback system (which provides duty-free treatment of imported intermediate goods for producing exported final goods).[8] We do not incorporate those issues explicitly mainly because of unavailability of appropriate data. While we do not expect NTBs or the bloc's duty drawback system to be the driving forces in our analysis, their effects are nevertheless subsumed in our estimations, which provide the net effect of preferences on external tariffs.[9]

3.1 Data

We work with a comprehensive data set that includes information on trade, MFN tariffs, and preferential tariffs, implemented and scheduled, for all 10 members of the ASEAN Free Trade Area. The information on preferential tariffs was provided by the ASEAN Secretariat.[10] The implemented rates are those actually employed by the member countries. The main novelty of the data set is the scheduled rates, which are the ones the members planned to apply in 1992, when the AFTA negotiations were concluded. The MFN tariffs and the trade data at the HS 6-digit level come from the World Integrated Trade System (WITS). An important advantage of our data is that they are very disaggregated, at the product (6-digit) level. Furthermore, we have a long sample, ranging from 1993 to 2007 (plus data in previous years for trade flows and MFN tariffs). On the negative side, the panel is unbalanced, with a significant amount of missing data, especially in the first half of the sample.

The aggregate trade data used in section 3.3 are from the International Monetary Fund's *Direction of Trade Statistics*. These data go back further than the WITS data, and a great effort was made to ensure that the data used captured aggregate bilateral flows.

3.2 Tariffs

Table 6.1 shows the (simple) average preferential and MFN tariffs, plus the difference between the two (margin), for each of the 10 ASEAN members since the outset of AFTA in 1993 (or since the entry year for the later entrants). Blank spaces reflect missing data (the year 2001 is not shown because preferential tariffs are missing for all members that year). The overall trend is of falling MFN and preferential rates, but this is not always the case, even though we are looking at average levels. The most notable exception is Thailand, where during the Asian crisis, MFN tariffs temporarily peaked at high levels.

These points become clearer when we look at figure 6.1, where we display the time series of the three variables from table 6.1 for the countries where data are available for most years, Indonesia, Malaysia, and the Philippines. The downward trend in preferential tariff rates is very transparent for all of them, although the speed and the magnitude of the changes vary, both being higher for the initially more protected countries, Indonesia and the Philippines. In those countries MFN tariffs have fallen as well, but the changes have been minimal since 2002. The pattern of the average MFN tariff in Malaysia has been more erratic, having gone up right after the Asian currency crisis and come down only slightly since 2005, but remaining above the pre-crisis level. With respect to the average margin of preference, the pattern again differs among the three countries: it is generally (but not always) increasing for Indonesia and Malaysia, and it is mostly (but not always) decreasing in the Philippines, reflecting the large drops in the MFN tariff there. Figure 6.1 therefore makes clear the large degree of variation in external and preferential tariffs in our sample, even when we look at average levels.

3.3 Aggregate Trade

We now look at aggregate trade data for the six original ASEAN members to examine how trade patterns change following the implementation of trade preferences.[11] The purpose is to identify whether there are significant trend changes in the trade growth with members and nonmembers subsequent to the agreement.

Figures 6.2.1 and 6.2.2 show the share of imports that stems from initial ASEAN members, collectively and for each of the six individual countries,

Table 6.1
MFN and Preferential Tariffs

Country (ASEAN-6)		1993	1994	1995	1996	1997	1998	1999	2000	2002	2003	2004	2005	2006	2007
Brunei Darussalam	MFN				3.75		2.76	2.71	2.68	2.63	2.63	2.60	2.14	2.11	2.61
	PREF	3.64	2.54	2.42	1.87		1.31	1.37	1.19	0.94	0.97	0.94			1.01
	Margin				1.88		1.45	1.34	1.49	1.69	1.66	1.66			1.60
Indonesia	MFN	17.88		15.06	13.57	12.35	12.35	8.81	8.25	6.89	6.90	6.95	6.95	6.95	6.91
	PREF	16.03	16.03	14.36	9.48	8.10	6.70	5.19	4.57	3.63	2.14	2.20	1.51	1.50	1.50
	Margin	1.85		0.70	4.09	4.25	5.65	3.62	3.68	3.26	4.76	4.75	5.44	5.45	5.41
Malaysia	MFN	11.06			6.77	6.21	6.26	8.17	8.36	8.35	8.35		7.35	7.18	7.18
	PREF	7.27	6.77	6.29	4.18	3.78	3.17	2.90	2.96	2.64	2.18		2.10	2.01	0.69
	Margin	3.79			2.59	2.43	3.09	5.27	5.40	5.71	6.17		5.25	5.17	6.49
Philippines	MFN	23.01	22.16	20.27	14.39	14.62	14.79	9.62	7.71	6.08	6.28	6.27	6.27		6.26
	PREF	12.41	11.36	10.62	9.57	9.22	7.78	7.37	5.09	4.05	1.98	2.05	2.05		1.97
	Margin	10.60	10.80	9.65	4.82	5.40	7.01	2.25	2.62	2.03	4.30	4.22	4.22		4.29
Singapore	MFN			0	0.32	0.07	0.07	0.06		0	0	0	0	0	0
	PREF			0						0	0	0	0	0	
	Margin			0						0	0	0	0	0	

	1	2	3	4	5	6	7	8	9	10	11	12
Thailand MFN	20.01	20.01	18.38	23.71	23.71	43.33	16.40	4.85	15.36	2.01		
PREF				14.09	10.30	9.75	5.96		2.00			
Margin				9.62	13.41	33.58	10.44		13.36			
Country (+4)												
Cambodia MFN							16.46	16.41	16.41	15.81	14.26	14.18
PREF								8.87	7.83		9.08	6.85
Margin								7.54	8.58		5.18	7.33
Lao PDR MFN					10.34	10.33	10.33	10.34		10.33	9.71	9.71
PREF							7.21			6.15	3.88	1.57
Margin							3.12			4.18	5.83	8.14
Myanmar MFN					5.54	5.51	5.49	5.51	5.51	5.51	5.60	5.60
PREF								4.80	4.81	4.26	4.29	3.36
Margin								0.71	0.70	1.25	1.31	2.24
Viet Nam MFN					4.47	12.43	13.08		16.03	16.81	16.81	16.81
PREF					3.71	7.39	7.54	6.86	6.57	5.50	4.08	2.35
Margin					0.76	5.04	5.54		9.46	11.31	12.73	14.46

Source: World Integrated Trade System (WITS) and ASEAN Secretariat.

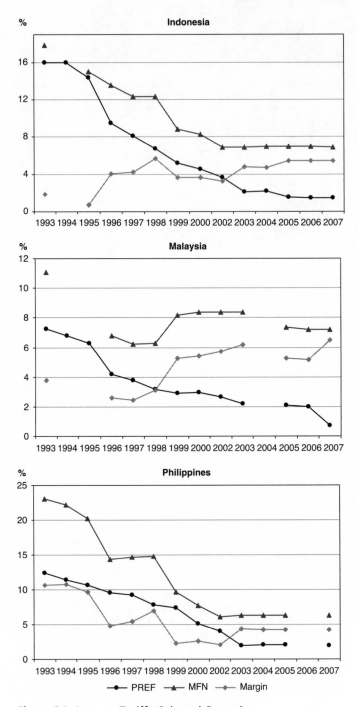

Figure 6.1 Average Tariffs, Selected Countries

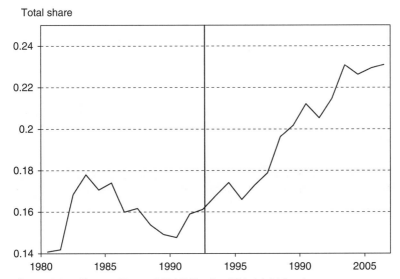

Figure 6.2.1 Share of Intra-ASEAN Trade: All Initial Members

13 years before and after the introduction of preferences in 1993. The figures show that, for the bloc as a whole and for most members, the share of imports coming from partner countries has increased steadily since 1993, although no clear trend is visible before that year. This suggests that the preferences were effective in affecting trade patterns. However, it does not hint at whether this reflects the prevalence of trade diversion or trade creation, since both imply an increase in the share of preferential imports.

In figures 6.3.1 and 6.3.2 we then plot, for the same period, the volumes of intra-AFTA imports and imports from outside the bloc. The figures suggest no evidence of important trade diversion, as imports from AFTA nonmembers kept increasing after the formation of the bloc in most years for all countries.[12] Imports from within the bloc increased at a higher pace, though, which explains the rise in the share of intra-AFTA trade. These trends are consistent with trade creation dominating trade diversion in AFTA, although other explanations are also plausible. The figures also make clear that import growth with members and with nonmembers are highly correlated, implying that other factors besides AFTA are important drivers of aggregate trade growth.

Table 6.2 shows the mean growth rates of imports from ASEAN partners and from the rest of the world before and after 1993. While several factors beyond AFTA have probably affected trade growth rates in the ASEAN countries (the currency crisis of 1997–1998 being only the most prominent one), a few regularities are worth noting. First, intra-AFTA trade grows faster than external trade in five of the six original members even in the pre-agreement period (the only exception being Indonesia). This suggests that

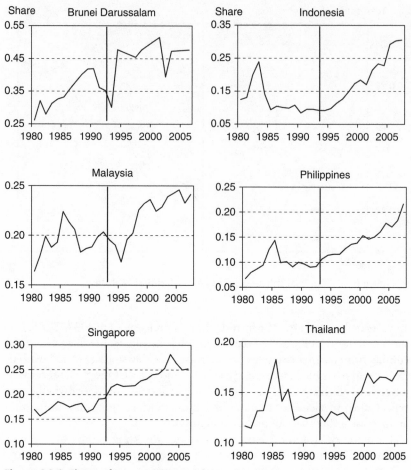

Figure 6.2.2 Share of Intra-ASEAN Trade: By Country

the choice of members was not random, but rather was influenced by their growing trade ties. In the post-agreement period, internal trade growth was faster than external import growth in all countries, and by a significantly larger margin than it was before 1993.

Although using aggregate trade data obviously makes the sample very small, we can still perform t-tests on the difference in the means of the pre-union and post-union growth rates and also between the growth rate of internal trade and trade with nonmembers. As the results reported in table 6.2 show, the t-tests of the difference in the mean growth rates before and after the agreement are not conclusive. On the other hand, the difference in the mean growth rates of imports from members and nonmembers are different enough for Indonesia and the Philippines in the post-AFTA period that the t-test on their difference is statistically significant, despite the very small sample.

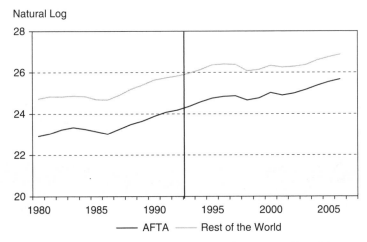

Figure 6.3.1 ASEAN Intra-Bloc and External Imports: All Initial Members

Furthermore, if increased trade with bloc members displaced imports from third countries, we would expect to see a decline in the correlation between internal and external trade growth subsequent to the formation of AFTA. However, as shown in the last column of table 6.2, the correlation between external trade growth and internal trade goes up in five out of the six countries—and by a large amount in Thailand and the Philippines. The correlation falls in the post-1993 period only in Brunei Darussalam, and the drop was minimal.

4 The Effect of Tariffs on Trade in ASEAN

Having looked at the pattern of aggregate trade and average tariffs in the ASEAN countries, we turn now to examine the relationship between imports and tariffs. Specifically, we study how MFN and preferential tariffs affect import growth from AFTA members and from outsiders.

For this exercise, as well as for our study of the relationship between the two types of tariffs in the next section, we aggregate the yearly data in three-year periods. This helps to downplay unnecessary noise in the data set due to missing data. The six periods are: (i) the pre-AFTA period (1990–1992); (ii) the early years of the agreement (1993–1995); (iii) the Asian crisis period (1996–1998); (iv) the post-crisis period (1999–2001); (v) the effective integration of the new members (2002–2004); and (vi) further intra-bloc liberalization by all members (2005–2007). We lose little with this approach, since the dataset remains very large.

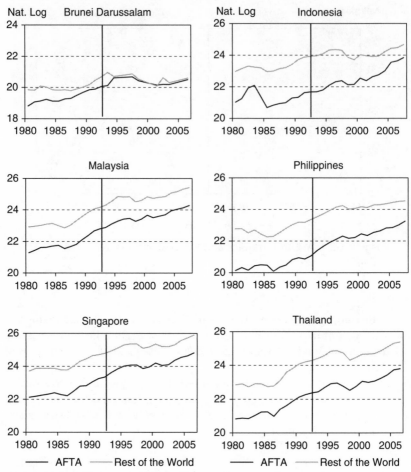

Figure 6.3.2 ASEAN Intra-Bloc and External Imports: By Country

Notes: Brunei Darussalam is on a different scale because imports are lower. The scale is drawn to make the magnitude of changes comparable with the other countries.

To control for other factors that might affect trade patterns, we run the following regression:

$$\Delta \ln(M_{ijtg}) = \gamma_{jtg} + \beta_1 \Delta PREF_{ijt} + \beta_2 \Delta MFN_{ijt} + \varepsilon_{ijt}, \qquad (1)$$

where M_{ijtg} corresponds to imports of product i, by country j, in period t, from group g = members or nonmembers; $PREF_{ijt}$ denotes the preferential tariff (in percentage points) enjoyed by exporters of good i to country j in period t, whereas MFN_{ijt} corresponds to the tariff (in percentage points) that non-ASEAN exporters have to incur; Δ indicates first difference; and γ_{jtg} is a country-period fixed effect for group g. The country-period effects control

Table 6.2
Growth Rates of ASEAN Imports

Country	ASEAN	ROW	t-test	p-value	Correlation
Brunei Darussalam					
1980–1993	10.45	6.91	0.85	0.41	0.351
1993–2007	5.37	(1.07)	0.49	0.64	0.330
t-test	0.62	0.68			
p-value	0.54	0.50			
Indonesia					
1980–1993	5.43	7.97	(0.28)	0.78	0.677
1993–2007	14.49	4.93	3.04	0.01	0.813
t-test	0.78	0.45			
p-value	0.44	0.66			
Malaysia					
1980–1993	12.57	10.37	0.81	0.43	0.786
1993–2007	9.87	8.40	0.78	0.45	0.886
t-test	0.53	0.33			
p-value	0.60	0.74			
Philippines					
1980–1993	7.78	4.97	0.53	0.61	0.575
1993–2007	14.51	7.81	3.50	0.00	0.836
t-test	1.01	0.48			
p-value	0.32	0.63			
Singapore					
1980–1993	10.21	8.93	0.59	0.57	0.819
1993–2007	10.43	7.95	1.41	0.18	0.900
t-test	0.04	0.19			
p-value	0.97	0.85			
Thailand					
1980–1993	12.94	12.01	0.21	0.84	0.647
1993–2007	10.19	7.79	1.14	0.27	0.900
t-test	0.40	0.58			
p-value	0.69	0.57			

( ) = negative.
Source: WITS.

for general liberalization and business cycle effects. To account for trends in country-specific demand for good i, we also try including country-product fixed effects in the regression. In addition, we run the regression using both the percentage point change in tariffs ($\Delta PREF$ and ΔMFN) and the percent change in tariffs ($\Delta \ln(1+MFN/100)$ and $\Delta \ln(1+PREF/100)$). The advantage of the percentage point change is that it puts more weight on large changes. The advantage of the percent change is that the coefficient can be interpreted as an elasticity.

Coefficient β_1 represents the quasi-elasticity or elasticity of imports from group g with respect to the preferential rate, *PREF,* for given *MFN* tariff.[13] A negative β_1 implies that, if *PREF* rises (thereby increasing the cost of imports from members and lowering the margin of preferences), imports from group g fall. We expect this to be the case when g = members, unless preferences are not being effectively used. In contrast, we expect $\beta_1 \geq 0$ when g = nonmembers, with a greater value indicating greater trade diversion effects. Coefficient β_2 represents the impact of changes in the *MFN* tariff, for given *PREF,* on changes in imports from group g. A negative β_2 implies that, if the *MFN* tariff rises (thereby increasing the cost of imports from nonmembers as well as the margin of preferences), imports from group g fall. We expect this to be the case when g = nonmembers. In contrast, an estimated β_2 of any sign is conceivable when g = members. If preferences are used for most products, $\beta_2 > 0$ for g = members is likely as a result of trade diversion. But if preferences are not effectively used, even imports from within the bloc are negatively affected by increases in the *MFN* rates.[14] In that case, $\beta_2 < 0$ for g = nonmembers as well.

Table 6.3 reports the results.[15] The first two columns show the outcomes of the regressions on tariffs in first differences. Imports from ASEAN outsiders are, as expected, negatively impacted by the members' MFN tariffs. Intra-ASEAN trade is negatively affected only by the preferential rates. Surprisingly, preferential tariffs appear also to lower imports from bloc outsiders. This is broadly consistent with some analyses that indicate that much of intra-ASEAN trade is in intermediate goods (e.g., Fouquin et al., 2006), with the implication that trade with bloc members and nonmembers is complementary.[16] Note, on the other hand, that the magnitudes are consistent with preferences in ASEAN being operative: imports from excluded countries appear to be more negatively affected by the MFN tariffs than by the preferential rates. The next two columns (3 and 4) report results with the percentage change in tariffs; the results are qualitatively similar.

Preferences may, however, be correlated with trends in country-specific demands for individual products. This would generate trends in imports; if tariffs are correlated with those trends, which is plausible, then regression (1) would be misspecified, misattributing part of the effects of such trends on trade to tariffs. To avoid this problem, we run equation (1) with country-product fixed effects. Columns 5–8 report the results. Only the statistically significant negative effect of MFN tariffs on imports from excluded countries remains intact, whether in first differences or percentage changes. Again, the results do not support evidence of significant trade diversion.

Finally, there is a danger of reverse causality if trade growth affects tariff changes. For example, an import surge could lead to higher MFN tariffs, thus leading to an upward bias in its coefficient. In the final four columns

Table 6.3
Table 3. The Effect of Tariffs on Trade

Explanatory Variables	Dependent Variables:											
	Δln M_{ROW} (1)	Δln M_{REG} (2)	Δln M_{ROW} (3)	Δln M_{REG} (4)	Δln M_{ROW} (5)	Δln M_{REG} (6)	Δln M_{ROW} (7)	Δln M_{REG} (8)	Δln M_{ROW} (9)	Δln M_{REG} (10)	Δln M_{ROW} (11)	Δln M_{REG} (12)
ΔMFN_{ijt}	-0.005***	0.001	—	—	-0.004***	0.002	—	—	-0.010***	-0.007	—	—
	[0.001]	[0.001]			[0.001]	[0.002]			[0.004]	[0.006]		
$\Delta PREF_{ijt}$	-0.003**	-0.006***	—	—	0.003	0	—	—	-0.022***	-0.049***	—	—
	[0.001]	[0.002]			[0.002]	[0.004]			[0.008]	[0.014]		
$\Delta \ln MFN_{ijt}$	—	—	-0.574***	0.203	—	—	-0.633***	0.19	—	—	-2.227***	-0.928
			[0.115]	[0.194]			[0.169]	[0.303]			[0.520]	[0.927]
$\Delta \ln PREF_{ijt}$	—	—	-0.426**	-0.925***	—	—	0.249	-0.273	—	—	-1.498	-6.520***
			[0.178]	[0.260]			[0.308]	[0.489]			[1.179]	[2.035]
Observations	65,386	51,891	53,749	42,301	65,386	51,891	53,749	42,301	46,739	37,919	36,927	29,726
R-squared	0.088	0.018	0.076	0.017	0.388	0.343	0.403	0.365	0.072	0.013	0.056	0.008
Fixed Effects:												
Country-Year	Yes	Yes	Yes	Yes	Yes	Yes	Yes	Yes	Yes	Yes	Yes	Yes
Country-Product					Yes	Yes	Yes	Yes			Yes	Yes

***Significant at 1% level
**Significant at 5% level
*Significant at 10% level

Note: Robust standard errors in brackets.

(9–12), we rerun the regressions using the lagged tariff changes as instruments for contemporaneous changes. The results point to stronger effects of tariff reductions on trade, suggesting that reverse causality is indeed a concern. Again, there is no evidence of reductions in preferential tariffs reducing trade from nonmembers.

However, to properly identify the impact of preferences in ASEAN, it is necessary to understand how those preferences affect the policies of ASEAN members toward outsiders. Members agreed on a schedule of preferential tariff reduction starting in 1992, updating and adjusting it over time. Meanwhile, most of them also cut their own MFN tariffs significantly, thus generating relatively low preferential margins. Were these large MFN tariff reductions influenced by the members' decision to liberalize preferentially? This is what we seek to answer in the next section.

5 Preferences and External Tariffs in ASEAN

We study in this section whether or how ASEAN governments altered their trade policies vis-à-vis outsiders following the introduction and deepening of preferences under AFTA. Naturally, several factors (political economy forces, currency crisis, fiscal needs, etc.) affect a country's external tariffs. We account for these factors by using a large variety of fixed effects, as in the trade regressions of the previous session. Those that are constant over time are eliminated in the regressions when we take first differences. Thus, we estimate the following regression:

$$\Delta MFN_{ijt} = \gamma_{ij} + \gamma_{jt} + \alpha \Delta PREF_{ijt} + \upsilon_{ijt}, \tag{2}$$

where γ_{ij} is a country-product fixed effect and γ_{jt} is a country-period fixed effect. Notice that, since equation (2) is specified in first-differences, these fixed effects correspond effectively to fixed trend effects, rather than fixed level effects. For robustness, we therefore report results both with and without these fixed effects. In equation (2), a positive coefficient α would support a "building blocs" view of preferential liberalization, where lower preferential tariffs are associated with lower external tariffs. In contrast, a negative α would support a "stumbling blocs" view of preferential liberalization, where lower preferential tariffs are associated with higher external tariffs.

Despite our large number of fixed (trend) effects, there may still be forces omitted in regression equation (2) that induce governments to alter both their preferential and external tariffs. This would tend to make our estimated coefficient α statistically significant, but causality would not follow from PREF to MFN. We adopt a number of strategies to check whether the results from the basic regression indeed correspond to causation.

First, we rerun (2) with lagged $\Delta PREF$. This neutralizes the effects of omitted variables that affect both MFN and PREF contemporaneously. Second, in the regression we introduce, in turn, $\Delta MFN_{ij,t-1}$ and $MFN_{ij,t-1}$, to control for autocorrelation in ΔMFN and for the fact that it is easier to lower MFN by more if it is high. Third, we replace lagged $\Delta PREF$ with the planned changes in preferential tariffs, agreed upon when AFTA was created, in 1992. Future shocks that might have affected the actual changes in $PREF$ and MFN did not play a role in the negotiation of the preferential rates in 1992 ($PREF92$), unless they were fully anticipated. Finally, we also regress ΔMFN on the lagged changes in preferential margins, defined as the difference between the MFN and the preferential rates. Notice that the interpretation of the coefficient on lagged changes in the preferential margins is different: a negative coefficient indicates tariff complementarity (a higher preferential margin induces lower MFN tariffs), while a positive coefficient suggests tariff substitutability.

Table 6.4 reports the results. All regressions indicate a strong complementarity between changes in preferential tariffs and changes in MFN rates: if the former falls, the latter falls as well. This is observed whether we look at the preferential rates directly, the planned preferential rates, or the preferential margins. In addition, the results are not sensitive to the inclusion of country-product fixed effects. The magnitudes are also economically significant, ranging from 0.24 to 0.47 for the preferential rates. This implies that a reduction of 10 percentage points in the intra-AFTA import tariff leads to a fall between 2.4 and 4.7 percentage points in the country's external tariff in the subsequent period. In the remaining regressions, to be conservative, we only report results with the full set of fixed effects.

As indicated earlier, a concern about ASEAN is that preferences may not be used if the difference between intra-ASEAN and MFN rates is not sufficiently large. If so, the economic and political channels through which intra-bloc liberalization affects governments' incentives to liberalize unilaterally against outsiders may be muted, or at least be weaker. Similarly, theory indicates that the impact of preferences on external tariffs should be more significant, the more important the intra-bloc imports are. Looking for differential effects in products where the margin of preference is meaningful, as well as where intra-bloc imports are more or less prominent, can therefore provide a finer test for our hypothesis that changes in MFN tariffs are indeed being driven by changes in preferences.

To look at these issues, we first construct the indicator variable $BIGM$, which is unity if the margin of preference is above x. We experiment with different thresholds: $x = \{2.5, 5, 7.5\}$. We then run the following regression:

$$\Delta MFN_{ijt} = \gamma_{ij} + \gamma_{jt} + \alpha \Delta PREF_{ijt-1} + \beta(\Delta PREF_{ijt-1} * BIGM_{ijt-1})$$
$$+ \rho BIGM_{ijt-1} + \upsilon_{ijt}. \tag{3}$$

Coefficient ρ tells us whether the presence of a large margin of preference has an independent impact on the changes in MFN tariffs. Coefficient β, on the interaction between $\Delta PREF$ and $BIGM$, indicates in turn whether the

Table 6.4
The Effect of Preferences on External Tariffs

Explanatory Variables	Dependent Variable: ΔMFN_{ijt}							
	(1)	(2)	(3)	(4)	(5)	(6)	(7)	(8)
$\Delta PREF_{ijt}$	0.34*** [0.01]	—	—	—	0.25*** [0.02]	—	—	—
$\Delta PREF_{ijt-1}$	—	0.33*** [0.01]	—	—	—	0.30*** [0.02]	—	—
$\Delta PREF92_{ijt-1}$	—	—	0.47*** [0.01]	—	—	—	0.28*** [0.03]	—
$\Delta MARGIN_{ijt-1}$	—	—	—	-0.24*** [0.01]	—	—	—	-0.36*** [0.01]
Observations	100,694	66,212	45,852	63,352	100,694	66,212	45,852	63,352
R-squared	0.40	0.34	0.32	0.384	0.58	0.56	0.50	0.72
Fixed Effects:								
Country-year	Yes	Yes	Yes	Yes	Yes	Yes	Yes	Yes
Country-product		Yes	Yes		Yes	Yes	Yes	Yes

*** Significant at 1% level
**Significant at 5% level
*Significant at 10% level

Note: Robust standard errors adjusted for clustering at the country-product level in brackets.

relationship between preferential and MFN tariffs is different in the presence of a large preferential margin.

Second, we define the variable *WGHT* as the share of imports coming from ASEAN members. Since this share is affected by the MFN tariffs after the introduction of AFTA, we use the share of imports from ASEAN members from the period right before AFTA came into force (1992 or the first period for which trade data are available prior to 1993). We then interact *WGHT* with *BIGM*:[17]

$$\Delta MFN_{ijt} = \gamma_{ij} + \gamma_{jt} + \alpha \Delta PREF_{ijt-1} + \beta(WGHT_{ij} * BIGM_{ijt-1}) + \upsilon_{ijt}. \tag{4}$$

This approach is analogous to that followed by Estevadeordal et al. (2008). If $\beta > 0$, it indicates that, when the margin of preference is significant, higher intra-bloc imports lead to higher external tariffs, or "tariff substitutability," whereas $\beta < 0$ reflects "tariff complementarity."

Results are displayed in table 6.5. The first three columns show the results for regression (3) for each of the considered thresholds for *BIGM*. The presence of a large margin of preference by itself induces a reduction in the MFN tariff. Furthermore, the tariff complementarity obtained in the previous regressions is considerably stronger when a large margin is present. In fact, as the first column of table 6.5 indicates, tariff complementarity vanishes for products where the preferential margin is below 2.5, confirming that margins that are too small are ineffectual. This result mirrors those obtained by Estevadeordal et al. (2008) for Latin America.

The last three columns (4–6) show the results for regression (4) for each of the three thresholds for *BIGM*. Again, we find tariff complementarity and that the presence of a large margin of preference by itself leads to reductions in the external tariff. We also observe that a higher intra-bloc share of imports is associated with reductions in the external tariffs. However, this effect is statistically significant only when the margin of preference is at least 7.5 percentage points. This result is in the same spirit as those of Estevadeordal et al. (2008) for Latin America,[18] but is quantitatively different, as there *WGHT* proved to play a role in pushing external tariffs down, even for margins that were just above 2.5 percentage points. One possible explanation for this difference is the level of aggregation. While our data for ASEAN is at the product level, the data of Estevadeordal et al.'s are much more aggregated, at the industry level (about 100 of them). Thus, the finding in the Latin America study that higher shares of intra-bloc imports drive MFN tariffs down, even for relatively small preferential margins, may be driven simply by its high level of aggregation.

Overall, our results in tables 6.4 and 6.5 provide extensive evidence that ASEAN countries dropped their MFN tariffs following reductions in preferential rates. Furthermore, our findings that this effect is stronger for goods where the margins and the (pre-agreement) share of intra-bloc imports are higher provide considerable support for a causal relationship. Still, if

Table 6.5
The Effect of Preferences on External Tariffs: High Preferential Margins and High Weights

Explanatory Variables	Dependent Variable: ΔMFN_{ijt}					
	Margin=2.5 (1)	Margin=5 (2)	Margin=7.5 (3)	Margin=2.5 (4)	Margin=5 (5)	Margin=7.5 (6)
$\Delta PREF_{ijt-1}$	-0.01	0.03**	0.07***	0.36***	0.36***	0.35***
	[0.01]	[0.01]	[0.01]	[0.02]	[0.02]	[0.02]
$\Delta PREF_{ijt-1} * BIGM_{ijt-1}$	0.36***	0.34***	0.32***	—	—	—
	[0.02]	[0.02]	[0.02]			
$BIGM_{ijt-1}$	-1.99***	-2.34***	-2.18***	-3.02***	-3.34***	-3.29***
	[0.13]	[0.15]	[0.19]	[0.17]	[0.19]	[0.21]
$WGHT_{ij} * BIGM_{ijt-1}$	—	—	—	-0.24	-0.49	-1.59**
				[0.74]	[0.75]	[0.77]
Observations	66,212	66,212	66,212	34,234	34,234	34,234
R-squared	0.58	0.59	0.58	0.55	0.55	0.55

*** Significant at 1% level
** Significant at 5% level
* Significant at 10% level

Notes: All regressions run with country-period and country-product fixed effects. Robust standard errors adjusted for clustering at the country-product level in brackets.

future changes in MFN tariffs are anticipated by the governments, their previous changes in preferential rates may simply reflect those anticipated lower MFN rates—that is, our regressions may be capturing reverse causality. Relatedly, omitted variables that affect changes in both external and (with a lag) intra-bloc tariffs may be affecting our results as well.

To address these issues, we adopt an IV approach, where we instrument actual changes in preferential tariffs with the planned ones by the original six members in 1992, as outlined in their original schedule. Moreover, we restrict the sample to period 4 (i.e., after 1998) onward. Our rationale is as follows: First, it is largely implausible that actual changes in MFN tariffs in the post-Asian crisis period were anticipated in 1992, affecting those planned changes in intra-bloc trade restrictions. The same is true for shocks that could have affected both ΔMFN and lagged $\Delta PREF$ after the Asian currency crisis. Second, while planned and actual preferential changes are clearly correlated (the correlation drops from 0.99 in period 2 to 0.34 in period 6, falling monotonically over time), one can safely argue that planned preferences in 1992 did not independently affect the willingness of governments to alter their external trade policies after the Asian crisis of 1997–1998.

We show the results for these IV regressions in the first two columns of table 6.6, where we instrument contemporaneous and lagged $\Delta PREF$ with contemporaneous and lagged $\Delta PREF92$, respectively.[19] The results reinforce our previous findings and in particular the causality mechanism: changes in preferential rates appear to have indeed caused subsequent changes in external tariffs in the same direction. Furthermore, this complementarity effect is stronger in the instrumented regressions.

Finally, in the last two columns of table 6.6 we adopt a generalized method of moments (GMM) procedure, adding lagged levels of preferential tariffs to instrument for lagged changes. In this specification, we also control for the lagged level of the MFN tariff to ensure that our results are not driven by the fact that high tariffs can be reduced more substantially. It is also instrumented with lags. The tariff complementarity results remain strong. In addition, we do find a negative coefficient on lagged MFN, suggesting that higher tariffs do tend to be reduced more.

6 Conclusion

In this chapter we study how the formation of the ASEAN Free Trade Agreement, established in 1993, has affected trade flows and trade policies vis-à-vis outsiders. AFTA provides a unique opportunity to analyze the effects of preferential trade integration, in that it involves 10 countries that have been lowering tariffs on each other's imports over time at very different paces across products. Moreover, very detailed data are available, and not only for the pace of actual preferential liberalization, but also for the members' planned schedule of liberalization at the inception of AFTA in 1992.

Table 6.6
The Effect of Preferential Tariffs on External Tariffs: IV and GMM

Explanatory Variables	Dependent Variable: ΔMFN_{ijt}			
	Method of Estimation:			
	IV(1)	IV(2)	GMM(3)	GMM(4)
$\Delta PREF_{ijt}$	0.77***	–	1.55***	–
	[0.04]		[0.03]	
$\Delta PREF_{ijt-1}$	–	0.54***	–	1.00***
		[0.02]		[0.03]
ΔMFN_{ijt-1}	–	–	−0.11***	−0.32***
			[0.01]	[0.01]
Observations	45,916	45,852	67,415	70,834
R-squared	0.05	0.10		

***Significant at 1% level
**Significant at 5% level
*Significant at 10% level

Notes: All regressions run with country-period and country-product fixed effects (demeaned in the IV regressions). Robust standard errors adjusted for clustering at the country-product level in brackets.

We find that AFTA has been broadly benign, in the sense that it does not seem to be promoting trade within the bloc at the expense of trade with nonmembers. Furthermore, we find strong evidence that AFTA members have been responding to lower internal tariffs by also reducing their tariffs on imports from outsiders. In this sense, AFTA has been clearly beneficial for the promotion of freer world trade.

These findings corroborate those of Estevadeordal et al. (2008) for Latin America, and to a lesser extent those of Lendle (2007) for some ASEAN members, reinforcing the view that regionalism promotes external liberalization and can be viewed as a "building bloc" toward free trade. On the other hand, our findings contrast sharply with those of Limão (2006) and Karacaovali and Limão (2008) for the US and the EU, which imply that regionalism constitutes a brake on external liberalization and should be regarded instead as a "stumbling bloc" to global free trade.

Why do we have such discrepant results across studies and trading blocs? While we cannot know for sure, one factor indeed that is very likely behind these divergent results is the stark difference between the countries analyzed in those studies. Since the multilateral system has not enforced much tariff reduction on developing countries, tariffs are relatively high there, creating a large potential for trade diversion. Lower external tariffs moderate that loss. The results of Estevadeordal et al. (2008) and of this study suggest that this force is important in explaining changes in MFN tariffs of developing countries involved in free trade areas. In contrast, Limão (2006) and Karacaovali and Limão (2008) focus on industrial countries. Tariffs were already quite low in the US and the EU at the onset of the Uruguay Round, which reduces the importance of this channel. In addition, the theoretical underpinnings that Limão uses to justify the importance of preferences in North-South agreements rely on regional blocs being formed for non-economic reasons—preferential treatment given in exchange for non-economic benefits, such as cooperation on migration, drug trafficking, or a global political agenda. This is not the case in South-South trade agreements, including AFTA, where the main goal is to exchange market access. Further research to confirm or disprove these presumptions would be very welcome.

Notes

1. Tariffs on outsiders may be constrained by WTO requirements, however.
2. Lee and Park (2005) develop a similar analysis, also predicting significant trade creation but no trade diversion from the formation of Asian RTAs, including the expansion of AFTA to incorporate the People's Republic of China, Japan and the Republic of Korea.
3. In a more structural approach, Krishna (2003) estimates trade diversion and trade creation in 24 hypothetical bilateral trade agreements, finding that in 80% of the cases, trade creation outweighs trade diversion. Furthermore, Baier and Bergstrand (2007) show that, if one takes into account the endogeneity in the formation of trading blocs, the trade impact of RTAs is much larger than conventional estimates suggest.
4. In CUs, unlike in FTAs, members are required to align their external tariffs. This can lead to very different tariff-setting behavior, as Estevadeordal et al. (2008) confirm to be the case for Latin America's trading blocs.
5. For example, agricultural goods were incorporated only in the early 2000s to the schedules. See Lendle (2007) for a brief description of those changes and http://www.aseansec.org/4920.htm for details.
6. Some significant changes in the liberalization trends can be observed in figures 6.2.1 and 6.2.2, which we discuss later.
7. On certain occasions, MFN rates have actually dropped below the preferential rates for AFTA members; see, for instance, Ando (2007). Naturally, preferences become redundant in those cases, and AFTA exporters simply use the prevailing MFN rate. Accordingly, in our empirical analysis we set the preferential tariffs to the level of their MFN counterparts when we observe such discrepancies.
8. We thank Fukunari Kimura for pointing this out.
9. NTBs are likely to weaken the relationship between preferential and MFN tariffs. For example, a large preferential margin may be innocuous in the presence of NTBs on intra-ASEAN trade, therefore having no effect on the governments' incentives to alter external tariffs. Similarly, if the NTBs are on non-ASEAN imports, MFN tariffs become less important, and governments may not bother to change them despite sizable preferential margins. Duty drawbacks

      may work in the opposite direction. As Cadot et al. (2003) show theoretically and confirm for MERCOSUR, duty drawbacks provide an additional reason for external tariffs to fall after the formation of a regional trading bloc.

10. We thank the ADB for very helpful assistance in obtaining the data.

11. Trade data for the four late entrants are available only for recent years.

12. The important exception is 1997, where trade flows fell significantly. That drop was largely unrelated to AFTA, however, reflecting instead the Asian currency crisis. In fact, in that year imports fell for members and nonmembers alike.

13. Notice that we look at the effect on $\ln(1+PREF/100)$ on $\ln(M)$. Thus, β_1 tells us how much M changes, in percentage terms, when $(1+PREF/100)$ increases by 1%. Since $PREF/100$ is in general small relative to unity, a 1% change in $(1+PREF/100)$ can be approximated by a one percentage point change in $PREF$. Similar interpretation applies to β_2.

14. A typical concern among ASEAN analysts is indeed that preferential margins have become too small in most sectors to have a practical effect. After all, eligibility for the preferential rate requires complying with complex rules of origin, which often imply large administrative costs. If the margin of preference is too low, it will then be best to simply use the MFN rate to avoid incurring such an administrative burden. Several scholars (for example, Baldwin, 2006) have indeed claimed that the utilization rates are very low in ASEAN, around just 5% to 10%. Manchin and Pelkmans-Balaoing (2008) note, however, that it is unclear what the primary source of this information is, since the ASEAN Secretariat does not publish information about utilization rates. Still, since a significant fraction of the preferential margins indeed seem too low to be useful, the preferential system under AFTA may have little practical importance for the trade flows in the region. In fact, Manchin and Pelkmans-Balaoing (2008) find that preferences have a positive effect on intra-bloc trade only when the preferential margins are very high—over 25 percentage points.

15. In these and the subsequent regressions, we use robust standard errors and cluster observations at the country-product level.

16. The negative effect of each tariff on imports from both bloc insiders and outsiders may also reflect income effects, in addition to the substitution effects they are designed to capture. We thank Warwick McKibbin for this observation.

17. Notice that, since $WGHT$ does not vary overtime, its independent effect is fully absorbed by the fixed effect γ_{ij}.

18. This result is related also to the findings of Manchin and Pelkmans-Balaoing (2008) that preferences affect intra-ASEAN trade only if the preferential margin is very high—in their case above 25 percentage points.

19. First-stage results, omitted, confirm the strong correlation between $\Delta PREF$ post-period 3 and $\Delta PREF92$.

References

Ando, M. 2007. Impacts of Japanese FTAs/EPAs: Preliminary Post Evaluation. *The International Economy*. 11. pp. 57–83.

Bagwell, K., and R. Staiger. 1999. Regionalism and Multilateral Tariff Cooperation. In J. Piggott, and A. Woodland, eds. *International Trade Policy and the Pacific Rim*. London: MacMillan.

Bagwell, K., and R. Staiger. 2004. Multilateral Trade Negotiations, Bilateral Opportunism and the Rules of GATT/WTO. *Journal of International Economics.* 63(1). pp. 1–29.

Baier, S., and J. Bergstrand. 2007. Do Free Trade Agreements Actually Increase Members' International Trade? *Journal of International Economics.* 71(1). pp. 72–95.

Baldwin, R. 2006. Managing the Noodle Bowl: The Fragility of East Asian Regionalism. *Centre for Economic and Policy Research (CEPR) Discussion Paper* 5561.

Bhagwati, J., and A. Panagariya. 1999. Preferential Trading Areas and Multilateralism: Strangers, Friends or Foes? In Panagariya, A., ed. *Regionalism in Trade Policy: Essays on Preferential Trading.* Singapore: World Scientific.

Bohara, A., K. Gawande, and P. Sanguinetti. 2004. Trade Diversion and Declining Tariffs: Evidence from Mercosur. *Journal of International Economics.* 64(1). pp. 65–88.

Bond, E., R. Riezman, and C. Syropoulos. 2004. A Strategic and Welfare Theoretic Analysis of Free Trade Areas. *Journal of International Economics.* 64(1). pp. 1–27.

Cadot, O., J. de Melo, and M. Olarreaga. 2003. The Protectionist Bias of Duty Drawbacks: Evidence from Mercosur. *Journal of International Economics.* 59(1). pp. 161–182.

Chang, W., and A. Winters. 2002. How Regional Blocs Affect Excluded Countries: The Price Effects of Mercosur. *American Economic Review.* 92(4). pp. 889–904.

Clausing, K. 2001. Trade Creation and Trade Diversion in the Canada–United States Free Trade Agreement. *Canadian Journal of Economics.* 34(3). pp. 677–696.

Estevadeordal, A., C. Freund, and E. Ornelas. 2008. Does Regionalism Affect Trade Liberalization towards Nonmembers? *Quarterly Journal of Economics.* 123(4). pp. 1531–1575.

Fouquin, M., D. Hiratsuka, and F. Kimuara. 2006. Introduction: East Asia's De Facto Economic Integration. In D. Hiratsuka, ed. *East Asia's De Facto Economic Integration.* New York: Palgrave Macmillan.

Frankel, J. 1997. *Regional Trade Blocs in the World Economic System.* Washington DC: Institute for International Economics.

Freund, C. 2000. Multilateralism and the Endogenous Formation of Preferential Trade Agreements. *Journal of International Economics.* 52(2). pp. 359–376.

Karacaovali, B., and N. Limão. 2008. The Clash of Liberalizations: Preferential *vs.* Multilateral Trade Liberalization in the European Union. *Journal of International Economics.* 74(2). pp. 299–327.

Krishna, P. 2003. Are Regional Trading Partners Natural? *Journal of Political Economy.* 111(1). pp. 202–226.

Lee, J-W., and I. Park. 2005. Free Trade Areas in East Asia: Discriminatory or Non-Discriminatory? *World Economy.* 28(1). pp. 21–48.

Lee, J-W., and K. Shin. 2006. Does Regionalism Lead to More Global Trade Integration in East Asia? *North American Journal of Economics and Finance.* 17(3). pp. 283–301.

Lendle, A. 2007. The ASEAN Free Trade Agreement: Building Block or Stumbling Block for Multilateral Trade Liberalization? *National Centre of Competence in Research (NCCR) Trade Working Paper* 2007/33.

Limão, N. 2006. Preferential Trade Agreements as Stumbling Blocks for Multilateral Trade Liberalization: Evidence for the US. *American Economic Review.* 96(3). pp. 896–914.

Manchin, M., and A. Pelkmans-Balaoing. 2008. Clothes without an Emperor: Analysis of the Preferential Tariffs in ASEAN. *Journal of Asian Economics*. 19(3). pp. 213–223.

Ornelas, E. 2005a. Trade Creating Free Trade Areas and the Undermining of Multilateralism. *European Economic Review*. 49(7). pp. 1717–1735.

Ornelas, E. 2005b. Endogenous Free Trade Agreements and the Multilateral Trading System. *Journal of International Economics*. 67(2). pp. 471–497.

Panagariya, A., and R. Findlay. 1996. A Political-Economy Analysis of Free-Trade Areas and Customs Unions. In R. Feenstra, G. Grossman, and D. Irwin, eds. *The Political Economy of Trade Reform: Essays in Honor of J. Bhagwati*. Cambridge: MIT Press.

Richardson, M. 1993. Endogenous Protection and Trade Diversion. *Journal of International Economics*. 34(3–4). pp. 309–324.

Viner, J. 1950. *The Customs Union Issue*. New York: Carnegie Endowment for International Peace.

7

Economic Integration in
Remote Resource-Rich Regions

Anthony J. Venables

This study was prepared for the Asian Development Bank and Hong Kong Institute for Monetary Research (ADB-HKIMR) workshop "Quantifying the Costs and Benefits of Regional Economic Integration." The work was also supported by the BP-funded Centre for the Analysis of Resource Rich Economies (OxCarre), Department of Economics, University of Oxford. Thanks to participants in the project conference and colleagues in OxCarre for valuable comments.

1 Introduction

Regional integration in Asia frequently focuses on the development of production networks and the linking of economies that are growing fast on the basis of exports of manufactures; but there is another Asian region containing economies with quite different characteristics. Central Asia contains countries that are landlocked and are, in some cases, rich in natural resources. The opportunities facing these countries are different from those facing East or South Asia, yet this region too is seeking to develop regional integration. Countries in the region are members of the Commonwealth of Independent States (CIS) Free Trade Agreement; and Kazakhstan, the Kyrgyz Republic, Tajikistan, and Uzbekistan are also members of the Eurasian Economic Community (EAEC). The integration process is also being driven forward by the Central Asia Regional Economic Cooperation (CAREC), which seeks to promote cross-border activities particularly in the areas of transportation, trade policy and trade facilitation, and energy. It currently has eight members: Afghanistan, Azerbaijan, Kazakhstan, the Kyrgyz Republic, Mongolia, Tajikistan, Uzbekistan, and the People's Republic of China (PRC), focusing on the Xinjiang Uygur Autonomous Region.

The characteristics of these countries raise issues for the analysis of economic integration that have received relatively little attention in the literature. The countries are remote, landlocked, with a restricted set of opportunities for engagement with the world economy, and little chance of following a manufacturing export route to economic development. At the same time, resource abundance ensures a flow of foreign exchange to the region, although it is uneven across countries and volatile over time. These circumstances make it natural to think that regional integration might be particularly valuable, but the debate on "natural trading partners" alerts us to the dangers of such thinking. Policy formulation needs to focus not on existing trade patterns, but on the alterations to trade flows that will be caused by policy change.

This chapter starts by sketching some of the key features of the region. It then highlights those features that are most important for trade policy formulation and undertakes some economic modeling to draw out their implications. The analysis is intended to offer some insights not just for Central Asia, but also for trade policy and regional integration in other remote resource-rich regions, for example, in the Common Market for Eastern and Southern Africa and in the proposals for deeper integration in the East African Community. Our results show that the effects of preferential and nonpreferential liberalization are quite different, with the former tending to benefit resource-poor countries in the region, and the latter benefiting countries that are resource-rich. Integration is therefore a powerful tool for spreading the benefits of resource wealth within the region, although it creates incentives for resource-poor countries to resist regional liberalization with the rest of the world.

2 Regional Characteristics

The remoteness of the landlocked Central Asian region is apparent, and the economic scale of this can be calculated in various ways. The World Bank's "Doing Business" database ranks six of the CAREC members (all except Mongolia and the PRC) in the bottom 10 of 181 countries for its "trade across borders" measure.[1] This is a composite of time taken, documents required, and direct costs of shipment; the average costs of importing a container to these six countries is around $3,000, compared to less than $1,000 in the East Asian and Pacific region and $450 for Singapore. The costs of shipping a container from the East Coast of the United States to Tajikistan reach $9,000, the leg from Georgia to Tajikistan accounting for two-thirds of this. By one estimate (World Bank, 2004) trade logistics costs amount to 23% of the value of Tajikistan's external trade and, including domestic movement of goods, total logistics costs amount to 27% of gross domestic product (GDP).

Economic geographers approach the problem by calculating measures of market access. The "foreign market potential" of a country, developed by Redding and Venables (2004), is a micro-founded way of measuring market access, and can be calculated from trade data and gravity modeling. Recent calculations by Mayer (2008) establish that, in a ranking of 196 countries (including a lot of small island states), six of the countries in the region rank in the range 131 (Kyrgyz Republic) to 168 (Uzbekistan).[2] The market potential of these countries is comparable to that of Uganda or Zambia, around six times less that of Malaysia or the Republic of Korea (Korea), or 90 times less that of Belgium, the top-ranked country. This means that if Tajikistan were—with its current endowments—relocated to Belgium, its exports would be 90 times their current level. Not only are the regional economies remote from external markets, they are also sparsely populated and generally lack good internal communications infrastructure.

A further way of seeing the impact of remoteness is to look at relative prices of commodities within the region. Table 7.1 gives these prices for

Table 7.1
Relative Prices in the Region

Category	Azerbaijan	Tajikistan
Food and non-alcoholic beverages	0.29	0.52
Alcoholic, beverages and tobacco	0.01	0.19
Clothing and footwear	0.59	0.88
Housing, water, electricity, gas and other fuels	−1.32	−1.60
Furnishings, household equipment and household maintenance	0.37	0.67
Health	−0.84	−1.24
Transport	0.03	0.47
Communications	0.46	0.71
Recreation and culture	−0.06	−0.17
Education	−1.34	−1.92
Restaurants and hotels	0.12	0.47
Miscellaneous goods and services	−0.18	−0.26
Collective consumption expenditure by government	−0.07	−0.50
Machinery and equipment	0.82	1.08
Construction	0.40	0.81
Other products	0.50	0.83

Note: The above figures are log deviations from world average prices, and are based on the price level indices of the *2005 International Comparison Program* (World Bank, 2008).

two countries, Azerbaijan and Tajikistan. The figures give log deviations from world average prices, and are based on the price-level indices of the *2005 International Comparison Program* (World Bank, 2008). For example, a positive deviation of 0.8 means that the price of machinery and equipment (relative to GDP) in Azerbaijan is 123% ($=100(e^{0.8} - 1)$) higher than it is on average in the world. Table 7.1 indicates the extremely high prices of tradable goods, such as machinery and equipment, clothing and footwear, transportation, and communications relative to nontraded goods, in particular services such as education, health, and utilities.

Despite, or perhaps because of, this natural protection, tariff barriers in the region are low (Figure 7.1). This reflects membership in the CIS free trade area and of the EAEC, although researchers point to the presence of nontariff (but manmade) barriers associated with customs clearance, transit fees, complicated systems of trade permits, "unofficial payments," and limited progress towards installation of modern information systems.

The second outstanding feature of the region is its resource wealth, as summarized in table 7.2. For Azerbaijan, Kazakhstan, and Mongolia, hydrocarbon and minerals account for more than 50% of exports and, in the case of oil and gas (Azerbaijan and Kazakhstan), more than 25% of fiscal revenue. The exports of Azerbaijan and Kazakhstan nearly quadrupled in value between 1999 and 2004, and these countries have had major resources and associated construction booms. However, the distribution of this resource wealth is uneven. Afghanistan, Tajikistan, Uzbekistan, and Xinjiang Uygur Autonomous Region have much lower levels of natural resource wealth; and the exports of the Kyrgyz Republic, Tajikistan, and Uzbekistan increased by less than 50% over the period 1999–2004.

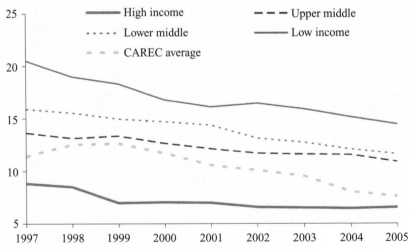

Figure 7.1 Trends in Import Tariffs: CAREC and Other Country Groupings
Source: IMF Trade Policy Database. Unweighted average import tariffs.

Table 7.2
Mineral Wealth of CAREC Countries

Country	Resource	Government Mineral/Hydrocarbon Revenues, 2000–2005		Mineral/Hydrocarbon Exports, 2000–2005		Population, 2005	GDP (PPP), 2005
		% Fiscal Revenue	% GDP	% Exports	% GDP	(million)	($ billion)
Afghanistan						32.7	35
Azerbaijan	Oil/gas	33.3	8.5	87.3	36.1	8.2	65
Kazakhstan	Oil/gas	25.1	6.3	52.6	24.1	15.3	168
Kyrgyz Republic	Gold	1.7	0.3	39.1	12.5	5.4	11
Mongolia	Copper/gold	8.2	2.9	51.2	26.3	3.0	9
Tajikistan						7.2	12
Uzbekistan	Oil/gas					27.3	64
	Gold			29.8	8.6		
Turkmenistan[a]	Oil/gas	43.2	8.7	83.5	28.7	5.2	27

Notes: CAREC = Central Asia Regional Economic Cooperation.

[a] Applicant for CAREC membership.

Sources: IMF *Guide on Resource Revenue Transparency* (2007), CIA *World Factbook.*

The overall implications of these facts for the region's trade have been studied by a number of authors, including Asian Development Bank (2006), Grafe et al. (2005), Grigoriou (2007), and Raballand (2003). Points made are: intra-regional trade is high relative to extra-regional trade; extra-regional exports are dominated by primary commodities, with natural resources taking a very large share; and equipment and capital goods account for a high share of imports from outside the region.

3 Trade Policy for Remote-Rich Economies

How do the features that we have sketched above shape trade and trade policy? The characteristics we have described dictate a number of issues that need to be put at the center of analysis of integration in the region.

3.1 Low Supply Response of External Exports

The first point is that both resource dependence and remoteness make it difficult to export non-resource based items outside the region. This means that the quantity response of exports to changes in trade policy is likely to be extremely small; the equilibrium elasticity of export volumes with respect to domestic costs will be low.

One reason for this is that natural resource exports are based on a fixed factor, so expanding supply faces sharply diminishing returns. Trade policy can be used to change the domestic price of imports and domestic goods and services (including labor and other inputs) relative to the price of oil or gold. But since local costs are a relatively small share of the value of such products, these changes in relative prices are unlikely to have much effect on the supply of oil or gold. This may apply most acutely to mineral and hydrocarbon exports, but also applies to agricultural products, the output of which is constrained by a sector-specific factor.

Another reason for the low responsiveness of export volumes to trade policy stems from remoteness and high trade costs. The coastal regions in developing Asia have attracted footloose export-oriented manufactures, and for these goods there is the possibility that small changes in trade policy and in competitiveness may lead to extremely large changes in the volume of exports. However, for Central Asia, remoteness means that the region is not on the cusp of an explosion of manufacturing exports. This constraint is further exacerbated by the large presence of resource exports that tend to raise the real exchange rate and create a "Dutch disease" problem for other exports. The combination of remoteness and resources therefore means that the region is left with a narrow base of inelastically supplied resource-based exports.

3.2 The Distribution of Natural Resources

The second point is that the supply of natural resources is unevenly distributed among the countries. This has implications for equity, and also

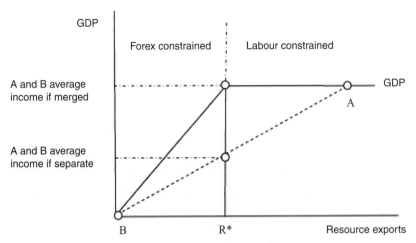

Figure 7.2 Income Loss from Uneven Distribution of Resources

for economic efficiency. Since the economic impact of resource revenues is likely to be subject to diminishing returns, their unequal distribution leads to an efficiency loss. A simple example makes the point. Suppose that every country consumes and produces a single nontradable good. Production of the good uses foreign exchange (imported oil or equipment) and domestic labor in fixed proportions. The only source of foreign exchange is resource revenues, and labor is in fixed supply. Real income in such an economy is illustrated in figure 7.2, in which resource revenue is measured on the horizontal axis. If resource exports are less than R^*, then production is foreign exchange constrained, and real income is given by the upward sloping section of the line (with slope equal to the foreign exchange content per unit GDP). If natural resource earnings are greater than R^*, then the economy is labor constrained, thus fixing income; further resource earnings beyond this point are simply accumulated as foreign assets. As a simplest case, suppose that one economy has no resource revenue (so is at point B) and another has resource revenue and is at point A. Average income—of the two separate countries—is the midpoint between A and B. Merger of the two economies would exactly double income, as illustrated.

This is an extreme example but serves to highlight some points. First, the resource-abundant country has run into diminishing returns in its ability to use resource revenues. In the example of figure 7.2, this economy has hit full employment, so no more labor is available to produce further income. The argument applies not just to labor, but to a range of inelastically supplied nontradable goods and services. For example, a resource boom often leads to inflation in the construction sector as supply bottlenecks are encountered. Spending bids up the price of these inputs and services but does not buy additional real services. More generally, spending from resource revenues will be met by a combination of increased output and crowding out of other expenditures. What are the expenditures that are crowded out? It may be exports, thus giving rise to the Dutch disease. Alternatively, monetary and exchange rate policy might be used to mitigate this problem, in which case crowding out will affect domestic activities, quite likely investment. If these activities are particularly valuable (as they would be if they are initially operating at a sub-optimal level) then crowding them out may actually reduce income.

The economy without resources exhibits the opposite characteristics. The wage is low, particularly relative to the price of imports, including imported capital equipment and inputs to production. Low wages might be expected to translate into a competitive position in other activities, but there are two obstacles to this. One is the need to use expensive imported inputs and capital equipment in production. And the other relates back to the remoteness of these economies. We argued above that low prices of nontraded inputs are unlikely to lead to a significant quantity response in the exports of landlocked Central Asian economies.

The logic of figure 7.2 seems to present a compelling case for regional integration. Simply merging the two economies has the effect of doubling income. Regional trade should mean that the resource-poor country can increase its foreign exchange earnings, while the resource-rich country can import goods that were previously supply constrained. However, we will show that it is likely that the distribution of gains between countries will be highly unequal. This creates real problems of undertaking integration in a region with these characteristics.

3.3 Regionally and Globally Traded Goods

The final point concerns the dichotomy between tradable and nontradable goods. We have argued that the set of goods that can be exported outside the region is quite small, but a much larger set may be traded within the region, where transport costs are lower. Similarly, on the import side, trade costs make the import of some goods from the rest of the world extremely expensive, although regional trade can substitute for some goods. Study of regional integration therefore requires that we distinguish between "globally traded" goods and "regionally traded" goods (as well as nontraded goods or factors). It is important that this is not an exogenously fixed distinction, but one that is set by barriers to trade—real trade costs, and also tariff and other trade barriers. In the model that follows, the division of products into globally and regionally traded goods will emerge endogenously from a continuum of goods facing different transport costs and tariffs.

The presence of an endogenously determined set of regionally traded goods has two important implications for trade policy. The first is that the terms of trade for these goods is endogenous. Even though the countries under study are price-takers on world markets, trade policy will change the price of regionally traded goods. This is a mechanism for distributing real income between countries in the region, and we will see that it is crucial in determining the international distribution of the effects of trade policy. The second implication concerns the analysis of trade creation and diversion in a regional integration scheme. The changing sets of goods produced domestically, imported from the region, or imported from the rest of the world provide an insightful way of capturing the trade creating and diverting effects of policy.

4 A Benchmark Model

The region we focus on contains two economies, A and B, each endowed with a fixed and equal quantity of labor, L, and with natural resources. These natural resources are the only exports to the rest of the world (i.e., outside the region) and are in fixed supply. The values of these exports are denoted N_A, N_B, and the only difference between the two countries—the only source of comparative advantage—is that country A has more of these exports than does country B, $N_A > N_B$. Clearly, fixing external exports is a strong assumption, but it serves the purpose of capturing the implications of unequal resource wealth and remoteness for the responsiveness of exports that we outlined above.

In addition to their natural resources, countries A and B produce and consume goods from a continuum of sectors, indexed by $z \epsilon [0, 1]$. For simplicity, we assume that all these sectors have identical technologies, using an imported intermediate good and labor. They have Cobb-Douglas technology with intermediate share μ, so the unit cost of output produced in country i is:

$$p_i(z) = w_i^{(1-\mu)} v^\mu, i = A, B, \tag{1}$$

where w_i is the wage and v the price of the imported intermediate. We take the world price of this intermediate as the numeraire and assume that it faces no tariff, so $v = 1$.

As well as being produced domestically, each good z can also be imported from the rest of the world with import price $q(z)$, strictly increasing in z. This variation with z can be thought of as capturing the different levels of transport costs for each good and, for simplicity, we set $q(z) = 1 + \alpha z$. In addition to importing from the rest of the world, goods may be traded intra-regionally, trade which faces transport costs but at a lower rate than external trade. The unit cost of importing a good from the partner country is then $r_i(z) = p_j(z)(1 + \beta z)$, $i, j = A, B, i \neq j$. External and internal trades face *ad valorem* tariffs at rates τ and t respectively, so consumer prices in country i are: for domestically produced goods, $p_i(z)$; for imports from the partner country, $p_j(z)(1 + t)(1 + \beta z)$; and for imports from the rest of the world, $(1 + \tau)(1 + \alpha z)$.

This structure gives an endogenous division of goods into a set that are nontraded; a set that are traded intra-regionally; and those goods that are

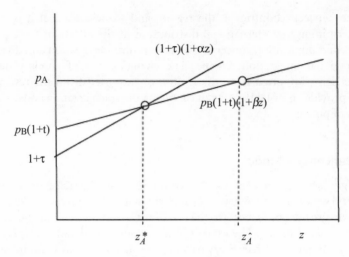

Figure 7.3.1 Market Division in Country A

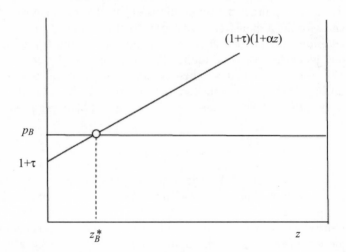

Figure 7.3.2 Market Division in Country B

imported from the rest of the world. Before turning to the general equilibrium of the model, we illustrate how this works, given values of prices, transport costs, and tariffs in each country. Figures 7.3.1 and 7.3.2 depict outcomes for country A and B, respectively. We draw the figures with $p_A > p_B$, a property that will surely be true in equilibrium with resource endowments $N_A > N_B$. These inequalities mean that resource-poor country B will import from the rest of the world, but not from country A. Resource-rich country A, in contrast, will import both from B and from the rest of the world. We look at country B, the lower panel, first.

The horizontal axis is the continuum of products, and the vertical axis the price of supply from different sources. The unit cost of domestic production is p_B, while imports from the rest of the world have unit cost $(1 + \alpha z)$ and tariff inclusive price $(1 + \tau)(1 + \alpha z)$, as illustrated by the upward sloping line. The economy imports goods with the lowest consumer price, so it imports a range of low transport cost goods, $z \epsilon [0, z_B^*]$, and supplies the rest from domestic production, $z \epsilon [z_B^*, 1]$. The dividing value is given by:

$$z_B^* = \frac{1}{\alpha} \left\{ \frac{p_B}{1 + \tau} - 1 \right\}. \tag{2}$$

For country A there may also be a range of products for which imports from the partner are cheapest. The tariff inclusive price of such products is $p_B(1 + t)(1 + \beta z)$, giving the flatter of the upward sloping lines in figure 7.3.1. In the situation illustrated, the goods with the lowest transport costs are imported from the rest of the world, $z \epsilon [0, z_A^*]$. Those with intermediate transport costs are imported from the partner country, $z \epsilon [z_A^*, z_A^\wedge]$, and domestic production supplies the remainder. The two critical values are given by:

$$z_A^* = \frac{(1 + \tau) - p_B(1 + t)}{\beta p_B(1 + t) - \alpha(1 + \tau)}, \tag{3}$$

$$z_A^\wedge = \frac{1}{\beta} \left\{ \frac{p_A}{p_B(1 + t)} - 1 \right\}. \tag{4}$$

The trade policy changes that we will explore operate by shifting these lines, thus changing the sources of supply to each market, which in turn will change demand for labor, wages, and prices. We now turn to closing the general equilibrium of the model to capture these price effects.

Consumers in each country have fixed coefficient preferences over the continuum of goods, $z \epsilon [0, 1]$ consuming an equal quantity of all goods, regardless of relative prices. We denote the equilibrium consumption of each product in each country by x_A, x_B. Given the production technology, labor market clearing is:

$$w_A L_A = (1 - \mu)(1 - z_A^\wedge) p_A x_A, \tag{5}$$

$$w_B L_B = (1 - \mu) p_B \left[x_B(1 - z_B^*) + x_A \int_{z_A^*}^{z_A^\wedge} (1 + \beta s) ds \right]. \tag{6}$$

In the first of these equations, the value of domestic output is $(1 - z_A^\wedge) p_A x_A$ and fraction $(1 - \mu)$ goes to labor rather than to imported intermediate goods. In the second, equation (6), demand for country B labor additionally comes from its exports to A, as captured by the integral of products in the interval $z \epsilon [z_A^*, z_A^\wedge]$. Notice also that trade costs are "iceberg"—they use up the good being shipped, thereby creating a demand for labor.

Finally, we have goods market clearing. Given the structure of preferences, this can be written simply using the budget constraint. We assume that all tariff revenue is distributed in a lump sum manner to consumers, so the budget constraint can be expressed as the equality of the value of imports to foreign exchange earnings,

$$x_A\left[\int_0^{z_A^*}(1+\alpha s)ds+p_B\int_{z_A^*}^{z_{\hat{A}}}(1+\beta s)ds\right]+\mu x_A p_A(1-z_{\hat{A}})=N_A \tag{7}$$

$$x_B\left[\int_0^{z_B^*}(1+\alpha s)ds+\mu p_B\left(1-z_B^*\right)\right]=N_B+(1-\mu)x_A p_B\int_{z_A^*}^{z_{\hat{A}}}(1+\beta s)ds. \tag{8}$$

For country A, foreign exchange earnings are simply the resource revenue, N_A. Imports are quantity x_A of each product imported times the unit cost, which depends on the source and on transport costs, as in the integrals. Additionally, the country has to import intermediate goods the value of which is fraction μ of the value of output. For country B, imports come only from one source, the rest of the world (products $z\epsilon[0, z_B^*]$ and intermediates $\mu p_B x_B$), but foreign exchange is earned on exports to A, (products $z\epsilon[z_A^*, z_{\hat{A}}]$, expressed net of imported intermediates), the final term in equation (8), as well as resource exports.

Equations (1)–(8) fully characterize equilibrium, giving prices, wages, consumption levels, and the three market-source dividing values, z_A^*, $z_{\hat{A}}$ and z_B^*. Notice also that the levels of consumption, x_A, x_B, can be used as the real income or utility index for each country. To develop intuition, it is helpful to think first about how resource wealth—an increase in N_A—will affect equilibrium. By raising demand in country A, this increase will raise consumption, x_A (equation [7]) and hence labor demand, wages, and prices (equation [5] with [1]). The increase in p_A makes imports from the partner country more competitive, increasing the range of products imported, $z_{\hat{A}}$ (as well as the quantity of each), as is clear from figure 7.3.1. This is the mechanism through which resource wealth in one country is transmitted to its neighbors; namely, through an increase in the range and quantity of locally traded goods. This extra foreign exchange accruing to country B raises income and x_B (equation [8]), thereby increasing wages and prices in country B (equation [6] with [1]). An increase in the p_B affects both figures 7.3.1 and 7.3.2, making imports from the rest of the world more competitive, thus raising z_A^* and z_B^* and the set of products imported.

5 Trade Liberalizations

5.1 Trade Policy and the Intra-Regional Terms of Trade

We start by drawing out some results about the quite different effects of reductions in external (τ) and internal tariff (t) on the terms of trade between the two economies. External trade liberalization will generally worsen the terms of trade of the resource-scarce country, while internal liberalization will improve its terms of trade (and conversely for the resource-rich country).

The point of reference is to consider the case in which traded goods are not used in domestic production, so $\mu = 0$. If we look just at equations (1)–(6) (or at figures 7.3.1 and 7.3.2) then it is apparent that a reduction in the external tariff, $(1 + \tau)$, if matched with an equal proportionate reduction in domestic prices p_A and p_B, will leave the division of markets, z_A^*, $z_{\hat{A}}$, and z_B^* unchanged. Can these changes be the full equilibrium response to the tariff reduction? With $\mu = 0$, remaining equilibrium conditions (goods market clearing) are:

$$x_A \left[\int_0^{z_A^*} (1 + \alpha s)ds + p_B \int_{z_A^*}^{z_{\hat{A}}} (1 + \beta s)ds \right] = N_A \qquad (7')$$

$$x_B \int_0^{z_B^*} (1 + \alpha s)ds = N_B + p_B x_A \int_{z_A^*}^{z_{\hat{A}}} (1 + \beta s)ds. \qquad (8')$$

Evidently, if there is no internal trade, that is $z_A^* = z_{\hat{A}}$, and if changes in $(1+\tau)$, p_A and p_B leave z_A^*, $z_{\hat{A}}$, and z_B^* constant, then these equations are unaffected. The change in the external tariff then has no real effect, leaving the pattern of production, trade, and consumption (x_A and x_B) unchanged.

This is an application of a result established in a more general model by Collier and Venables (2010). They show that, in a resource-rich economy with inelastic export supply, an import tariff has no real effect apart from shifting revenues between recipients of resource rents and trade taxes. So, for example, a tariff reduction simply shifts resource revenues from the government's tariff revenue account to its resource revenue account. The reason is that the demand for imports has to be held constant, given fixed foreign exchange earnings, and this means that a tariff reduction must be matched by an equal proportion reduction in domestic prices. Real wages are unchanged, tariff revenue falls, but the domestic purchasing power of resource rents is increased. (The argument may alternatively be seen by Lerner symmetry, the equivalence of import tariffs and export taxes. An export tax is fully shifted to the owners of the resource, so it redistributes rent but has no effect on relative prices or on any quantities). As we saw above, the effect applies in this model under the assumptions that $\mu = 0$ and that there is no intra-regional trade (or alternatively, if we were to collapse the model down to a single country).

With this as the benchmark, what is the effect of the reduction in $(1 + \tau)$ when there is intra-regional trade? Since this trade takes the form of exports from the resource-poor to the resource-rich, the reduction in p_B is a terms of trade loss for the resource-poor economy. Its real income effects are obvious, and seen clearly from equations (7') and (8'); a reduction in p_B must be associated with an increase in x_A and fall in x_B. In line with Collier and Venables (2008), a reduction in the tariff redistributes real income toward resource owners, here the resource-rich country. Of course these changes in x_A and x_B cause further changes for equilibrium to be restored (as they must, see equations [5] and [6]), and we examine the full changes in more detail below. But these changes will not reverse the terms of trade effect outlined above.

Can a similar argument be made for a change in the internal tariff, t? The argument is less clear cut, but it is apparent that the effect must be in the opposite direction. There is no direct effect on the division of market A if a reduction in $(1 + t)$ is met by an equi-proportionate increase in p_B. By inspection of equations (3) and (4) we see (holding market shares constant) that changes in $(1 + \tau)$ and in $(1 + t)$ have opposite effects on p_B, the intra-regional terms of trade. Whereas a reduction in external tariffs $(1 + \tau)$ redistributes real income to the resource-rich (via a fall in p_B), a reduction in the internal tariff $(1 + t)$ enables an increase in p_B and hence the terms of trade of the resource-poor country.

With these general arguments established, we now turn to a more detailed analysis of the effects of trade policy, and also restore the possibility that imports are used in production, $\mu > 0$.

5.2 Trade Policy: General Equilibrium Outcomes

We want to explore the interaction between various trade policy experiments and resource wealth. We focus initially on the impact on real income (utility) in each country, and summary results are shown in figures 7.4.1 and 7.4.2. These, and all subsequent results, are derived from numerical simulation.[3] The horizontal axis gives resource income relative to non-resource income in country A. The exogenous variable that changes as we move along the horizontal axis is country A resource wealth, N_A, but for ease of interpretation we report this relative to non-resource income $N_A / w_A L_A$. N_B is held constant at 50% of the lowest value that we use for N_A.

Looking first at the resource poor country, figure 7.4.2 reports real income, x_B, as a function of N_A under three different trade regimes. The bottom line is the initial high tariff regime where trade—between A and B and with the rest of the world—is subject to a 50% tariff ($t = 0.5$, $\tau = 0.5$). At low levels of N_A these tariffs are sufficient to choke off all trade between A and B, so country B utility is invariant with respect to country A resource wealth, and x_B is constant. Once N_A becomes large enough (exceeding 60% of non-resource income in our example), the price differential, p_A / p_B, becomes wide enough that intra-regional trade begins, raising real consumption and, by linking the two economies, making utility in B an increasing function of that in A.

The higher two lines in figure 7.4.2 report x_B under nonpreferential free trade (middle line, $t = 0$, $\tau = 0$) and regional integration ($t = 0$, $\tau = 0.5$). There are several points to note. Both forms of trade liberalization bring benefits, and both increase the degree of linkage from the resource-rich to

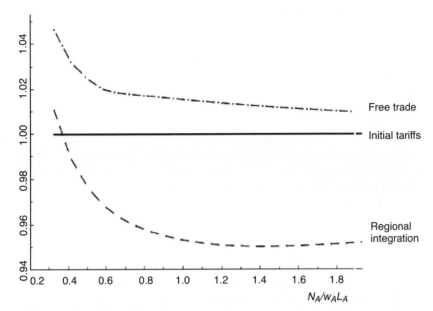

Figure 7.4.1 Country A Real Income

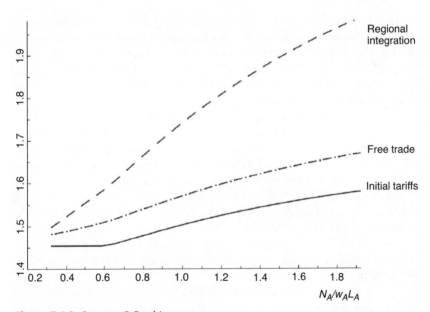

Figure 7.4.2 Country B Real Income

the resource-poor country. However, regional integration brings much larger gains than nonpreferential liberalization. The main reason is the different terms of trade effects that we discussed above.

Figure 7.4.1 reports real income for the resource-rich country, x_A, but with variables expressed relative to their value in the tariff regime. (This is for ease of viewing; otherwise the figure is dominated by the direct effect of additional resource wealth). There are three points. First, regional integration, the lower curve, brings gains only at low levels of resource wealth, and losses at higher levels, because of its adverse terms of trade effect. Second, regional integration is dominated by free trade (the upper curve) at all levels of resource wealth. And finally, the gains from trade liberalization relative to initial tariffs decline with resource wealth, although this relative effect is driven largely by the direct effect of additional resources on country A real income.

Combining the results of figures 7.4.1 and 7.4.2, we conclude that the opposite effects of nonpreferential liberalization and regional integration that we discussed above (the terms of trade effect) are not overturned by the full general equilibrium analysis. While gains to each country vary with the trade regime, the aggregate gains are quite clear. The aggregate real consumption of countries A and B combined is highest under free trade, followed by regional integration, and lowest with the initial restrictive tariff policy.

5.3 Non-Resource Income and Within-Country Income Distribution

We now turn to concentrating on the effect of the different trade regimes on real wages plus tariff receipts (which are transferred to workers), stripping out the direct impact of the resource income itself. The experiment is useful, both because it makes our main results very clear-cut, and because it sheds some light on potential within-country conflicts of interests between workers and recipients of resource revenues.

The different impacts of regional integration and nonpreferential liberalization are seen by comparison of figures 7.5.1 and 7.5.2. For the resource-poor country the pattern of non-resource income is, unsurprisingly, very similar to real consumption (x_B, figure 7.4.2), with regional integration yielding much the largest gains. For the resource-rich country (A, figure 7.5.1), the effect is very different. We see that real non-resource income is highest under the restrictive tariff policy, then is less under regional integration, and is lowest under free trade. The reason is the downward pressure that openness places on wages. Recipients of resource revenues are major beneficiaries from lower prices, but openness reduces the real income of those dependent on wages and tariff revenues.

One final point comes from comparison of figure 7.5.1 with 7.5.2. The level of real wages in country B remains below that in country A at all corresponding points on the figures. However, under free trade the difference is a function simply of intra-regional trade costs, β. As $\beta \to 0$, the economies

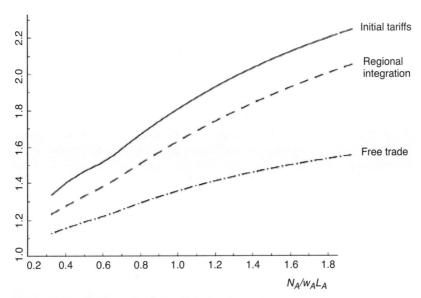

Figure 7.5.1 Country A Real Non-Resource Income

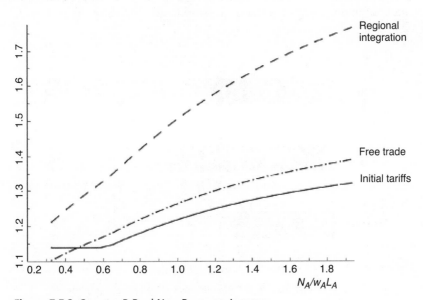

Figure 7.5.2 Country B Real Non-Resource Income

become fully integrated and wages become equalized, thereby involving real wage gain in country B and real wage decline in country A.

5.4 Trade Creation and Trade Diversion

There are three mechanisms underlying the effects of alternative trade policies. They are changes in the intra-regional terms of trade, trade creation, and trade diversion. The particular features of remote resource-rich economies that we have captured in the model are crucial to these effects. These countries are price-takers in world markets, but their remoteness and the consequent importance of regional trade means that the terms of trade within the region are endogenous. And it is movement of the margin between regional and global trade that creates trade diversion.

We argued above that the effects of regional integration and of nonpreferential trade liberalization have opposite effects on the terms of trade, and we see this come through most clearly in figures 7.5.1 and 7.5.2. Trade creation and diversion effects are drawn out in figure 7.6. The figure illustrates changing sources of supply to country A at a fixed intermediate value of N_A, the three rows corresponding to the different trade regimes. Comparing regional integration with the initial situation, there is an increase in the share of imports coming from the partner country, and this is largely—from the standpoint of country A—trade diversion; goods that were being imported from the rest of the world are now imported from the partner. Comparing free trade with regional integration, we see trade creation, with expansion of the market shares of imports from the rest of the world and from the partner country.

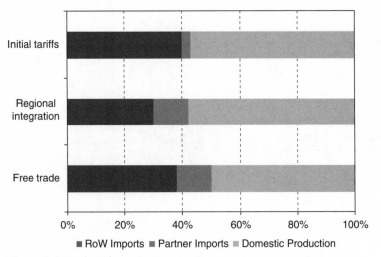

Figure 7.6 Market Shares in Country A
Note: Boundaries between lines are z_A^*, $z_A^{\hat{}}$.

The latter arises because country B's opening to imports reduces p_B, increasing the competitiveness of imports from the partner country.

In country B (not illustrated) the share of the market taken by imports (i.e., fraction z_B^*) goes from 11% under the tariff regime to 34% with regional integration and 39% with free trade. The regional integration regime nevertheless yields the highest country B real consumption because of terms of trade effects; country B prices are some 40% higher under regional integration than free trade, thus increasing the volume of rest of the world imports than can be purchased.

6 Policy Implications

The real income of the region as a whole—the resource-poor and resource-rich countries combined—is maximized by free trade, as must be the case in a framework where the region as a whole is a price-taker on world markets and there are no market failures. But comparing the trade options we have studied, there are large changes in relative prices and wages and large redistributions of income between the cases, creating incentives for deviations from free trade.

Within the resource-rich country, tariff reductions reduce wages and the cost of living. The move to free trade, in particular, has a negative effect on real wages and non-resource incomes, while increasing the domestic purchasing power of resource rents. This points to the importance of paying attention to who receives the resource rents. The direct effects of the tariff reduction may occur entirely within government: transfers are between its resource revenue accounts and tariff accounts. Nevertheless, the fall in real wages associated with the move to free trade makes it essential that trade liberalization is accompanied by measures to use resource revenues for the benefit of workers, either directly or through investments in human capital or other measures that enhance productivity and thereby raise wages.

The resource-poor country gains more from regional integration than it does from a regional movement to nonpreferential free trade. Essentially, this is because of the terms of trade improvement that it gets as a consequence of duty-free access to the resource-rich partner. This effect points to the importance of regional integration as a way of spreading the benefits of unevenly distributed resource wealth. Of course, there are other channels for spreading these benefits—notably migration—but trade alone can deliver a substantial part of the benefits. However, the fact that the benefits of regional integration exceed those of free trade raises the danger that regional preferences may become an obstacle to more general liberalization. The way to overcome this obstacle is to look for other policy measures that can accompany nonpreferential opening. This could include direct sharing of resource wealth between countries, but most important is the use of resource wealth to develop regional infrastructure. In this way the competitive position of the resource-poor country can be maintained at the same time as external opening takes place.

7 Conclusion

Remote resource-poor economies are disadvantaged in exporting outside their region, and as a consequence are critically short of the foreign exchange needed to finance essential imports. In many cases foreign aid has to fill this gap. Yet, in many regions of the world, they have neighbors that are resource-rich. These countries are possibly concerned about the "resource curse," including the damage that large foreign exchange windfalls might inflict on other sectors of their economies. Regional integration appears to be a way of solving both problems, and this chapter has presented a highly stylized model to investigate the issue. It turns out that the gains from integration are so unevenly distributed, particularly compared to other trade policies, that it may be difficult to achieve.

Better integration with a resource-rich economy is extremely valuable for the resource-poor. Remote and landlocked developing countries have very limited export potential with the external world, but need foreign exchange to purchase inputs for production—equipment and basic energy needs—as well as consumption goods. Regional integration enables them to earn foreign exchange via their exports to the resource-rich partner. The benefits arise as the prices of these regionally traded goods are bid up, raising wages and creating a terms of trade gain for the resource-poor economy.

However, resource-rich economies lose (or at best have very modest gains) from regional integration. The terms of trade gain for the resource-poor country is, of necessity, a terms of trade loss for the resource-rich economy. Added to terms of trade effects are trade creation and diversion. The resource-rich economy runs into diminishing returns as it seeks to spend its resource revenues, and trade is a way to relax this constraint. But these gains come from nonpreferential opening, and regional integration leads preponderantly to trade diversion.

The analysis points to the potential for conflicts of interest between resource-poor countries that seek regional integration, and resource-rich countries seeking nonpreferential opening. A way to resolve this conflict is to accompany nonpreferential opening with regional infrastructure improvement. Lower intra-regional trade costs bring real income benefits to both countries, although their capital costs are of course project specific (and beyond the scope of the modeling exercise of this chapter). ·

The framework that has been developed in this chapter provides some new insights on the core issues of trade policy, but many other aspects of the economic integration of remote resource-rich economies remain to be studied. Diminishing returns to resource wealth occur not just because of long run supply constraints, but also because of short run absorption and macro-economic problems as the economy seeks to adjust to resource wealth, because of the way the economy handles volatility, and for numerous political economy reasons. Each of these sources of diminishing returns may be relaxed if the resource rent is spread over a wider economic space. Analysis of regional integration needs to be extended to look at these other issues, and also at integration tools beyond trade policy, including labor mobility, regional infrastructure, and macro-economic and monetary issues.

Notes

1. http://www.doingbusiness.org/EconomyRankings/
2. In increasing order: Uzbekistan, Tajikistan, Afghanistan, Kazakhstan, Azerbaijan, and the Kyrgyz Republic. Mongolia and the PRC as a whole rank considerably higher.
3. Parameter values are: $L_A = 1$, $L_B = 1$, $N_A \epsilon [1, 10]$, $N_B = 0.5$, $\alpha = 2$, $\beta = 0.2$, $\mu = 0.2$.

References

Asian Development Bank. 2006. *Central Asia: Increasing Gains from Trade through Regional Cooperation in Trade Policy, Transport, and Customs Transit.* Manila: Asian Development Bank.

Collier, P., and A. J. Venables. 2010. Illusory Revenues: Import Tariffs in Resource-Rich and Aid-Rich Economies. *Journal of Development Economics.* Forthcoming.

Grafe, C., M. Raiser, and T. Sakatsume. 2005. Beyond Borders: Reconsidering Regional Trade in Central Asia. *European Bank for Reconstruction and Development (EBRD) Working Paper* 95.

Grigoriou, C. 2007. Landlockedness, Infrastructure and Trade: New Estimates for Central Asian Countries. *World Bank PR Working Paper* 4335.

Mayer, T. 2008. Market Potential and Development. *CEPR Discussion Paper* 6798.

Raballand, G. 2003. Determinants of the Negative Impact of Being Landlocked on Trade: An Empirical Investigation through the Central Asian Case. *Comparative Economic Studies.* 45(4). pp. 520–536.

Redding, S. J., and A. J. Venables. 2004. Economic Geography and International Inequality. *Journal of International Economics.* 62(1). pp. 53–82.

World Bank. 2004. *Tajikistan Trade Diagnostic Study.* http://siteresources.worldbank.org/INTTLF/Resources/Tajikistan_Final_Report.pdf.

World Bank. 2008. *Global Purchasing Power Parities and Real Expenditures: 2005 International Comparison Programme.* http://siteresources.worldbank.org/ICPINT/Resources/icp-final.pdf.

8

Regional Trade Integration and Multinational Firm Strategies

Pol Antràs and C. Fritz Foley

This chapter was prepared for the workshop "Quantifying the Costs and Benefits of Regional Economic Integration," held on January 19–20, 2009, in Hong Kong, China. The statistical analysis of firm-level data on US multinational companies was conducted at the Bureau of Economic Analysis (BEA), US Department of Commerce, under arrangements that maintain legal confidentiality requirements. The views expressed are those of the authors and do not reflect official positions of the US Department of Commerce. We are grateful to Eduardo Morales for superb research assistance and to Robert Barro, Elhanan Helpman, Jong-Wha Lee, Emanuel Ornelas, Bill Zeile, and seminar participants at Harvard and the Asian Development Bank for helpful suggestions.

1 Introduction

Regional trade agreements significantly affect the structure of international trade flows. Existing research emphasizes the costs and benefits inherent in the trade creation and trade diversion effects of these agreements and considers whether they generate incentives for trading partners to promote or thwart the development of an open multilateral trading system. Most existing analyses fail to consider the effect of regional trade agreements on patterns of foreign direct investment (FDI). In this chapter, we study these effects.

Our empirical analysis focuses on the behavior of multinational firms based in the United States (US) around the time of a single event, the signing of the Association of Southeast Asian Nations (ASEAN) Free Trade Area

(AFTA) in January of 1992. We begin by reviewing aggregate data on US multinationals and then use some broad trends in those data to guide the development of a model of how multinationals based outside of a region respond to the formation of a free trade agreement in the region. This model builds on the work of Helpman et al. (2004) and incorporates firm-level heterogeneity to generate predictions of how lower regional trade costs affect the intensive and extensive margins of foreign direct investor activity. In addition to highlighting effects on levels of activity, the theory delivers implications for the share of multinational affiliate activity directed toward serving different markets. Departing from previous approaches that used only aggregate data, we test these predictions using the firm-level results of the benchmark Survey of US Direct Investment Abroad conducted by the Bureau of Economic Analysis (BEA).

The ASEAN agreement of 1992 was signed by six countries: Brunei Darussalam, Indonesia, Malaysia, the Philippines, Singapore, and Thailand. In subsequent years, four additional countries joined AFTA; Viet Nam in 1995, Lao People's Democratic Republic (PDR) and Myanmar in 1997, and Cambodia in 1999. The original agreement outlined a program of progressive tariff reductions to be carried out through 2008, but the member countries subsequently decided to accelerate reforms and make AFTA fully operational on January 1, 2003. We analyze data on US multinational operations in ASEAN and other Asian countries in the 1989 and 1994 benchmark survey years. Doing so allows for a comparison of the changing structure of multinational activity in countries that signed AFTA in 1992 and in other similar countries. Our tests therefore attempt to rule out the possibility that changes in activity in ASEAN countries are driven by factors unrelated to AFTA, like technological shocks or other general drivers of US multinational expansion. While ASEAN tariff reductions continued after 1994, substantial progress had been made by that time, and it is plausible that US multinationals would have started responding to the process of regional trade integration shortly after the signing of the agreement in 1992. Although the results are robust to analyzing longer time frames, our main analysis does not use data from the 1999 benchmark survey because a subset of AFTA's signing countries experienced a severe financial crisis in 1997, which affected FDI into the region for reasons quite distinct from those analyzed here.

Section 2 of the chapter describes broad patterns regarding the operations of US multinational firms in Asia in 1989 and 1994. The data indicate a surge in the level of activity in ASEAN countries around the time of the formation of AFTA that exceeds levels of growth in other Asian countries. Analysis of growth among affiliates that were active both before and after the creation of AFTA and net entry of affiliates reveals that both types of growth contributed to the higher levels of relative expansion in ASEAN countries. More specifically, about one-third of the growth in US multinational activity is due to growth in the number of affiliates, while the remaining two-thirds is due to growth in the levels of activity at the affiliate level. Some interesting changes in the direction of US multinational affiliate sales also emerge around the time of the creation of AFTA. In particular, it is possible to distinguish between affiliate sales to their host markets, sales to the US, and sales to third countries. In ASEAN countries, sales to third countries increased substantially between 1989 and 1994, while this share remained virtually unchanged in other Asian countries. The growth in the third-country sales share among ASEAN affiliates is driven by both an increase in the share of third-country sales of affiliates that were active before AFTA and the fact that new affiliates in the area direct more of their sales to third countries than other affiliates.

These broad patterns guide the formulation of some theory, which is presented in section 3. We develop a simple three-country extension of the model of FDI with heterogeneous firms developed in Helpman et al. (2004). The main innovation of our model is the introduction of third-market sales, and our main theoretical results concern the responses of multinational firms based in one country (the West) to a reduction of trade barriers between the other two countries in the model (the South and the East). We interpret this change as regional trade integration between these other two countries. The model predicts an increase in the number of Western firms engaging in FDI in the South-East area. Furthermore, the model indicates that there should be growth on the intensive margin because affiliates that operate before and after the regional trade agreement should expand. The theory also predicts that regional trade agreements lead to gross entry and exit of Western affiliates operating in the South-East area, with the net effect depending on the distribution of productivity across firms. With a Pareto distribution of productivity, gross entry exceeds gross exit and the extensive margin responds positively to the agreement. The model also has clear implications for the effects of the regional trade agreements on the sales of Western affiliates to countries other than their host country. In particular, lowering trade barriers between the East and the South increases the share of affiliate sales going to third countries for three reasons. First, new Western affiliates in the South-East area sell more to third markets than the average Western-owned affiliate does. Second, some Western firms that were active in both the South and the East before the agreement consolidate activity in one of these countries after the formation of the free trade area and serve the country they leave through regional trade. Finally, affiliates of US parents that are active in only one market (the South or the East) before and after the regional trade agreement also increase the share of affiliate sales going to third markets.

These predictions are consistent with the broad patterns described in section 2 of the chapter, and section 4 presents a more rigorous analysis of them. Difference-in-difference estimates illustrate statistically distinctive behavior of US multinational affiliates in ASEAN and other Asian countries. Affiliates that existed in 1989 and 1994 grew faster in ASEAN countries than other countries. Consistent with the theoretical results obtained under a Pareto distribution of productivity, levels of US multinational activity measured at the country/industry level also increase as a result of AFTA.

Predictions concerning the direction of affiliate sales also receive support in the data, and there is evidence that the channels by which free trade agreements affect the direction of sales described above are operative. These results hold controlling for other time-varying country-specific factors that might confound the results, like differences in gross domestic product (GDP) per capita growth and changes in tax rates.

These findings contribute to two main literatures. First, they point out a neglected consequence of regional trade agreements, that is, such agreements affect FDI from countries outside the region. Traditional theoretical analyses of regional trade agreements build on the work of Viner (1950) and focus on the welfare consequences of trade creation and trade diversion effects. Krueger (1999) reviews the theoretical and empirical literature on preferential trade agreements, but this review does not consider effects related to FDI. Some theoretical work does point out implications for FDI responses. Motta and Norman (1996), Krugman and Venables (1996), Puga and Venables (1997), and Ekholm et al. (2007) each provide a basis by which a reduction in tariffs between two countries would increase foreign investment from third countries. Although relatively few studies empirically test for effects of regional trade agreements on FDI from outside the region, Chen (2009) is an exception. The results in Chen (2009) indicate marginally significant effects of free trade agreements that do not include the US on aggregate levels of US multinational affiliate sales. Although our theory generates subtle predictions regarding aggregate levels of affiliate sales, our results confirm and expand on those in Chen (2009).

The effects of regional trade agreements on FDI are likely to have significant welfare consequences given the unique nature of multinational firms. Several strands of the literature indicate benefits for host countries. Aitken et al. (1996) and Heyman et al. (2007) find that multinational firms pay their workers a premium relative to comparable domestic firms, and Aitken and Harrison (1999) and Smarzynska (2004) show that these firms are also more productive than comparable domestic firms. A large body of work, including recent papers by Smarzynska (2004) and Haskel et al. (2007), also points out that multinationals can generate spillovers for other firms through a variety of channels. Depending on the nature of the relation between the foreign and domestic activity of multinationals, the formation of regional trade agreements could also have consequences for the home countries of multinationals that increase their regional investment. Desai et al. (2009) find that domestic and foreign activities are complements, suggesting that increased foreign activity in response to a regional trade agreement could yield some benefits to countries that are the source of FDI.

Our study also enhances the literature that introduces firm heterogeneity to models of trade and multinational activity. Theoretical attempts at understanding the existence and behavior of multinationals have emphasized horizontal, vertical, and export-platform motivations.[1] Only recently have researchers attempted to incorporate firm level heterogeneity in these types of models. Helpman et al. (2004), Antràs and Helpman (2004), Nocke and Yeaple (2008), and Yeaple (2008a, 2008b) are notable examples of work in this vein. Our model introduces the possibility of export-platform behavior into a model that is similar to the one in Helpman et al. (2004). It then confronts this theory with detailed firm-level data by analyzing how multinationals respond to a specific change in trade costs. By using a detailed panel data set, we are able to explore firm-level responses at both the intensive and extensive margins.

A couple of limitations of our study should be pointed out. Our empirical tests focus on the formation of a single free trade agreement, and the response to this reform may not be representative. Furthermore, given the limited number of countries that signed this agreement and the limited variation in characteristics among them, we have not empirically explored any asymmetries in the effects on FDI between countries. Our theory, however, could be used to generate further predictions related to country characteristics. Further, we only examine the response of foreign direct investors based in the US. While this is largely a consequence of data limitations, it is worth pointing out that the US was by no means a small investor in the area during the period under study. Although it is difficult to find comparable data on measures of foreign investment across host and source countries, the Organisation for Economic Co-operation and Development's (OECD) *International Direct Investment Statistics* database provides information on the outward FDI position of many OECD countries in ASEAN countries. The coverage in this database is reasonably complete, but data are missing for a number of countries that were OECD members during the 1989–1994 period, including Belgium, Greece, Iceland, Ireland, Luxembourg, Mexico, Spain, Sweden, and Turkey. Among those countries reporting investment in the ASEAN region, the US held a 22%–27% share of aggregated investment position over the 1989–1994 period. Only Japan (with a share of roughly 50%) featured higher levels of FDI in the ASEAN area during that time period.

2 A First Look at the Data

In this section, we provide a broad description of US multinational activity in ASEAN countries around the time that AFTA was formed. Aggregate data reveal if levels of US multinational activity increased in ASEAN countries relative to other Asian countries when AFTA was created and if the nature of multinational activity appears to have changed as the costs of serving regional customers fell. In this section, we document some broad empirical trends that help guide the development of the theory and that we later test in a more rigorous manner.

Data on multinationals are drawn from the BEA benchmark surveys of US Direct Investment Abroad. In our main analyses, we use data on nonbank affiliates and their parents from the 1989 and 1994 surveys, as these years span the formation of AFTA and avoid the 1997 Asian financial crisis.[2]

These surveys provide a panel of data on the financial and operating characteristics of US multinational firms operating abroad. US direct investment abroad is defined as the direct or indirect ownership or control by a single US legal entity of at least 10% of the voting securities of an incorporated foreign business enterprise or the equivalent interest in an unincorporated foreign business enterprise. A US multinational entity is the combination of a single US legal entity that has made the direct investment, called the US parent, and at least one foreign business enterprise, called the foreign affiliate. As a result of confidentiality assurances and penalties for noncompliance, BEA believes that coverage is close to complete and levels of accuracy are high.

The survey forms that US multinational enterprises (MNE) are required to complete track basic information on affiliate sales, assets, employment compensation, and net property plant and equipment (PPE). In addition, for majority-owned affiliates, the survey forms also capture the direction of sales. More specifically, the survey results provide information on the level of affiliate sales to persons in the affiliate's host country, to persons in the US, and to persons in third countries.

Table 8.1 presents measures of aggregate activity in ASEAN countries and in other Asian countries for the years 1989 and 1994.[3] The formation of AFTA in 1992 appears to have induced a surge in US MNE activity in the ASEAN countries relative to the rest of Asia, and this surge appears to be a consequence of growth on the intensive and extensive margins. Between 1989 and 1994, the number of affiliates in ASEAN countries increased from 740 to 1,065, or by a factor of 44%. Other Asian countries showed an increase in the number of affiliates of only 26%. In addition to high growth in the number of affiliates in the ASEAN region, there is also a sizable increase in the number of parent firms. In 1989, there were 309 parent firms with operations in ASEAN countries, and by 1994 this number had grown to 403. This rate of growth exceeded the growth in the number of parent firms that were active in other Asian countries. Therefore, a part of the large relative US MNE activity growth in ASEAN countries comes from growth on the extensive margin.

Measures of firm size and factor use increase by larger amounts than affiliate counts. In the ASEAN region, levels of affiliate sales, assets, employment compensation, and net PPE all increase by 125% or more between 1989 and 1994, but they increase by only 32%–54% in other Asian countries. These patterns illustrate that growth on the intensive margin is also important in explaining the increase in US MNE activity. In particular, the figures in table 8.1 indicate that about two-thirds of the growth in affiliate sales is accounted for by increases in average sales per affiliate (intensive margin), while the remaining one-third is explained by growth in the number of affiliates (extensive margin).

Tables 8.2 and 8.3, respectively, present additional analysis of the intensive and extensive margins of growth. Table 8.2 presents information similar to that in table 8.1, but it only aggregates measures of activity for affiliates that exist in 1989 and survive until 1994. For this group of affiliates, aggregate

Table 8.1
Effect on Aggregate Activity

	1989	1994	Growth Rate
ASEAN Countries			
Number of Affiliates	740	1,065	44%
Number of Parents	309	403	30%
Aggregate Sales	36,939,740	83,218,640	125%
Aggregate Assets	28,103,986	68,206,904	143%
Aggregate Employment Compensation	2,216,711	5,346,706	141%
Aggregate Net PPE	11,903,194	27,964,768	135%
Other Asian Countries			
Number of Affiliates	2,417	3,052	26%
Number of Parents	775	934	21%
Aggregate Sales	233,633,360	308,670,176	32%
Aggregate Assets	171,856,768	258,032,128	50%
Aggregate Employment Compensation	25,960,936	37,153,888	43%
Aggregate Net PPE	59,890,208	92,479,056	54%

Notes: This table presents measures of US multinational aggregate activity in ASEAN and other Asian countries in 1989 and 1994. The sample includes nonbank affiliates that filed long or short survey forms. Number of Affiliates and Number of Parents are, respectively, the number of US MNE affiliates and parents operating in the region. Net PPE measures the net property, plant, and equipment of MNE affiliates. Growth rates are computed by taking the difference between 1994 and 1989 values and dividing by 1989 values.

levels of sales, assets, employment compensation, and net PPE more than double in ASEAN countries but increase by much lower amounts in other Asian countries.

Table 8.3 displays aggregate measures of activity for affiliates that either exit or enter the data. The first column shows 1989 measures for affiliates that exist in the 1989 data but that leave the sample before 1994. The second column shows 1994 measures for affiliates that report in 1994 but that did not exist in the data in 1989. Comparing the first and second columns therefore provides insights about the effects of net entry on the extent of US MNE activity. As suggested by the aggregate data, net entry is much greater in ASEAN than in other Asian countries. In ASEAN countries, the count of 558 new affiliates in 1994 is about 2.4 times the count of 233 affiliates that exit the data. In other Asian countries, however, the ratio of entering affiliates to exiting affiliates is only about 1.8. Aggregate measures of sales, assets, employment compensation, and net PPE are approximately 3 times larger for entering than exiting affiliates in ASEAN countries. In other Asian countries, these measures are similar for entering and exiting affiliates. Thus, the large increase in US

Table 8.2
Effects on Aggregate Activity: Intensive Margin

	1989	1994	Growth Rate
ASEAN Countries			
Number of Affiliates	507	507	0%
Aggregate Sales	31,365,546	67,467,664	115%
Aggregate Assets	22,387,278	49,965,720	123%
Aggregate Employment Compensation	1,806,404	3,898,378	116%
Aggregate Net PPE	9,720,393	19,589,564	102%
Other Asian Countries			
Number of Affiliates	1,591	1,591	0%
Aggregate Sales	181,131,168	256,260,880	41%
Aggregate Assets	131,140,912	201,230,736	53%
Aggregate Employment Compensation	20,550,656	30,694,388	49%
Aggregate Net PPE	46,193,692	69,387,904	50%

Notes: This table presents measures of US multinational aggregate activity in ASEAN and other Asian countries in 1989 and 1994 for affiliates that report activity in both years. The sample includes nonbank affiliates that filed long or short survey forms. Number of Affiliates is the number of US MNE affiliates operating in the region. Net PPE measures the net property, plant, and equipment of MNE affiliates. Growth rates are computed by taking the difference between 1994 and 1989 values and dividing by 1989 values.

MNE activity in ASEAN countries around the time of the signing of AFTA reflects an increase in the size of affiliates that existed in 1989 and survive until 1994, as well as higher levels of entry relative to exit in ASEAN countries.

For majority-owned affiliates, the BEA data also include information on sales by destination, including sales to persons in the affiliate's host country, sales to persons in the US, and sales to persons in third countries. Sales to third countries would include sales by affiliates to persons in ASEAN countries other than the affiliate's host country, and the theory developed in the next section indicates that these kinds of sales should increase around the formation of AFTA. Table 8.4 presents descriptive statistics on sales shares that are computed using aggregate data. For the top panel, data on all affiliates are used to compute sales shares for different types of sales for firms in ASEAN and other Asian countries.[4] Compared to affiliates in other Asian countries, affiliates in ASEAN countries direct a smaller fraction of their sales to their host market and larger fractions to the US and to third countries.

Examining changes in sales patterns suggests that AFTA did indeed increase the share of sales to third countries for affiliates in the ASEAN region relative to affiliates in the rest of Asia. The share of sales to third countries for affiliates in ASEAN countries increased from 28.3% to 32.5% between 1989 and 1994,

Table 8.3
Effects on Aggregate Activity: Extensive Margin

	Exiting Affiliate 1989 Activity	Entering Affiliate 1994 Activity
ASEAN Countries		
Number of Affiliates	233	558
Aggregate Sales	5,574,194	15,750,973
Aggregate Assets	5,716,708	18,241,180
Aggregate Employment Compensation	410,307	1,448,328
Aggregate Net PPE	2,182,801	8,375,202
Other Asian Countries		
Number of Affiliates	826	1,461
Aggregate Sales	52,502,180	52,409,312
Aggregate Assets	40,715,852	56,801,392
Aggregate Employment Compensation	5,410,280	6,459,498
Aggregate Net PPE	13,696,517	23,091,148

Notes: This table presents measures of US multinational aggregate activity in ASEAN and other Asian countries in 1989 and 1994 for affiliates that report activity only in either 1989 or 1994. The sample includes nonbank affiliates that filed long or short survey forms. The first column provides 1989 aggregates for affiliates that exit the sample after 1989 and before 1994, and the second column provides 1994 aggregates for affiliates that enter the sample after 1989 and before 1994. Number of Affiliates is the number of US MNE affiliates operating in the region. Net PPE measures the net property, plant, and equipment of MNE affiliates.

while this share decreased slightly in other Asian countries, equaling 12.8% in 1989 and 11.2% in 1994. Accompanying these changes, the share of sales to persons in the affiliate's host country increased by slightly higher amounts in other Asian countries. The share of sales to the US fell for affiliates in both sets of countries and by larger amounts in ASEAN as opposed to other Asian countries.

Panels B and C of table 8.4 provide information on the direction of sales for affiliates that exist in 1989 and 1994 as well as for affiliates that enter and exit. Panel B displays data for the survivors, and it reveals patterns that are very similar to those observed for the whole sample. The share of sales to third countries disproportionately increases for affiliates in ASEAN countries. In Panel C, the first column displays 1989 sales shares for affiliates that appear in 1989 but exit before 1994, and the second column displays 1994 sales shares for affiliates that do not appear in 1989 but enter in 1994. In ASEAN countries, new entrants are more focused on selling to third countries and less focused on selling to the host market and the US than exiting affiliates. Indeed, 41.2%

Table 8.4
Effects on Aggregate Sales Patterns (%)

Panel A: All Affiliate Activity	1989	1994
ASEAN Countries		
Share of Sales to the Host Country Market	45.8	47.1
Share of Sales to the US	25.9	20.4
Share of Sales to Third Countries	28.3	32.5
Other Asian Countries		
Share of Sales to the Host Country Market	78.6	83.1
Share of Sales to the US	8.6	5.7
Share of Sales to Third Countries	12.8	11.2

Panel B: Surviving Affiliates	1989	1994
ASEAN Countries		
Share of Sales to the Host Country Market	43.8	45.9
Share of Sales to the US	28.4	21.9
Share of Sales to Third Countries	27.8	32.2
Other Asian Countries		
Share of Sales to the Host Country Market	79.9	81.5
Share of Sales to the US	9.0	6.1
Share of Sales to Third Countries	11.1	12.4

Panel C: Entrants and Exits	Exiting Affiliates 1989 Activity	Entering Affiliate 1994 Activity
ASEAN Countries		
Share of Sales to the Host Country Market	46.5	41.2
Share of Sales to the US	20.1	17.6
Share of Sales to Third Countries	33.3	41.2
Other Asian Countries		
Share of Sales to the Host Country Market	74.4	85.0
Share of Sales to the US	9.6	4.8
Share of Sales to Third Countries	16.0	10.1

Notes: This table presents information on the direction of sales of affiliates in ASEAN and other Asian countries. The sample includes majority-owned nonbank affiliates that filed long or short survey forms. The top panel presents data on the activities of all affiliates, the second panel presents data only on those affiliates that appear in both the 1989 and 1994 samples, and the bottom panel presents data on affiliates that exit and enter the sample between 1989 and 1994. In order to avoid the potential disclosure of confidential information, the top panel was constructed using published data that do not include figures for Brunei Darussalam, but the other panels cover all ASEAN countries. In the bottom panel, the first column provides 1989 figures for affiliates that appear in the 1989 sample but not in the 1994 sample, and the second column provides 1994 figures for affiliates that appear in the 1994 sample but not the 1989 sample. Share of Sales to the Host Country Market measures the ratio of sales to persons in the affiliate's host country to affiliate total sales. Share of Sales to the US and Share of Sales to Third Countries respectively measure the share of sales to persons in the US and to countries other than the US and the affiliate's host country.

of the 1994 sales of new entrants is directed to third countries, but only 33.3% of exiting affiliate 1989 sales is directed to these markets. However, an opposite pattern appears for entries and exits in other Asian countries. In these countries, 10.1% of the 1994 sales of new entrants is directed to third markets, and this share is 16.0% for the affiliates that exited. Therefore, growth in the share of sales to third countries among affiliates in the ASEAN region in part reflects growth in this share for surviving affiliates and in part reflects growth that is a consequence of new affiliates having relatively high shares of third-country sales.

Further unreported analysis suggests that models of horizontal FDI are more salient in explaining the response of US multinationals than models of vertical FDI. If multinationals increased their vertical specialization within regions that entered into a trade agreement, one should observe firms expand into several regional countries and increase their level of sales by affiliates in one part of the region to affiliates in other parts of the region. While US multinational firms do appear to expand within the ASEAN region, those firms that increase the number of countries in which they operate do not appear to have high or increasing levels of intrafirm regional transactions.

In summary, aggregated descriptive statistics indicate that US multinational activity in the ASEAN region disproportionately increased at the time of the formation of AFTA. This increase reflects growth on the intensive and extensive margins. Within the ASEAN region, the share of affiliate sales to countries other than host countries also increased, and it appears that the increase is a consequence of changes among affiliates that operated before AFTA, as well as changes in the composition of activity because of net entry. These aggregate patterns do not, however, indicate the statistical significance of differences in firm behavior. Furthermore, because aggregate measures are particularly sensitive to the activities of large firms, the patterns in the aggregates might not indicate the experiences of the typical firm. Aggregate patterns could also reflect other trends in ASEAN and other Asian countries, like difference in per capita growth rates or changes in tax policy. In order to address these considerations, it is helpful to employ the firm-level data in more rigorous regression analysis. However, before doing so, we develop some theory that serves as a guide to the analysis.

3 Theoretical Framework

In this section, we develop a simple model to illustrate the effects of a regional trade agreement on the patterns of FDI in the set of countries signing the agreement. Our goal in developing the model is to provide a simple rationale for the broad empirical patterns described in the previous section and to formally develop a set of hypotheses that are explored econometrically in the next section.

3.1 A Simple Model of FDI

Our model is a simple variant of the framework in Helpman et al. (2004).[5] We consider a world of three countries: the West, the East, and the South. The model studies the optimal international organization of production from the point of view of firms based in the West, which in the empirical analysis we associate with the US. These firms own the technology to produce a differentiated good with demand

$$y = A^j p^{-\sigma}$$

in country $j = W, E, S$. There is a continuum of firms based in the West, which we index by their heterogeneous productivity level φ, and we let the cumulative distribution function of productivity be $G(\varphi)$.

Final goods are produced combining skilled and unskilled labor. We allow firms to produce their final good in each of the three countries, which we index by $l = W, E, S$. The unit variable cost of production for a firm with productivity φ producing in country l is given by:

$$c^l(\varphi) = \frac{1}{\varphi} \left(w_S^l \right)^{\beta} \left(w_U^l \right)^{1-\beta},$$

where w_S^l denotes the wage rate of skilled workers in the country where the good is produced, and w_U^l denotes the analogous wage rate for unskilled workers.

Although our main results are unchanged when all countries have the same factor prices, we shall assume that the unskilled-labor wage is lower in the South than in the East or the West, that is,

$$w_U^W = w_U^E > w_U^S.$$

For simplicity, we assume that the wage of skilled workers is identical in all three countries and we set it equal to one (so skilled labor is the numeraire in the model), that is,

$$w_S^W = w_S^E = w_S^S = 1.$$

It is straightforward to develop a general equilibrium version of the model that produces these factor prices as equilibrium prices. In terms of our empirical application, one can think of the East as being a relatively skilled-labor abundant Southeast Asian country (such as Singapore) and the South as being a relatively unskilled-labor abundant Southeast Asian country (such as the Philippines).[6]

Production entails a fixed cost f^l in terms of skilled labor (the numeraire), and the size of this fixed cost depends on the location of production. In particular, we assume that firms in the West need to incur a higher fixed cost when operating in the East or the South than when operating in their home country (i.e., the West), consistent with the assumptions in

Helpman et al. (2004). For simplicity, we set the fixed cost of production in the West equal to 0, and we let

$$f^E = f^S = f > 0.$$

Final goods are tradable, but at a variable cost equal to $\bar{\tau}$ between the West and each of the two other countries and equal to $\underline{\tau} < \bar{\tau}$ between the East and the South. We shall interpret a regional trade agreement between the East and the South as a drop in $\underline{\tau}$ while holding $\bar{\tau}$ constant.[7] For reasons that will become apparent below, we shall also assume that the following inequality holds (though we discuss what happens when this assumption is relaxed):

Assumption 1:

$$\underline{\tau} > \left(\frac{w_U^E}{w_U^S} \right)^{(1-\beta)}.$$

We next compute the profits associated with the different organizational strategies of a firm in the West with productivity φ. A first convenient implication of Assumption 1 is that it ensures that the Western market is necessarily served domestically, that is from a plant located in the West.[8] Hence, the key organizational decision in the model is whether to also have a plant in the East and/or the South. Because the profits obtained from sales in the West are independent of this organizational decision, we ignore them hereafter.

Consider first the case in which the firm in the West has only one plant and this plant is located in the West. In such a case, the East and the South are serviced through exports from the West. Given the demand levels in the East and the South and the unit variable cost of production $c^l(\varphi) = \frac{(w_U^W)^{1-\beta}}{\varphi}$, it is straightforward to compute the joint profits associated with this strategy:

$$\pi^X(\varphi) = \frac{1}{\sigma} \left(\frac{(\sigma - 1)\varphi}{\sigma} \right)^{\sigma-1} \frac{\bar{\tau}^{1-\sigma}(A^E + A^S)}{\left(w_U^W\right)^{(1-\beta)(\sigma-1)}}. \tag{1}$$

Alternatively, the firm in the West could decide to open one plant in the East. This option would not affect the variable unit cost of production ($w_U^W = w_U^E$) and would increase fixed costs by an amount f, but it would also reduce shipping costs associated with servicing the East and the South.[9] The profits in the East and the South associated with this option are:

$$\pi^{I_E}(\varphi) = \frac{1}{\sigma} \left(\frac{(\sigma - 1)\varphi}{\sigma} \right)^{\sigma-1} \left(\frac{A^E + \underline{\tau}^{1-\sigma} A^S}{\left(w_U^E\right)^{(1-\beta)(\sigma-1)}} \right) - f. \tag{2}$$

Similarly, the firm in the West could decide to set up one plant in the South, an option that would generate joint profits in the East and the South equal to:

$$\pi^{I_S}(\varphi) = \frac{1}{\sigma} \left(\frac{(\sigma - 1)\varphi}{\sigma} \right)^{\sigma - 1} \left(\frac{\underline{\tau}^{1-\sigma} A^E + A^S}{\left(w_U^S \right)^{(1-\beta)(\sigma-1)}} \right) - f. \tag{3}$$

The final alternative available to firms in the West is to set up production plants in both the East and the South, in which case each of the three markets is serviced through local sales. Straightforward calculations deliver a joint profit level in the East and the South equal to:

$$\pi^{I_{ES}}(\varphi) = \frac{1}{\sigma} \left(\frac{(\sigma - 1)\varphi}{\sigma} \right)^{\sigma - 1} \left(\frac{A^E}{\left(w_U^E \right)^{(1-\beta)(\sigma-1)}} + \frac{A^S}{\left(w_U^S \right)^{(1-\beta)(\sigma-1)}} \right) - 2f. \tag{4}$$

3.2 Analysis

Having computed the profits associated with each of these options, we next analyze how the optimal organizational form of firms varies with levels of productivity φ. In particular, we will identify the organizational mode $k \in \{X, I_E, I_S, I_{ES}\}$ that maximizes profits $\pi^k(\varphi)$. For that purpose, it proves convenient to follow Helpman et al. (2004) and Antràs and Helpman (2004) in expressing the profit function associated with each alternative as a linear function of the modified productivity measure $\varphi^{\sigma-1}$, that is:

$$\pi^k(\varphi) = \psi^k \varphi^{\sigma-1} - f^k, \tag{5}$$

where f^k is the fixed cost associated with option k and where ψ^k can be backed out from equations (1) through (4).

Our first observation is that because the fixed cost associated with the strategies I_E and I_S is identical, the choice between these two options depends only on the relative magnitude of ψ^{I_E} and ψ^{I_S} and is thus independent of productivity. Manipulation of equations (2) and (3) indicates that investing only in the East dominates investing only in the South whenever

$$\frac{A^E + \underline{\tau}^{1-\sigma} A^S}{\underline{\tau}^{1-\sigma} A^E + A^S} > \left(\frac{w_U^E}{w_U^S} \right)^{(1-\beta)(\sigma-1)}. \tag{6}$$

Other things being equal, investment in the East is more likely to be chosen if the market size of the East is large relative to the South (if A^E is large relative to A^S) and if the cost of production in the East is not disproportionately high relative to the South, which is true when wage differences are small (i.e., when w_U^E / w_U^S is low) or when production is relatively skill-intensive (when β is high). Finally, a high shipping cost between the East and the South (a high $\underline{\tau}$) also favors FDI in the East provided that $A^E > A^S$, while it favors FDI in the South whenever $A^S > A^E$. Intuitively, when there is only one plant in the South-East area, higher transport costs between the South and the East generate an incentive to concentrate production in the larger country. By the same argument, a fall in $\underline{\tau}$ reduces the importance of market size in determining the location of MNE activity and increases the role of factor cost considerations.

We next compare the option of exporting from the West with the three alternative FDI strategies. Combining equation (5) with equations (1)–(4) and using Assumption 1, it is simple to establish that the following inequalities hold:

$$\psi^{IES} > max\{\psi^{IE}, \psi^{IS}\} > min\{\psi^{IE}, \psi^{IS}\} > \psi^{X},$$

and

$$f^{IES} = 2f > f^{IE} = f^{IS} = f > f^{X} = 0.$$

These rankings immediately imply that a sufficiently productive Western firm chooses some form of FDI over exporting, while a firm with a sufficiently low productivity level necessarily prefers exporting to any form of FDI.[10] These results parallel those obtained by Helpman et al. (2004), but our analysis permits a comparison of single-plant FDI with multiple-plant FDI and allows for the possibility of affiliate exports. The rankings above immediately imply that only the most productive firms find it profitable to establish affiliates in both the East and the South, while firms with intermediate levels of productivity may decide to undertake FDI in just one of the two countries.[11]

We use figure 8.1 to illustrate these results. As in Helpman et al. (2004) and Antràs and Helpman (2004), we plot the profit functions of all four possible

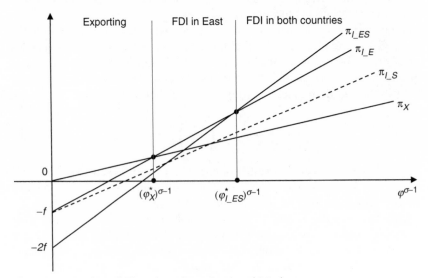

Figure 8.1 Sorting of Firms into Organizational Modes

organizational modes as a function of the modified productivity measure $\varphi^{\sigma-1}$. As is clear from figure 8.1, firms with low productivity φ ($\varphi < \varphi_X^*$) find it optimal to service both the East and the South via exporting. Conversely, firms above a certain productivity threshold ($\varphi > \varphi_{I_{ES}}^*$) optimally choose to set up plants in both countries. Finally, firms with intermediate productivity levels, shown as $\varphi \in (\varphi_X^*, \varphi_{I_{ES}}^*)$, have one plant in either the East or the South and will not export from the West. The location of this plant depends on whether condition (6) holds. Figure 8.1 illustrates the case in which condition (6) holds (perhaps because the Eastern market size is larger or because the good is relatively skill-intensive) and the plant is located in the East.

3.3 Effects of a Regional Trade Agreement

We can now consider the effects of a regional trade agreement between the East and the South, which we associate with a fall in $\underline{\tau}$ in the model, holding other parameters constant.[12] Notice that the profits associated with the exporting decision and the multiple-plant FDI decision are independent of $\underline{\tau}$, while the profitability of each of the two FDI strategies involving one plant is positively affected by the fall in $\underline{\tau}$. Although the free trade area does not increase the sales and profits in the market where the affiliate is located, it does increase the attractiveness of this plant as an export-platform to the other country in the FTA. In terms of figure 8.1, the slopes of the functions π^{I_E} and π^{I_S} necessarily increase, which translates into a fall in the threshold φ_X^* and entry of new Western affiliates in the South-East area. This in turn implies that, consistent with the findings reported in table 8.1:

Prediction 1: An FTA between the East and the South increases the number of Western firms engaging in FDI in the South-East area.

A second implication of the increase in the slopes of the profit functions π^{I_E} and π^{I_S} is that the threshold $\varphi_{I_{ES}}^*$ necessarily goes up as a result of the regional trade agreement. Consequently, some Western firms that initially had two affiliates in the South-East area now optimally choose to shut down one of their plants and concentrate the location of production in only one country in the area. The model thus predicts gross entry and exit as a result of the FTA, and in general the net effect on the number of Western affiliates located in the South-East area is ambiguous. However, when the distribution of productivity across firms is Pareto distributed (an assumption consistent with available evidence), it is possible to show that gross entry of affiliates exceeds gross exit. Under this assumption, the model predicts an increase in the number of Western affiliates operating in the South-East area (see the appendix at the end of this chapter for details). Consistent with the findings described in section 2, we have:

Prediction 2: An FTA between the East and the South generates gross entry and gross exit of Western affiliates in the South-East area. Furthermore, when firm productivity follows a Pareto distribution, the FTA generates a net increase in the number of Western affiliates in the South-East area.

We next consider the effects of the regional trade agreement on measures of affiliate activity. Although in section 2 we document changes in four alternative measures of activity, we focus for the most part on deriving predictions for affiliate sales, which is the measure most easily retrievable from the model. It is simplest to first discuss predictions at the affiliate level. In our model, because firm-level sales are proportional to firm-level operating profits, it follows from our discussion above that affiliates that exist before the regional trade agreement (weakly) increase their level of sales as a result of the fall in South-East trade barriers. This increase is qualified with the word "weakly" because firms with two affiliates before and after the FTA are not predicted to change their activity as a result of the FTA. Noting that factor prices are independent of τ and that the variable cost function is homothetic, we can also conclude that other measures of affiliate activity, such as assets, employment compensation, and net PPE also (weakly) increase as a result of the FTA. Hence, we can state:

Prediction 3: Conditional on survival, an FTA between the East and the South weakly increases economic activity (in terms of sales, assets, employment compensation, and net PPE) at the affiliate level.

This prediction is consistent with the intensive margin results in table 8.2, but the prediction is more nuanced in that we predict growth at the affiliate level, rather than just an increase in affiliate sales among surviving affiliates. We test this prediction in the next section.

Does prediction 3 necessarily imply, as we documented in section 2, that aggregate affiliate sales in the South-East area increase as a result of the FTA? Not necessarily. As shown above, the FTA leads to gross exit of some plants in the area, as some two-plant MNEs become one-plant MNEs. Affiliate sales for this group of MNEs necessarily fall as a result of the FTA, and this decrease may not be offset by the increase in sales of surviving affiliates. The overall effect on aggregate affiliate sales depends on the distribution of productivity in the population, just as our prediction on the number of affiliates does. We show in the appendix that when productivity follows a Pareto distribution, aggregate affiliate sales are indeed decreasing in $\underline{\tau}$. In sum, we have:

Prediction 4: When firm productivity follows a Pareto distribution, the FTA leads to an increase in aggregate affiliate sales in the South-East area.

We can derive further predictions by studying the direction of sales implied by the model. Notice that Western firms with affiliates in both the East and the South will have affiliates that sell all of their output in their local market. Hence, the level of affiliate third-country sales is zero both for exporters and for two-plant MNEs. On the other hand, under condition (6), firms with productivity $\varphi \in \left(\varphi_X^*, \varphi_{I_{ES}}^*\right)$ sell an amount

$$\left(\frac{(\sigma - 1)\varphi}{\sigma}\right)^{\sigma-1} \frac{A^E}{\left(w_U^E\right)^{(1-\beta)(\sigma-1)}}$$

in the Eastern (local market) and an amount

$$\left(\frac{(\sigma - 1)\varphi}{\sigma}\right)^{\sigma-1} \frac{\tau^{1-\sigma} A^S}{\left(w_U^E\right)^{(1-\beta)(\sigma-1)}}$$

in the Southern market. The ratio of affiliate third-market sales to local sales is thus given by $\frac{\tau^{1-\sigma} A^S}{A^E}$. It is independent of productivity and decreasing in τ. When condition (6) does not hold, single-affiliate firms operate in the South, but the share of third-country sales by affiliates is either 0 or a positive number that decreases in τ. Putting all the pieces together, we can conclude:

Prediction 5: An FTA between the East and the South increases the share of affiliate sales going to third countries for three reasons. First, new entrants into the South-East area sell more to third markets than the average Western-owned plant in the area. Second, firms that consolidate two affiliates into one have affiliates with positive sales to third markets, which they did not have before. Third, firms with only one affiliate before and after the FTA also increase the share of affiliate sales going to third markets.

In table 8.4 we presented broad patterns consistent with these predictions, but we test these predictions more formally in the next section.

4 Econometric Evidence

The first prediction from the theory is that the formation of the FTA increases the number of US MNEs operating there. The number counts in table 8.1 suggest that this is the case. There is also evidence for Prediction 2 in that the number of affiliates in the ASEAN region increases, and the rate of increase exceeds the rate of increase in other Asian countries. In order to consider the evidence for the other predictions, we turn to detailed firm level data. Table 8.5 provides descriptive statistics for these data.

Prediction 3 of the theory holds that affiliates that exist before the formation of the FTA and survive should increase their activity. The specifications presented in table 8.6 test for this effect. The tests explain growth in measures of US MNE activity over the 1989–1994 period using measures of changes at the affiliate level. Therefore, the data only measure growth on the intensive margin because changes can only be measured for affiliates that are observed in both 1989 and 1994. The sample includes observations from all ASEAN countries as well as other Asian countries. The main coefficient of interest is the one on the ASEAN dummy; it reveals whether affiliate growth within the ASEAN region is larger than growth elsewhere in Asia. The specifications

Table 8.5
Descriptive Statistics

	Mean	Standard Deviation
Affiliate Measures of Growth		
Sales Growth	0.4052	0.6670
Asset Growth	0.4178	0.6003
Employment Compensation Growth	0.4778	0.7102
Net PPE Growth	0.3222	0.8691
Growth in Sales due to Local Sales	0.2920	0.5906
Growth in Sales due to US Sales	0.0185	0.2839
Growth in Sales due to Third Country Sales	0.0824	0.3700
Country/Industry Measures of Growth		
Sales Growth	0.4780	0.8052
Asset Growth	0.5092	0.8017
Employment Compensation Growth	0.5203	0.8329
Net PPE Growth	0.4941	0.9513
Direction of Sales		
Share of Sales to Local Market	0.7894	0.3519
Share of Sales to US	0.0709	0.2201
Share of Sales to Third Countries	0.1397	0.2790
Controls		
Per Capita GDP Growth	0.1583	0.1430
Changes in Tax Rate	−0.0298	0.0390
Log of per capita GDP	9.3365	1.3979
Tax Rate	0.3146	0.1249

Notes: This table provides descriptive statistics for the variables used in the regression analysis. The top panel displays measures of affiliate activity that are used in the analysis presented in tables 8.6 and 8.8. Growth rates of sales, assets, employment compensation and net property plant and equipment are measured by taking the difference between end and beginning of period values and dividing by the average of end and beginning of period values. Growth in sales due to sales to a particular location are computed by taking the difference between end and beginning of period values of sales to that location and dividing by the average of end and beginning of period values of total sales. The second panel displays country/industry measures of growth used in the analysis presented in Table 8.7. The third panel displays affiliate measures of the direction of affiliate sales in 1994 used in the analysis presented in Table 8.9. Data on the direction of sales are only reported by majority-owned affiliates.

also control for per capita GDP growth and changes in the corporate tax rate. Heteroskedasticity-consistent standard errors that allow for clustering at the country level are computed and appear in parentheses.

The dependent variable in the first two columns is sales growth, and it is measured by taking the difference between end and beginning of period values of sales and dividing by average values. The 0.1638 coefficient on the

Table 8.6
Affiliate Level Responses

Dependent Variable	Sales Growth		Asset Growth		Employment Compensation Growth		Net PPE Growth	
	(1)	(2)	(3)	(4)	(5)	(6)	(7)	(8)
ASEAN Dummy	0.1638	0.0842	0.2014	0.1829	0.2118	0.1380	0.1520	0.1738
	(0.0630)	(0.0383)	(0.0601)	(0.0546)	(0.0961)	(0.0737)	(0.1009)	(0.0853)
Per Capita GDP Growth		0.6323		0.1634		0.6064		−0.1468
		(0.1941)		(0.2064)		(0.3133)		(0.1760)
Changes in Tax Rate		0.9047		0.6883		1.0420		0.5478
		(0.8479)		(0.7199)		(1.0668)		(1.2317)
Constant	0.3654	0.3116	0.3690	0.3681	0.4274	0.3806	0.2853	0.3195
	(0.0486)	(0.0627)	(0.0503)	(0.0617)	(0.0800)	(0.0962)	(0.0814)	(0.1001)
No. of Obs.	2,090	2,090	2,090	2,090	2,023	2,023	2,068	2,068
R-Squared	0.011	0.034	0.021	0.025	0.016	0.035	0.006	0.006

Notes: This table presents the results of specifications explaining measures of US MNE affiliate growth computed using data at the affiliate level. The dependent variable is sales growth in the first two columns, asset growth in the second two columns, employment compensation in the third two columns, and growth in net property plant and equipment in the last two columns. The ASEAN Dummy is equal to one for ASEAN members, and zero for other Asian countries. Per Capita GDP Growth measures the growth of GDP per capita in constant dollar terms. Changes in Tax Rate measures the change in the tax rate paid on corporate income by US MNEs. All growth rates are measured by taking the difference between end and beginning of period values and dividing by the average of end and beginning of period values. Heteroskedasticity-consistent standard errors that allow for clustering by country appear in parentheses.

ASEAN dummy in column 1 is positive and significant, as is the coefficient on this variable in column 2. The specifications in columns 3–8 explain asset growth, employment compensation growth, and growth in net PPE, and the coefficient on the ASEAN dummy is positive and significant in each of the specifications except those presented in columns 6 and 7.[13] These results imply that affiliates that were active in the ASEAN region before and after the formation of AFTA increase their activity by larger amounts than surviving affiliates that operate in other Asian countries over a similar period. These findings are consistent with the claim that FTAs have a positive effect on the level of activity of affiliates that existed before the FTA and remain active after its formation.

The theory does not make decisive predictions concerning how the formation of an FTA affects overall levels of multinational production and sales. Although new firms enter the FTA region and surviving affiliates expand, fixed costs of investment can induce some firms to close an affiliate and serve that affiliate's host country through trade, thereby reducing aggregate sales. Prediction 4 indicates, however, that the latter effect is dominated in the plausible case of a Pareto distribution of productivity. In order to empirically analyze the net impact of these effects, we perform the tests presented in table 8.7. These tests are similar to those in table 8.6, but the data are aggregated to the country/industry level. Therefore, the estimates of the coefficient on the ASEAN dummy captures growth that is due to the net entry of affiliates in addition to the growth of surviving affiliates. These coefficients are slightly larger in the specifications in table 8.7 relative to table 8.6, and they are all significant except the one in column 2. The slightly larger estimates on the ASEAN dummy indicate that part of the disproportionately high levels of growth of US MNE activity in ASEAN countries is a consequence of net entry, or the extensive margin. Consolidation of activity by firms following the formation of AFTA is more than offset by the entry of new firms. This result would be predicted under many distributions of productivity, like a Pareto distribution, as indicated in Prediction 4.

Prediction 5 suggests that a part of growth in affiliate sales observed in table 8.6 is due to growth in sales to third countries. Specifically, the theory indicates that surviving affiliates of those firms that are active in only one country after the formation of AFTA should increase their sales to third countries. Such firms include both those that were active in more than one country prior to AFTA and consolidated activity and those that operated in one country both before and after the formation of AFTA.

The specifications presented in table 8.8 test for this possibility. The dependent variables are components of sales growth; they are measures of growth due to sales to the host country, to the US, and to third countries. Each component of growth is measured by scaling the first difference in sales to a particular location by the average of beginning and end of period aggregate affiliate sales. Therefore, the three components of sales growth sum to the measure of affiliate sales growth analyzed in columns 1 and 2 of table 8.6.

Table 8.7
Country/Industry Level Responses

Dependent Variable	Sales Growth		Asset Growth		Employment Compensation Growth		Net PPE Growth	
	(1)	(2)	(3)	(4)	(5)	(6)	(7)	(8)
ASEAN Dummy	0.2214	0.1213	0.2530	0.2178	0.3085	0.2082	0.3027	0.3095
	(0.1125)	(0.0914)	(0.0759)	(0.0857)	(0.1100)	(0.0850)	(0.0941)	(0.1079)
Per Capita GDP Growth		1.1134		0.4645		1.2034		0.0999
		(0.4337)		(0.4094)		(0.3575)		(0.4875)
Changes in Tax Rate		−0.0679		0.3763		0.5470		0.9626
		(1.2377)		(1.1181)		(0.9244)		(1.5739)
Constant	0.4071	0.2285	0.4282	0.3610	0.4215	0.2395	0.3975	0.3991
	(0.0690)	(0.0609)	(0.0602)	(0.0553)	(0.0745)	(0.0591)	(0.0830)	(0.0887)
No. of Obs.	665	665	665	665	662	662	664	664
R-Squared	0.017	0.044	0.022	0.028	0.030	0.065	0.022	0.025

Notes: This table presents the results of specifications explaining measures of US MNE affiliate growth computed using data at the country/industry level. The dependent variable is sales growth in the first two columns, asset growth in the second two columns, employment compensation in the third two columns, and growth in net property plant and equipment in the last two columns. The ASEAN Dummy is equal to one for ASEAN members, and zero for other Asian countries. Per Capita GDP Growth measures the growth of GDP per capita in constant dollar terms. Changes in Tax Rate measures the change in the tax rate paid on corporate income by US MNEs. All growth rates are measured by taking the difference between end and beginning of period values and dividing by the average of end and beginning of period values. Heteroskedasticity-consistent standard errors that allow for clustering by country appear in parentheses.

The specifications in the odd-numbered columns are similar to those in previous tables, but those in the even-numbered columns differ in that they include the ASEAN dummy interacted with a dummy that is equal to one for firms that operate in only a single ASEAN country after the formation of AFTA. In these specifications, the coefficient on the ASEAN dummy captures the effects of being in an ASEAN country around the time of the formation of AFTA, and the coefficient on the interaction term identifies if the effects of being in an ASEAN country differ for firms that operate in a single ASEAN country in 1994. We introduce this interaction because our model predicts a growth in third-market sales only for the subset of affiliates owned by US multinational firms with a single affiliate in ASEAN countries after the formation of AFTA.

The -0.0018 coefficient on the ASEAN dummy in column 1 indicates that AFTA did not increase sales to the host country. In the second column, this coefficient remains insignificant, and the coefficient on the interaction term is also insignificant, indicating that AFTA did not differentially affect the local sales of firms operating in one ASEAN country after the formation of AFTA. The next two columns analyze the growth in sales due to US sales. The positive and significant coefficient on the ASEAN dummy in column 3 and the positive and marginally significant coefficient on it in column 4 suggest that sales to the US increased around the time AFTA was created. There does not appear to be any differential effect for firms that compete in only a single ASEAN country after the formation of AFTA. While interesting, this result is beyond the scope of the theory. The final two columns analyze the growth in sales due to third country sales, which the model emphasizes. The 0.0391 coefficient in column 5 is positive but not significant, suggesting that the share of sales to third countries does not increase on average for all affiliates. The positive and significant coefficient on the interaction term in the specification in column 6 is consistent with prediction 4. AFTA appears to increase the third country sales of affiliates of firms that operate in a single ASEAN country after the FTA, either because they have consolidated or maintained their activities.

Prediction 5 also asserts that the share of sales to third countries should increase in response to the formation of an FTA in part because new affiliates sell more to third countries than preexisting affiliates. The tests presented in table 8.9 consider this possibility. The specifications explain the share of sales to the host country, to the US, and to third countries for the sample of affiliates in Asia in 1994. The specifications include an ASEAN dummy, a dummy for new affiliates, the interaction of these two, and controls for the log of per capita GDP and the corporate tax rate. In these specifications, the coefficients on the ASEAN dummy estimate the difference in sales shares for ASEAN as opposed to other Asian affiliates, the coefficient on the new affiliate dummy picks up differences in sales shares for new affiliates, and the coefficient on the interaction term identifies whether new affiliates have distinctive sales patterns relative to preexisting affiliates in ASEAN countries.

Table 8.8
Decomposition of Sales Growth

Dependent Variable	Growth in Sales Due to Local Sales		Growth in Sales Due to US Sales		Growth in Sales Due to Third Country Sales	
	(1)	(2)	(3)	(4)	(5)	(6)
ASEAN Dummy	−0.0018	0.0274	0.0224	0.0230	0.0391	0.0284
	(0.0564)	(0.0524)	(0.0106)	(0.0132)	(0.0382)	(0.0368)
ASEAN Dummy × Dummy if in One ASEAN Country in 1994		−0.1622		−0.0035		0.0593
		(0.1110)		(0.0317)		(0.0237)
Per Capita GDP Growth	0.5002	0.5134	0.0684	0.0687	0.1989	0.1941
	(0.1667)	(0.1591)	(0.0333)	(0.0324)	(0.1677)	(0.1650)
Changes in Tax Rate	0.6840	0.6439	−0.0719	−0.0728	0.3278	0.3425
	(0.6291)	(0.6208)	(0.1434)	(0.1424)	(0.3479)	(0.3420)
Constant	0.2327	0.2299	−0.0008	−0.0008	0.0497	0.0508
	(0.0449)	(0.0441)	(0.0091)	(0.0090)	(0.0381)	(0.0377)
No. of Obs.	1,620	1,620	1,620	1,620	1,620	1,620
R-Squared	0.020	0.024	0.003	0.003	0.014	0.015

Notes: This table presents the results of specifications explaining components of the growth of US MNE affiliates measured using data at the affiliate level. The dependent variable is growth in sales due to local sales in the first two columns, the growth in sales due to sales to the US in the second two columns, and the growth in sales due to sales to countries other than the US and the affiliate's host country in the last two columns. The ASEAN Dummy is equal to one for ASEAN members, and zero for other Asian countries. The Dummy if in One ASEAN Country in 1994 is a dummy equal to one for firms that were active in only one ASEAN country in 1994. Per Capita GDP Growth measures the growth of GDP per capita in constant dollar terms. Changes in Tax Rate measures the change in the tax rate paid on corporate income by US MNEs. All growth rates are measured by taking the difference between end and beginning of period values and dividing by the average of end and beginning of period values. Heteroskedasticity-consistent standard errors that allow for clustering by country appear in parentheses.

Prediction 5 suggests that the coefficient on this interaction term should be positive in specifications explaining the share of sales to third countries.

The new affiliate dummy is defined in two ways. In the odd-numbered columns, this variable is equal to one for all affiliates that appear in the data in 1994 but not in 1989. In the theory, firms that establish new affiliates in response to the formation of an FTA establish a single affiliate. However, the theory does not consider a variety of factors that might induce a firm to enter many ASEAN markets after the creation of AFTA. For example, firms could face trade costs within the ASEAN region that reflect nontariff costs of moving their goods. Such firms may be induced to enter two or more ASEAN countries following the introduction of AFTA, directing a large fraction of their sales to the host country. In the even-numbered columns, the new affiliate dummy is defined to equal one for new affiliates in ASEAN countries provided that the affiliate's firm operates in only a single ASEAN country in 1994. It is also equal to one for all new affiliates in other Asian countries. The interaction term therefore isolates effects for the type of new affiliate that is considered in the theory.

The coefficients on the ASEAN dummies indicate that surviving affiliates in ASEAN countries have a lower share of host country sales and a higher share of US and third country sales than surviving affiliates in other Asian countries. The coefficients on the dummy for new affiliates are all insignificant, implying that new affiliates in other Asian countries do not exhibit a pattern of sales that is distinctive from surviving affiliates in those countries. The coefficients on the interaction terms are also insignificant, except for the one in the last column. The positive and significant 0.0738 coefficient implies that new affiliates in ASEAN countries that are a part of firms that operate in only a single ASEAN country have higher shares of sales to third countries than other affiliates in ASEAN countries. This difference in the direction of sales for new affiliates is not observed in the rest of Asia. These results are consistent with Prediction 5.

These empirical results are subject to a number of reasonable concerns, and we have conducted several robustness tests to address them. A couple of issues might distort the findings on affiliate growth presented in tables 8.6 and 8.7. First, the disproportionate growth of affiliate activity in ASEAN countries could reflect low levels of affiliate growth in other Asian countries rather than high levels of affiliate growth in ASEAN countries. Several factors could induce such a pattern. For example, the formation of AFTA may attract US foreign investment away from other regional countries. In order to consider this possibility, we conduct the tests presented in tables 8.6 and 8.7 using a sample that is comprised of affiliates in ASEAN countries and affiliates in European countries. The results obtained using this sample are qualitatively similar to the results presented in the study, with the exception that the coefficient on the ASEAN dummy in the specification presented in column 8 of table 8.6 is no longer significant.[14] The results in each table are also largely robust to removing Australia and Japan from the sample of other Asian countries; these

Table 8.9
Direction of Sales of New Affiliates

Dependent Variable	Share of Sales to Local Market		Share of Sales to US		Share of Sales to Third Countries	
	(1)	(2)	(3)	(4)	(5)	(6)
ASEAN Dummy	-0.1787	-0.1368	0.0582	0.0410	0.1205	0.0958
	(0.0524)	(0.0555)	(0.0180)	(0.0193)	(0.0419)	(0.0413)
New Affiliate Dummy	0.0314	0.0319	-0.0091	-0.0093	-0.0223	-0.0226
	(0.0245)	(0.0245)	(0.0106)	(0.0106)	(0.0143)	(0.0143)
ASEAN Dummy × New Affiliate Dummy	0.0216	-0.1220	-0.0121	0.0482	-0.0095	0.0738
	(0.0309)	(0.0812)	(0.0119)	(0.0497)	(0.0210)	(0.0371)
Log of Per Capita GDP	-0.0388	-0.0371	0.0105	0.0098	0.0283	0.0273
	(0.0125)	(0.0126)	(0.0052)	(0.0054)	(0.0104)	(0.0103)
Tax Rate	0.7745	0.7662	-0.2061	-0.2026	-0.5684	-0.5636
	(0.1873)	(0.1899)	(0.0843)	(0.0859)	(0.1137)	(0.1148)
Constant	0.9495	0.9356	0.0251	0.0310	0.0254	0.0333
	(0.0956)	(0.0951)	(0.0422)	(0.0438)	(0.0824)	(0.0815)
In ASEAN countries, new affiliates include all affiliates?	Y	N	Y	N	Y	N
In ASEAN countries, new affiliates include all new affiliates of firms operating in one ASEAN country in 1994?	N	Y	N	Y	N	Y
No. of Obs.	3,299	3,299	3,299	3,299	3,299	3,299
R-Squared	0.103	0.103	0.022	0.022	0.083	0.084

Notes: This table presents the results of specifications explaining the direction of sales of new affiliates. The sample includes affiliates in ASEAN and other Asian countries that appear in the data in 1994. The dependent variable is the share of sales to persons in the affiliate's host country in the first two columns, the share of sales to persons in the US in the second two columns and the share of sales to persons in countries other than the US and the affiliate's host country in the last two columns. The ASEAN Dummy is equal to one for ASEAN members, and zero for other Asian countries. The New Affiliate Dummy is equal to one for all new affiliates in Columns 1, 3, and 5. In Columns 2, 4, and 6, for affiliates in ASEAN countries, it is equal to one for new affiliates of firms that operate in only one ASEAN country in 1994, and for affiliates in other Asian countries, it is equal to one for all new affiliates. Log of Per Capita GDP is the log of per capita GDP, and Tax Rate measures the corporate income tax rate. Heteroskedasticity-consistent standard errors that allow for clustering by country appear in parentheses.

nations are large and developed, and multinational activity in them may be distinctive.

Second, many of the provisions of the AFTA did not take effect until after 1994, so it is potentially informative to study growth in activity over the 1989 to 1999 period as opposed to the 1989 to 1994 period. We have conducted the tests presented in tables 8.6 and 8.7 of the chapter using this longer sample period. The coefficients on the ASEAN dummy in these specifications generally maintain their significance, but these coefficients are insignificant in the specifications presented in columns 5 and 6 of table 8.6, and the coefficient on the ASEAN dummy in the specification presented in column 6 of table 8.7 is only marginally significant.

The specifications presented include a parsimonious set of controls. Other country characteristics could be changing at the same time that AFTA is formed, and these might confound our results regarding patterns in affiliate growth. For example, the extent to which countries place restrictions on FDI or changes in political regimes could be coincident with the formation of AFTA and explain patterns in US multinational growth. To address this issue, we have conducted the analysis in tables 8.6 and 8.7 including controls for changes in FDI restrictions drawn from Shatz (2000) and for political regime changes drawn from Marshall and Jaggers (2009).[15] Some results are only marginally significant when these controls are included, but for the most part the results are little changed by them. We do not include these controls in the specifications we present because these data cover only a subset of the countries in the BEA data.

Although the BEA data include firms in all industries, the theory envisions a firm that produces a physical good that is costly to trade. Therefore, the predictions might be more relevant to manufacturing firms than they are to firms in other industries. We have performed the analysis in tables 8.6–8.8 limiting the sample to affiliates in manufacturing industries. The results of the tests in tables 8.6 and 8.7 are stronger than those obtained using the full sample, but the tests presented in column 6 of tables 8.8 and 8.9 are no longer significant, perhaps because the sample size is smaller.

Finally, we have rerun all of the specifications, dropping each ASEAN country in turn, to see if activity related to a particular country drives the results. Although this yields some variation in the estimates, no single ASEAN country is central to the results.

5 Conclusion

Even though existing studies of regional trade agreements focus on their impact on trade flows, these agreements appear to have large effects on the level and nature of multinational firm activity. In this chapter we build on recent theoretical work to develop a model of the behavior of heterogeneous firms based in one country when there is a reduction in the tariffs on trade between two other countries. This model generates a series of predictions that we consider in the context of how US multinational firms responded to the formation of the ASEAN free trade agreement. Examination of aggregate data and more detailed firm-level analysis indicates that measures of US multinational activity increase at the time AFTA is created. Specifically, the number of US firms that are active in the region increases at a faster rate than the number of US firms active in other Asian countries. Affiliates within the ASEAN region grow by larger amounts than affiliates elsewhere. There are also distinct shifts in the direction of sales of ASEAN affiliates. These affiliates increase the share of sales to countries other than the US and the affiliate's host country. This increase reflects two channels for firms that focus their activity in a single ASEAN country after the formation of AFTA. First, there are high levels of growth in third-country sales for affiliates that are active before and after the formation of AFTA. In addition, new affiliates in ASEAN countries direct a larger share of their sales to third countries than new affiliates elsewhere in Asia. These findings are consistent with the model's predictions.

Our results have significant implications for the welfare effects of regional trade agreements. Increased multinational firm activity in a regional free trade area is likely to generate benefits within the region as multinationals typically exhibit high levels of productivity, pay high wages, and create positive spillovers for other firms. Policy makers from excluded countries have reason to support the creation of regional trade agreements because firms from excluded countries can benefit through the use of foreign direct investment.

The findings also point out the relevance of incorporating firm level heterogeneity into models of multinational firms. Only recently have these theories been confronted with firm-level data that allow for a careful analysis of intensive and extensive responses to shifts in environmental factors.

6 Appendix

In this appendix we briefly discuss the effects of the regional trade agreement in the model for the case in which the distribution of productivity $G(\varphi)$ is Pareto, so that

$$G(\varphi) = 1 - \left(\frac{b}{\varphi}\right)^k,$$

with $k > \sigma - 1$, a condition needed for the distribution of sales revenue to have finite variance. Given our results in the model, Western parents with productivity lower than φ_X^* have no affiliates in the South-East area, those with productivity between φ_X^* and $\varphi_{I_{ES}}^*$ have one affiliate, and those with productivity higher than $\varphi_{I_{ES}}^*$ have two. Normalizing the total measure of US firms to 1, we have that the measure of affiliates in the South-East area is given by:

$$n = G\left(\varphi_{IES}^*\right) - G\left(\varphi_X^*\right) + 2\left(1 - G\left(\varphi_{IES}^*\right)\right)$$

$$= 2 - \left(G\left(\varphi_x^*\right) + G\left(\varphi_{IES}^*\right)\right) = \left(\frac{b}{\varphi_{IES}^*}\right)^k + \left(\frac{b}{\varphi_X^*}\right)^k.$$

It then follows that

$$\frac{\partial n}{\partial \underline{\tau}} = -kb^k\left[\left(\varphi_{IES}^*\right)^{-k-1}\frac{\partial \varphi_{IES}^*}{\partial \underline{\tau}} + \left(\varphi_X^*\right)^{-k-1}\frac{\partial \varphi_X^*}{\partial \underline{\tau}}\right],$$

which at first sight appears ambiguous since $\frac{\partial \varphi_X^*}{\partial \underline{\tau}} > 0$ but $\frac{\partial \varphi_{IES}^*}{\partial \underline{\tau}} < 0$. However, using the definitions of φ_X^* and φ_{IES}^*, that is,

$$\varphi_X^* = \left(\frac{f}{\psi^{IE} - \psi^X}\right)^{\frac{1}{\sigma-1}} \tag{A1}$$

and

$$\varphi_{IES}^* = \left(\frac{f}{\psi^{IES} - \psi^{IE}}\right)^{\frac{1}{\sigma-1}}, \tag{A2}$$

we find that

$$\frac{\frac{\partial \varphi_X^*}{\partial \underline{\tau}}}{\frac{\partial \varphi_{IES}^*}{\partial \underline{\tau}}} = -\left(\frac{\varphi_X^*}{\varphi_{IES}^*}\right)^\sigma,$$

and thus

$$\frac{\partial n}{\partial \underline{\tau}} = kb^k\frac{\frac{\partial \varphi_{IES}^*}{\partial \underline{\tau}}}{\left(\varphi_{IES}^*\right)^\sigma}\left[\left(\varphi_X^*\right)^{-(k-(\sigma-1))} - \left(\varphi_{IES}^*\right)^{-(k-(\sigma-1))}\right] < 0,$$

which is negative because $\frac{\partial \varphi_{IES}^*}{\partial \underline{\tau}} < 0$, $k > \sigma - 1$, and $\varphi_{IES}^* > \varphi_X^*$.

We next study the effect of the agreement on aggregate affiliate sales. Aggregate sales of Western multinationals with one affiliate are given by

$$R^{IE} = \int_{\varphi_X^*}^{\varphi_{IES}^*} \sigma \psi^{IE} \varphi^{\sigma-1} dG(\varphi)$$

$$= \sigma \psi^{IE} \int_{\varphi_X^*}^{\varphi_{IES}^*} \varphi^{\sigma-1} kb^k \varphi^{-k-1} d\varphi$$

$$= \sigma \psi^{IE} \frac{kb^k}{k-(\sigma-1)}\left[\left(\varphi_X^*\right)^{-(k-(\sigma-1))} - \left(\varphi_{IES}^*\right)^{-(k-(\sigma-1))}\right]$$

On the other hand, aggregate sales of affiliates of Western multinational firms with two affiliates are given by:

$$R^{IES} = \int_{\varphi^*_{IES}}^{\infty} \sigma \psi^{IES} \varphi^{\sigma-1} dG(\varphi)$$

$$= \sigma \psi^{IES} \int_{\varphi^*_X}^{\infty} \varphi^{\sigma-1} kb^k \varphi^{-k-1} d\varphi$$

$$= \sigma \psi^{IES} \frac{kb^k}{k-(\sigma-1)} \left(\varphi^*_{IES}\right)^{-(k-(\sigma-1))}.$$

Aggregate affiliate sales are then given by

$$R = \Theta \left\{ \psi^{IE} \cdot \left(\varphi^*_X\right)^{-(k-(\sigma-1))} + (\psi^{IES} - \psi^{IE}) \cdot \left(\varphi^*_{IES}\right)^{-(k-(\sigma-1))} \right\},$$

where Θ is a constant. Using (A1) and (A2), we can write this expression as

$$R = \Theta \left\{ \psi^{Ix} \cdot \left(\varphi^*_X\right)^{-(k-(\sigma-1))} + f \cdot \left(\varphi^*_X\right)^{-k} + f \cdot \left(\varphi^*_{IES}\right)^{-k} \right\}.$$

But note that ψ^{Ix} is independent of $\underline{\tau}$, $\left(\varphi^*_X\right)^{-(k-(\sigma-1))}$ is decreasing in $\underline{\tau}$ (for $k > \sigma - 1$), while in our derivations regarding the number of affiliates above, we have shown that $(\varphi^*_X)^{-k} + (\varphi^*_{IES})^{-k}$ is also decreasing in $\underline{\tau}$. Hence, we can conclude that when productivity follows a Pareto distribution, a regional trade agreement between the South and the East (i.e., a fall in $\underline{\tau}$) increases affiliate sales in the area.

Notes

1. The horizontal FDI view represents FDI as the replication of capacity in multiple locations in response to factors such as trade costs, as in Markusen (1984), Brainard (1997), and Markusen and Venables (2000). The vertical FDI view represents FDI as the geographic distribution of production globally in response to the opportunities afforded by different markets, as in Helpman (1984) and Yeaple (2003). Caves (1996) and Markusen (2002) provide particularly useful overviews of this literature.
2. Our sample includes nonbank affiliates that filed long or short survey forms; it excludes estimates for affiliates that did not file a survey report. Our sample therefore differs from the data used to produce aggregates published by BEA. Only majority-owned nonbank affiliates report data used in the analysis presented in tables 8.4, 8.8, and 8.9, so smaller samples are used in creating the results reported in these tables.
3. The other Asian countries include all non-ASEAN countries in the Asia and Pacific grouping used by BEA.
4. In order to avoid the possible disclosure of confidential information, published aggregate data that exclude Brunei Darussalam are used to compute the figures in the top panel.

5. Similar extensions are developed by Yeaple (2003, 2008a, 2008b) and Grossman et al. (2006), but the focus of those papers is very different.

6. As explained in the introduction, our empirical analysis does not study these country asymmetries. We, however, found it natural to develop a theoretical framework that can be used for future empirical investigations.

7. Although a free trade area would drive trade policy costs to 0, natural trade barriers would still imply $\underline{\tau} > 1$.

8. It is clear that as long as $w_U^W = w_U^E$, a firm would never want to service the West with exports from a plant located in the East because this would entail positive transport costs and a higher fixed cost. Provided that w_U^S or $\bar{\tau}$ is sufficiently high (as Assumption 1 imposes), servicing the West from a plant in the South is not optimal either.

9. Because $\bar{\tau} > \underline{\tau}$, the firm would choose to service the South via exports from the plant in the East. Hence, under this strategy, exports from the West are equal to 0.

10. In particular, note that $\pi^{I_E}(\varphi) - \pi^X(\varphi)$, $\pi^{I_S}(\varphi) - \pi^X(\varphi)$ and $\pi^{I_{ES}}(\varphi) - \pi^X(\varphi)$ all increase unboundedly with φ. Furthermore, as $\varphi \to 0$, only the exporting option remains profitable.

11. When Assumption 1 does not hold, the operating profits associated with setting up only one affiliate in the South are strictly higher than those obtained when setting up only one affiliate in the East and when setting up an affiliate in both the East and the South. In such a case, the least productive firms export, while the most productive firms engage in single-plant FDI in the South. No other organizational mode is optimal in equilibrium.

12. In reality, an FTA would be likely to affect other variables in the model, such as wage rates and the demand level. We attempt to control for these factors in the econometric exercises in section 4.

13. Statements about levels of significance are based on the large sample properties of t-statistics. If one assumes that the degrees of freedom equal the number of clusters, which is 22 (the number of countries in the data), results presented in column 8 of table 8.6 and column 6 of table 8.9 are only significant at the 6% level.

14. Although it is less clear why these considerations might bias the results in tables 8.8 and 8.9, we have also checked the robustness of our results in those tables, and the results are similar.

15. Changes in FDI restrictions are measured as changes in a dummy that is set equal to one if the acquisition or sector scores in Shatz (2000) are less than 3. Regime changes are measured as changes in the Polity2 variable in Marshall and Jaggers (2009).

References

Aitken, B., G. Hanson, and A. Harrison. 1996. Wages and Foreign Ownership: A Comparative Study of Mexico, Venezuela, and the United States. *Journal of International Economics*. 40(3–4). pp. 345–371.

Aitken, B., and A. Harrison. 1999. Do Domestic Firms Benefit from Foreign Direct Investment? Evidence from Panel Data. *American Economic Review*. 89(3). pp. 605–618.

Antràs, P., and E. Helpman. 2004. Global Sourcing. *Journal of Political Economy*. 112(3). pp. 552–580.

Brainard, S. L. 1997. An Empirical Assessment of the Proximity-Concentration Trade-off Between Multinational Sales and Trade. *American Economic Review.* 87(4). pp. 520–544.

Caves, R. 1996. *Multinational Enterprise and Economic Analysis.* Second Edition. New York: Cambridge University Press.

Chen, M. 2009. Regional Economic Integration and Geographic Concentration of Multinational Firms. *European Economic Review.* 53(3). pp. 355–375.

Desai, M., C. F. Foley, and J. Hines Jr. 2009. Domestic Effects of the Foreign Activities of US Multinationals. *American Economic Journal: Economic Policy.* 1(1). pp. 181–203.

Ekholm, K., R. Forslid, and J. Markusen. 2007. Export-Platform Foreign Direct Investment. *Journal of the European Economic Association.* 5(4). pp. 776–795.

Grossman, G., E. Helpman, and A. Szeidl. 2006. Optimal Integration Strategies for the Multinational Firm. *Journal of International Economics.* 70(1). pp. 216–238.

Haskel, J., S. Pereira, and M. Slaughter. 2007. Does Inward Foreign Direct Investment Boost the Productivity of Domestic Firms? *Review of Economics and Statistics.* 89(3). pp. 482–496.

Helpman, E. 1984. A Simple Theory of International Trade with Multinational Corporations. *Journal of Political Economy.* 92(3). pp. 451–471.

Helpman, E., M. Melitz, and S. Yeaple. 2004. Export versus FDI with Heterogeneous Firms. *American Economic Review.* 94(1). pp. 300–316.

Heyman, F., F. Sjöholm, and P. G. Tingvall. 2007. Is There Really a Foreign Ownership Wage Premium? Evidence from Matched Employer-Employee Data. *Journal of International Economics.* 73(2). pp. 355–376.

Krugman, P., and A. Venables. 1996. Integration, Specialization, and Adjustment. *European Economic Review.* 40(3–5). pp. 959–967.

Krueger, A. 1999. Are Preferential Trading Arrangements Trade-Liberalizing or Protectionist? *The Journal of Economic Perspectives.* 13(4). pp. 105–124.

Markusen, J. 1984. Multinationals, Multi-Plant Economies, and the Gains from Trade. *Journal of International Economics.* 16(3–4). pp. 205–226.

Markusen, J., and A. Venables. 2000. The Theory of Endowment, Intra-Industry and Multi-National Trade. *Journal of International Economics.* 52(2). pp. 209–234.

Markusen, J. 2002. *Multinational Firms and the Theory of International Trade.* Cambridge, MA: MIT Press.

Marshall, M., and K. Jaggers. 1999. Polity IV Project. Data set available at: http://www.systemicpeace.org/polity/polity4.htm.

Motta, M., and G. Norman. 1996. Does Economic Integration Cause Foreign Direct Investment? *International Economic Review.* 37(4). pp. 757–783.

Nocke, V., and S. Yeaple. 2008. An Assignment Theory of Foreign Direct Investment. *Review of Economic Studies.* 75(2). pp. 529–557.

Puga, D., and A. Venables. 1997. Preferential Trading Agreements and Industrial Location. *Journal of International Economics.* 43(3–4). pp. 347–358.

Shatz, H. 2000. The Location of US Multinational Affiliates. PhD dissertation, Harvard University.

Smarzynska, B. 2004. Does Foreign Direct Investment Increase the Productivity of Domestic Firms? In Search of Spillovers through Backward Linkages. *American Economic Review.* 94(3). pp. 605–627.

Viner, J. 1950. *The Customs Union Issue.* New York: Carnegie Endowment for International Peace.

Yeaple, S. 2003. The Complex Integration Strategies of Multinationals and Cross Country Dependencies in the Structure of FDI. *Journal of International Economics.* 60(2). pp. 293–314.

Yeaple, S. 2008a. Firm Heterogeneity and the Structure of US Multinational Activity: An Empirical Analysis. *NBER Working Paper* 14072.

Yeaple, S. 2008b. Firm Heterogeneity, Central Locations, and the Structure of Foreign Direct Investment. In E. Helpman, D. Marin, and T. Verdier, eds. *The Organization of Firms in a Global Economy.* Cambridge, MA: Harvard University Press, pp. 602–611.

9

A World Factory in Global Production Chains: Estimating Imported Value-Added in Exports by the People's Republic of China

Robert Koopman, Zhi Wang, and Shang-Jin Wei

This study was prepared for the Asian Development Bank and Hong Kong Institute for Monetary Research (ADB-HKIMR) project "Quantifying the Costs and Benefits of Economic Integration." The authors are grateful to Robert Barro, Jong-Wha Lee, Prakash Loungani, Leonard Cheng, Judith Dean, Pieter Bottelier, Peter Dixon, Kun-fu Zhu, conference participants at the ADB-HKIMR conference in January 2009, and seminar participants at the International Trade Commission for helpful comments. The views in this chapter are those of the authors and are not the official views of the United States International Trade Commission, or of any other organization that the authors are or have been affiliated with.

1 Introduction

Walking into any shopping mall in the United States (US), one is rarely surprised to see a product with a "Made in China" label. Increasingly, many products that are supposed to be technically sophisticated and therefore likely to be associated with exports from high-income countries, such as digital cameras and computers, also carry that label. Since the most salient characteristic of the factor endowment in the People's Republic of China (PRC) is a vast supply of unskilled labor relative to either physical or human capital, is the country's actual export structure inconsistent with the predictions from the international trade theory based on its endowment? A possible resolution to the puzzle is that the PRC is simply the last section of a long global production chain that ends up assembling components from various countries into a final product before it is exported to the US market. Indeed, a MacBook computer carries a label at its back (in small type) that reads "Designed by Apple in California; Assembled in China." This label is likely to be oversimplified already, as it reports only the head and the tail of a global production chain, but skips many other countries that supply other components that go into the product.

The PRC is the archetype of a national economy that is well integrated into a global production chain. It imports raw material, equipment, and intermediate inputs, and then exports a big fraction of its output (on the order of 37% of gross domestic product [GDP] in 2006) to the world market. The PRC is not the only country whose production and exports are a part of a global chain; Japan, the Republic of Korea (Korea), Singapore, and Malaysia are some other examples of countries that participate actively in the international divisions of labor. However, the PRC is noteworthy due to its sheer size. In addition, its export/GDP ratio, at 35% or higher in recent years, is extraordinarily high for a large economy, when compared with 8% for the US and 13% for India. With a reputation as a "world factory," the PRC is a top supplier of manufacturing outsourcing for many global companies.

Imported inputs used in production for exports reduce the share of value-added generated by domestic producers. Consider the example of iPod, which the PRC assembles for Apple and exports to the US and other countries. In its trade statistics, the export value for a unit of a 30 gigabyte video model in 2006 was about $150. However, the best estimate of the value-added attributable to producers in the PRC was only $4, with the remaining value-added coming from the US, Japan, and other countries (Linden et al., 2007; Varian, 2007).

For many policy issues, it is important to assess the extent of domestic content in exports. For example, what is the effect of a currency appreciation on a country's exports? The answer depends crucially on the share of domestic content in the exports. Other things being equal, the lower the share of domestic content in the exports, the smaller the effect on trade volume a given exchange rate appreciation would have. As another example, what is the effect of trading with the PRC on US income inequality? The answer depends in part on whether the PRC simply exports products that are intensive in low-skilled labor or whether its exports are more sophisticated. Rodrik (2006) notes that the per capita income typically associated with the kind of goods bundle that the PRC exports is much higher than the country's actual income. He interprets this as evidence that the skill content of its exports is likely to be much higher than its endowment may imply. Schott (2008) documents an apparent rapid increase in the similarity between the PRC's export structure and that of high-income countries, and interprets it as evidence of a rise in the level of sophistication embedded in the country's exports. Wang and Wei (2008a) use disaggregated regional data to investigate the determinants of the rise in export sophistication. Indeed, many other observers have expressed fear that the PRC is increasingly producing and exporting sophisticated products and may be providing wage competition for mid- to high-skilled workers in the US and Europe. However, the calculations by Rodrik (2006) and Schott (2008) do not take into account the imported content in the country's exports. If the domestic content in exports from the PRC is low, especially in sectors that would have been considered sophisticated or high-skilled in the US, then imports from the PRC may still generate a large downward pressure on the wage of the low-skilled Americans after all (as pointed out by Krugman, 2008). These are important policy questions and have implications for both developing and developed countries. A good understanding of the nature and extent of global supply chains can provide important insights for economists and policy makers.

How would one assess foreign versus domestic content in a country's exports? Hummels et al. (2001) (HIY in subsequent discussion) propose a concept of vertical specialization (VS) in a country's trade, defined as "the imported input content of exports, or equivalently, foreign value-added embodied in exports," and provide a formula to compute VS share based exclusively on a country's input-output (IO) table. For a sample of 14 countries (not including the PRC), they calculate that the average share of foreign value-added in exports was about 21% in 1990. Yi (2003) shows that a dramatic increase in vertical specialization after World War II is likely to have been responsible for a faster growth of world trade relative to world GDP over the last five decades. Other recent applications of the vertical specialization concept include Goh and Olivier (2004), Chinn (2005), National Research Council (2006), Dean et al. (2007), and Koopman et al. (2008).

A key assumption needed for the HIY formula to work is that the intensity in the use of imported inputs is the same between production for exports and production for domestic sales. This assumption is violated in the presence of processing exports. Processing exports are characterized by imports for exports with favorable tariff treatment: firms import parts and other intermediate materials from abroad, with tariff exemptions on the imported inputs and other tax preferences from local or central governments, and, after processing or assembling, export the finished products. The policy preferences for processing exports usually lead to a significant difference in the intensity of imported intermediate inputs in the production of processing exports and that in other demand sources (for domestic final sales and normal exports). Since processing exports have accounted for more than 50% of exports from the PRC every year at least since 1996 (see column 1 of table 9.1 for detail), the HIY formula is likely to lead to a significant under-estimation of the share of foreign value-added in its exports. In fact, most economies offer tariff reductions or exemptions on imported intermediate inputs used in production for exports. Ignoring processing exports (or duty drawbacks) is likely to lead to estimation errors, especially for economies that engage in a massive amount of tariff/tax-favored processing trade, such as the PRC, Mexico, and Viet Nam.

In this chapter, we aim to make three points. First, we review a formula in Koopman et al. (2008) for computing shares of foreign and domestic

Table 9.1

Processing Manufacturing Exports (excluding HS Chapters 1–27), 1996–2006

Year	Share of Processing Exports in Total Exports (100*PE/TE)	Share of Processing and Assembling	Share of Processing with Imported Materials	Share of Processing Imports in Total Imports	Ratio of Processing Imports to Processing Exports (100*PM/PE)	Processing Trade Surplus as Share of Processing Exports (100*[PE-PM]/PE)
1996	62.1	18.0	44.1	47.6	71.1	28.9
1997	60.2	17.9	42.3	53.1	67.0	33.0
1998	62.0	18.3	43.7	52.0	63.3	36.7
1999	61.2	19.9	41.3	47.9	64.7	35.3
2000	59.6	17.9	41.7	46.6	65.9	34.1
2001	59.7	17.2	42.5	43.0	62.7	37.3
2002	58.8	15.6	43.2	45.6	67.4	32.6
2003	58.5	13.2	45.4	44.0	66.7	33.3
2004	58.0	12.0	46.0	45.3	66.6	33.4
2005	57.0	11.3	45.7	48.3	64.6	35.4
2006	54.5	9.9	44.6	47.9	61.7	38.3

Source: Customs Trade Statistics, General Customs Administration, PRC.

value-added in a country's exports when processing exports are pervasive. We develop this formula because the production technology and input sourcing differ between goods produced for general domestic consumption and general exports, compared to those produced under export processing regimes. The HIY formula is a special case of this general formula. Second, we apply our methodology to the PRC using data for 1997, 2002, and 2006.[1] We estimate that the share of foreign value-added in its manufactured exports is about 50%, almost twice as high as that implied by the HIY formula. There are also interesting variations across sectors. Those sectors that are likely labeled as relatively sophisticated such as computers, telecommunication equipments, and electronic devices have particularly high foreign content (about 80%). Third, we develop a method that estimates the amount of foreign content that originates in key individual foreign supplying countries by taking advantage of an international IO table. Computers and home electronics (such as TVs, radios, and cell phones), two of the country's largest export categories in recent years, account for 17% of manufacturing exports; our estimates suggest that Japan; the US; Hong Kong, China; and the European Union (EU) supplied about 60% of their foreign input content.

By our estimation, the imported content in total merchandise exports of the PRC experienced a modest increase in recent years (from 47.7% in 1997 to 49.3% in 2006). The imported content in manufactured goods exports experienced a modest decline (from 52.4% in 1997 to 50.6% in 2006). However, the average imported content in exports masks an interesting divergence between normal versus processing exports. For processing exports, there was a decline in imported content (or an increase in domestic content) from 1997 to 2002 (though this is reversed in more recent years). As domestic input suppliers increase both number of varieties and qualities over time, processing trade producers may decide to increase local sourcing of their inputs. This is consistent with the conjecture in Aziz and Li (2007) of a rising domestic content in processing trade based on an increase in their estimated price elasticity over time. However, for normal exports, the imported content has been increasing. This is because the PRC has progressively lowered import barriers on foreign inputs, largely in association with its accession to the World Trade Organization in 2001, which has encouraged producers to buy more imported inputs. In addition, the reductions in the country's trade barriers also reduced the tariff advantage associated with the processing trade. As a result, processing exports as a share of total exports declined steadily from 60.2% in 1997 to 54.5% in 2006. These two opposing forces balance each other out and result in a relatively stable overall share of imported content in PRC exports. Looking ahead, the share of imported content in exports could fall or rise, depending on the relative speed with which domestic input suppliers can step up their quality and variety versus the extent of additional reductions in the cost of using imported inputs.

In addition to discussions on vertical specialization in the international trade literature, this chapter is also related to the IO analyses. In particular,

Chen et al. (2004) and Lau et al. (2007) are the first to develop a "non-competitive" type IO model for the PRC (i.e., one in which imported and domestically produced inputs are accounted for separately) and to incorporate processing exports explicitly. However, these papers do not describe a systematic way to compute separate input-output coefficients for production of processing exports versus those for other final demands. It is therefore difficult for others to replicate their estimates or apply their methodology to other countries. In addition, they use an aggregated version of the PRC's 1995 and 2002 input-output tables to perform their analysis, with 20-some goods-producing industries. We provide a more up-to-date and more disaggregated assessment of foreign and domestic values added in the country's exports with 83 goods-producing industries. Finally, they impose an assumption in estimating the import use matrix from the competitive type IO table published by the PRC National Statistical Bureau: within each industry, the mix of the imported and domestic inputs is the same in capital formation, intermediate inputs, and final consumption. We relax this assumption by refining a method proposed in Dean et al. (2007) that combines the PRC's processing imports statistics with the United Nations Broad Economic Categories (UN BEC) classification.

The rest of the chapter is organized as follows: Section 2 reviews a conceptual framework in Koopman et al. (2008) for estimating shares of domestic and foreign value-added in a country's exports when processing exports are pervasive. Section 3 presents the estimation results for the PRC's exports. Section 4 develops a method to further slice up foreign content to account for supplies from individual foreign countries, while section 5 applies it to the country's exports. Finally, section 6 offers concluding remarks.

2 Conceptual Framework and Estimation Method

2.1 When Special Features of Processing Exports Are Not Taken into Account

We first discuss how domestic and foreign contents in a country's exports can be computed when it does not engage in any processing trade. The discussion follows the input-output literature, and is the approach adopted (implicitly) by Hummels et al. (2001) and Yi (2003). Along the way, we will point out a clear connection between the domestic content concept and the concept of vertical specialization.[2]

When imported and domestically produced intermediate inputs are accounted separately, an input-output model can be specified as follows:[3]

$$A^D X + Y^D = X, \tag{1}$$

$$A^M X + Y^M = M, \tag{2}$$

$$u A^D + u A^M + A_v = u, \tag{3}$$

where $A^D = [a_{ij}^D]$ is an $n \times n$ matrix of direct input coefficients of domestic products; $A^M = [a_{ij}^M]$ is an $n \times n$ matrix of direct inputs of imported goods; Y^D is an $n \times 1$ vector of final demands for domestically produced products, including usage in gross capital formation, private and public final consumption, and gross exports; Y^M is an $n \times 1$ vector of final demands for imported products, including usages in gross capital formation, private and public final consumption; X is an $n \times 1$ vector of gross output; M is an $n \times 1$ vector of imports; $A_v = [a_j^v]$ is a $1 \times n$ vector of each sector j's ratio of value-added to gross output; $\hat{A}_V$ is an $n \times n$ diagonal matrix with a_j^v as its diagonal elements; finally, u is a $1 \times n$ unity vector. Subscripts i and j indicate sectors, and superscripts D and M represent domestically produced and imported products, respectively.

Equations (1) and (2) define two horizontal balance conditions for domestically produced and imported products, respectively. A typical row k in equation (1) specifies that total domestic production of product k should be equal to the sum of the sales of product k to all users in the economy (to be used as intermediate inputs or for final sales to these users); the final sales include domestic consumption and capital formation, plus exports of product k. A typical row h in equation (2) specifies that the total imports of product h should be equal to the sum of the sales of product h to all users in the economy, including intermediate inputs for all sectors, plus final domestic consumption and capital formation. Equation (3) is both a vertical balance condition, and an adding-up constraint for the input-output coefficients. It implies that the total output (X) in any sector k has to be equal to the sum of direct value-added in sector k, and the cost of intermediate inputs from all domestically produced and imported products.

From equation (1) we have

$$X = (I - A^D)^{-1} Y^D. \tag{4}$$

$(I - A^D)^{-1}$ is the well-known Leontief Inverse, a matrix of coefficients for the total domestic intermediate product requirement. Define a vector of share of domestic content, or domestic value-added, in a unit of domestically produced products, $DVS = \{dvs_j\}$, a $1 \times n$ vector, as the additional domestic value-added generated by one additional unit of final demand of domestic products $(\Delta Y^D = u')$:

$$DVS = \hat{A}_V \Delta X / \Delta Y^D = \hat{A}_V (I - A^D)^{-1} = A_v (I - A^D)^{-1}. \tag{5}$$

Equation (5) indicates that the domestic content for an IO industry is the corresponding column sum of the coefficient matrix for total domestic intermediate goods requirement, weighted by the direct value-added coefficient of each industry.

Under the condition that all exports and domestic sales have the same input-output coefficients, the share of domestic content in final demand and the share of domestic content in total exports should be the same. So equation (5) is also the formula for the share of domestic content in total exports for each industry. As Chen et al. (2004) point out, there is good intuition behind the *DVS* formula. When one extra unit of product for final demand is produced at home, both direct and indirect value-added are generated. The indirect value-added comes from the domestic value-added that is embedded in all the domestically produced intermediate inputs. Each of them is produced with direct and indirect value-added involved. Therefore, the total domestic value-added induced by one extra unit of domestic product is equal to the sum of direct domestic value-added and multiple rounds of indirect domestic value-added. Expressing this process mathematically, we have:

$$
\begin{aligned}
DVS &= A_v + A_v A^D + A_v A^D A^D + A_v A^D A^D A^D + \cdots \\
&= A_v (I - A^D)^{-1}.
\end{aligned}
\tag{6}
$$

The last step invokes the formula for the convergence of matrix power series of A^D.

Define a vector of share of foreign content (or foreign value-added) in final demand for domestically produced products by $FVS = u - DVS$. By making use of equation (3), it can be verified that

$$
FVS = u - A_v (I - A^D)^{-1} = u A^M (I - A^D)^{-1}.
\tag{7}
$$

This turns out to be the same formula used to compute vertical specialization by Hummels et al. (2001). In other words, the concepts of vertical specialization and of foreign content are identical.

2.2 Domestic Content in Exports When Processing Trade Is Prevalent

We now turn to the case in which tariff-favored processing exports are prevalent; these exports have a different intensity in the use of imported inputs than do domestic final sales (and normal exports). Conceptually, we wish to keep track separately of the IO coefficients of the processing exports and those of domestic final sales and normal exports. For now, we ignore the fact that these IO coefficients may not be directly available, and will discuss a formal approach to estimate them in the next subsection.

The expanded IO table with a separate account for processing exports is represented by figure 9.1. We use superscript P and D, respectively, to represent processing exports on one hand, and domestic sales and normal exports on the other. Define z_{ij}^{dd} = domestically produced intermediate good i used by sector j for domestic sales and normal exports; z_{ij}^{dp} = domestically produced intermediate good i used by sector j for processing exports;

| | | Dimension | Intermediate Use | | Final Use (C+I+G+E) | Gross Output or Imports |
			Production for Domestic Use and Normal Exports	Production for Processing Exports		
			1, 2,...,N	1, 2,...,N	1	1
Domestic Intermediate Inputs	Production for Domestic Use and Normal Exports (D)	1 ⋮ N	Z^{DD}	Z^{DP}	Y^D	$X - E^P$
	Processing Exports (P)	1 ⋮ N	0	0	E^P	E^P
Intermediate Inputs from Imports		1 ⋮ N	Z^{MD}	Z^{MP}	Y^M	M
Value-Added		1	V^D	V^P		
Gross Output		1	$X - E^P$	E^P		

Figure 9.1 Input-Output Table with Separate Production Account for Processing Trade
Source: Authors' construction.

z_{ij}^{md} = imported intermediate good i used by sector j for domestic sales and normal exports; z_{ij}^{mp} = imported intermediate good i used by sector j for processing exports; v_j^d = direct value-added by domestic and normal export production in industry j; v_j^p = direct value-added by processing export production in industry j. Then direct IO coefficients for this expanded model can be written:

$$A^{DD} = \left[a_{ij}^{dd} \right] = \left[\frac{z_{ij}^{dd}}{x_j - e_j^p} \right], A^{MD} = \left[a_{ij}^{md} \right] = \left[\frac{z_{ij}^{md}}{x_j - e_j^p} \right],$$

$$A_v^D = \left[a_j^{vd} \right] = \left[\frac{v_j^d}{x_j - e_j^p} \right],$$

$$A^{DP} = \left[a_{ij}^{dp} \right] = \left[\frac{z_{ij}^{dp}}{e_j^p} \right], A^{MP} = \left[a_{ij}^{mp} \right] = \left[\frac{z_{ij}^{mp}}{e_j^p} \right], A_v^P = \left[a_j^{vp} \right] = \left[\frac{v_j^p}{e_j^p} \right],$$

where i represents a row and j represents a column. This expanded IO model can be formally described by the following system of equations:

$$\begin{bmatrix} I - A^{DD} & -A^{DP} \\ 0 & I \end{bmatrix} \begin{bmatrix} X - E^P \\ E^P \end{bmatrix} = \begin{bmatrix} Y^D \\ E^P \end{bmatrix},$$
(8)

$$A^{MD}(X - E^P) + A^{MP}E^P + Y^M = M,$$
(9)

$$uA^{DD} + uA^{MD} + A_v^D = u,$$
(10)

$$uA^{DP} + uA^{MP} + A_v^P = u.$$
(11)

This is a generalization of the model discussed in the previous subsection. Equations (8) and (9) are a generalization of equations (1) and (2), and equations (10) and (11) are a generalization of equation (3), with a separate account for processing exports. In a slight abuse of notation, we now re-define Y^D to be final domestic sales plus normal exports while excluding processing exports. Equations (10) and (11) are also the new adding-up constraint for the IO coefficients.

The analytical solution of the system is:

$$\begin{bmatrix} X - E^P \\ E^P \end{bmatrix} = \begin{bmatrix} I - A^{DD} & -A^{DP} \\ 0 & I \end{bmatrix}^{-1} \begin{bmatrix} Y^D \\ E^P \end{bmatrix}.$$
(12)

The generalized Leontief inverse for this expanded model can be computed as follows:

$$B = \begin{bmatrix} I - A^{DD} & -A^{DP} \\ 0 & I \end{bmatrix}^{-1} = \begin{bmatrix} B^{DD} & B^{DP} \\ B^{PD} & B^{PP} \end{bmatrix} = \begin{bmatrix} (I - A^{DD})^{-1} & (I - A^{DD})^{-1}A^{DP} \\ 0 & I \end{bmatrix},$$
(13)

Substituting equation (13) into equation (12), we have:

$$X - E^P = (I - A^{DD})^{-1}Y^D + (1 - A^{DD})^{-1}A^{DP}E^P.$$
(14)

Substituting equation (14) into equation (9), the total demand for imported intermediate inputs is:

$$M - Y^M = A^{MD}(I - A^{DD})^{-1}Y^D + A^{MD}(1 - A^{DD})^{-1}A^{DP}E^P + A^{MP}E^P.$$
(15)

It has three components: the first term is total imported content in final domestic sale and normal exports, and the second and the third terms are indirect and direct imported content in processing exports, respectively.

We can compute vertical specialization (VS) or foreign content share in processing and normal exports in each industry separately:

$$\begin{vmatrix} VSS^D \\ VSS^P \end{vmatrix}^T = \begin{vmatrix} uA^{MD}(I - A^{DD})^{-1} \\ uA^{MD}(1 - A^{DD})^{-1}A^{DP} + uA^{MP} \end{vmatrix}^T.$$
(16)

The total foreign content share in a particular industry is the sum of the two weighted by the share of processing and nonprocessing exports s^P and $u - s^P$, where both s and u are a 1 by n vector:

$$\overline{VSS} = (u - s^P, s^P) \begin{vmatrix} VSS^D \\ VSS^P \end{vmatrix}. \tag{17}$$

The foreign content (or foreign value-added) share in a country's total exports is:

$$TVSS = uA^{MD}(I - A^{DD})^{-1} \frac{E - E^P}{te} + u(A^{MD}(1 - A^{DD})^{-1}A^{DP} + A^{MP}) \frac{E^P}{te}, \tag{18}$$

where te is a scalar, the country's total exports. Equation (17) is a generalization of equation (7), the formula to compute industry-level share of vertical specialization. Equation (18) is a generalization of the formula for country-level share of vertical specialization proposed by Hummels et al. (2001, p. 80). In particular, either when $A^{DD} = A^{DP}$ and $A^{MD} = A^{MP}$, or when $E^P/te = 0$, equation (18) reduces to the HIY formula for VS.

Similarly, the domestic content share for processing and normal exports at the industry level can be computed separately:

$$\begin{vmatrix} DVS^D \\ DVS^P \end{vmatrix}^T = \bar{A}_v B = (A_v^D \quad A_v^P) \begin{bmatrix} (I - A^{DD})^{-1} & (I - A^{DD})^{-1}A^{DP} \\ 0 & I \end{bmatrix} \tag{19}$$

$$= \begin{vmatrix} A_v^D(I - A^{DD})^{-1} \\ A_v^D(I - A^{DD})^{-1}A^{DP} + A_v^P \end{vmatrix}^T.$$

The total domestic content share in a particular industry is a weighted sum of the two:

$$\overline{DVS} = (u - s^P, s^P) \begin{vmatrix} DVS^D \\ DVS^P \end{vmatrix}. \tag{20}$$

The domestic content share in a country's total exports is:

$$TDVS = A_V^D(I - A^{DD})^{-1} \frac{E - E^P}{te} + (A_V^D(1 - A^{DD})^{-1}A^{DP} + A_V^P) \frac{E^P}{te}. \tag{21}$$

Either when $A^{DD} = A^{DP}$ and $A_v^D = A_v^P$, or when $E^P/te = 0$, equation (20) reduces to the HIY formula in equation (5). Note that we can easily verify that for both processing and normal exports, the sum of domestic and foreign content shares is unity.

2.3 Estimation Issues

Equations (19)–(21) allow us to compute the shares of domestic content in processing and normal exports for each industry, as well as in a country's total exports. However, statistical agencies typically only report a traditional IO matrix, A^D, and sometimes A^M, but not A^{DP}, A^{DD}, A^{MP}, and A^{MD} separately.

Koopman et al. (2008) present a mathematical programming procedure to estimate these matrices that utilizes both detailed trade data that separate processing and normal trade and a conventional IO table.

3 Estimation Results on Domestic and Foreign Content in Exports of the PRC

After describing the data sources, we report and discuss the estimation results for shares of domestic and foreign content in both normal and processing exports by the PRC and compare our estimation with results from HIY formula at the aggregate level.

3.1 Data

Inter-industry transaction and (direct) value-added data are from 1997 and 2002 benchmark IO tables for the PRC published by the National Bureau of Statistics (NBS). We use detailed exports and imports data from 1997, 2002, and 2006 from the General Customs Administration to help differentiate the processing and normal trade in each sector. The trade statistics are first aggregated from the 8-digit HS level to the IO industry level, and then used to compute the share of processing exports in each IO industry. Modifying a method from Dean et al. (2007), we partition all imports in a given industry into three parts based on the distinction between processing and normal imports in the trade statistics, and on the UN BEC classification scheme: (i) intermediate inputs in producing processing exports; (ii) intermediate inputs for normal exports and other domestic final sales; and (iii) those used in gross capital formation and final consumption. A summary of these trade statistics as a share of the PRC's total imports during 1996–2006 is reported in table 9.2, which shows a downward trend for the use of imported inputs in producing processing exports, but a moderately upward trend in their use in producing normal trade and domestic final sales.

3.2 Domestic and Foreign Contents in Total Exports

Table 9.3 shows decomposition results for foreign and domestic value-added shares in 1997 and 2002. Preliminary estimates for 2006 are also included.[4] For comparison, the results from the HIY formula that ignore processing trade are also reported. The aggregate domestic value-added share in PRC's merchandise exports was 52.3% in 1997, and 50.7% in 2006. For manufacturing products, these shares are slightly lower in levels but trending upward moderately at 47.6% in 1997 and 49.4% in 2006, respectively, indicating that the country uses more imported intermediate inputs to produce manufacturing goods than other exports. In general, the direct domestic value-added shares are less than half of the total domestic

Table 9.2
Final Use of Imports by Producers in the People's Republic of China (% of Total Imports), 1996–2006

Year	Share of Intermediates		Share of Capital Goods		Share of Final Consumption
	For Processing Exports	For Normal Use	For Processing Exports	For Normal Use	
1996	46.2	26.8	8.1	16.7	2.2
1997	51.2	28.2	12.1	7.3	1.2
1998	50.8	28.2	10.0	9.8	1.3
1999	43.7	34.9	11.2	8.3	1.9
2000	39.4	41.2	9.1	8.5	1.7
2001	36.6	41.2	11.6	8.7	1.8
2002	38.3	38.5	10.3	11.1	1.8
2003	35.4	41.2	11.0	10.8	1.6
2004	35.1	42.3	9.1	12.0	1.5
2005	36.6	42.9	8.2	10.8	1.5
2006	35.7	43.5	10.0	9.1	1.7

Source: Authors' calculations based on the UN BEC classification scheme, and trade statistics on normal and processing imports.

value-added shares. However, the indirect foreign value-added share was relatively small; most of the foreign content comes from directly imported foreign inputs.

Relative to the numbers from the HIY method, our procedure produces a much higher share of foreign value-added in the country's gross exports (approximately double) and shows a different trend over time. To be more precise, estimates from the HIY method show that the foreign content share (total VS share) increased steadily from 17.6% in 1997 to 26.3% in 2006 for all merchandise exports, and from 19.0% to 27.1% for manufacturing goods only during the same period. In contrast, our estimates reveal no clear trend for foreign content (with the share of foreign value-added in all merchandise exports falling from 47.7% in 1997 to 46.1% in 2002, and bouncing back to 49.3% in 2006, and a similar fluctuation for the share in manufacturing exports, falling from 52.4% in 1997 to 48.7% in 2002 but bouncing back to 50.6% in 2006. Overall, the HIY method appears to incorrectly estimate both the level and the trend in domestic versus foreign content in the PRC's exports.

Table 9.4 reports our estimates of the shares of domestic and foreign value-added in normal and processing exports, separately. Clearly, the share of domestic value-added is high in normal exports (between 88%–95%), but low in processing exports (between 18%–26%). This is true for both manufacturing exports and all merchandise exports.

Table 9.3

Shares of Domestic and Foreign Value-Added in Total Exports by the People's Republic of China (%)

	The HIY Method			The KWW Method		
	1997	2002	2006	1997	2002	2006
All Merchandise						
Total Foreign Value-Added	17.6	25.1	26.3	47.7	46.1	49.3
Direct foreign value-added	8.9	14.7	15.7	46.1	42.4	45.7
Total Domestic Value-Added	82.4	74.9	73.7	52.3	53.9	50.7
Direct domestic value-added	29.4	26.0	25.3	23.7	20.1	19.2
Manufacturing Goods Only						
Total Foreign Value-Added	19.0	26.4	27.1	52.4	48.7	50.6
Direct foreign value-added	9.7	15.6	16.3	50.9	45.0	47.0
Total Domestic Value-Added	81.1	73.6	72.9	47.6	51.3	49.4
Direct domestic value-added	27.5	24.6	24.6	21.2	18.5	18.4

Notes: The HIY method refers to estimates from using the approach in Hummels et al. (2001). The KWW method refers to estimates from using the approach developed in this paper that takes into account special features of processing exports. The estimates for 2006 are preliminary as they use the trade statistics in 2006 but the IO table in 2002, which is the latest available. The next benchmark table (2007) is scheduled to be released in 2010.

Source: Authors' calculation.

4 Slicing Up the Value Chains along Multiple Countries: Methodology

In this and the next sections, we attempt to disaggregate foreign value-added (FVA) in the PRC's exports into that which originates from selected key economies and the rest of the world. We also separate PRC's indirect domestic value-added (DVA) via third countries that use PRC-made intermediate inputs themselves to produce their exports from the PRC's total DVA. This exercise is made possible by taking advantage of a rare international input-output table that records the source of input use in a sector in any one of nine East Asian economies plus the US from each sector in each of the other countries in the group and the rest of the world. We first explain the conceptual framework in this section, following Wang and Wei (2008b) and then report the empirical results in the next section.

While VS measures the imported content in a country's exports, a separate indicator (called VS1 in Hummels et al., 2001) measures the extent of a country's exports used by other countries as inputs in their exports. The primary conceptual contribution of this section is to extend both measures of vertical specialization (VS and VS1) into a framework that includes many

Table 9.4
Domestic and Foreign Value-Added: Processing and Normal Exports (% of Total Exports)

	Normal Exports			Processing Exports		
	1997	2002	2006	1997	2002	2006
All Merchandise						
Total Foreign Value-Added	5.3	10.8	11.3	81.9	74.3	81.9
Direct foreign value-added	1.9	4.5	4.6	81.7	72.5	80.9
Total Domestic Value-Added	94.7	89.2	88.7	18.1	25.7	18.1
Direct domestic value-added	34.4	31.0	29.3	15.0	11.4	10.5
Manufacturing Goods Only						
Total Foreign Value-Added	5.7	11.6	11.7	82.3	74.9	82.3
Direct foreign value-added	2.1	4.9	4.8	82.2	73.0	81.4
Total Domestic Value-Added	94.3	88.4	88.3	17.7	25.1	17.7
Direct domestic value-added	30.9	28.5	28.3	15.0	9.5	10.4

Notes: The estimates for 2006 are preliminary as they use the trade statistics in 2006 but the IO table in 2002, which is the latest available. The next benchmark IO table—the 2007 table—is scheduled to be released in 2010.

Source: Authors' calculations.

countries based on an international input-output model. This extended measure allows us to estimate each country's net contribution of value-added in the East Asia production network at industry level.

It is relatively rare to use an international IO table to evaluate the growth of vertical specialization and to slice up value-added along an industrial supply chain across countries. We know of only one related paper, Pula and Peltonen (2008), entitled "Has Emerging Asia Decoupled? An Analysis of Production and Trade Linkage Using the Asian International Input-Output Table." They estimate the dependence of each country's GDP on domestic, intra-East Asia, and extra-regional demand based on an aggregate Asia IO table, and conclude that there is no support for the "decoupling" view. These authors do not connect their exercise with the HIY measure of vertical specialization and do not conduct any analysis at the industry level.

Recall that two key (but implicit) assumptions are needed for the HIY measure to work. First, the intensity in the use of imported inputs is the same between production for export and production for domestic final demand. Second, the foreign value-added in all imported intermediate inputs is 100%.[5] That is, there is no indirect domestic content in a country's imports. The first assumption is violated when processing exports are pervasive. The second assumption is violated because the essence of a global production chain is that any country's exports could contain inputs coming from many other countries. By this logic, imported inputs (e.g., imported computer parts by the PRC) could very well contain domestic value-added that is embedded in the country's intermediate goods exports.

When data on processing trade are utilized, one can relax the first assumption. Koopman et al. (2008) provide a methodology to re-compute domestic and foreign value-added in this case, and the first part of this paper summarizes the empirical results for the PRC's exports. An interregional input-output (IRIO) table permits the relaxation of the second assumption. In particular, such a table would have information on: (i) transaction flows of intermediate products and final goods within and between each country in the world at industry level; (ii) the direct value-added of each industry in all countries; and (iii) the gross output for each industry in all countries.

In the next two subsections, we will use an international input-output model to illustrate how value-added along a multi-country production chain can be decomposed into the sum of each participating country's net contributions.

4.1 When a World Input-Output Table (That Covers All Countries) Is Available

Assume there are G countries, with N sectors in each country. Production in each sector in any country can potentially use intermediate inputs from any sector (including its own) in any country. Products in the same sector from two countries are imperfect substitutes. A world IO table is a comprehensive account of annual product and payment flows within and between countries. With a slight abuse of notations, we will recycle the symbols in section 2; in most instances, a given notation in this section is a multi-country generalization of the same object for a single country case in section 2. To be precise, we use the following notations to describe the elements of the world IO table (expressed in annual values): x_i^r = gross output of industry i in country r; v_j^s = direct value-added by production of industry j in country s; z_{ij}^{sr} = delivery of good i produced by country s and used as an intermediate by sector j in country r; and y_{ik}^{sr} = delivery of good i produced in country s for final use in final demand type k in country r (the total number of final demand types is H). Then the following two accounting identities describe the relationship among elements of each row (i, r) and column (j, s) of the international IO table:

$$\sum_{s=1}^{G}\sum_{j=1}^{N} z_{ij}^{sr} + \sum_{s=1}^{G}\sum_{k=1}^{H} y_{ik}^{sr} = x_i^r. \tag{22}$$

$$\sum_{r=1}^{G}\sum_{i=1}^{N} z_{ij}^{rs} + v_j^s = x_j^s. \tag{23}$$

The economic meanings of the two equations are straightforward. A typical row in equation (22) states that total gross output of commodity i in country r is equal to the sum of all deliveries to intermediate and final users in all countries (including itself) in the world. Equation (23) defines the value of gross output for commodity j in production country s as the sum of the values from all of its (domestic plus imported) intermediate and primary factor inputs. Equations (22) and (23) must hold for all $i, j \in N, k \in H$ and $s, r \in G$ in each year. In addition, this World IO account has to be consistent with each country's national IO account and official trade statistics, which requires the following accounting identities to be satisfied each year:

$$\sum_{k=1}^{H}\sum_{s=1}^{G} y_{ik}^{sr} = y_i^{\cdot r}, \tag{24}$$

$$\sum_{s=1}^{G} z_{ij}^{sr} = z_{ij}^{\cdot r}, \tag{25}$$

$$\sum_{s\neq r}^{G}\sum_{j=1}^{N} z_{ij}^{sr} + \sum_{s\neq r}^{G}\sum_{k=1}^{H} y_{ik}^{sr} = e_i^s, \tag{26}$$

$$\sum_{s\neq r}^{G}\sum_{j=1}^{N} z_{ij}^{sr} + \sum_{s\neq r}^{G}\sum_{k=1}^{H} y_{kj}^{sr} = m_j^r, \tag{27}$$

where $y_i^{\cdot r}$= total final domestic demand of product i of destination country r; $z_{ij}^{\cdot r}$ = total intermediate demand of product i by sector j in destination country r; e_i^s = exports of sector i of production country s; and m_j^r = imports of product j of destination country r.

Equation (24) indicates that each country's total final demand for commodity i must be met by final goods and services shipped from all nations, including its own. Equation (25) states that each country's total intermediate use of product i in sector j must be equal to the total input-output flow from sector i to sector j in the IO table of the destination country r. Equations (26) and (27) simply represent the fact that all intermediate and final goods and services exported to and imported from all foreign countries have to equal the country's total exports to and imports from the world market.

Define $a_{ij}^{rr} = z_{ij}^{rr}/x_j^{rr}$ as the direct input coefficients of the domestic products of country r, $a_{ij}^{sr} = z_{ij}^{sr}/x_j^{rr} s\neq r$ as intermediate input-output coefficients of good i produced in source country s for use in sector j by destination country r; and $av_j^r = v_j^r/x_j^r$ as each sector j's ratio of value-added to gross output for each country r; then using matrix notation, equations (22) and (23) could be re-written as:

$$AX + Y = X, \tag{28}$$

$$A^T X + \hat{A}_v X = X, \tag{29}$$

where A is an NG by NG square matrix with G^2 number of N by N block sub matrices. It shows inter-industry input-output coefficients not only within each country, but also across all countries.

$$A = \begin{bmatrix} A^{11} & \cdots & A^{1G} \\ \vdots & \ddots & \vdots \\ A^{G1} & \cdots & A^{GG} \end{bmatrix}$$

$A^{rr} = \left[a_{ij}^{rr} \right]$ are $n \times n$ matrices at the diagonal, $A^{sr} = \left[a_{ij}^{sr} \right] s \neq r$ are also $n \times n$ matrices but at the off-diagonal. $\hat{A}_V$ is a diagonal block matrix of NG by NG whose diagonal elements are row vectors of the corresponding country's ratio of value-added to gross output (value-added coefficients).

$$\hat{A}_v = \begin{bmatrix} AV^1 & 0 & 0 \\ 0 & \ddots & 0 \\ 0 & 0 & AV^G \end{bmatrix},$$

where $AV^r = \left[av_j^r \right]$ is an n by n diagonal block matrix and X is an RG by one output vector

$$X = \begin{bmatrix} x_1^1 & \cdots & x_n^1 & \cdots & x_1^r \cdots & x_n^r & \cdots & x_1^G \cdots & x_n^G \end{bmatrix}^T.$$

The adding up condition on the input-output coefficients in equations (30) and (31) can be written as

$$uA + A_v = u, \tag{30}$$

where u and A_v are a one by NG unit vector and a value-added coefficient vector respectively. Equation (30) implies that the direct value-added coefficients and intermediate input-output coefficients from all domestically produced and imported products in any sector j and country r must sum to unity.

As in section 2, from equation (28) we have

$$X = (I - A)^{-1} Y. \tag{31}$$

$B = (I - A)^{-1} = \left[b_{ij}^{sr} \right]$ is the Leontief inverse. Its jth column in the rth block states how much the production of each industry in all countries is induced when the final demand for j^{th} industry in country r increases by one unit (total requirement coefficient). Y is an NG by H final demand matrix, usually including private and government consumption, capital formation, and inventory changes.

Based on the definition of the value-added coefficient, the incremental increase in value-added induced by a one unit increase in final demand is given by:

$$\Delta V = \hat{A}_v \Delta X = \hat{A}_v (I - A)^{-1} \Delta Y = \hat{A}_v (I - A)^{-1}. \tag{32}$$

Define a G by NG matrix VAS as the value-added share distribution in a unit of final product. Each row r represents the value-added share contributed to industry i by corresponding country r. It can be computed by summing across rows (along the column) of the NG by NG matrix ΔV:

$$VAS = V_0 (I - A)^{-1} = V_0 B \quad V_0 = S \cdot \hat{A}_v, \tag{33}$$

where S is a G by NG block diagonal summation matrix with G one by N unit vectors as its diagonal block. Its elements are the column sum of products between value-added coefficients and total requirement coefficients:

$$VAS = \left[vas_i^{sr} \right] = \left[\sum_{j=1}^{N} av_j^s b_{ji}^{sr} \right]. \tag{34}$$

Intuitively, this equals pre-multiplying the Leontief inverse by the value-added ratio and summing them over the column (industries) for each bilateral transaction in every country and industry, so we obtain the amount of value-added generated directly and indirectly in one unit of final product for each industry in each country. The contributed value-share from all countries for a particular industry equals unity. The VAS matrix can be written as a G block G by N matrix as follows,

$$VAS = \left[VAS_1^1 \quad \cdots \quad VAS_i^r \quad \cdots \quad VAS_N^G \right], \tag{35}$$

where $VAS_i^r = \left[vas_i^{sr} \right]$ is a G by G matrix . For each VAS_i^s the off-diagonal elements (for all $s \neq r$) of source country s and destination country r (hold production country s constant) are the terms capturing exported intermediate inputs from source country s used in the output of destination country r at the 2nd, 3rd, 4th, ... stages before becoming embodied in final goods delivered to other countries. Therefore the sum over destination country r weighted by the corresponding final goods from all G countries consumed in country r will be similar to the VS1 measure proposed by HIY, but without the restrictive assumption that the exported intermediates are 100% domestically sourced. This revised VS1 measures how much of source country s domestic value-added is embodied in its indirect intermediate exports to third countries that then export final goods consumed in the destination countries. It can be computed at each sector i as

$$vs1_i^s = \sum_{r}^{G} vas_i^{sr} y_i^{sr} = \sum_{r}^{G} \sum_{j=1}^{N} \sum_{k}^{H} av_j^s b_{ij}^{sr} y_{ik}^{sr}. \tag{36}$$

The off-diagonal elements of destination country r and source country s (holding the destination country r constant) in the VAS matrix are the terms capturing imported intermediate inputs from source country s in the output of destination country r at the 2nd, 3rd, 4th, ... stages before becoming embodied in the final goods imported by destination country r. Therefore, the sum over source country s is similar to the VS measure proposed by HIY without the assumption that the imported intermediates be 100% foreign-sourced. This revised VS measure decomposes the foreign value-added embodied in direct exports of the exporting country s to its destination country r into its original value-added sources and can be computed at sector level as

$$vs_i^r = \sum_s^G vas_i^{sr} y_i^{sr} = \sum_s \sum_{j=1}^N \sum_k^H av_j^s b_{ij}^{sr} y_{ik}^{sr}. \tag{37}$$

For the destination country r, vs_i^r is the domestic content of its imports, that is, its own domestic content that was previously exported and has come back into the country through its imports from other countries. The diagonal elements of each VAS_i^s matrix captures the domestic intermediate inputs in domestic output of country r at the 2nd, 3rd, 4th, ... stages before it becomes embodied in final goods delivered to other countries plus the revised VS1, the domestic value-added embodied in its exports used by any third country to produce exports to a destination for final consumption. Therefore, the domestic value-added share derived from HIY VS share measure (one minus HIY VS share) will underestimate domestic value-added by neglecting both the domestic value-added embodied in the imports of the home country and indirect exports to the destination country via indirect intermediate exports to third countries. It can be computed at sector i for each country as follows:

$$dv_i^r = \sum_s^G vas_i^{rr} y_i^{sr} = \sum_s \sum_{j=1}^N \sum_k^H av_j^r b_{ij}^{rr} y_{ik}^{sr}. \tag{38}$$

The aggregate measure of revised VS, VS1 and domestic value-added DV at each country or each sector level can be obtained by sum over sector (country) weighted by final consumption. For example,

$$VS^r = \sum_s^G \sum_i^N vas_i^{sr} y_i^{sr} = \sum_s \sum_i^N \sum_{j=1}^N \sum_k^H av_j^s b_{ij}^{sr} y_{ik}^{sr}, \tag{39}$$

$$VS_i = \sum_s^G \sum_r^G vas_i^{sr} y_i^{sr} = \sum_s \sum_r^G \sum_{j=1}^N \sum_k^H av_j^s b_{ij}^{sr} y_{ik}^{sr}. \tag{40}$$

Just as our revised VS measure provides a way to further decompose VS to all its original source countries, our revised VS1 measure provides a way to further decompose domestic value-added into that which is embodied in a country's direct exports to its consumption destination and that which is embodied in its indirect intermediate exports via third countries to its final destination. When all the off-diagonal block matrices in A are equal to zero, our VAS matrix reduces to HIY's VS measure. Our measure also allows us to relax the assumption that HIY made for their computations that each country's imports are of 100% foreign content.

Obviously, our total value chain measure, VAS, is an extension of the vertical specialization measure (VS and VS1) proposal by HIY into as many as G countries. It includes both domestic value-added share (in the diagonal) and foreign value-added share from all other countries, and a country's exports of intermediates embodied in all other countries' exports, and thus combines VS and VS1 in a consistent framework. The detailed distribution of foreign value-added in both a source country's direct and indirect exports to a destination country revealed by this systematic measure will enable us to quantify the "length" (how many participating countries) and "thickness" (value-added share for each participating country) of the regional or global production chain. In addition, it relaxes the unrealistic assumption that a country's imported intermediate inputs have to be 100% foreign content and the first country's exports have to be 100% domestic content. Our revised VS measure takes all the back-and-forth trade of intermediates across borders into account, something that cannot be captured with only single country IO tables.

4.2 Working with an Interregional Input-Output Table (for a Subset of Countries)

International IO tables are rare because of the tremendous amount of data required to compile them, as well as differences in statistical classifications across countries. Available IRIO tables, such as the Asian International Input-Output tables (AIO), usually cover only a select set of economies and treat other countries in the rest of the world (without IO accounts) as exogenous blocks. To estimate total value chains based on such tables, our model specified in the previous section has to be modified.

Dividing the G countries into a set of M endogenous and another set of $G-M$ exogenous countries, the model specified by equations (24) and (25) becomes:

$$\sum_{s=1}^{M}\sum_{j=1}^{N} z_{ij}^{sr} + \sum_{s=1}^{M}\sum_{k=1}^{H} y_{ik}^{sr} + \sum_{s=G-M}^{G} e_{i}^{sr} = x_{i}^{r}, \tag{41}$$

$$\sum_{s=1}^{M}\sum_{i=1}^{N} z_{ij}^{sr} + \sum_{s=G-M}^{G}\sum_{i=1}^{N} m_{ij}^{sr} + v_{j}^{r} = x_{j}^{r}, \tag{42}$$

where e_{i}^{sr} = exports of product i from country s to country r; m_{ij}^{sr} = imports of product i used in sector j in an endogenous country r from an exogenous country s.

This is a modified international IO model. The computation of VAS in such a model is similar to equation (33) but with different dimensionality for the related matrices. (Matrix A reduces to NM with M^2 number of N by N blocks. $\hat{A}_V$ reduces to a diagonal block matrix of NM by NM, and the block diagonal summation matrix S reduces to M by NM).

To estimate the value-added contribution from exogenous countries in the rest of the world (which does not have an input-output account), we need to assume imported intermediate inputs from the $G-M$ exogenous countries are 100% foreign sourced, similar to HIY. Then the contribution of value-added share from the $G-M$ exogenous countries in each of the N industries is computed as follows:

$$VSS = M_0(I - A)^{-1}, \tag{43}$$

where VSS is a $G-M$ by $N(G-M)$ matrix, with each row i giving the contribution of value-added share from a corresponding exogenous country to each of the N industries.

$$M_0 = \begin{bmatrix} M_0^{M+1} & 0 & 0 \\ 0 & \ddots & 0 \\ 0 & 0 & M_0^G \end{bmatrix}$$

M_0 is also a diagonal block matrix of $G-M$ by $N(G-M)$ whose diagonal blocks are $1 \times n$ row vectors $M_0^r = [m_{0j}^r]$, and each element m_{0j}^r is the column sum of the direct import coefficients of the corresponding exogenous country. In other words, $M_0^r = uM^r$ where $M^r = [m_{ij}^{sr}]$ is an n by n import coefficient matrix and u is a $1 \times n$ vector of ones. Intuitively, the amount of imports from the rest of the world required directly and indirectly by one unit of final demand (including exports to the rest of the world) can be obtained by pre-multiplying the Leontief inverse by the imported intermediate IO coefficient matrix.

The column sum of VAS and VSS is always equal to one by using the adding up condition of the international IO model. In other words, the column sum of domestic input/output coefficients, import input/output coefficients, and the value-added ratio for each industry in each endogenous country has to equal unity.

5 Empirical Estimates on Value-Added along Production Chains

5.1 Data Source

The AIO are the main source of data. These table are compiled by the Institute of Development Economies (IDE) affiliated with Japan's Ministry of Economics, Trade and Industry in collaboration with national statistical institutions in eight other economies in Asia (Indonesia; Korea; Malaysia; the

PRC; the Philippines; Singapore; Taipei,China; and Thailand) plus the US. The AIO provides the origin and destination of all transaction flows within and across these the economies at the industry level, and reports trade flows with Hong Kong, China and the rest of the world. It specifies intermediate and/or final use for all such flows. The table is available for 1990 and 2000. The 2000 table separates the EU15 from the rest of the world.

Sixty-four sectors, including 36 non-food-processing manufactures sectors, appear in both the 1990 and 2000 tables after careful concordance. Final demand in the AIO has four components (i.e., H=4): private consumption, government consumption, gross domestic fixed capital formation, and changes in inventories. Direct value-added in the AIO includes wages and salary, operating surplus, gross fixed capital formation, and indirect taxes less subsidies.

5.2 Comparing the PRC with Other Asian Economies in Production Chain

Table 9.5 provides a comparison of the PRC vis-à-vis other major economies in East Asia. Columns 2 and 3 report the current dollar value of final and intermediate goods exports by each of the nine economies in 1990 and 2000, relying on BEC classifications. Column 4 gives the estimated share of intermediate exports in total manufacturing exports $(4) = (3)/[(2) + (3)]$. In 2000, the median value of this share is 52.9% (Malaysia). Four economies that exported a greater portion of intermediate goods that year are Korea (63.5%), the Philippines (61.2%), Singapore (59.9%), and Taipei,China (61.6%). It is noteworthy that in 2000 the PRC's intermediate export share is the lowest of the economies in our Asian sample. Indeed, comparing 2000 with 1990, it stands out as the only economy that experienced a decline in the share of intermediates in exports. All other economies experienced an increase, with the increment exceeding 10 percentage points for five of them. By this metric, it seems that the PRC's participation in the Asian (plus the US and EU) production chains declined, but it may indicate that the PRC is located at the end of this production chain, with a significant portion of its exports consisting of final goods exports to the US and EU markets.

However, the share of intermediate goods in a country's total exports can be a misleading yardstick to judge international integration. We suggest a more informative statistic might be the shares of domestic and foreign content in a country's exports; these are reported in columns 5 and 6 in table 9.5. The foreign content share exceeds 40% for Malaysia, the Philippines, Singapore, Taipei,China and Thailand in 2000. This suggests that these economies are heavy users of imported intermediates in the production of their exports. On the other end of the spectrum is Japan, whose foreign content is less than 10% of its exports. This indicates that Japan primarily specializes in producing intermediate inputs for other countries' exports, but uses relatively

Table 9.5
Foreign and Domestic Value-Added in East Asia Manufacturing Exports to the United States ($ million)

Source Country (1)	Final Goods Exports (2)	Intermediate Goods Exports (3)	Intermediate Share in Gross Exports (4)	Total Domestic Value-Added (%) (5)	Total Foreign Value-Added (%) (6)
			1990		
China, People's Rep. of	3,870	2,672	40.8	81.2	18.8
Indonesia	886	538	37.8	76.9	23.1
Japan	53,446	28,473	34.8	91.6	8.4
Korea, Rep. of	11,298	5,450	32.5	68.3	31.8
Malaysia	2,051	2,091	50.5	52.8	47.2
Philippines	1,361	596	30.5	55.0	45.0
Singapore	5,306	3,599	40.4	39.9	60.1
Thailand	2,641	1,189	31.0	56.9	43.2
Taipei;China	13,280	8,411	38.8	63.6	36.4
Total	94,139	53,019	36.0	86.0	14.0
			2000		
China, People's Rep. of	37,991	22,060	36.7	76.5	23.6
Indonesia	3,730	2,424	39.4	75.4	24.6
Japan	66,680	53,438	44.5	90.5	9.5
Korea, Rep. of	16,661	19,260	53.6	66.2	33.8
Malaysia	9,681	10,860	52.9	35.1	64.8
Philippines	3,674	5,785	61.2	55.4	44.5
Singapore	6,074	9,072	59.9	41.8	58.1
Thailand	5,909	5,912	50.0	54.9	45.0
Taipei;China	12,300	19,761	61.6	54.5	45.5
Total	162,700	148,571	47.7	84.5	15.5

Source: Authors' calculations based on the Asia Input-Output Table, originally compiled by the Institute of Development Economics, Ministry of Economics, Trade and Industry, Japan.

few foreign-sourced inputs in its own final goods exports. In comparison, the foreign content share for the PRC's exports is estimated to be 23.6%, which is on the low end of the spectrum when compared with most other East Asian economies.

It is important to note that the estimates reported in table 9.5 do not distinguish between processing and normal exports; they underestimate the true extent of foreign content in exports. For the PRC, as the first part of this chapter shows, the foreign content share is on the order of 50% once the higher reliance on imported inputs by processing exports is taken into account. As the use of processing exports is more intensive in the PRC than in many other Asian economies, it is likely that the adjustment needed is smaller for those economies. For example, for both Japan and Singapore, since their tariff rates on manufactured inputs are already low, the estimation errors are probably small, and the estimated foreign content shares reported in table 9.5 are likely to be reliable.

5.3 Slicing Up Production Chains across Countries

A major advantage of the international IO tables is that they allow for further breakdown of the foreign content in a country's exports according to the origins of countries that supply intermediate goods. This is done with the help of the formulas in equations (39) and (43),[6] and reported in table 9.6.

Each row represents a breakdown of the supply chain, for a given county's exports to the US, of all foreign countries that contribute value-added to its production. For example, the first row shows that in 1990 Indonesia contributed 1.1% to the foreign content of PRC's exports to the US. Hong Kong, China; Japan; and the US are the most significant suppliers of intermediate inputs for the PRC's exports to the US, accounting for 51.3%, 13.0% and 6.8% of the foreign content, respectively. Comparing 2000 with 1990, we can see the share of Hong Kong, China in the foreign content in PRC's exports has declined substantially (to 10.5% in 2000). On the other hand, the shares by Japan; Korea; Taipei,China; and the US in the foreign content in PRC's exports have each increased by more than two percentage points during the same period. The biggest increase in the contribution to the foreign content comes from the rest of the world, including Europe. In other words, sourcing of inputs by companies in the PRC to be used in production for exports has become more dispersed geographically, and there is significantly less reliance on inputs from Hong Kong, China. These countries increasingly export value-added to the US indirectly by exporting intermediate inputs to the PRC to be used in its exports to the US market.

Across the rows in table 9.6, we can compare the geographic sourcing patterns in exports for nine major economies in East Asia. A number of interesting patterns emerge. First, Japan is the dominant supplier of inputs used in the production of other Asian economies' exports to the US market, accounting for 20% of foreign content in nearly all other Asian

Table 9.6

Tracing Sources of Foreign Value-Added in Exports for Exports to the United States for Individual Exporting Countries

Source country (1)	China, People's Rep. of (2)	Indonesia (3)	Japan (4)	Korea, Rep. of (5)	Malaysia (6)	Taipei, China (7)	Philippines (8)	Singapore (9)	Thailand (10)	United States (11)	Hong Kong, China (12)	Rest of World (13)	Total (14)
						1990 (%)							
China, People's Rep. of	—	1.1	13.0	1.4	1.7	3.5	0.1	0.4	0.9	6.7	51.3	20.0	100
Indonesia	3.2	—	12.2	8.2	1.6	5.9	0.3	1.7	0.7	11.3	3.3	51.6	100
Japan	2.6	3.7	—	2.9	1.7	2.6	0.8	0.7	1.5	18.6	1.2	63.6	100
Korea, Rep. of	0.2	1.5	26.5	—	2.8	2.2	0.3	0.5	0.6	20.7	1.5	43.2	100
Malaysia	2.1	1.3	21.1	2.3	—	5.8	0.5	7.2	1.0	12.3	3.8	42.5	100
Taipei, China	0.2	1.2	28.2	2.0	1.4	—	0.4	1.0	0.5	17.7	3.3	44.1	100
Philippines	1.3	1.1	16.4	3.9	1.1	10.8	—	1.9	0.5	18.1	10.4	34.4	100
Singapore	1.6	1.3	32.8	2.7	5.6	4.0	0.9	—	1.6	19.6	4.4	25.4	100
Thailand	2.4	0.8	22.4	2.5	2.0	3.3	0.3	3.8	—	17.5	2.3	42.6	100
Total	3.6	1.1	56.3	8.6	1.7	9.5	0.9	2.5	1.8	3.8	1.0	9.2	100

2000 (%)

China, People's Rep. of	–	1.6	15.5	8.4	1.6	7.9	0.5	1.2	1.0	8.9	10.5	42.9	100
Indonesia	5.4	–	11.5	6.3	2.3	4.2	0.2	1.4	1.6	8.4	2.3	56.4	100
Japan	6.1	3.6	–	4.6	2.5	4.5	1.3	1.1	2.7	18.4	2.3	52.8	100
Korea, Rep. of	6.0	1.7	21.5	–	1.7	2.7	0.7	1.3	0.8	17.5	3.2	42.9	100
Malaysia	3.4	1.8	21.1	3.8	–	4.6	1.5	6.8	2.6	17.9	5.1	31.3	100
Taipei,China	3.8	1.7	26.0	5.3	2.4	–	1.4	1.9	1.2	13.8	3.2	39.3	100
Philippines	5.0	2.5	17.0	6.2	2.0	8.9	–	2.0	2.9	13.5	9.8	30.2	100
Singapore	4.3	1.4	23.6	3.3	7.1	2.8	0.5	–	1.7	15.0	2.9	37.6	100
Thailand	6.2	2.1	22.1	4.2	3.4	4.0	0.8	3.3	–	13.2	3.2	37.5	100
Total	18.8	2.2	41.5	8.0	2.7	5.2	1.5	2.1	2.4	3.7	1.3	10.5	100

Notes: The first column lists individual exporting countries. Each row reports estimated percentage contributions to the foreign content embedded in that country's exports to the US by individual economies and the rest of the world.

Source: Authors' calculations.

exporters' goods. This role by Japan has declined only moderately over time. Second, the US itself is often a major input supplier to Asian countries' exports to the US market. Its role is relatively stable over time, though with some fluctuations for individual exporters. Third, Korea and Taipei,China are the next two most significant Asian suppliers of inputs in other Asian economies' exports.

5.4 Multinational Value-Added Chains in the PRC for Disaggregated Export Categories

The extent of participation in a global production chain varies by sectors. One of the findings in Koopman et al. (2008) is that for the PRC's exports, those sectors that are considered relatively sophisticated, such us consumer electronics and computers, often have a relatively high foreign content. In this subsection, we apply the methodology in section 4 to sector-level exports data of the PRC, and report the estimation results in table 9.7.

The sectors are listed in descending order by the value of the PRC's exports in 2002, reported in column 2 of table 9.7. The top three sectors in absolute value are "television, radios, audios and communication equipments" (or "electronics" for short), "electronic computing equipment" (or "computers" for short), and "wearing apparel." Columns 3 and 4 report the share of a sector's exports in the country's total manufacturing exports, and the share of processing exports in that sector's exports, respectively. The top three sectors (out of 64 manufacturing sectors) account for about one-quarter of total manufacturing exports. The degree of processing trade differs across sectors. For example, 90% of electronics exports are in the processing trade category, and virtually all computer exports (99%) are processing exports. In comparison, about 45% of wearing apparel exports are processing exports.

Columns 5 and 6 report an estimated breakdown between domestic and foreign content (as a share of a sector's exports) according to the Koopman et al. (KWW) method, as summarized in section 2, (i.e., taking into account the difference between processing and normal exports). The numbers reported in these two columns are the sector level counterpart for national aggregate estimates reported in the second to the last column (i.e., for 2002) of table 9.3 for manufacturing goods only. The foreign content share is 65% for electronics and 83% for computers, but only 33% for wearing apparel. These examples illustrate the more general pattern that Chinese exports from relatively sophisticated sectors are more likely to have a high foreign content share.

The remaining columns (columns 7–15 of table 9.7) list the contribution of key foreign economies as a percentage of foreign content in PRC's exports using the KWW methodology described in section 4. These estimates are the sector-level counterparts to the national aggregate estimates reported in the first row of table 9.6. It is useful to note the maintained assumptions in the construction of this chapter. First, when it comes to partitioning a

Table 9.7
Slicing Up Value-Added Chains in Manufacturing Exports by Sector (2002)

Industries (1)	Export Value in 2002 ($ million) (2)	Share in PRC's Manufacturing Exports (%) (3)	Share of Processing Exports (%) (4)	Domestic Content Share (%) (5)	Foreign Content Share (%) (6)	Sources of Foreign Value-Added in PRC's Exports to the US in 2000								
						Japan (7)	Korea Rep. of (8)	Taipei, China (9)	Singapore (10)	Other ASEAN (11)	United States (12)	Hong Kong, China (13)	EU15 (14)	Rest of the world (15)
Television, radios, audios and communication equipment	32,713	10.2	89.8	35.0	65.0	16.2	7.2	7.8	1.8	4.6	11.1	16.9	16.5	17.8
Electronic computing equipment	22,450	7.0	99.1	16.9	83.1	15.9	7.0	8.3	2.6	6.5	12.6	16.5	13.0	17.6
Wearing apparel	22,450	7.0	45.1	67.0	33.0	19.4	10.6	10.3	0.6	3.9	6.1	7.3	9.7	32.1
Knitting	18,601	5.8	31.6	72.9	27.1	17.0	10.3	10.0	0.4	4.1	5.5	8.5	8.9	35.4
Lighting fixtures, batteries, wiring and others	17,960	5.6	66.8	46.1	53.9	14.1	5.8	6.1	0.7	3.5	7.8	5.6	12.1	44.3
Other manufacturing products	16,036	5.0	64.2	55.0	45.0	15.3	8.4	8.0	0.7	4.7	7.1	6.9	11.6	37.3
Leather and leather products	14,432	4.5	54.3	48.8	51.2	9.6	15.6	9.8	0.4	3.1	10.0	6.8	16.6	28.1
Metal products	14,111	4.4	43.2	57.9	42.1	16.6	6.7	7.4	0.5	3.3	5.7	3.6	11.2	45.1

(*Continued*)

Table 9.7
(continued)

Industries (1)	Export Value in 2002 ($ million) (2)	Share in PRC's Manufacturing Exports (%) (3)	Share of Processing Exports (%) (4)	Domestic Content Share (%) (5)	Foreign Content Share (%) (6)	Sources of Foreign Value-Added in PRC's Exports to the US in 2000								
						Japan (7)	Korea Rep. of (8)	Taipei, China (9)	Singapore (10)	Other ASEAN (11)	United States (12)	Hong Kong, China (13)	EU15 (14)	Rest of the world (15)
Other electronics and electronic products	13,791	4.3	93.4	19.2	80.8	18.6	7.3	7.4	1.1	4.2	8.7	9.8	14.2	28.7
General machinery	11,225	3.5	43.7	58.5	41.5	17.6	6.5	7.0	0.7	3.6	7.2	5.1	14.0	38.3
Semiconductors and integrated circuits	10,904	3.4	89.7	22.2	77.8	16.2	7.6	8.4	1.7	5.0	10.3	13.9	14.0	23.0
Wooden furniture	8,980	2.8	36.7	76.3	23.7	13.5	7.6	6.8	0.4	10.5	6.8	5.1	13.5	35.9
Plastic products	7,697	2.4	64.5	37.6	62.4	16.0	8.7	9.3	1.3	4.2	9.0	4.8	13.6	33.2
Basic industrial chemicals	6,414	2.0	11.7	80.2	19.8	14.6	7.6	5.1	0.5	4.5	7.6	3.0	13.1	43.9
Household electrical equipment	6,094	1.9	79.1	37.2	62.8	16.9	7.0	7.5	1.0	4.1	8.4	7.3	14.0	33.8
Other chemical products	6,094	1.9	42.7	60.2	39.8	13.3	7.0	6.0	1.0	5.5	8.3	3.5	13.3	42.0
Precision machines	5,773	1.8	68.6	42.2	57.8	18.5	6.2	6.7	1.0	3.8	10.2	9.5	14.5	29.4
Tires and tubes	5,131	1.6	53.1	61.0	39.0	14.4	7.4	7.4	0.8	6.2	6.2	4.9	12.6	40.3

Other food products	1.5	4,811	26.7	74.9	25.1	10.0	4.4	4.0	0.8	7.6	11.2	3.2	12.7	46.2
Specialized machinery	1.4	4,490	38.5	63.4	36.6	18.9	6.3	7.1	0.8	3.3	7.4	4.4	16.1	35.8
Other transport equipment	1.3	4,169	40.2	61.0	39.0	17.7	6.7	7.2	0.8	3.6	6.7	4.4	13.3	39.7
Fish products	1.3	4,169	41.6	82.9	17.1	12.9	5.8	4.7	0.6	5.8	7.6	3.5	13.5	45.6
Non-metallic ore and quarrying	1.3	4,169	16.4	85.0	15.0	14.0	5.3	5.3	0.7	4.7	6.7	4.7	16.7	42.0
Non-ferrous metal	1.2	3,849	45.6	61.8	38.2	9.9	4.2	4.5	0.5	3.1	6.3	3.4	9.4	58.6
Refined petroleum and its products	1.1	3,528	24.2	65.3	34.7	4.0	1.7	1.4	0.3	6.6	2.0	1.2	5.5	77.2
Other non-metallic mineral products	1.1	3,528	12.9	84.5	15.5	12.3	5.8	5.8	0.6	5.2	7.1	3.9	13.5	45.8
Heavy electrical equipment	0.9	2,886	76.8	39.6	60.4	17.9	6.0	6.3	0.7	3.3	7.5	5.6	15.2	37.6
Motor vehicles	0.8	2,566	35.2	67.8	32.2	23.0	5.3	5.6	0.6	2.8	6.5	3.1	21.7	31.4
Iron and steel	0.7	2,245	26.3	79.9	20.1	13.9	6.0	6.0	0.5	3.5	4.5	3.0	9.5	53.2
Drugs and medicine	0.7	2,245	16.9	81.4	18.6	14.0	6.5	5.4	0.5	4.8	9.1	4.3	16.7	38.7
Shipbuilding	0.6	1,924	95.8	56.7	43.3	18.7	5.8	6.2	0.7	3.2	7.9	4.4	18.2	34.9
Slaughtering, meat products and dairy products	0.6	1,924	17.5	88.9	11.1	11.7	4.5	4.5	0.9	5.4	11.7	4.5	13.5	43.2
Pulp and paper	0.5	1,604	50.7	58.9	41.1	10.9	7.5	5.1	0.5	8.5	12.2	5.1	12.9	37.2
Glass and glass products	0.5	1,604	33.0	71.1	28.9	14.5	6.6	5.2	0.7	5.2	7.3	3.8	12.5	44.3
Crude petroleum and natural gas	0.5	1,604	3.4	93.6	6.4	15.6	6.3	6.3	1.6	4.7	7.8	4.7	14.1	39.1

(*Continued*)

Table 9.7
(continued)

Industries (1)	Export Value in 2002 ($ million) (2)	Share in PRC's Manufacturing Exports (%) (3)	Share of Processing Exports (%) (4)	Domestic Content Share (%) (5)	Foreign Content Share (%) (6)	Sources of Foreign Value-Added in PRC's Exports to the US in 2000								
						Japan (7)	Korea Rep. of (8)	Taipei, China (9)	Singapore (10)	Other ASEAN (11)	United States (12)	Hong Kong, China (13)	EU15 (14)	Rest of the world (15)
Boilers, engines and turbines	1,283	0.4	26.6	75.8	24.2	18.2	5.8	5.8	0.4	2.9	7.9	3.7	18.6	36.8
Printing and publishing	962	0.3	83.0	43.1	56.9	11.2	7.6	5.3	0.5	8.3	12.3	5.4	13.2	36.2
Chemical fertilizers and pesticides	962	0.3	5.6	78.7	21.3	14.6	6.6	6.1	0.9	4.2	8.5	4.2	14.1	40.8
Beverage	641	0.2	16.9	80.8	19.2	13.5	5.7	5.7	0.5	5.7	10.9	4.2	13.5	40.1
Metal working machinery	641	0.2	13.3	83.5	16.5	18.2	6.1	7.3	0.6	3.6	7.3	4.8	14.5	37.6
Livestock and poultry	641	0.2	2.8	94.8	5.2	11.5	3.8	3.8	0.0	5.8	11.5	3.8	13.5	46.2
Other metallic ore	321	0.1	7.2	85.4	14.6	15.1	6.2	6.2	0.7	4.1	7.5	4.8	13.7	41.8
Cement and cement products	321	0.1	7.0	86.5	13.5	16.3	6.7	6.7	0.7	4.4	7.4	4.4	13.3	40.0
Fishery	321	0.1	1.2	94.4	5.6	12.5	5.4	5.4	0.0	5.4	7.1	3.6	14.3	46.4
Tobacco	321	0.1	5.0	95.7	4.3	11.6	7.0	7.0	0.0	7.0	11.6	4.7	14.0	37.2

Source: Authors' calculations.

sector's exports into domestic and foreign content share, the KWW method is feasible and preferred, therefore we report the estimates using the KWW method in columns 5 and 6. Second, when it comes to slicing up the foreign content across different foreign sources, we do not have information on a breakdown between processing and normal trade for these economies, except the PRC.

Consequently, we assume that the distribution of foreign content across the source countries as estimated in table 9.7 is not affected by the estimated share of foreign content in a country's total exports.

In any case, for both electronics and computers (two major sectors with a low share of local content), Japan; Hong Kong, China; EU15; and the US are the primary sources for the foreign content in the PRC's exports, collectively accounting for about 60% of it. For wearing apparel, domestic content share is high (67%), and the foreign content comes from a diverse set of countries. Japan, Korea, and Taipei,China are the main supplies of foreign content in East Asia, but account for only 40% of the total foreign content; another 40% come from EU15 and rest of the world.

6 Conclusion

Segmentation of production across countries allows for reductions in production costs and more efficient allocation of resources. The opening-up of the PRC has likely facilitated this process. A quantitative assessment of the extent of its participation in global production chains allows us to get a better grasp of many policy questions, including the effect of an exchange rate change on bilateral trade balances. This chapter reviews and extends a conceptual framework that allows one to estimate domestic and foreign content in a country's exports, and to further assign foreign content into contributions from individual foreign economies. This framework is then applied to the data for the PRC.

We find several interesting patterns. First, we report from Koopman et al. (2008) that the estimated level of foreign content in exports from the PRC is close to 50%, almost twice as high as that calculated using the HIY formula. Second, we report interesting heterogeneity across sectors: those sectors that are likely to be labeled as sophisticated or high-skilled, such as computers, electronic devices, and telecommunication equipment, tend to have notably low shares of domestic content. Conversely, many sectors that are relatively intensive in low-skilled labor, such as apparel, are likely to exhibit a high share of domestic content in the country's exports. Finally, we find that Japan; the US; and Hong Kong, China are the primary suppliers of foreign content in the PRC's exports in several top export categories that may be considered relatively sophisticated. In other export sectors that are relatively less sophisticated, Korea and Taipei,China become more important, in addition to Japan.

Notes

1. Note that the 2002 Input-Output (IO) Table is the latest such table available; the next table—the 2007 benchmark IO table—is scheduled to be released in 2010. Our 2006 estimates make use of the 2006 trade statistics but use the 2002 IO table.
2. We use the terms "domestic value-added" and "domestic content" interchangeably. Similarly, we use the terms "foreign value-added," "foreign content," and "vertical specialization" to mean the same thing.
3. Such a model is called a "non-competitive" model in the IO literature. HIY (2001) do not specify this system explicitly but go straight to the implied Leontief inverse, while Chen et al. (2004) specify only the first two equations. A fully specified model facilitates better understanding of the connection between vertical specialization and domestic content, and a comparison with the model in the next subsection that features processing exports.
4. We consider the estimates preliminary because the calculation relies on the trade statistics from 2006 but the IO table from 2002. The 2002 IO table is the most recent benchmark table currently available. The next benchmark table—the 2007 table—is scheduled to be released in 2010.Therefore, 2006 estimates are not directly comparable to 1997 and 2002 estimates.
5. This is equivalent to the assumption that the first exporting country's exports have to be 100% domestic sourced when computing VS1 in HIY framework.
6. In columns 2–11, the shares of the 10 endogenous countries are computed using equation (39), while in columns 12 and 15, the shares for Hong Kong, China and the rest of the world are computed according to equation (43). These shares are then treated equally when re-scaled (to ensure that they sum to 100%).

References

Aziz, J., and X. Li. 2007. China's Changing Trade Elasticities. *IMF Working Paper* 07/266.

Chen, X., L. Cheng, K. C. Fung, and L. J. Lau. 2004. The Estimation of Domestic Value-Added and Employment Induced by Exports: An Application to Chinese Exports to the United States. *Stanford University Working Paper.*

Chinn, M. D. 2005. Supply Capacity, Vertical Specialization and Tariff Rates: The Implications for Aggregate US Trade Flow Equations. *NBER Working Paper Series* 11719.

Dean, J. M., K. C. Fung, and Z. Wang. 2007. Measuring the Vertical Specialization in Chinese Trade. *US International Trade Commission, Office of Economics Working Paper* 2007–01-A.

Goh, A-T., and J. Olivier. 2004. International Vertical Specialization, Imperfect Competition and Welfare. *HEC School of Management (France) Working Paper.*

Hummels, D., J. Ishii, and K. Yi. 2001. The Nature and Growth of Vertical Specialization in World Trade. *Journal of International Economics.* 54(1). pp. 75–96.

Koopman, R., Z. Wang, and S-J. Wei. 2008. How Much of Chinese Exports Is Really Made in China? Assessing Foreign and Domestic Value-Added in Gross Exports. *NBER Working Paper Series* 14109.

Krugman, P. 2008. Trade and Wages, Reconsidered. Paper prepared for the Brookings Papers on Economic Activity, Princeton University. Available at: http://www.princeton.edu/~pkrugman/pk-bpea-draft.pdf.

Lau, L. J., X. Chen, L. K. Cheng, K. C. Fung, Y. Sung, C. Yang, K. Zhu, J. Pei, and Z. Tang. 2007. Non-Competitive Input-Output Model and Its Application: An Examination of the China-US Trade Surplus. *Social Science in China.* 5. pp. 91–103 (in Chinese).

Linden, G., K. L. Kraemer, and J. Dedrick. 2007. What Captures Value in a Global Innovation System? *The Paul Merage School of Business Working Paper,* University of California, Irvine.

National Research Council. 2006. *Analyzing the US Content of Imports and the Foreign Content of Exports.* Committee on Analyzing the US Content of Imports and the Foreign Content of Exports. Center for Economics, Governance, and International Studies, Division of Behavioral and Social Sciences and Education. Washington, DC: The National Academies Press.

Pula, G., and T. Peltonen. 2008. Has Emerging Asia Decoupled? An Analysis of Production and Trade Linkages Using the Asian International Input-Output Table. *European Central Bank Working Paper* 993.

Rodrik, D. 2006. What's So Special about China's Exports? *China & World Economy.* 14(5). pp. 1–19.

Schott, P. 2008. The Relative Sophistication of Chinese Exports. *Economic Policy.* 53. pp. 5–49.

Varian, H. R. 2007. An iPod Has Global Value. Ask the (Many) Countries That Make it. *The New York Times.* 28 June.

Wang, Z., and S-J. Wei. 2008a. What Accounts for the Rising Sophistication of China's Exports? *NBER Working Paper Series* 13771.

Wang, Z., and S-J. Wei. 2008b. A Method to Slice Up the Value Chain Based on an International Input-Output Table. *Unpublished ITC Working Paper.*

Yi, K-M. 2003. Can Vertical Specialization Explain the Growth of World Trade? *Journal of Political Economy.* 111(1). pp. 52–102.

Index